Multi-moment Asset Allocation
and Pricing Models

For other titles in the Wiley Finance Series
please see www.wiley.com/finance

Multi-moment Asset Allocation and Pricing Models

Edited by

Emmanuel Jurczenko and Bertrand Maillet

John Wiley & Sons, Ltd

Other Wiley Editorial Offices

John Wiley & Sons Inc., 111 River Street, Hoboken, NJ 07030, USA

Jossey-Bass, 989 Market Street, San Francisco, CA 94103-1741, USA

Wiley-VCH Verlag GmbH, Boschstr. 12, D-69469 Weinheim, Germany

John Wiley & Sons Australia Ltd, 42 McDougall Street, Milton, Queensland 4064, Australia

John Wiley & Sons (Asia) Pte Ltd, 2 Clementi Loop #02-01, Jin Xing Distripark, Singapore 129809

John Wiley & Sons Canada Ltd, 22 Worcester Road, Etobicoke, Ontario, Canada M9W 1L1

Library of Congress Cataloging in Publication Data

Multi-moment asset allocation and pricing models / edited by Emmanuel Jurczenko and Bertrand Maillet.
    p. cm. — (Wiley finance series)
Includes bibliographical references and index.
ISBN-13: 978-0-470-03415-6 (cloth : alk. paper)
ISBN-10: 0-470-03415-7 (cloth : alk. paper)
1. Investments—Mathematical models. 2. Asset allocation—mathematical models.
3. Capital assets pricing model. I. Jurczenko, Emmanuel. II. Maillet, Bertrand.
HG4515.2.M84 2006
332.601′5195—dc22   2006017994

British Library Cataloguing in Publication Data

A catalogue record for this book is available from the British Library

ISBN-13 978-0-470-03415-6 (HB)
ISBN-10 0-470-03415-7 (HB)

Typeset in 10/12pt Times by Integra Software Services Pvt. Ltd, Pondicherry, India
Printed and bound in Great Britain by Antony Rowe Ltd, Chippenham, Wiltshire
This book is printed on acid-free paper responsibly manufactured from sustainable forestry
in which at least two trees are planted for each one used for paper production.

To our wives and children
and specifically to Manon and Viktor:
welcome to our skewed and leptokurtic world . . .

Contents

6   **The Four-moment Capital Asset Pricing Model: Between Asset Pricing and Asset Allocation**   **113**
    Emmanuel Jurczenko and Bertrand Maillet

9   A Test of the Homogeneity of Asset pricing Models   223

Giovanni Barone-Adesi, Patrick Gagliardini   and Giovanni Urga

About the Contributors

Gustavo M. de Athayde. After receiving his PhD in Economics (EPGE/Fundação Getulio Vargas), Gustavo joined the *Banco Itaú* technical staff in order to build up an advanced quantitative finance unit. Nowadays, as Senior Quantitative Manager, he is the top derivative designer and analyst at the bank. His interests comprise portfolio theory and design, incorporating higher moments, the econometrics of risk management, exotic and fixed-income derivatives; areas where he regularly publishes.

Giovanni Barone-Adesi is Professor of Finance Theory at USI in Lugano (Switzerland). Since graduating from the University of Chicago, he has taught at the University of Alberta, University of Texas, City University and the University of Pennsylvania. His main research interests are derivative securities and risk management. He is the author of several models for valuing and hedging securities; especially well known are his contributions to the pricing of American commodity options. He advises several exchanges and other business organisations and is the advisory editor of the *Journal of Banking and Finance*.

François Desmoulins-Lebeault has just completed his PhD thesis at the University of Paris-9 (Dauphine), where he also teaches Financial Management and Financial Econometrics. His research interests are in the study of statistical distributions in finance and their impact on portfolio selection and securities pricing.

Renato G. Flôres Jr is a specialist in dynamic econometrics, mathematical finance and international economics, and works at the PhD programme of the Graduate School of Economics, *Fundação Getulio Vargas*. His fruitful collaboration with Gustavo Athayde dates back from when he was Gustavo's PhD adviser, and has given way to their generalisation of Markowitz's portfolio choice theory, which they continue to expand. Professor Flôres holds several visiting positions in European universities and research centres; he has published extensively in leading academic journals for several years.

Patrick Gagliardini is Junior Professor of Economics at the University of St Gallen. He studied at the ETH in Zurich, where he got a degree in Physics in 1998. In 2003 he received a PhD in economics at the University of Lugano for a thesis on financial econometrics. He subsequently spent one year at CREST (Paris) with a post-doctoral fellowship from the Swiss

National Science Foundation. His main research interests are financial econometrics and quantitative methods in finance, especially credit risk modelling, asset pricing, nonparametric methods and time series analysis. In these areas, his current research focuses on rating migration models and estimation of derivative prices. He is a co-author of some recent research articles published in the *Journal of Econometrics*, the *Journal of Business and Economic Statistics* and the *Journal of Banking and Finance*.

Eric Jondeau is Professor of Finance at HEC-Lausanne and FAME research fellow. He is a graduate of the French National School of Statistics and Economics (*ENSAE*, Paris) and was awarded a PhD in Economics from the University of Paris-Dauphine. He is also a fellow of the French Actuaries Institute. Until August 2004, he was a researcher at the Research Department of the Banque de France and Associate Professor at the University of Paris-12 (Val-de-Marne). His research interests are mainly related to econometric modelling of asset prices, portfolio allocation under non-normality and the estimation of rational expectation models.

Emmanuel Jurczenko is Quantitative Analyst within AAAdvisors-QCG, Head of Analysts within Variances and Associate Professor in Finance at the ESCP-EAP. He graduated in Economics and Finance, and holds a PhD in Economics (*Multi-moment Asset Pricing Models*) from the University of Paris-1 (Panthéon-Sorbonne). He gained market experience for several years as a Quantitative Analyst within a subsidiary of ABN Amro dedicated to funds of funds. He has been an Associate Professor of Finance at the ESCP-EAP European School of Management since 2000, where he teaches Portfolio Management, Financial Mathematics, Options and Other Derivatives and Corporate Finance. His interests mainly concern portfolio management, asset pricing and applications of statistics in finance. He is also Associate Researcher at CES/CNRS (Centre for National Research) at the University of Paris-1.

Bertrand Maillet is CEO and Head of Research within AAAdvisors-QCG (ABN Amro Group) and Variances, and Lecturer in Economics at the University of Paris-1. He graduated in Economics, Finance and Statistics, and holds a PhD in Economics (*Market Efficiency and Performance Measurements*) from the University of Paris-1 (Panthéon-Sorbonne). After qualifying as a Lecturer in Economics at the same university in 1997 (lectures in financial econometrics, international finance and microeconomics), and being appointed Professor of Finance at the ESCP-EAP European School of Management (lectures in risk and portfolio management), he developed consulting activities in various financial institutions before joining the ABN Amro Group as Head of Research in a multi-fund activity. His domain of expertise covers risk management, performance measurement, portfolio management and asset pricing. He has published several articles in academic journals such as *Quantitative Finance*, *Review of International Economics* and *The European Journal of Finance*, chapters in books published by John Wiley & Sons, Springer-Verlag and Kluwer Academics, and serves as a referee for several international leading journals. He is currently Associate Researcher at CES/CNRS (Centre for National Research) of the University of Paris-1 and at the Financial Markets Group of the London School of Economics. He is also affiliated as a Junior Academic Fellow to the Europlace Institute of Finance.

Yannick Malevergne is an Assistant Professor of Finance at ISFA Graduate School of Actuarial Sciences (University of Lyon, France). He also teaches at EM-Lyon Graduate School of Management. Alumnus of Ecole Normale Supérieure de Lyon, *Agrégé de l'Université* in physics, he holds a PhD in Science from the University of Nice. His research is mainly devoted to the study of extreme risks in financial markets, to their modelling and to the development of new portfolio management methods allowing for a better understanding of this class of risks. Yannick regularly publishes articles in both professional journals and peered academic reviews. He has also recently co-authored a book on financial risk management methods with Didier Sornette.

Paul Merlin is Quantitative Analyst within AAAdvisors-QCG and Variances. He is also a PhD candidate in Finance at CES/CNRS (Centre for National Scientific Research) at the University of Paris-1. His thesis *Asset Allocation, Risk Control and Neural Network Applications in the Hedge Fund Universe* focuses on hedge fund strategies and financial risks. He graduated in Mathematics from the University of Paris-1 (Panthéon-Sorbonne) and in Finance from the University of Evry. His interests mainly concern portfolio and risk management and computational finance.

Michael Rockinger is Professor of Finance at HEC Lausanne (FAME), and a former scientific consultant at the Banque de France. He earned a PhD in Economics at Harvard University after graduating in mathematics from the Swiss Federal Institute of Technology. He is the author of several books as well as of several scientific articles. He has also been a visiting professor at the New Economic School in Moscow, the London Business School, Amos Tuck Business School at Dartmouth College, as well as at the University of California San Diego. His research interests are split into various strands: modelling asset-price behaviour, portfolio allocation under non-normality and the volume–volatility–trading activity relation.

Didier Sornette. After graduating from Ecole Normale Superieure (ENS Ulm, Paris), and getting a PhD in Physical Sciences in 1985, Didier became Staff Researcher and then Research Director at CNRS, University of Nice, France. In 1996 he obtained an additional joint appointment at UCLA of Los Angeles, California, where he teaches the theory of complex systems. He was the Director of Research at X-RS R&D (1988–1995) and Scientific Advisor to Thomson-Marconi Sonar until 1997. He has consulted for the world's major aerospace industrial companies, banks, investment and reinsurance companies. He is the author of two books on the theory of complex systems and on stock market crashes, and has a third in press (with co-author Y. Malevergne) on extreme financial risks. His research interests span the physics of complex systems and pattern formation in spatio-temporal structures, dynamical systems theory, pattern recognition, self-organised criticality, the prediction of complex systems, novel time series analysis, the prediction of rupture and of earthquakes, the prediction of financial bubbles and crashes, the theory and insurance of large risks, the theory of derivatives, portfolio optimisation, trading strategies, agent-based models, market microstructures, macroeconomics, behavioural finance and decision theory.

Luisa Tibiletti is Associate Professor in Applied Mathematics for Economics and Finance at the Department of Statistics and Mathematics of the University of Torino (Italy). Her main research interests include financial risk management, risk measures, modelling of dependence in risk management and stochastic optimisation. She is the author of numerous articles published in academic journals and books.

Giovanni Urga joined Cass Business School as Senior Lecturer in Financial Econometrics, was promoted to Reader in May 2001 and to Professor of Finance and Econometrics in May 2002, where he is also Director of the PhD programme and Director of the Centre for Econometric Analysis (CEA@Cass). He is visiting Professor of Econometrics at the Economics Department of Bergamo University (Italy). Formerly, he was at London Business School from October 1994 to July 1999 as Research Fellow of the Centre for Economic Forecasting, Visiting Professor of Econometrics at the New Economic School (Moscow) in 1996–1999, Lecturer at Queen Mary and Westfield College (London) in 1992–1994 and Research Officer at the Institute of Economics and Statistics (Oxford) in 1991–1992. His research concentrates on econometric methodology, the econometrics of panel data, financial econometrics, the economics and econometrics of investment, modelling structural breaks, modelling common stochastic trends, emerging markets and transition economy stock markets. Recent publications include papers in the *Journal of Econometrics*, *Journal of Applied Econometrics*, *Journal of Business and Economic Statistics*, *Journal of Comparative Economics*, *Oxford Bulletin of Economics and Statistics* and *Oxford Economic Papers*.

Foreword

This book of articles on multi-moment portfolio choice and asset pricing is long overdue. The theoretical ideas behind these articles have long been available, dating back 30 years, to the 1970s. Yet, only recently have academics paid attention to them.

There are many reasons for believing investors care about higher-order moments such as skewness and *kurtosis*. Harry Markowitz (1959) himself, in his book on mean–variance portfolio theory, acknowledges that a superior approach, were it not for its intractability, would be a mean–semi-variance trade-off, which places greater weight on avoiding downside losses. Following Markowitz's earlier insights (1952), Prospect Theory, developed by Kahneman and Tversky (1979), departs from normal decision theory by tying the utility of future wealth to current wealth level and by imposing an asymmetric preference for deviations from current wealth. Basic results in utility theory from simple experiments governing choices between riskless and risky lotteries are explained by individual preferences for positive skewness. For instance, if investors have decreasing absolute risk aversion, then they must have a preference for positive skewness. Ample empirical evidence, much of it casual, also points in the direction of a concern for skewness and *kurtosis*. Several papers examining betting at horserace tracks show that "long shots" (horses with positively skewing betting outcomes) are over-bet and "short shots" (horses with negatively skewed betting outcomes) are under-bet. The so-called "skew" in the pricing of index options (although the name derives from the shape of the "smile" not the implied risk-neutral probability density function) also makes more sense under loss aversion: purchased out-of-the-money puts have significant pricing premiums relative to at-the-money options than the Black and Scholes model (1973) would suggest. Of course, it is precisely these securities which provide concentrated protection against downside risk. The same asymmetry may partially explain the high promised interest rate default spreads on low grade corporate bonds, which seem to be otherwise excessive compensation for the probability of default.

The set of utility functions exhibiting constant proportional risk aversion, so popular in theoretical work on asset pricing, exhibits a positive preference toward all odd moments (including skewness) and an aversion toward all even moments (including *kurtosis*). Pursuit of positive skewness and avoidance of *kurtosis* seem to go together. It would be interesting to directly examine this connection (although I am not aware that such an analysis has been conducted). In other words, I would like to know what are the necessary and sufficient conditions (that is, the class of the utility functions) for rational investors to like positive skewness and dislike *kurtosis*. Casual empiricism suggests that investors, if they understand the potential for loss as well as profit, will shy away from investments that have high *kurtosis*. *Kurtosis* can be created in two ways: (1) by a continuous stochastic price process with stochastic volatility, and (2) by jumps. Investors are particularly averse to situations in which *kurtosis* is created in the second way since they cannot then avoid the effects of *kurtosis* by liquidating before small losses expand into large losses.

So, given the obvious significance of higher-order moments in portfolio choice (and, therefore, probably in equilibrium asset pricing models), why have financial economists taken so long to give this subject its due? I think the first reason was the original fascination with the comparative tractability of mean–variance choice and the elegance of the mean–variance capital asset pricing model (CAPM). Scientists notoriously worship at the altar of theoretical elegance and simplicity at the sacrifice of empirical realism. But as the poor fit of the CAPM to observations became progressively apparent, a number of other modifications to the CAPM were attempted, but the suggestion that it just might be important for investors to think about higher-order moments was little pursued. Even survey papers of the CAPM which would recount potentially interesting modifications to the original model were silent about incorporating higher-order moments even after the theory for this had been worked out.

I remember having a conversation, in about 1977, with Barr Rosenberg, then a professor at Berkeley, who had built his own, very successful company (BARRA) around the idea of the mean–variance trade-off. I pointed out that modifying the CAPM to account for preference for higher-order moments could easily be accomplished with little sacrifice to elegance. The usual CAPM equation can be written:

$$\mu_i = r_f + (\mu_M - r_f)\beta_i \quad \text{with } \beta_i = \text{Cov}(r_i, r_M)/\sigma_M^2$$

where μ_i and μ_M represent, respectively, the expected return on a risky security i and on the market portfolio, r_f stands for the risk-free return and β_i is the beta of asset i with respect to the market portfolio. It can be easily shown that incorporating preference for all odd higher-order moments and aversion for all even higher-order moments can be accomplished by simply redefining β_i as:[1]

$$\beta_i = \text{Cov}(r_i, -r_M^{-b})/\text{Cov}(r_M, -r_M^{-b})$$

where $b > 0$ is the measure of constant proportional risk aversion. Although this adds another parameter (b) that needs to be evaluated, many might value that added flexibility; if not, one could simplify the model even further by imposing logarithmic representative utility function, in which case the risk aversion parameter b is set to 1, so that:

$$\beta_i = \text{Cov}(r_i, -r_M^{-1})/\text{Cov}(r_M, -r_M^{-1})$$

and one has an equation that is only very slightly different than the original CAPM but has the right sign-preference toward higher-order moments. Barr Rosenberg agreed that in principle this model would be better. But in practice he thought not. First, it gave him just another complication to explain (when mean–variance theory was difficult enough), and it did not buy him much since his clients, primarily pension funds and money managers, were not into high positive or negative skewness investments. Most were much like "closet indexers". The CAPM, as justified by the joint normality hypothesis, assumes preference for skewness by

---

[1] A result recently supported by further analysis by Hayne Leland (1998).

making it impossible to obtain. All portfolios – which must be constructed from securities which all have jointly normal returns – must have returns that are normally distributed. As Henry Ford once remarked, his customers could buy cars of all colors from him provided the cars were black. While by the 1970s, it would have been a poor assumption to suppose that only black cars were for sale, it was perhaps not such a misleading presumption to assume that only portfolios with zero skewness (in their logarithmic returns) were available.

But today I think this situation has changed. First, institutional investors now find the mean–variance model second nature and its jargon (alpha, beta, Sharpe ratio, efficient set, and so on) is more or less widely understood even by many non-professionals – so in contrast to the 1970s they are better prepared for greater sophistication. Second, the development of very active exchange-traded option markets has made the purchase of skewness-oriented securities a simple matter. Third, the creation of skewed outcomes (even at the portfolio level) by using systematic dynamic trading strategies (an observation perhaps first made by Markowitz in his 1952 paper cited above) is now a standard practice. Fourth, in the last few years, hedge fund strategies have become popular which intentionally (and often unintentionally) pursue skewed or highly kurtotic outcomes. Under these circumstances, if investor preference toward higher-order moments is not considered, then using mean–variance analysis, funds with high mean returns and low variance will appear to have good performance when all they have done is to achieve this end at the sacrifice of negative skewness and high *kurtosis*.

Mark Rubinstein
May 20, 2006

REFERENCES

Black, F. and M. Scholes (1973) The pricing of options and corporate liabilities, *Journal of Political Economy* **81**, 637–654.

Kahneman, D. and A. Tversky (1979) Prospect theory: An analysis of decision under risk, *Econometrica* **47**, 263–291.

Leland, H. (1998) Beyond mean-variance: Risk and performance measurement in a nonsymmetrical world, *Financial Analysts Journal*, January–February, 27–36.

Markowitz, H. (1952) The utility of wealth, *Journal of Political Economy* **60**, 151–158.

Markowitz, H. (1959) *Portfolio Selection*, Blackwell, 384 pages.

Preface

Concern for higher-order moments than the variance in finance can be traced back to Kendall and Hill (1953), Mandelbrot (1963a and 1963b), Cootner (1964) and Fama (1965), who discovered the presence of significant skewness and excess *kurtosis* in empirical asset return distributions, and to Arditti (1967 and 1971), who documented the individual investor's preference for positive skewness.

These empirical findings led, in the seventies, to the development of a new area of research dedicated to the introduction of higher moments in portfolio theory and asset pricing models, whose fathers are, respectively, Samuelson (1970) and Rubinstein (1973).

In the field of portfolio theory, Samuelson (1970), following the general work by Marschak (1938) on a three-moment decision criterion and Levy (1969) in the case of a cubic utility, was the first to consider in an expected utility framework the importance of higher moments for the individual portfolio analysis. Then, Jean (1971, 1972 and 1973), Ingersoll (1975) and Schweser (1978) studied the mean–variance–skewness efficient portfolio frontier with a risk-free asset. Arditti and Levy (1975) also considered the extension of the three-moment portfolio analysis to a multiperiodic setting.

In the field of asset pricing, Rubinstein (1973) was the first to propose a multi-moment asset pricing model. He extended the traditional Sharpe–Lintner–Mossin CAPM (see Sharpe, 1964, Lintner, 1965 and Mossin, 1966) a vérifer to take into account the effect of the systematic coskewness on the asset valuation. Note that the ideas of an asset pricing relation without a risk-free asset, the related zero-beta portfolio,[1] and the possible extension of the traditional analysis with higher moments than skewness were already present in his seminal paper. A confirmation of this original idea is to be found, later on, in the paper published by Kraus and Litzenberger (1976), reformulating the original idea and adding the first empirical study of the 3-CAPM on the American stock market. A few years later, Ang and Chua (1979) developed a three-moment absolute risk-adjusted performance measure.

The eighties and nineties also saw a great deal of active academic research dedicated to multi-moment asset allocation and pricing models. For instance, Barone-Adesi (1985) established the link between the three-moment CAPM and the Arbitrage Pricing Theory of Ross (1976), while Graddy and Homaifar (1988) and Fang and Lai (1997) extended the mean–variance–skewness asset allocation and pricing framework to take into account the *kurtosis* of the asset return distributions. Diacogiannis (1994) and Athayde and Flôres (1997)

---

[1] Which appeared independently at about the same time as Black's (1972) zero-beta mean–variance paper.

proposed in their turn compact and tractable expressions for investors' portfolio moments and associated gradients that greatly simplified the numerical solutions of the multi-moment portfolio optimisation programme. Another approach to asset allocation with higher moments was given by Lai (1991) and Chunhachinda *et al.* (1997), who applied the Polynomial Goal Programming approach (PGP) to portfolio selection with skewness.

In parallel with these theoretical extensions, various empirical tests have been conducted during the past two decades on the three and four-moment CAPM using different asset classes, time periods and timescales (see, for instance, Friend and Westerfield, 1980; Sears and Wei, 1988; Lim, 1989; Hwang and Satchell, 1999). While these studies have led to rather mixed results, most recent empirical studies have proven the ability of systematic higher co-moments to increase the explicative power of the traditional CAPM model and to explain some well-known financial anomalies such as the book-to-market, size and industry effects (see Harvey and Siddique, 2000a and 2000b; Christie-David and Chaudhry, 2001 and Dittmar, 2002).

Despite this amount of research, only recently have multi-moment asset allocation and pricing models become popular amongst academics and practitioners. The recent explosion of interest in this area of research can be explained by the fast-growing concerns of investors for extreme risks, the recent success of non-normally distributed assets such as hedge funds or guaranteed products, and advances in decision theory, econometric and statistical models that look promising for multi-moment asset allocation and pricing models.

The aim of this monograph is to present the state of the art in multi-moment asset allocation and pricing models and to provide, in a single volume, new developments, collecting in a unified framework theoretical results and applications previously scattered throughout the financial literature.

This book is organised as follows. In Chapter 1, Jurczenko and Maillet present the theoretical foundations of multi-moment asset allocation and pricing models in an expected utility framework. Then, in Chapter 2, Athayde and Flôres derive analytically the unconstrained minimum variance portfolio frontier in the mean–variance/*kurtosis*–skewness spaces when a risk-free rate exists, using compact tensor notation for the portfolio moments. In Chapter 3, Jurczenko, Maillet and Merlin propose a nonparametric methodology to determine the set of Pareto-optimal portfolios in the four-moment space, with an application to hedge fund asset allocation. In Chapter 4, Tibiletti introduces a family of coherent risk measures based on one-sided higher moments that overcome some of the drawbacks of centred higher moments. In Chapter 5, Desmoulins-Lebeault describes alternative portfolio selection criteria with skewness and *kurtosis*, using a Gram–Charlier Type A statistical series expansion to approximate the investor's portfolio return distribution. In Chapter 6, Jurczenko and Maillet generalise the traditional CAPM relation in the four-moment framework, with or without a riskless asset. In Chapter 7, Malevergne and Sornette present alternative multi-moment/cumulant capital asset pricing models with homogeneous and heterogeneous agents when a risk-free asset exists. Jondeau and Rockinger introduce, in Chapter 8, a flexible copula-based multivariate distributional specification that allows for wide possibilities of dynamics for conditional systematic (co)higher-moments. Finally, in Chapter 9, Barone-Adesi, Gagliardini and Urga introduce a quadratic market specification to model the coskewness of an individual asset with the market portfolio and explain the size effect on the US stock market.

All the contributions included in this book are amended and extended versions of papers that were originally presented at the *Multi-moment Capital Asset Pricing Models and Related Topics* Workshop organised by the association Finance sur Seine in Paris on the 29th April

2002 at the ESCP-EAP European Business School. We would like to thank all the authors for providing chapters in a timely fashion and for their patience. Each chapter has been reviewed by referees, and we specifically would like to thank Nicolas Gaussel, Thierry Michel, Sébastien Laurent, Patrice Poncet and Philippe Spieser for their help with this important task. We would also like to thank Michael Rockinger for his constant support. Furthermore, we would like to thank Emily Pears and the staff of John Wiley & Sons for their encouragement, patience and support during the preparation of the book. Our last vote of thanks is warmly addressed to (Pr.) Thierry Chauveau, without whom none of this would have been possible.

With this book we hope to have expanded the fast-growing multi-moment asset allocator and pricer community a little more. The usual disclaimers apply here.

Emmanuel Jurczenko and Bertrand Maillet

REFERENCES

Ang, J. and J. Chua (1979) Composite Measures for the Evaluation of Investment Performance, *Journal of Financial Quantitative Analysis* **14**, 361–383.

Arditti, F. (1967) Risk and the Required Return on Equity, *Journal of Finance* **22**, 19–36.

Arditti, F. (1971) Another Look at Mutual Fund Performance, *Journal of Financial Quantitative Analysis* **6**, 913–924.

Arditti, F. and H. Levy (1975) Portfolio Efficiency Analysis in Three Moments: The Multiperiod Case, *Journal of Finance* **30**, 797–809.

Athayde, G. and R. Flôres (1997) A CAPM with Higher Moments: Theory and Econometrics, Discussion Paper EPGE-FGV, 23 pages.

Barone-Adesi, G. (1985) Arbitrage Equilibrium with Skewed Asset Returns, *Journal of Financial and Quantitative Analysis* **20**, 299–311.

Black, F. (1972) Capital Market Equilibrium with Restricted Borrowing, *Journal of Business* **45**, 444–454.

Christie-David, R. and M. Chaudhry (2001) Coskewness and Cokurtosis in Futures Markets, *Journal of Empirical Finance* **8**, 55–81.

Chunhachinda, P., K. Dandapani, K. Hamid and S. Prakash (1997) Portfolio Selection and Skewness: Evidence from International Stock Markets, *Journal of Banking and Finance* **21**, 143–167.

Cootner, P. (Ed.) (1964), *The Random Character of Stock Market Prices*, MIT Press.

Diacogiannis, G. (1994) Three-parameter Asset Pricing, *Managerial and Decision Economics* **15**, 149–158.

Dittmar, R. (2002) Nonlinear Pricing Kernels, Kurtosis Preference and Evidence from the Cross-Section of Equity Returns, *Journal of Finance* **57**, 369–403.

Fama, E. (1965) The Behaviour of Stock-Market Prices, *Journal of Business* **38**, 34–105.

Fang, H. and T. Lai (1997) Co-kurtosis and Capital Asset Pricing, *Financial Review* **32**, 293–307.

Friend, I. and R. Westerfield (1980) Co-skewness and Capital Asset Pricing, *Journal of Finance* **30**, 897–913.

Graddy, D. and G. Homaifar (1988) Equity Yields in Models Considering Higher Moments of the Return Distribution, *Applied Economics* **20**, 325–334.

Harvey, C. and S. Siddique (2000a) Conditional Skewness in Asset Pricing Tests, *Journal of Finance* **54**, 1263–1296.

Harvey, C. and S. Siddique (2000b) Time-Varying Conditional Skewness and the Market Risk Premium, *Research in Banking and Finance* **1**, 25–58.

Hwang, S. and S. Satchell (1999) Modelling Emerging Market Risk Premia Using Higher Moments, *International Journal of Finance and Economics* **4**, 271–296.

Ingersoll, J. (1975) Multidimensional Security Pricing, *Journal of Financial and Quantitative Analysis* **10**, 785–798.

Jean, W. (1971) The Extension of Portfolio Analysis to Three and More Parameters, *Journal of Financial and Quantitative Analysis* **6**, 505–515.

Jean, W. (1972) Distribution Moments and Equilibrium: Reply, *Journal of Financial and Quantitative Analysis* **7**, 1435–1437.

Jean, W. (1973) More on Multidimensional Portfolio Analysis, *Journal of Financial and Quantitative Analysis* **8**, 475–490.

Kendall, M. and B. Hill (1953) The Analysis of Economic Time-series – Part I: Prices, *Journal of the Royal Statistical Society Series A* **116** (1), 11–34.

Kraus, A. and R. Litzenberger (1976) Skewness Preference and the Valuation of Risk Assets, *Journal of Finance* **31**, 1085–1099.

Lai, T. (1991) Portfolio with Skewness: A Multiple-objective Approach, *Review of Quantitative Finance and Accounting* **1**, 293–305.

Levy, H. (1969) A Utility Function Depending on the First Three Moments, *Journal of Finance* **24**, 715–719.

Lim, K. (1989) A New Test of the Three-moment Capital Asset Pricing Model, *Journal of Financial and Quantitative Analysis* **24**, 205–216.

Lintner, J. (1965) The Valuation of Risk Assets and the Selection of Risky Investments in Stock Portfolios and Capital Budgets, *Review of Economics and Statistics* **13**, 13–37.

Mandelbrot, B. (1963a) The Variation of Certain Speculative Prices, *Journal of Business* **36**, 394–419.

Mandelbrot, B. (1963b) New Methods in Statistical Economics, *Journal of Political Economy* **71**, 421–440.

Marschak, J. (1938) Money and the Theory of Assets, *Econometrica* **6** (4), 311–325.

Mossin, J. (1966) Equilibrium in a Capital Market, *Econometrica* **34**, 768–783.

Ross, S. (1976) The Arbitrage Theory of Capital Asset Pricing Theory, *Journal of Economic Theory* **13**, 341–360.

Rubinstein, M. (1973) The Fundamental Theorem of Parameter-preference Security Valuation, *Journal of Financial and Quantitative Analysis* **8**, 61–69.

Samuelson, P. (1970) The Fundamental Approximation Theorem of Portfolio Analysis in Terms of Means, Variances and Higher Moments, *Review of Economic Studies* **37**, 537–543.

Schweser, C. (1978) Multidimensional Security Pricing: A Correction, *Journal of Financial and Quantitative Analysis* **30**, 177–183.

Sears, R. and K. Wei (1988) The Structure of Skewness Preferences in Asset Pricing Models with Higher Moments: An Empirical Test, *Financial Review* **23**, 25–38.

Sharpe, W. (1964) Capital Asset Prices: A Theory of Market Equilibrium under Conditions of Risk, *Journal of Finance* **19**, 425–442.

1

Theoretical Foundations of Asset Allocation and Pricing Models with Higher-order Moments

Emmanuel Jurczenko and Bertrand Maillet

ABSTRACT

The purpose of this chapter is to present the theoretical foundations of multi-moment asset allocation and pricing models in an expected utility framework. Using an infinite-order Taylor series expansion, we first recall the link between the expected utility and higher moments of the investment return distribution (Tsiang, 1972; Loistl, 1976 and Lhabitant, 1997). Following the approach of Benishay (1987, 1989 and 1992) and Rossi and Tibiletti (1996), we next develop a quartic utility specification to obtain an exact mean–variance–skewness–*kurtosis* decision criterion. We also present the behavioural and distributional conditions under which the preference of a rational agent can be approximated by a fourth-order Taylor series expansion. The Taylor approach and the polynomial utility specification are then compared when justifying a moment-based decision criterion.

1.1 INTRODUCTION

The definition of a decision's criterion under uncertainty is a prerequisite for the derivation of an equilibrium asset pricing relation. Multi-moment asset allocation and pricing models assume that investors determine their investment by taking into account only the first N moments of the portfolio return distribution. Agents are supposed to maximise their expected utility[1], which can be represented by an indirect function that is strictly concave and decreasing with even moments and strictly concave and increasing with odd moments.

Despite the tractability and economic appeal of such models, their theoretical justifications are far from simple. First, it is not always possible to translate individual preferences into a function that depends on the entire sequence of the moments of the portfolio return distribution (Loistl, 1976; Lhabitant, 1997 and Jurczenko and Maillet, 2001). Most importantly, agents who maximise their expected utility do not, in general, have preferences that can be translated into a simple comparison of the first N moments of their investment return

---

[1] The expected utility criterion remains the traditional one for rational individual decisions in a risky environment.

distribution. Brockett and Kahane (1992) show[2] that it is always possible to find two random variables such that the probability distribution of the first random variable dominates statistically[3] the second one with respect to the first N moments, but is stochastically dominated to the Nth order[4] for some rational investors. Since Nth degree stochastic dominance implies a lexicographic order over the first N moments (Fishburn, 1980; O'Brien, 1984 and Jean and Helms, 1988), the preference ordering will coincide with a moment-based ranking only when all the moments up to order $(N - 1)$ are equal.[5]

Although there is no bijective relation between the expected utility theory and a moment-based decision criterion, it is, however, possible, by suitably restricting the family of distributions and von Neumann–Morgenstern utility functions, to translate individual preferences into a partial moment ordering. Conditional on the assumption that higher moments exist, the expected utility can then be expressed – approximately or exactly – as an increasing function of the mean and the skewness, and a decreasing function of the variance and the *kurtosis* of the portfolio return distribution.[6]

The purpose of this first chapter is to present the theoretical foundations of a mean–variance–skewness–*kurtosis* decision criterion. To achieve this, we consider investors endowed with utility functions relevant for the fourth-order stochastic dominance (Levy, 1992 and Vinod, 2004). We first recall the link that exists between the expected value function and the moments of the probability distribution. This leads us to specify the interval of convergence of the Taylor series expansion for most of the utility functions used in the finance field and to characterise the maximum skewness–*kurtosis* domain for which density functions exist (Hamburger, 1920 and Widder, 1946). We then introduce a quartic parametric utility function to obtain an exact mean–variance–skewness–*kurtosis* decision criterion (Benishay, 1987, 1989 and 1992). Following the approach of Rossi and Tibiletti (1996) and Jurczenko and Maillet (2001), we show how such polynomial specification can satisfy – over a realistic range of returns – the five desirable properties of utility functions stated by Pratt (1964), Arrow (1970) and Kimball (1990) – non-satiation, strict risk aversion, strict decreasing absolute risk aversion (DARA), strict decreasing absolute prudence (DAP) and constant or increasing relative risk aversion (CRRA or IRRA). We then present the conditions under which rational preferences can be approximated by a fourth-order Taylor series expansion.

Even though Taylor series approximations or polynomial utility specifications have already been considered to deal with the non-normalities in the asset return distributions (see, for instance, Levy, 1969; Hanoch and Levy, 1970; Rubinstein, 1973 and Kraus and Litzenberger, 1976), this contribution constitutes – to the best of our knowledge – the first one that considers in detail the theoretical justifications of multi-moment asset allocation and pricing models.

The chapter is organised as follows. In Section 1.2 we review the link between the expected utility function and the centred moments of the terminal return distribution. In Section 1.3 we study the preference and distributional restrictions that enable us to express the expected

---

[2] See also Brockett and Garven (1998), Gamba and Rossi (1997, 1998a and 1998b) and Lhabitant (1997).

[3] In the sense that it is characterised – for instance – by a higher expected value, a lower variance, a higher skewness and a lower *kurtosis*.

[4] For a survey on stochastic dominance literature, see Levy (1992).

[5] The mean–variance portfolio selection suffers the same flaw, since a mean–variance ordering does not constitute a necessary condition for second-order stochastic dominance (Hanoch and Levy, 1969).

[6] Throughout this chapter, we restrict our attention only to the first four moments since there is no clear economic justification concerning the link between the expected utility function and the fifth and higher-order centred moments of the investment return distribution. Moreover, even though most empirical works show that moments up to fourth order exist in (un)conditional asset return distributions (see, for instance, Lux, 2000 and 2001 and Jondeau and Rockinger, 2003a), there remains an issue concerning the existence of moments beyond the fourth. Another problem is the poor sampling properties of higher moments' empirical estimators due to high powers in the expectation operator (Vinod, 2001 and 2004).

utility criterion as an exact function of the mean, variance, skewness and *kurtosis* of the portfolio return density. Section 1.4 presents the theoretical justifications of a four-moment expected utility approximation. Section 1.5 concludes. Proofs of all the theorems presented in the chapter are given in the appendices.

1.2 EXPECTED UTILITY AND HIGHER-ORDER MOMENTS

We consider a one-period single exchange economy with one consumption good serving as *numeraire*. Each agent has an initial endowment, W_0, arbitrarily fixed to one without any loss of generality, and a von Neumann–Morgenstern utility function $U(.)$ defined over its final wealth and denoted W_F, from $I \subset IR$ to IR. The preference function is assumed to belong to the class of utility functions, called D_4, relevant for the fourth-order stochastic dominance (abbreviated to 4SD)[7], satisfying:

$$D_4 = \left\{ U \,\middle|\, U^{(1)}(.) > 0,\, U^{(2)}(.) < 0,\, U^{(3)}(.) > 0,\, U^{(4)}(.) < 0 \right\} \tag{1.1}$$

where $U^{(i)}(.)$ with $i = [1, \ldots, 4]$ are the derivatives of order i of $U(.)$.

At the beginning of the period, each agent maximises the expected utility of its end-of-period investment gross rate of return, denoted R, such that:

$$E[U(R)] = \int_{-\infty}^{+\infty} U(R)\, dF(R) \tag{1.2}$$

where $F(.)$ is the continuous probability distribution of $R = W_F / W_0$.

If the utility function is arbitrarily continuously differentiable in I, one can express the utility of the investor $U(.)$ as an Nth order Taylor expansion, evaluated at the expected gross rate of return on the investment, that is, $\forall R \in I$:

$$U(R) = \sum_{n=0}^{N} (n!)^{-1} U^{(n)}[E(R)][R - E(R)]^n + \varepsilon_{N+1}(R) \tag{1.3}$$

where $E(R)$ is the expected simple gross rate of return, $U^{(n)}(.)$ is the nth derivative of the utility function and $\varepsilon_{N+1}(.)$ is the Lagrange remainder defined as:

$$\varepsilon_{N+1}(R) = \frac{U^{(N+1)}(\xi)}{(N+1)!}[R - E(R)]^{(N+1)}$$

where $\xi \in\,]R, E(R)[$ if $R < E(R)$, or $\xi \in\,]E(R), R[$ if $R > E(R)$, and $N \in IN^*$.

---

[7] Let X and Y be two continuous random variables defined by their probability distributions $F_X(.)$ and $F_Y(.)$. The variable X is said to dominate stochastically the variable Y to the fourth-order – that is, X is preferred over Y for the class D_4 of utility functions – if and only if, whatever p:

$$\begin{cases} \displaystyle \int_{-\infty}^{p} [F_X(z) - F_Y(z)]\, dz \le 0 \\[2ex] \displaystyle \int_{-\infty}^{p} \int_{-\infty}^{q} [F_X(z) - F_Y(z)]\, dz\, dq \le 0 \\[2ex] \displaystyle \int_{-\infty}^{p} \int_{-\infty}^{q} \int_{-\infty}^{r} [F_X(z) - F_Y(z)]\, dz\, dq\, dr \le 0 \end{cases}$$

with $(p \times q \times r) = (IR)^3$ and at least one strict inequality over the three for some p.

If we assume, moreover, that the Nth Taylor approximation of $U(.)$ around $E(R)$ converges absolutely towards $U(.)$, that the integral and summand operators are interchangeable, and that the moments of all orders exist and determine uniquely the return distribution, taking the limit of N towards infinity and the expected value on both sides in (1.3) leads[8] to:

$$E[U(R)] = \int_{-\infty}^{+\infty} \left\{ \lim_{N \to \infty} \left[\sum_{n=0}^{N} (n!)^{-1} U^{(n)} [E(R)] [R - E(R)]^n + \varepsilon_{N+1}(R) \right] \right\} dF(R)$$

$$= U[E(R)] + \frac{1}{2} U^{(2)}[E(R)] \sigma^2(R) + \frac{1}{3!} U^{(3)}[E(R)] s^3(R) \qquad (1.4)$$

$$+ \frac{1}{4!} U^{(4)}[E(R)] \kappa^4(R) + \sum_{n=5}^{\infty} \frac{1}{n!} U^{(n)}[E(R)] m^n(R)$$

where $\sigma^2(R) = E\left\{[R - E(R)]^2\right\}$, $s^3(R) = E\left\{[R - E(R)]^3\right\}$, $\kappa^4(R) = E\left\{[R - E(R)]^4\right\}$ and $m^n(R) = E\{[R - E(R)]^n\}$ are, respectively, the variance, the skewness, the *kurtosis*[9] and the nth centred higher moment of the investor's portfolio return distribution, and:

$$\lim_{N \to \infty} \varepsilon_{N+1}(R) = 0$$

There are three conditions under which it is possible to express a continuously differentiable expected utility function as a function depending on all the moments of the return distribution.

The first condition implies that the utility function $U(.)$ is an analytic function[10] at $E(R)$ and that the realised returns must remain within the absolute convergence interval of the infinite-order Taylor series expansion of the utility function considered (Tsiang, 1972; Loistl, 1976; Hasset *et al.*, 1985 and Lhabitant, 1997).

Theorem 1   *A sufficient condition for a Taylor series expansion of an infinitely often differentiable utility function $U(.)$ around the expected gross rate of return $E(R)$ to converge absolutely is that the set of realisations of the random variable R belongs to the open interval J defined by:*

$$|R - E(R)| < \zeta \qquad (1.5)$$

---

[8] Under the same set of conditions, it is also possible to express the generic expected utility as a function of the non-centred moments of the return distribution through a MacLaurin series expansion (see, for instance, Levy and Markowitz, 1979; Rossi and Tibiletti, 1996 and Lhabitant, 1997).

[9] These definitions of skewness and *kurtosis*, as third- and fourth-order centred moments, differ from the statistical ones as standardised centred higher moments, that is:

$$\alpha_n = E\left\{\left[\frac{R - E(R)}{\sigma(R)}\right]^n\right\}$$

with $n = [3, 4]$.

[10] A real function $f(x)$ is analytic at $x = a$ if there exists a positive number ζ such that $f(.)$ can be represented by a Taylor series expansion in the interval $]-\zeta, \zeta[$, centred around a; that is, if $\forall x \in]-\zeta, \zeta[$, we have:

$$f(x) = \sum_{n=0}^{N} (n!)^{-1} f^{(n)}(a) \times (x - a)^n$$

where ζ is called the radius of convergence of the Taylor series of $f(.)$ around a, and $f^{(n)}(.)$ is the nth derivative of the function $f(.)$.

with:

$$\zeta = \lim_{N \to \infty} \left| \frac{(N+1)! \, U^{(N)} \left[E(R) \right]}{N! \, U^{(N+1)} \left[E(R) \right]} \right|$$

where ζ is a positive constant corresponding to the radius of convergence of the Taylor series expansion of $U(.)$ around $E(R)$ and $N \in IN$.

Proof   *see Appendix A*

The region of absolute convergence of a Taylor series expansion depends on the utility function considered. For instance, condition (1.5) does not require any specific restriction on the return range for exponential and polynomial utility functions since their convergence intervals are defined on the real line, whilst it entails the following restriction for logarithm-power type utility functions (see Table 1.1):

$$0 < R < 2E(R)$$

Even though this condition is not binding for traditional asset classes when short-sale is forbidden, it may be too restrictive for some applications on alternative asset classes due to their option-like features and the presence of leverage effects (Weisman, 2002 and Agarwal and Naik, 2004). In this case, *ex post* returns might lie outside of the convergence interval (1.5).

The second condition entails shrinking the interval of absolute convergence (1.5) slightly so that the infinite-order Taylor series expansion of $U(.)$ around $E(R)$ converges uniformly towards $U(.)$ and the integral and summand operators are interchangeable in the investor's objective function[11] (Loistl, 1976; Lhabitant, 1997 and Christensen and Christensen, 2004).

Table 1.1   Taylor series expansion absolute convergence interval

Utility function $U(R)$	Radius of absolute convergence ζ	Convergence interval
HARA $\frac{\gamma \left(b + \frac{a}{\gamma} R \right)^{(1-\gamma)}}{(1-\gamma)}$	$\|-\gamma\| \left(\frac{b}{a} + \frac{E(R)}{\gamma} \right)$	$\left\{ \begin{array}{l} \left] -\frac{\gamma b}{a}, \frac{\gamma b + 2aE(R)}{a} \right[\\ \text{or} \\ \left] \frac{\gamma b + 2aE(R)}{a}, -\frac{\gamma b}{a} \right[\end{array} \right.$
CARA $-\exp(-aR)$	$+\infty$	IR
CRRA $\frac{R^{(1-\gamma)}}{(1-\gamma)}$	$E(R)$	$]0, 2E(R)[$
CRRA $\ln(R)$	$E(R)$	$]0, 2E(R)[$
Polynomial of order N $\left(\frac{1-N}{N} \right) \left(b + \frac{aR}{1-N} \right)^N$	$+\infty$	IR

---

[11] Uniform convergence is a sufficient condition for a term-by-term integration of an infinite series of a continuous function.

Theorem 2   *A sufficient condition for a Taylor series expansion of an infinitely often differentiable utility function U(.) around the expected gross rate of return E (R) with a positive radius of convergence ζ to converge uniformly is that the set of realisations of the random variable R remains in the closed interval J^* defined by (using previous notation):*

$$|R - E(R)| \leq \zeta^* \tag{1.6}$$

$\forall \zeta^* \in \,]0, \zeta[$, *where ζ is defined in (1.5).*

Proof   *see Appendix B.*

The third condition is related to the Hamburger moment problem (1920), that is, to the question of the existence and uniqueness, for a sequence of non-centred moment constraints (μ^k), of an absolutely continuous positive distribution probability function $F(.)$ such that[12] $\forall k \in IN^*$:

$$\mu^k = \int_p^q R^k \, dF(R) \tag{1.7}$$

where $p := -\infty$, $q := +\infty$ and $\mu^0 = 1$.

If $F(.)$ is unique, the Hamburger moment problem is said to be "determinate", since the probability distribution function is uniquely determined by the sequence of its moments.

Theorem 3   *(Hamburger, 1920; Widder, 1946 and Spanos, 1999). The sufficient conditions[13] for a sequence of non-centred moments (μ^k), with $0 \leq k \leq 2N$, to lead to a unique continuous positive probability distribution[14] are that:*

$$\begin{cases} E\left[|R - E(R)|^k\right] < \infty & \text{(existence of the moments of order k)} \\ \det(\boldsymbol{\mu}^n) \geq 0 \; \forall n \in [0, \ldots, N] & \text{(existence of the density function)} \\ -(1+R)^{-2} \int_{-\infty}^{+\infty} \ln f(R) \, dR = \infty & \text{(Krein's uniqueness condition)} \end{cases} \tag{1.8}$$

where $\boldsymbol{\mu}^n$ is the $[(n+1) \times (n+1)]$ Hankel matrix of the non-centred moments defined as:

$$\boldsymbol{\mu}^n = \begin{pmatrix} \mu^0 & \mu^1 & \cdots & \mu^n \\ \mu^1 & \mu^2 & \cdots & \mu^{n+1} \\ \vdots & \vdots & \ddots & \vdots \\ \mu^n & \mu^{n+1} & \cdots & \mu^{2n} \end{pmatrix}$$

with elements (μ^{i+j}) with coordinates (i, j), where $(i, j) = [0, \ldots, n]^2$, $\mu^0 = 1$; $N \in IN^*$ and $f(.)$ is the continuous density function of the gross rate of return R.

Proof   *see Widder, 1946, p. 134 and Spanos, 1999, pp. 113–114.*

---

[12] The moment problem (1.7) in the case where $p := 0$ and $q := +\infty$ is called the Stieltjes moment problem (Stieltjes, 1894), while in the case where $p := 0$ and $q := 1$, we talk about the little Hausdorff moment problem (Hausdorff, 1921a and 1921b).

[13] For necessary and sufficient conditions for uniqueness in the Hamburger moment problem, see Lin (1997) and Stoyanov (1997 and 2000).

[14] This approach is based on functional analysis. Another approach to the moment problem involves Padé approximants (see, for instance, Baker and Graves-Morris, 1996).

Conditional on the existence of the moments, the existence of a density function means, for $k = 4$, that the sequence of determinants of the associated Hankel matrices (μ^{i+j}), with $(i \times j) = [1, 2]^2$, must satisfy:

$$\det \begin{pmatrix} \mu^0 & \mu^1 \\ \mu^1 & \mu^2 \end{pmatrix} \geq 0 \text{ and } \det \begin{pmatrix} \mu^0 & \mu^1 & \mu^2 \\ \mu^1 & \mu^2 & \mu^3 \\ \mu^2 & \mu^3 & \mu^4 \end{pmatrix} \geq 0 \qquad (1.9)$$

with $\mu^0 = 1$.

Using the following results (Kendall, 1977, p. 58):

$$\begin{cases} \mu^2 = \sigma^2 (R) + [E(R)]^2 \\ \mu^3 = s^3 (R) + 3E(R) \sigma^2 (R) + [E(R)]^3 \\ \mu^4 = \kappa^4 (R) + 4E(R) s^3 (R) + 6[E(R)]^2 \sigma^2 (R) + [E(R)]^4 \end{cases} \qquad (1.10)$$

the positive definiteness of (1.9) implies the following restriction for the four-moment problem:

$$(\gamma_1)^2 \leq \gamma_2 + 2 \qquad (1.11)$$

where γ_1 and γ_2 are the Fisher parameters for the skewness and the *kurtosis*:

$$\gamma_1 = \frac{s^3 (R)}{\sigma^3 (R)} \quad \text{and} \quad \gamma_2 = \frac{\kappa^4 (R)}{\sigma^4 (R)} - 3$$

This relation confirms that, for a given level of standardised *kurtosis*, only a finite range of standardised skewness may be spanned. That is, for $\gamma_2 \geq (-2)$, the possible standardised skewness belongs to $[-\gamma_1^*, \gamma_1^*]$, where:

$$\gamma_1^* = \sqrt{\gamma_2 + 2} \qquad (1.12)$$

Figure 1.1 represents the skewness–*kurtosis* domain ensuring the existence of a density function[15] compared to some empirical couples of Fisher coefficient estimates. The curve corresponds to the theoretical maximum domain of the Fisher parameters γ_1 and γ_2, for which density functions exist when the first four moments are given.

While the domain of existence of a density (1.12) is large, the solution of the Hamburger moment problem, if it exists, may not be unique. The Krein's integral test (third line in equation (1.8)) is not fulfilled by all probability distributions. For instance, the lognormal distribution has finite centred moments of all orders and verifies the inequality (1.11) but is not uniquely determined by its moments. It is indeed straightforward to show that the probability distribution whose density function is given by:

$$f(R) = (2\pi)^{-1/2} R^{-1} \exp\left[-\frac{1}{2} (\ln R)^2\right] \times [1 + a \sin(2\pi \ln R)] \qquad (1.13)$$

---

[15] In the case of a standardised random variable with a zero mean and a unit variance, condition (1.11) leads to (see Jondeau and Rockinger, 2003a):

$$(\mu^3)^2 \leq \mu^4 - 1$$

where $\mu^0 = 1$ and $\mu^1 = 0$.

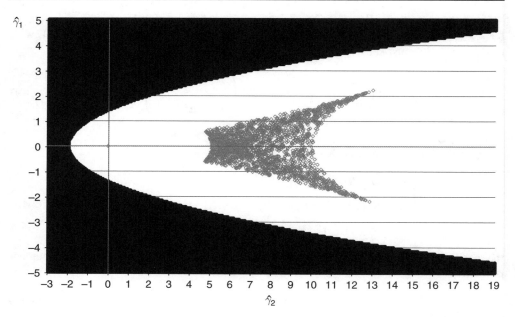

Figure 1.1 Realistic Fisher coefficients domain for return density functions. This figure illustrates the boundaries of $\hat{\gamma}_1$ and $\hat{\gamma}_2$ Fisher coefficients ensuring the existence of a density function when the first four moments are given (see Equation 1.12). The black (white) region in the figure represents (60 000) simulated couples of Fisher $(\hat{\gamma}_1, \hat{\gamma}_2)$ parameters that violate (or respect) the condition of existence of a density function in the four-moment case. The grey lozenges correspond to the (2432) simple weekly rolling (overlapping) estimates of the two first Fisher coefficients on the daily returns of random constrained (positive and unitary sum) portfolios composed with close-to-close CAC40 stocks on the period 01/95 to 08/04. See Jondeau and Rockinger (2003a, Figure 5, p. 1707) for a comparison with normalised variables and generalised *t*-student skewness and *kurtosis* boundaries.

for $|a| < 1$, has exactly the same sequence of moments as the lognormal distribution obtained by substituting $a = 0$ in (1.13) – see Heyde (1963).

Under these regular conditions, any investor with a utility function belonging to the D_4 class displays a preference for the expected return and the (positive) skewness, and an aversion to the variance and the *kurtosis*, since differentiating equation (1.4) with respect to $E(R)$, $\sigma^2(R)$, $m^3(R)$ and $\kappa^4(R)$, leads to, $\forall R \in [E(R) - \zeta^*, E(R) + \zeta^*]$:

$$
\begin{cases}
\dfrac{\partial E[U(R)]}{\partial E(R)} = (n!)^{-1} \displaystyle\sum_{n=0}^{\infty} U^{(n+1)}[E(R)] m^n(R) = E\left[U^{(1)}(R)\right] \quad (>0) \\[12pt]
\dfrac{\partial E[U(R)]}{\partial \sigma^2(R)} = (2!)^{-1} U^{(2)}[E(R)] \quad (<0) \\[12pt]
\dfrac{\partial E[U(R)]}{\partial s^3(R)} = (3!)^{-1} U^{(3)}[E(R)] \quad (>0) \\[12pt]
\dfrac{\partial E[U(R)]}{\partial \kappa^4(R)} = (4!)^{-1} U^{(4)}[E(R)] \quad (<0)
\end{cases}
\tag{1.14}
$$

where ζ^* is defined as in (1.6).

Standard risk aversion (see Kimball, 1993) and strict consistency in the direction of preference for higher moments (see Horvath and Scott, 1980) constitute two sufficient, but non-necessary, conditions to establish a mean–variance–skewness–*kurtosis* preference ordering for a non-satiable and risk-averse investor.

Indeed, Kimball (1993) shows that decreasing absolute risk aversion (DARA) and decreasing absolute prudence (DAP) are sufficient conditions for any monotonically increasing and strictly concave utility function to belong to the standard risk-aversion utility class. This implies the mean–variance–skewness–*kurtosis* preference relation (1.14), since, $\forall R \in J^*$:

$$
\begin{cases}
\dfrac{\mathrm{d}\left(-U^{(2)}(R)/U^{(1)}(R)\right)}{\mathrm{d}R} = \dfrac{\left\{-U^{(3)}(R)\,U^{(1)}(R) + \left[U^{(2)}(R)\right]^2\right\}}{\left[U^{(1)}(R)\right]^2} < 0 \Longrightarrow U^{(3)}(R) > 0 \\[4mm]
\dfrac{\mathrm{d}\left(-U^{(3)}(R)/U^{(2)}(R)\right)}{\mathrm{d}R} = \dfrac{\left\{-U^{(4)}(R)\,U^{(2)}(R) + \left[U^{(3)}(R)\right]^2\right\}}{\left[U^{(2)}(R)\right]^2} < 0 \Longrightarrow U^{(4)}(R) < 0
\end{cases}
$$

$$(1.15)$$

with $U^{(1)}(.) > 0$ and $U^{(2)}(.) < 0$.

Horvath and Scott (1980) reach a similar result under the hypotheses of non-satiation, risk aversion and strict consistency in preference direction for higher moments. Strict consistency of an investor's preference with respect to higher moments requires that all the nth derivatives of $U(.)$ are either always negative, always positive or everywhere zero for any $n \geq 3$ and every possible return. That is, $\forall n \geq 3$ and $\forall R \in J^*$:

$$
\begin{cases}
U^{(n)}(R) < 0 \\
U^{(n)}(R) = 0 \quad \text{or} \\
U^{(n)}(R) > 0
\end{cases}
$$

$$(1.16)$$

where J^* is the interval of uniform convergence of the Taylor series expansion of $U(.)$ around $E(R)$ defined in (1.6). Under non-satiation and risk aversion, the next preference restrictions then follow from the mean-value theorem (see Horvath and Scott, 1980, p. 916):

$$(-1)^n U^{(n)}(R) < 0 \qquad (1.17)$$

$\forall n \geq 3$ and $\forall R \in J^*$. In particular, if $U^{(3)}(R) < 0 \ \forall R \in J^*$, the assumption of positive marginal utility is violated for all feasible gross rates of return; so we must have $U^{(3)}(R) > 0 \ \forall R \in J^*$. Likewise, $U^{(4)}(R) > 0 \ \forall R \in J^*$, would violate the assumption of strict risk aversion.

More generally, non-satiation, risk aversion and strict consistency of agent preferences towards higher moments imply a preference for expected return and (positive) skewness and an aversion for variance and *kurtosis*, and more generally a preference for odd higher-order centred moments and an aversion to even higher-order centred moments.

Provided that the utility functions of agents belong to the class of the analytic utility functions relevant for the fourth-order stochastic dominance, that the realisations of the investment returns remain in the interval of the uniform convergence of the Taylor series expansions of the utility functions, and that the Hamburger moment problem is "determinate", it is then possible to express the expected utility criterion as a function that depends positively on the mean, skewness and odd higher-order moments and negatively on the variance, *kurtosis* and even higher-order moments of investment rates of return.

1.3   EXPECTED UTILITY AS AN EXACT FUNCTION OF THE FIRST FOUR MOMENTS

While, under some behavioural and distributional restrictions, individual preferences are linked with the first four moments of the investment return distribution, the expected utility of such investors also depends upon all the other moments of their portfolio returns, so that the mean–variance–skewness–*kurtosis* approach is necessarily restrictive.[16] As in the mean–variance case, there are two ways one can theoretically justify an exact four-moment decision criterion in an expected utility framework: the first theoretical justification consists in restricting asset return distributions to a specific four-parameter distribution class, while the second one consists in restricting investors' utility functions to a quartic polynomial specification.

The first theoretical justification of a mean–variance–skewness–*kurtosis* decision criterion is to assume that the asset return distributions belong to a four-parameter family of probability distributions that allows for finite mean, variance, skewness and *kurtosis*. Without pretence of exhaustivity, we can underline the choice of skew-student distributions (Azzalini and Capitanio, 2003; Branco *et al.*, 2003; Adcock, 2003 and Harvey *et al.*, 2004), normal inverse Gaussian (Barndorff-Nielsen, 1978 and 1997 and Eriksson *et al.*, 2004), confluent U hypergeometric distributions (Gordy, 1998), generalised beta distributions of the second kind (Bookstaber and McDonald, 1987; McDonald and Xu, 1995 and Dutta and Babbel, 2005), Pearson type IV distributions (Bera and Premaratne, 2001), four-moment maximum entropy distributions (Jondeau and Rockinger, 2002; Bera and Park, 2003 and Wu, 2003), Gram–Charlier and Edgeworth statistical series expansions (Jarrow and Rudd, 1982; Corrado and Su, 1996a and 1996b; Capelle-Blanchard *et al.*, 2001 and Jurczenko *et al.*, 2002a, 2002b and 2004), copula-based multivariate non-elliptical distributions (Patton, 2001 and 2004; Xu, 2004) and multivariate separable skewed fat-tailed distributions (Ortobelli, 2001 and Ortobelli *et al.*, 2000 and 2002).

But, if the normal density is perfectly and uniquely defined by its first two moments, this is not the case when some other density functions are considered. This last point leads, in fact, to real difficulties. For instance, as shown by Brockett and Kahane (1992), Simaan (1993) and Brockett and Garven (1998), it is unlikely to determine, on *a priori* grounds, the sign of sensitivities of the objective function with respect to the moments of the portfolio return distribution. Indeed, when higher-order moments are not orthogonal one to another, the effect on the utility function of increasing one of them becomes ambiguous. Moreover, even if the considered density function can be in accordance with some of the stylised facts highlighted in the literature[17], additional utility assessments

---

[16] The mean–variance criterion suffers the same flaw (see Markowitz, 1952).

[17] Such as leptokurticity, asymmetry, time-aggregation properties of the process, the leverage effect and clustering in the volatility (Cont, 2001).

are required to obtain an ordering consistent with the fourth-order stochastic dominance criterion.

A second theoretical justification of the mean–variance–skewness–*kurtosis* analysis is to consider a fourth-order polynomial utility specification. In this case, conditional on the assumption that *kurtosis* exists and provided that the range of returns is well-restricted, the expected utility ordering can be translated exactly into a four-moment ordering.

A quartic parametric utility function can be defined as follows[18] (see Benishay, 1987, 1989 and 1992):

$$U(R) = a_0 + a_1 R + a_2 R^2 + a_3 R^3 + a_4 R^4 \tag{1.18}$$

with $a_i \in IR^*$, $i = [1, \ldots, 4]$.

Since all partial derivatives above the fourth order are equal to zero, taking the expected value of (1.18) yields:

$$E[U(R)] = a_0 + a_1 E(R) + a_2 E(R^2) + a_3 E(R^3) + a_4 E(R^4) \tag{1.19}$$

Using the results about uncentred moment definitions recalled from (1.10), we obtain:

$$
\begin{aligned}
E[U(R)] = {} & a_0 + a_1 E(R) + a_2 E(R)^2 + a_3 E(R)^3 + a_4 E(R)^4 \\
& + \left[a_2 + 3a_3 E(R) + 6a_4 E(R)^2 \right] \sigma^2(R) \\
& + \left[a_3 + 4a_4 E(R) \right] s^3(R) + a_4 \kappa^4(R)
\end{aligned}
\tag{1.20}
$$

When the first four moments exist and determine uniquely the return distributions (see above), the investors' preferences can then be expressed as an exact function of the mean, variance, skewness and *kurtosis* of their portfolio returns. Taking the first four derivatives of the quartic utility function and using the behavioural requirements associated with the fourth-order stochastic dominance criterion defined in (1.1) leads to the following theorem.

Theorem 4   *The necessary and sufficient conditions for a quartic utility function $U(.)$ to belong to the class D_4 of utility functions relevant for the fourth-order stochastic dominance are given by the following system:*

---

[18] Since a von Neumann–Morgenstern utility function is uniquely defined up to an increasing affine transformation, it is always possible to give a simpler and equivalent expression for the quartic utility function. Substracting a_0 to equation (1.18) and dividing it by a_1, we have:

$$U(R) = R + bR^2 + cR^3 + dR^4$$

where $b = a_2/a_1$, $c = a_3/a_1$, $d = a_4/a_1$ and $a_1 > 0$.

$$\begin{cases} \begin{cases} a_1 > 0 \\ \left(-\dfrac{a_3^2}{16a_4^2} + \dfrac{a_2}{6a_4}\right)^3 + \left(\dfrac{a_3^3}{16a_4^3} + \dfrac{a_1}{8a_4} - \dfrac{a_2 a_3}{16a_4^2}\right)^2 > 0 \quad (\textit{non-satiable individuals}) \\ R < -\dfrac{a_3}{4a_4} + \dfrac{K + \left(9a_3^2 - 24a_4 a_2\right) K^{-1}}{12a_4} \end{cases} \\[2em] \begin{cases} \begin{cases} 0 > a_2 \geq \left(\dfrac{3a_3^2}{8a_4}\right) \\ R < -\dfrac{a_3}{4a_4} + \dfrac{\sqrt{9a_3^2 - 24a_4 a_2}}{12a_4} \text{ and } R > -\dfrac{a_3}{4a_4} \\ \quad - \dfrac{\sqrt{9a_3^2 - 24a_4 a_2}}{12a_4} \end{cases} \quad (\textit{risk-averse agents}) \\ \text{or } a_2 < \left(\dfrac{3a_3^2}{8a_4}\right) \end{cases} \\[2em] \begin{cases} a_3 > 0 \\ R < -\left(\dfrac{a_3}{4a_4}\right) \end{cases} \qquad (\textit{prudent investors}) \\[1.5em] a_4 < 0 \qquad (\textit{temperant people}) \end{cases} \tag{1.21}$$

with:

$$K = \left(\frac{A + \sqrt{-108\left(3a_3^2 - 8a_4 a_2\right)^3 + A^2}}{2}\right)^{1/3}$$

and:

$$A = \left(-54a_3^3 - 432a_4^2 a_1 + 216a_4 a_3 a_2\right)$$

where $a_i \in IR^*, i = [1, \dots, 4]$.

Proof   *see Appendix C.*

Any investor with a D_4 class quartic utility function has a preference for the mean, an aversion to the variance, a preference for the (positive) skewness and an aversion to the *kurtosis*, that is:

$$\begin{cases} \dfrac{\partial E\left[U\left(R\right)\right]}{\partial E\left(R\right)} = a_1 + 2a_2 E\left(R\right) + 3a_3 E\left(R^2\right) + 4a_4 E\left(R^3\right) > 0 \\[1em] \dfrac{\partial E\left[U\left(R\right)\right]}{\partial \sigma^2\left(R\right)} = a_2 + 3a_3 E\left(R\right) + 6a_4 \left[E\left(R^2\right) + \sigma^2\left(R\right)\right] < 0 \\[1em] \dfrac{\partial E\left[U\left(R\right)\right]}{\partial m^3\left(R\right)} = a_3 + a_4 E\left(R\right) > 0 \\[1em] \dfrac{\partial E\left[U\left(R\right)\right]}{\partial \kappa^4\left(R\right)} = a_4 < 0 \end{cases} \tag{1.22}$$

The regularity conditions in (1.22) lead, nevertheless, to some restrictions on the asset return realisations. Indeed, when we restrict investors' preferences to a quartic specification, we have to make sure that the asset return realisations belong to the interval where the utility function exhibits non-satiety, strict risk aversion, strict prudence and strict temperance. In other words, the *ex post* investor's portfolio gross rate of return must respect the following system of inequalities:

$$R < -\frac{a_3}{4a_4} + \min\left[\Delta, \frac{K + \left(9a_3^2 - 24a_4a_2\right)K^{-1}}{12a_4}\right]$$ (1.23)

with:

$$\Delta = \min\left(\frac{\sqrt{9a_3^2 - 24a_4a_2}}{12a_4}, 0\right)$$

and:

$$\begin{cases} \left(-\frac{a_3^2}{16a_4^2} + \frac{a_2}{6a_4}\right)^3 + \left(\frac{a_3^3}{16a_4^3} - \frac{a_2a_3}{16a_4^3} + \frac{a_1}{8a_4}\right)^2 > 0 \\ (-1)^i\, a_i < 0 \end{cases}$$

where $a_i \in IR^*, i = [1, \ldots, 4]$.

Figure 1.2 represents three particular quartic utility functions and the evolution of their first derivatives with respect to the gross rate of return on a realistic range of returns.

These restrictions constitute necessary, but not sufficient, conditions for the quartic utility function (1.18) to satisfy simultaneously the properties of decreasing absolute risk aversion (DARA), decreasing absolute prudence (DAP) and constant or increasing relative risk aversion (CRRA or IRRA) with respect to the gross rate of return, R. The necessary and sufficient conditions are that the expressions Δ^*, Δ^{**} and Δ^{***} respect the following system:

$$\begin{cases} \Delta^* = \left[-\frac{\partial U(R)}{\partial R}\frac{\partial^3 U(R)}{\partial R^3} + \left(\frac{\partial^2 U(R)}{\partial R^2}\right)^2\right] < 0 \quad (DARA) \\ \Delta^{**} = \left[-\frac{\partial^2 U(R)}{\partial R^2}\frac{\partial^4 U(R)}{\partial R^4} + \left(\frac{\partial^3 U(R)}{\partial R^3}\right)^2\right] < 0 \quad (DAP) \\ \Delta^{***} = \left[R\Delta^\circ - \frac{\partial^2 U(R)}{\partial R^2}\left(\frac{\partial U(R)}{\partial R}\right)^{-1}\right] \geq 0 \quad (CRRA\ or\ IRRA) \end{cases}$$ (1.24)

This system of inequalities leads to the following theorem.

Theorem 5 *The necessary and sufficient conditions for a quartic utility function $U(.)$ to exhibit a decreasing absolute risk aversion (DARA), a decreasing absolute prudence (DAP)*

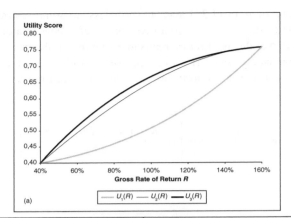

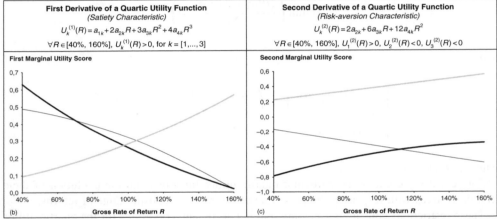

Figure 1.2 Quartic utility function illustrations. (a) displays examples of realistic quartic utility functions: $U_k(R) = a_{0k} + a_{1k}R + a_{2k}R^2 + a_{3k}R^3 + a_{4k}R^4$ for the cases of: 1. $k = 1$ non-satiable, risk seeker, prudent and intemperant investor; 2. $k = 2$ non-satiable, risk averse, imprudent and intemperant investor; 3. $k = 3$ non-satiable, risk averse, prudent and temperant investor; with:

$$\begin{cases} U_1(R) : a_{01} = 0.3774;\ a_{11} = 0.0250;\ a_{21} = 0.0605;\ a_{31} = 0.0450;\ a_{41} = 0.0002 \\ U_2(R) : a_{02} = 0.1954;\ a_{12} = 0.5230;\ a_{22} = -0.0013;\ a_{32} = -0.0695;\ a_{42} = 0.0019 \\ U_3(R) : a_{03} = 0.0714;\ a_{13} = 1.0165;\ a_{23} = -0.5400;\ a_{33} = 0.1400;\ a_{43} = -0.0200 \end{cases}$$

where coefficient a_{jk} values, $j = [0, \ldots, 4]$, result from a grid search on the possible domain, before being rescaled in order to get, for the three utility functions, the same minimum (0.4) and maximum (0.758) score values when the gross return stands respectively at 40 % and 160 % (corresponding to the maximum drawdown and maximum run-up observed on the CAC40 index for six-month series on the period 01/95 to 06/04). See, for comparison, real-market GMM estimates of a_{2k} and a_{3k} (with $a_{0k} = 0$, $a_{1k} = 1$ and a_{4k} unconstrained) in the case of a cubic utility function, in Levy *et al.* (2003), Table 2 and Figure 1, pp. 11 and 13. The four graphs in (b), (c), (d) and (e) show the evolution of the first derivatives of the three considered quartic utility functions with respect to the gross rate of return on a realistic range of gross returns.

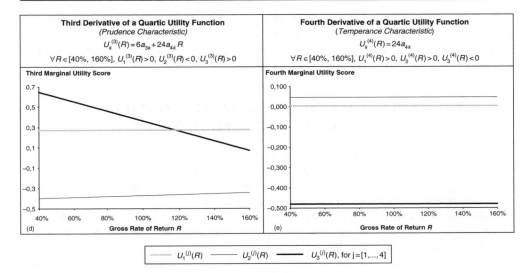

Figure 1.2 Continued

and a constant or increasing relative risk aversion (CRRA or IRRA) with respect to the gross rate of return R are given by:

$$
\begin{cases}
8a_4^2 R^4 + 8a_4 a_3 R^3 + 3a_3^2 R^2 + 2\left(a_3 a_2 - 2a_4 a_1\right)R + \frac{2}{3}a_2^2 - a_3 a_1 < 0 & (DARA)\\[2mm]
\begin{cases}
-\dfrac{a_3}{4a_4} + \dfrac{\sqrt{\left(-9a_3^2 + 24a_4 a_2\right)}}{12a_4} < R < -\dfrac{a_3}{4a_4} - \dfrac{\sqrt{\left(-9a_3^2 + 24a_4 a_2\right)}}{12a_4} \\[3mm]
a_2 < \left(\dfrac{3a_3^2}{8a_4}\right)
\end{cases} & (DAP)\\[6mm]
120\left(a_4\right)^2 R^4 + 120 a_3 a_4 R^3 + 3\left[9\left(a_3\right)^2 + 16 a_2 a_4\right]R^2 \\
\quad + 6\left(3a_2 a_3 + 2a_4 a_1\right)R + 3a_3 a_1 + 2\left(a_2\right)^2 \geq & (CRRA\ or\ IRRA)\\
\left(12 a_4 R^2 + 6 a_3 R + 2a_2\right)\left(4a_4 R^4 + 3a_3 R^3 + 2a_2 R^2 + a_1 R\right)^{-1}
\end{cases}
$$

$$(1.25)$$

where $a_i \in IR^*$, $i = [1, \ldots, 4]$.

Proof   *see Appendix D.*

These requirements constitute the traditional limits of using a polynomial utility function[19] to represent individual preferences (Levy, 1969 and Tsiang, 1972). We can note, however, that, contrary to the quadratic one, the quartic specification is compatible – for some values of parameters – with the five desirable properties of utility functions: non-satiation, risk aversion, decreasing absolute risk aversion, decreasing absolute prudence and constant or increasing relative risk aversion (Pratt, 1964; Arrow, 1970 and Kimball, 1990 and 1993).

---

[19] For a study of the properties of the cubic utility function see Levy (1969), Hanoch and Levy (1970), Rossi and Tibiletti (1996), Gamba and Rossi (1997, 1998a and 1998b), Jurczenko and Maillet (2001) and Bellalah and Selmi (2002).

The theoretical conditions of an exact mean–variance–skewness–*kurtosis* decision criterion presented, in the next section we consider the conditions under which the mean–variance–skewness–*kurtosis* analysis can provide a satisfactory approximation rather than an exact solution of the expected utility optimisation problem.

1.4   EXPECTED UTILITY AS AN APPROXIMATING FUNCTION OF THE FIRST FOUR MOMENTS

While it is possible, by assuming specific parametric return distributions or utility functions to transform the expected utility principle into a mean–variance–skewness–*kurtosis* analysis, academics generally prefer to explore the conditions under which a fourth-order Taylor series expansion of the utility function can provide an accurate approximation of the investor's objective function. However, since the conventional utility theory does not generally translate into a simple comparison of the first N moments, this alternative approach is in fact as restrictive as the previous one. Indeed, additional preference and distributional restrictions are needed to ensure that a quartic approximation of the expected utility provides an accurate and consistent local approximation of the individual objective function.

To address this issue, we consider the set of utility functions that display hyperbolic absolute risk aversion (HARA)[20] and belong to the D_4 class. These utility functions are defined as:

$$U(R) = \frac{\gamma}{(1-\gamma)}\left(b + \frac{a}{\gamma}R\right)^{(1-\gamma)} \tag{1.26}$$

with:

$$\begin{cases} b + \dfrac{a}{\gamma}R > 0 \\[2mm] \dfrac{1}{\gamma} > -\dfrac{1}{2} \end{cases}$$

where, if γ is a negative integer then $\gamma \leq -3$ and $\gamma \neq 0$ otherwise, $a > 0$ and $b \geq 0$. It is easy to check that (1.26) satisfies the fourth-order stochastic dominance requirements, since:

$$\begin{cases} U^{(1)}(R) = a\left(b + \dfrac{a}{\gamma}R\right)^{-\gamma} \quad (>0) \\[3mm] U^{(2)}(R) = -a^2\left(b + \dfrac{a}{\gamma}R\right)^{-(\gamma+1)} \quad (<0) \\[3mm] U^{(3)}(R) = a^3\left(\dfrac{\gamma+1}{\gamma}\right)\left(b + \dfrac{a}{\gamma}R\right)^{-(\gamma+2)} \quad (>0) \\[3mm] U^{(4)}(R) = -a^4\dfrac{(\gamma+1)(\gamma+2)}{\gamma^2}\left(b + \dfrac{a}{\gamma}R\right)^{-(\gamma+3)} \quad (<0) \end{cases} \tag{1.27}$$

---

[20] For a study of the general HARA utility class, see Feigenbaum (2003) and Gollier (2004).

The HARA class relevant for the fourth-order stochastic dominance subsumes most of the popular functional forms of utility used in finance, including the constant absolute risk aversion (CARA) class, the constant relative risk aversion (CRRA) class and some functions belonging to the subclass of quartic utility and higher-degree polynomial utility functions.

The CRRA power and logarithmic utility functions can be obtained from (1.26) by selecting $\gamma > 0$ and $b := 0$, that is:

$$U(R) = \begin{cases} \frac{1}{(1-\gamma)} R^{(1-\gamma)} & \text{if } \gamma \neq 1 \\ \ln(R) & \text{if } \gamma = 1 \end{cases} \tag{1.28}$$

where γ is the constant investor's relative risk-aversion coefficient. As for any HARA utility function, with $\gamma > 0$, the CRRA utility functions are also characterised by a decreasing absolute risk aversion with respect to the gross rate of return R.

If $\gamma := +\infty$ and $b := 1$, we obtain the (CARA) negative exponential utility function, that is:

$$U(R) = -\exp(-aR) \tag{1.29}$$

where a measures the constant investor's absolute risk aversion.

For $\gamma := -(N-1)$ and $b > 0$, (1.26) reduces to a polynomial utility function of degree N, that is:

$$U(R) = \frac{(1-N)}{N} \left(\frac{a}{1-N} R + b \right)^N \tag{1.30}$$

where $N \in IN^* - \{1, 2, 3\}$ with $\gamma \leq -3$. This last specification covers only a subset of the quartic and higher-order polynomial utility functions (those with increasing absolute risk aversion) since HARA utility functions only have three free parameters, whereas a polynomial of degree N, with $N \geq 4$, has $(N+1)$ parameters.

The quartic utility functions obtained from (1.26) by selecting $\gamma := -3$ and $b > 0$, have the following general form:

$$U(R) = R - \frac{3}{2} cR^2 + c^2 R^3 - \left(\frac{c}{2} \right)^3 R^4 \tag{1.31}$$

with:

$$c = 3 \left(\frac{b}{a} \right)$$

where $c > 0$.

If the gross rate of return belongs to the interval of absolute of convergence of the Taylor series expansion of the HARA[21] utility function (1.26) around the expected gross rate of return, the investor's utility can be expressed as:

$$U(R) = \sum_{n=0}^{N} \frac{1}{n!} (1-\gamma)^{-1} \gamma^{-(n-1)} \left[\frac{\prod_{i=0}^{n-1} (1-\gamma-i)}{(1-\gamma) \gamma^{(n-1)}} \right] (a)^n \tag{1.32}$$

$$\times \left[b + \frac{a}{\gamma} E(R) \right]^{-(\gamma+n-1)} [R - E(R)]^n$$

---

[21] HARA utility functions are analytic functions.

with:

$$|R - E(R)| < \zeta$$

where ζ is the positive radius of absolute convergence of the Taylor series expansion of $U(.)$ around $E(R)$ defined in (1.5), which is equal here to:

$$\zeta = |-\gamma| \left(\frac{b}{a} + \frac{E(R)}{\gamma} \right)$$

and $N \in IN$.

Provided the existence of the *kurtosis* and supposing that the investment probability distribution is uniquely determined by its moments, taking the limit of N towards infinity and the expected value on both sides in (1.32) leads to:

$$E[U(R)] = \sum_{n=0}^{\infty} \frac{1}{n} (1 - \gamma)^{-1} \gamma^{-(n-1)} \left[\frac{\prod_{i=0}^{n-1} (1 - \gamma - i)}{(1 - \gamma) \gamma^{(n-1)}} \right] (a)^n \qquad (1.33)$$

$$\times \left[b + \frac{a}{\gamma} E(R) \right]^{-(\gamma+n-1)} E\{[R - E(R)]^n\}$$

with:

$$|R - E(R)| \le \zeta^*$$

where $\zeta^* \in \,]0, \zeta[$ and ζ is defined as in (1.5).

Focusing on terms up to the fourth, the expected utility can then be approximated by the following four-moment function[22]:

$$E[U(R)] \cong \frac{\gamma}{(1 - \gamma)} \left[b + \frac{a}{\gamma} E(R) \right]^{(1-\gamma)} - \frac{a^2}{2} \left[b + \frac{a}{\gamma} E(R) \right]^{-(\gamma+1)} \sigma^2(R)$$

$$+ \frac{a^3}{3!} \frac{(\gamma+1)}{\gamma} \left[b + \frac{a}{\gamma} E(R) \right]^{-(\gamma+2)} s^3(R) \qquad (1.34)$$

$$- \frac{a^4}{4!} \frac{(\gamma+1)(\gamma+2)}{\gamma^2} \left[b + \frac{a}{\gamma} E(R) \right]^{-(\gamma+3)} \kappa^4(R)$$

with (using previous notation):

$$|R - E(R)| \le \zeta^*$$

where $\gamma \in IR^*$, $a > 0$ and $b \ge 0$; $\sigma^2(R)$, $m^3(R)$, $\kappa^4(R)$ are respectively the second, the third and the fourth centred moment of the returns R, $\zeta^* \in \,]0, \zeta[$ with ζ defined as in (1.5).

This expression is consistent with our earlier comments regarding investors' preference direction for higher moments, since the expected utility (1.34) depends positively on the expected return and skewness, and negatively on the variance and *kurtosis*, so that a positive skew in the returns distribution and less *kurtosis* lead to higher expected utility.

---

[22] For quartic HARA utility functions, i.e. $\gamma := -3$ and $b > 0$, the Taylor series expansion of (1.26) leads to an equality in (1.34).

For the CARA and CRRA[23] class preference specifications, the fourth-order Taylor approximation of the expected utility leads to the following analytical expressions (see Tsiang, 1972; Hwang and Satchell, 1999; Guidolin and Timmermann, 2005a and 2005b and Jondeau and Rockinger, 2003b, 2005 and 2006):

$$
\begin{cases}
E\left[(1-\gamma)^{-1} R^{(1-\gamma)}\right] \cong (1-\gamma)^{-1} E(R)^{(1-\gamma)} - \dfrac{\gamma}{2} E(R)^{-(\gamma+1)} \sigma^2(R) \\[2mm]
\qquad + \dfrac{\gamma(\gamma+1)}{3!} E(R)^{-(\gamma+2)} s^3(R) - \dfrac{\gamma(\gamma+1)(\gamma+2)}{4!} \\[2mm]
\qquad \times E(R)^{-(\gamma+3)} \kappa^4(R) \\[2mm]
E[\ln(R)] \cong \ln[E(R)] - \dfrac{1}{2} E(R)^{-2} \sigma^2(R) + \dfrac{2}{3!} E(R)^{-3} s^3(R) \\[2mm]
\qquad - \dfrac{6}{4!} E(R)^{-4} \kappa^4(R) \\[2mm]
E[-\exp(-aR)] \cong -\exp[-aE(R)] \times \left[1 + \dfrac{a^2}{2}\sigma^2(R) - \dfrac{a^3}{3!}s^3(R) + \dfrac{a^4}{4!}\kappa^4(R)\right]
\end{cases}
$$

$$(1.35)$$

with (using previous notation):

$$|R - E(R)| \le \zeta^* < \zeta$$

where $\zeta^* \in \,]0, \zeta[$ and ζ is defined as in (1.5).

Through a fourth-order Taylor approximation, the investor's decision problem under uncertainty can be simplified, but additional restrictions on the individual preferences and asset return distributions are required for guaranteeing the theoretical validity and practical interest of such an approach. Indeed, besides the necessary restrictions for the uniform convergence of the Taylor series expansion of $U(.)$ around $E(R)$, extra distributional conditions are required to guarantee the smoothness of the convergence of the Taylor polynomial towards the investor's utility so that the quartic objective function (1.34) will perform uniformly better than the quadratic one. From the risk aversion property of the HARA utility functions, we get the following theorem.

Theorem 6 *A necessary condition[24] for a fourth-order Taylor expansion of a HARA utility function of the class D_4, around $E(R)$, to lead to a better expected utility approximation than a second-order one is that, $\forall n \in IN^*$:*

$$
[(2n+1)!]^{-1} \times U^{(2n+1)}[E(R)] \times E\left\{[R - E(R)]^{2n+1}\right\}
$$
$$
< -[(2n+2)!]^{-1} \times U^{(2n+2)}[E(R)] \times E\left\{[R - E(R)]^{2n+2}\right\} \qquad (1.36)
$$

---

[23] Despite its prominence in the finance field, the usefulness of the CRRA class of utility functions for asset allocation with higher moments is limited due to the small responsiveness of CRRA investors to skewness and tail events (see Chen, 2003; Jondeau and Rockinger, 2003b and Cremers *et al.*, 2005).

[24] This condition is more general than the one proposed by Berényi (2001) since it is valid for any analytic utility function relevant for the fourth-order stochastic dominance and any probability distribution with finite variance and uniquely determined by the sequence of its moments.

with (using previous notation):

$$U^{(n)}\left[E\left(R\right)\right] = (1-\gamma)^{-1}\,\gamma^{-(n-1)}\left[\frac{\prod_{i=0}^{n-1}(1-\gamma-i)}{(1-\gamma)\,\gamma^{(n-1)}}\right] \times (a)^n\left[\frac{a}{\gamma}E\left(R\right)+b\right]^{-(\gamma+n-1)}$$

and:

$$\left|R - E\left(R\right)\right| \leq \zeta^*$$

where $\zeta^* \in\,]0, \zeta[$ and ζ, a, b and γ are defined respectively in (1.5) and (1.26).

Proof   *see Appendix E.*

Another approach is to consider that the relative risk borne by investors, defined as the ratio of standard deviation by mean return, is so large that we cannot neglect it. In this case, Tsiang (1972) shows that, for most of the utility functions that belong to the HARA class, a suitable interval on which the relative risk is defined can be found, such that a quartic objective function provides a better approximation of the expected utility than a quadratic function. This approach is, however, less satisfactory than the last one, since it does not provide *a priori* any clue regarding the limits of validity of the mean–variance–skewness–*kurtosis* decision criterion.

Following Samuelson (1970), it can also be shown that the speed of convergence of the Taylor series expansion towards the expected utility increases with the compactness of the portfolio return distribution and the length of the trading interval. That is, the smaller the trading interval and the absolute risk borne by individuals are, the less terms are needed in (1.34) to achieve an acceptable result.

Furthermore, since the conventional utility theory does not generally translate into a simple comparison of the first N moments, supplementary preference and distributional restrictions are needed to ensure that the quartic approximation (1.34) preserves individual preference ranking.

Theorem 7   *A necessary condition for the mean–variance–skewness–kurtosis function (1.34) to lead exactly to the same preference ordering as the expected utility criterion for an investor with a HARA utility of the D_4 class is that the absolute risk aversion is decreasing ($\gamma > 0$), asset return distributions are negatively skewed and odd (even) higher-order moments are positive nonlinear functions of skewness (kurtosis), that is[25], $\forall\,(i, n) \in (IN^*)^2$:*

$$\begin{cases} m^{2n+1}\left(R_i\right) = (p_{2n+1})^{\frac{2n+1}{3}}\left[s^3\left(R_i\right)\right]^{\frac{2n+1}{3}} \\ m^{2n+2}\left(R_i\right) = (q_{2n+2})^{\frac{n+1}{2}}\left[\kappa^4\left(R_i\right)\right]^{\frac{n+1}{2}} \end{cases} \tag{1.37}$$

---

[25] Similar statistical restrictions have been considered to simplify the mathematics of the mean–variance–skewness and mean–variance–*kurtosis* efficient frontiers (see Athayde and Flôres, 2002, 2003 and 2004).

with:

$$\begin{cases} p_3 = q_4 = 1 \\ p_{2n+1} > 0 \\ q_{2n+2} > 0 \\ s^3(R_i) < 0 \end{cases}$$

and:

$$|R_i - E(R_i)| \le \zeta_i^*$$

where $\zeta_i^* \in]0, \zeta_i[$ with ζ_i the radius of absolute convergence of the Taylor series expansion of $U(.)$ around $E(R_i)$, $i = [1, \ldots, N]$ and $(p_{2n+1} \times q_{2n+2}) = (IR_+^*)^2$.

Proof   *see Appendix F.*

Nevertheless, whatever the truncation order chosen in (1.33), the accuracy of the approximation of the expected utility must be determined empirically (see Hlawitschka, 1994).

It has been shown on using different data, utility and parameter sets that a second-order Taylor expansion is an accurate approximation of the expected utility or the value function. For instance, using, respectively, annual returns on 149 US mutual funds and monthly returns on 97 randomly selected individual stocks from the CRSP database, Levy and Markowitz (1979) and Markowitz (1991) show that mean–variance portfolio rankings are highly correlated with those of the expected utility for most of the HARA utility functions and absolute risk-aversion levels. Moreover, using annual returns on 20 randomly selected stocks from the CRSP database, Kroll *et al.* (1984) find that mean–variance optimal portfolios are close to the ones obtained from the maximisation of the expected utility function when short-sales are forbidden, whatever leverage levels are considered. Similar results are obtained by Pulley (1981 and 1983), Reid and Tew (1987), Rafsnider *et al.* (1992), Ederington (1995)[26] and Fung and Hsieh (1999) on different settings. Simaan (1997) also suggests that the opportunity cost of the mean–variance investment strategy is empirically irrelevant when the opportunity set includes a riskless asset, and very small in the absence of a riskless asset. Amilon (2001) and Cremers *et al.* (2004) extend the previous studies when short-sales are allowed. Working with monthly data on 120 Swedish stocks and five different families of utility functions, Amilon (2001) shows the opportunity cost of the mean–variance strategy remains relatively small for most of the investors in the presence of limited short-selling and option holding. Using monthly data on five different asset classes, Cremers *et al.* (2004) reach the same conclusions when the utility functions of the investors are logarithmic and the estimation risk is taken into account in the portfolio optimisation process.

Other recent empirical studies also show, however, that a fourth-order Taylor series expansion can improve significantly the quality of the investor's expected utility approximation.

---

[26] Nonetheless, working with bootstrapped quarterly returns on 138 US mutual funds, Ederington (1995) finds that for strongly risk-averse investors, a Taylor series expansion based on the first four moments approximates the expected utility better than a Taylor series based on the first two moments.

For instance, working with monthly data on 54 hedge funds from the TASS database, Berényi (2002 and 2004) reports an increase of the correlation level between performance-based portfolio orderings and expected utility portfolio rankings when the considered performance measure takes into account the effect of the higher-order moments for various leverage levels and utility specifications. Jondeau and Rockinger (2003b and 2006) show that the mean–variance–skewness–*kurtosis* portfolio selection criterion leads to more realistic risky asset allocations than the mean–variance approach for some US stocks at a weekly frequency and emerging markets at a monthly frequency when investors have CARA or CRRA preferences and are short-sale constrained.[27] Considering the tactical asset allocation of a US CRRA investor with holding periods ranging from one month to one year, Brandt *et al.* (2005) also find that approximated asset allocations obtained through the optimisation of a quartic objective function are closer to the true asset allocations than the ones obtained through the maximisation of a quadratic function and lead to lower certainty equivalent return losses than the second-order approximation, irrespective of the risk-aversion level and the investment horizon considered. The importance of higher moments for tactical asset allocation increases with the holding period and decreases with the level of the relative risk-aversion coefficient.[28]. Moreover, using ten years of monthly data on 62 hedge funds from the CIDSM database, Cremers *et al.* (2005) show that the mean–variance approach results in significant utility losses and unrealistic asset allocations for investors with bilinear or S-shaped value functions.

1.5   CONCLUSION

In this chapter we derive the theoretical foundations of multi-moment asset allocation and pricing models in an expected utility framework. We recall first the main hypotheses that are necessary to link the preference function with the centred moments of the unconditional portfolio return distribution. We then develop a quartic utility specification to obtain an exact mean–variance–skewness–*kurtosis* decision criterion. We also present the behavioural and distributional conditions under which the expected utility can be approximated by a fourth-order Taylor series expansion.

Our main conclusion is that, despite its widespread use in multi-moment asset allocation (see, for instance, Guidolin and Timmermann, 2005a and 2005b; Brandt *et al.*, 2005 and Jondeau and Rockinger, 2003b, 2005 and 2006b) and capital and consumption asset pricing models (see, for instance, Kraus and Litzenberger, 1980; Fang and Lai, 1997; Hwang and Satchell, 1999; Dittmar, 2002 and Semenov, 2004), the Taylor series approach displays no general theoretical superiority over a polynomial utility specification to justify a moment-based decision criterion. Indeed, extra restrictions on the risky asset return distributions are required to ensure that a fourth-order Taylor series expansion preserves the preference ranking, while in the quartic case the opportunity set and utility parameters must be severely restricted to satisfy the five desirable properties of utility functions (see Pratt, 1964; Arrow, 1970 and Kimball, 1990). Moreover, additional requirements are necessary to guarantee the convergence of the (in)finite-order Taylor series expansions.

---

[27] Patton (2001 and 2004) finds similar results in a conditional setting for small and large capitalisation US stock indices with monthly data and with or without short-sales.
[28] Jondeau and Rockinger (2003b) investigate a similar risk-aversion effect when a risk-free asset exists.

Thus, the introduction of the third- and fourth-order centred moment in a portfolio selection criterion is theoretically justifiable when the utility function is quartic, and when the support of the portfolio distribution is well restricted or when individuals exhibit decreasing HARA utility functions, the time interval between actions and consequences is small but finite, and all the odd and even centred moments of investment returns can be expressed respectively as positive nonlinear functions of the (negative) skewness and the *kurtosis*. Under these conditions, it is then theoretically possible to derive a multi-moment asset pricing relation (see, for instance, Chapter 6).

APPENDIX A

Theorem 1   *A sufficient condition for a Taylor series expansion of an infinitely often differentiable utility function U(.) around the expected gross rate of return $E(R)$ to converge absolutely is that the set of realisations of the random variable R belongs to the open interval J defined by:*

$$|R - E(R)| < \zeta$$

with:

$$\zeta = \lim_{N \to \infty} \left| \frac{(N+1)! U^{(N)}[E(R)]}{N! U^{(N+1)}[E(R)]} \right|$$

where ζ is a positive constant corresponding to the radius of convergence of the Taylor series expansion of U(.) around $E(R)$ and $N \in IN$.

Proof   Let $P_N[E(R)]$ be the Taylor approximation of order N around $E(R)$ of an arbitrarily often differentiable utility function $U(.)$ on a subset I of IR, that is:

$$P_N[E(R)] = \sum_{n=0}^{N} \frac{1}{n!} U^{(n)}[E(R)][R - E(R)]^n \tag{1.38}$$

According to the quotient test, the Taylor polynomial (1.38) converges if:

$$q = \lim_{N \to \infty} \left| \frac{N! U^{(N+1)}[E(R)]}{(N+1)! U^{(N)}[E(R)]} \times \frac{[R - E(R)]^{N+1}}{[R - E(R)]^N} \right| \tag{1.39}$$

$$= \lim_{N \to \infty} \left| \frac{N! U^{(N+1)}[E(R)]}{(N+1)! U^{(N)}[E(R)]} \right| |R - E(R)| < 1$$

That is, the Taylor series expansion of $U(.)$ around the expected gross rate of return $E(R)$ is absolutely convergent when:

$$|R - E(R)| < \lim_{N \to \infty} \left| \frac{(N+1)! U^{(N)}[E(R)]}{N! U^{(N+1)}[E(R)]} \right| \tag{1.40}$$

■

APPENDIX B

Theorem 2   *A sufficient condition for a Taylor series expansion of an infinitely often differentiable utility function U(.) around the expected gross rate of return $E(R)$ with a positive radius of convergence ζ, to converge uniformly is that the set of realisations of the random variable R remains in the closed interval J^* defined as:*

$$|R - E(R)| \leq \zeta^*$$

$\forall \zeta^* \in]0, \zeta[$.

Proof   Consider the Taylor approximation of order N of an infinitely often differentiable utility function $U(.)$ defined on an open interval J such that:

$$P_N[E(R)] = \sum_{n=0}^{N} \frac{1}{n!} U^{(n)}[E(R)][R - E(R)]^n \tag{1.41}$$

where $N \in IN^*$ and $J =]E(R) - \zeta, E(R) + \zeta[$ with ζ the radius of convergence of the Taylor series expansion of $U(.)$ around $E(R)$, e.g.:

$$\zeta = \lim_{N \to \infty} \left| \frac{(N+1)! U^{(N)}[E(R)]}{N! U^{(N+1)}[E(R)]} \right|$$

For any $R \in [E(R) - \zeta^*, E(R) + \zeta^*]$, we must have:

$$|P[E(R)] - P_N[E(R)]| = \left| \sum_{n=N+1}^{\infty} \frac{1}{n!} U^{(n)}[E(R)][R - E(R)]^n \right|$$

$$\leq \sum_{n=N+1}^{\infty} \left| \frac{1}{n!} U^{(n)}[E(R)][R - E(R)]^n \right| \tag{1.42}$$

$$\leq \sum_{n=N+1}^{\infty} \left| \frac{1}{n!} U^{(n)}[E(R)][\zeta^* - E(R)]^n \right|$$

with:

$$P[E(R)] = \sum_{n=0}^{\infty} \frac{1}{n!} U^{(n)}[E(R)][R - E(R)]^n$$

where $\zeta^* \in]0, \zeta[$.
    That is:

$$\sup_{R \in [E(R) - \zeta^*, E(R) + \zeta^*]} \{|P[E(R)] - P_N[E(R)]|\} \leq \sum_{n=N+1}^{\infty} \left| \frac{1}{n!} U^{(n)}[E(R)][\zeta^* - E(R)]^n \right| \tag{1.43}$$

Since the infinite-order Taylor series expansion of $U(.)$ around $E(R)$ is absolutely convergent on J, we get:

$$\lim_{N \to \infty} \sum_{n=N+1}^{\infty} \left| \frac{1}{n!} U^{(n)}[E(R)][\zeta^* - E(R)]^n \right| = 0 \tag{1.44}$$

We can thus make $|P(.) - P_N(.)|$ as small as possible, $\forall R \in [E(R) - \zeta^*, E(R) + \zeta^*]$, by choosing N sufficiently large and independent of R. So that the Taylor series expansion of $U(.)$ around $E(R)$ converges uniformly[29] on the interval $[E(R) - \zeta^*, E(R) + \zeta^*]$.   ■

APPENDIX C

Theorem 3 *The necessary and sufficient conditions for a quartic utility function $U(.)$ to belong to the class D_4 of utility functions relevant for the fourth-order stochastic dominance are:*

$$
\begin{cases}
U^{(1)}(.) > 0 \Leftrightarrow
\begin{cases}
a_1 > 0 \\[2mm]
\left(-\dfrac{a_3^2}{16a_4^2} + \dfrac{a_2}{6a_4} \right)^3 + \left(\dfrac{a_3^3}{16a_4^3} - \dfrac{a_2 a_3}{16a_4^2} + \dfrac{a_1}{8a_4} \right)^2 > 0 \\[4mm]
R < -\dfrac{a_3}{4a_4} + \dfrac{K + \left(9a_3^2 - 24a_4 a_2\right) K^{-1}}{12 a_4}
\end{cases}
\\[18mm]
U^{(2)}(.) < 0 \Leftrightarrow
\begin{cases}
\begin{cases}
0 > a_2 \geq \left(\dfrac{3a_3^2}{8a_4} \right) \\[3mm]
R < -\dfrac{a_3}{4a_4} + \dfrac{\sqrt{9a_3^2 - 24a_4 a_2}}{12a_4} \ \text{and} \ R > -\dfrac{a_3}{4a_4} - \dfrac{\sqrt{9a_3^2 - 24a_4 a_2}}{12a_4}
\end{cases} \\[6mm]
\text{or } a_2 < \left(\dfrac{3a_3^2}{8a_4} \right)
\end{cases}
\\[18mm]
U^{(3)}(.) > 0 \Leftrightarrow
\begin{cases}
a_3 > 0 \\[2mm]
R < -\left(\dfrac{a_3}{4a_4} \right)
\end{cases}
\\[8mm]
U^{(4)}(.) < 0 \Leftrightarrow a_4 < 0
\end{cases}
$$

with:

$$
K = \left(\frac{A + \sqrt{-108\left(3a_3^2 - 8a_4 a_2\right)^3 + A^2}}{2} \right)^{1/3}
$$

and:

$$
A = \left(-54a_3^3 - 432a_4^2 a_1 + 216 a_4 a_3 a_2 \right)
$$

---

[29] An infinite series $\{\sum_{n=0}^{\infty} a_n x^n\}$ is said to converge uniformly on an interval J^* if, for each $\epsilon > 0$, we can find a positive integer N_0 such that, $\forall N \geq N_0$ and $\forall x \in J^*$:

$$
\left| \sum_{n=0}^{\infty} a_n x^n - \sum_{n=0}^{N} a_n x^n \right| \leq \epsilon
$$

This is equivalent to saying that $\{\sum_{n=0}^{\infty} a_n x^n\}$ converges uniformly on an interval J^* if, for each $\epsilon > 0$, we can find a positive integer N_0 such that, $\forall N \geq N_0$:

$$
\sup_{x \in J^*} \left| \sum_{n=0}^{\infty} a_n x^n - \sum_{n=0}^{N} a_n x^n \right| \leq \epsilon
$$

where $U^{(1)}(.)$, $U^{(2)}(.)$, $U^{(3)}(.)$ and $U^{(4)}(.)$ *are the first four partial derivatives of U (.) and* $a_i \in IR^*$ *with* $i = [1, \ldots, 4]$.

Proof   Consider the following general quartic utility function:

$$U(R) = a_0 + a_1 R + a_2 R^2 + a_3 R^3 + a_4 R^4 \tag{1.45}$$

with $a_i \in IR^*$, $i = [1, \ldots, 4]$.

The first, second, third and fourth derivatives of (1.45) are given, respectively, by:

$$\begin{cases} U^{(1)}(R) = a_1 + 2a_2 R + 3a_3 R^2 + 4a_4 R^3 \\ U^{(2)}(R) = 2a_2 + 6a_3 R + 12a_4 R^2 \\ U^{(3)}(R) = 6a_3 + 24a_4 R \\ U^{(4)}(R) = 24a_4 \end{cases} \tag{1.46}$$

Imposing $U^{(4)}(.) < 0$ and $U^{(3)}(.) > 0$ yields the following set of requirements:

$$\begin{cases} \begin{cases} a_3 > 0 \\ R < -\left(\dfrac{a_3}{4a_4}\right) \end{cases} \\ a_4 < 0 \end{cases} \tag{1.47}$$

Depending on the sign of the discriminant of the quadratic expression of $U^{(2)}(.)$ in (1.46), the risk-aversion property $U^{(2)}(.) < 0$ leads to:

$$\begin{cases} \begin{cases} 0 > a_2 \geq \left(\dfrac{3a_3^2}{8a_4}\right) \\ R < -\dfrac{a_3}{4a_4} + \dfrac{\sqrt{9a_3^2 - 24a_4 a_2}}{12a_4} \text{ and } R > -\dfrac{a_3}{4a_4} - \dfrac{\sqrt{9a_3^2 - 24a_4 a_2}}{12a_4} \end{cases} \\ \text{or } a_2 < \left(\dfrac{3a_3^2}{8a_4}\right) \end{cases} \tag{1.48}$$

From the non-satiation property, $U^{(1)}(.) < 0$, we obtain the final system of parameter restrictions, that is:

$$\begin{cases} a_1 > 0 \\ \left(-\dfrac{a_3^2}{16a_4^2} + \dfrac{a_2}{6a_4}\right)^3 + \left(\dfrac{a_3^3}{16a_4^3} - \dfrac{a_2 a_3}{16a_4^2} + \dfrac{a_1}{8a_4}\right)^2 > 0 \\ R < -\dfrac{a_3}{4a_4} + \dfrac{K + \left(9a_3^2 - 24a_4 a_2\right)K^{-1}}{12a_4} \end{cases} \tag{1.49}$$

with:

$$K = \left(\frac{A + \sqrt{-108\left(3a_3^2 - 8a_4 a_2\right)^3 + A^2}}{2}\right)^{1/3}$$

and:

$$A = \left(-54a_3^3 - 432a_4^2a_1 + 216a_4a_3a_2\right).$$

Combining (1.47), (1.48) and (1.49) leads to the desired result.   ∎

APPENDIX D

Theorem 4   *The necessary and sufficient conditions for a quartic utility function $U(.)$ to exhibit a decreasing absolute risk aversion (DARA), a decreasing absolute prudence (DAP) and a constant or increasing relative risk aversion (CRRA or IRRA) with respect to the gross rate of return R are given by:*

$$
\begin{cases}
8a_4^2R^4 + 8a_4a_3R^3 + 3a_3^2R^2 + 2\left(a_3a_2 - 2a_4a_1\right)R + \dfrac{2}{3}a_2^2 - a_3a_1 < 0 & \text{(DARA)} \\[2mm]
\begin{cases}
-\dfrac{a_3}{4a_4} + \dfrac{\sqrt{\left(-9a_3^2 + 24a_4a_2\right)}}{12a_4} < R < -\dfrac{a_3}{4a_4} - \dfrac{\sqrt{\left(-9a_3^2 + 24a_4a_2\right)}}{12a_4} \\[2mm]
a_2 < \left(\dfrac{3a_3^2}{8a_4}\right)
\end{cases} & \text{(DAP)} \\[4mm]
\begin{aligned}
& 120\left(a_4\right)^2R^4 + 120a_3a_4R^3 + 3\left[9\left(a_3\right)^2 + 16a_2a_4\right]R^2 \\
& + 6\left(3a_2a_3 + 2a_4a_1\right)R + 3a_3a_1 + 2\left(a_2\right)^2 \geq \\
& \left(12a_4R^2 + 6a_3R + 2a_2\right)\left(4a_4R^4 + 3a_3R^3 + 2a_2R^2 + a_1R\right)^{-1}
\end{aligned} & \text{(CRRA or IRRA)}
\end{cases}
$$

where $a_i \in IR^*$, with $i = [1, \ldots, 4]$.

Proof   Imposing the decrease of absolute risk-aversion coefficient with respect to the gross rate of return, that is:

$$\left[-\frac{\partial U(R)}{\partial R}\frac{\partial^3 U(R)}{\partial R^3} + \left(\frac{\partial^2 U(R)}{\partial R^2}\right)^2\right] < 0 \tag{1.50}$$

we obtain, from the derivative expressions (1.46) of the quartic utility function, that the DARA property is verified when:

$$8a_4^2R^4 + 8a_4a_3R^3 + 3a_3^2R^2 + 2\left(a_3a_2 - 2a_4a_1\right)R + \frac{2}{3}a_2^2 - a_3a_1 < 0 \tag{1.51}$$

Imposing the decrease of absolute prudence coefficient with respect to the gross rate of return gives:

$$\left[-\frac{\partial^2 U(R)}{\partial R^2}\frac{\partial^4 U(R)}{\partial R^4} + \left(\frac{\partial^3 U(R)}{\partial R^3}\right)^2\right] < 0 \tag{1.52}$$

In the quartic case, this inequality translates into (see 1.46):

$$24a_4^2 R^2 + 12a_4a_3R + 3a_3^2 + 4a_4a_2 < 0 \tag{1.53}$$

Depending on the sign of the discriminant in (1.53), we find that the DAP is achieved for quartic utility functions when:

$$
\begin{cases}
\begin{cases}
-\dfrac{a_3}{4a_4} + \dfrac{\sqrt{(-9a_3^2 + 24a_4a_2)}}{12a_4} < R < -\dfrac{a_3}{4a_4} - \dfrac{\sqrt{(-9a_3^2 + 24a_4a_2)}}{12a_4} \\[2ex]
a_2 < \left(\dfrac{3a_3^2}{8a_4}\right)
\end{cases} \\[4ex]
\text{or } a_2 > \left(\dfrac{3a_3^2}{8a_4}\right)
\end{cases}
\tag{1.54}
$$

Finally, the increase or constancy of relative risk-aversion coefficient with respect to the gross rate of return leads to the following restriction:

$$\left\{ R \times \left[-\frac{\partial^2 U(R)}{\partial R^2} \frac{\partial^4 U(R)}{\partial R^4} + \left(\frac{\partial^3 U(R)}{\partial R^3} \right)^2 \right] - \frac{\partial^2 U(R)}{\partial R^2} \left(\frac{\partial U(R)}{\partial R} \right)^{-1} \right\} \geq 0 \tag{1.55}$$

Using the derivative expressions (1.46), this property requires, for the fourth-order polynomial utility function, that:

$$8a_4^2 R^5 + 8a_4a_3R^4 + 3a_3^2R^3 - 2\left[a_4a_1 - 2a_3a_2 - 6\left(a_1 + 2a_2R + 3a_3R^2 + 4a_4R^3\right)^{-1} a_4 \right] R^2$$
$$- \left[a_3a_1 - \frac{2}{3}a_2^2 + 6\left(a_1 + 2a_2R + 3a_3R^2 + 4a_4R^3\right)^{-1} a_3 \right] R$$
$$- 2a_2 \left(4a_4R^3 + 3a_3R^2 + 2a_2R + a_1\right)^{-1} \leq 0 \tag{1.56}$$

■

APPENDIX E

Theorem 5 *A necessary condition for a fourth-order Taylor expansion of a HARA utility function of D_4 utility class around $E(R)$ to lead to a better expected utility approximation than a second-order one is that, $\forall n \in IN^*$:*

$$[(2n+1)!]^{-1} U^{(2n+1)} [E(R)] \times E\left\{ [R - E(R)]^{2n+1} \right\}$$
$$< -[(2n+2)!]^{-1} U^{(2n+2)} [E(R)] \times E\left\{ [R - E(R)]^{2n+2} \right\}$$

with (using previous notation):

$$U^{(n)} [E(R)] = (1-\gamma)^{-1} \gamma^{-(n-1)} \left[\frac{\prod_{i=0}^{n-1}(1-\gamma-i)}{(1-\gamma)\gamma^{(n-1)}} \right] \times (a)^n \left[\frac{a}{\gamma} E(R) + b \right]^{-(\gamma+n-1)}$$

and:

$$
\begin{cases}
b + \dfrac{a}{\gamma} R > 0 \\[2mm]
\dfrac{1}{\gamma} > -\dfrac{1}{2} \\[2mm]
|R - E(R)| \le \zeta^*
\end{cases}
$$

where $\gamma \le -3$ if γ is a negative integer and $\gamma \ne 0$ otherwise, $a > 0$, $b \ge 0$, and $\zeta^* \in]0, \zeta[$ with ζ the radius of convergence of the Taylor series expansion of $U(.)$ around $E(R)$.

Proof   If all the centred moments exist and uniquely determine the return distribution, it is possible to express the expected utility of any investor with HARA preference as[30]:

$$
E[U(R)] = U[E(R)] + \Phi[E(R)] \tag{1.57}
$$

with:

$$
\Phi[E(R)] = \sum_{n=2}^{\infty} \frac{1}{n!} U^{(n)}[E(R)] \, m^n(R)
$$

and:

$$
|R - E(R)| \le \zeta^*
$$

where $\zeta^* \in]0, \zeta[$, ζ is the positive radius of absolute convergence of the Taylor series expansion of $U(.)$ around $E(R)$, $\Phi(.)$ is negative by the risk-aversion property of HARA utility functions[31], and $m^n(R) = E\{[R - E(R)]^n\}$, corresponds to the nth centred moment of R.

If, moreover, the centred higher-order moments of the gross rate of return distribution, denoted $m^n(R)$, verify $\forall n \in IN^*$:

$$
[(2n+1)!]^{-1} \times U^{2n+1}[E(R)] \times m^{2n+1}(R) < -[(2n+2)!]^{-1} \times U^{2n+2}[E(R)] \times m^{2n+2}(R) \tag{1.58}
$$

then, the nth order Taylor approximation of the expected utility of an agent with HARA-type preference must converge smoothly towards its objective function, since, $\forall N \in IN^*$ and $R \in [E(R) - \zeta^*, E(R) + \zeta^*]$:

$$
\frac{1}{2} U^{(2)}[E(R)] \sigma^2(R) + \sum_{n=3}^{2N+2} \frac{1}{n!} U^{(n)}[E(R)] \, m^n(R) < 0 \tag{1.59}
$$

and:

$$
E[U(R)] < U[E(R)].
$$

---

[30] HARA utility functions are analytic real functions.
[31] The risk aversion property entails, for any risky investment, that: $E[U(R)] < U[E(R)]$.

It follows that the fourth-order Taylor series expansion of a HARA utility function which belongs to the D_4 class will lead to a better approximation of the expected utility criterion than the one obtained through a second-order Taylor series expansion, $\forall R \in [E(R) - \zeta^*, E(R) + \zeta^*]$.   ∎

APPENDIX F

Theorem 6   *A necessary condition for the mean–variance–skewness–kurtosis function (1.34) to lead exactly to the same preference ordering as the expected utility criterion for an investor with a HARA utility $U(.)$ of the D_4 utility class is that the absolute risk aversion is decreasing $(\gamma > 0)$, asset return distributions are negatively skewed and odd (even) higher-order moments are positive nonlinear functions of skewness (kurtosis), that is, $\forall (i, n) \in (IN^*)^2$:*

$$\begin{cases} m^{2n+1}(R_i) = (p_{2n+1})^{\frac{2n+1}{3}} \left[s^3(R_i) \right]^{\frac{2n+1}{3}} \\ m^{2n+2}(R_i) = (q_{2n+2})^{\frac{n+1}{2}} \left[\kappa^4(R_i) \right]^{\frac{n+1}{2}} \end{cases}$$

with:

$$\begin{cases} p_3 = q_4 = 1 \\ p_{2n+1} > 0 \\ q_{2n+2} > 0 \\ s^3(R_i) < 0 \end{cases}$$

and:

$$|R_i - E(R_i)| \leq \zeta_i^*$$

where $\zeta_i^* \in \,]0, \zeta_i[$ with ζ_i the positive radius of absolute convergence of the Taylor series expansion of $U(.)$ around $E(R_i)$, $i = [1, \ldots, N]$, and $(p_{2n+1} \times q_{2n+2}) = (IR_+^*)^2$.

Proof   Consider a HARA utility function $U(.)$ of the D_4 class and two negatively skewed distributed random returns $R_1 \in [\zeta_1^* - E(R_1), \zeta_1^* + E(R_1)]$ and $R_2 \in [\zeta_2^* - E(R_2), \zeta_2^* + E(R_2)]$, with finite moments such that:

$$\begin{cases} E(R_1) \geq E(R_2) \\ \sigma^2(R_1) \leq \sigma^2(R_2) \\ s^3(R_1) \geq s^3(R_2) \\ \kappa^4(R_1) \leq \kappa^4(R_2) \end{cases} \qquad (1.60)$$

with at least one strict inequality[32], and $\forall i \in [1, 2]$ and $\forall n \in IN^*$:

$$\begin{cases} m^{2n+1}(R_i) = (p_{2n+1})^{\frac{2n+1}{3}} \left[s^3(R_i)\right]^{\frac{2n+1}{3}} \\ m^{2n+2}(R_i) = (q_{2n+2})^{\frac{n+1}{2}} \left[\kappa^4(R_i)\right]^{\frac{n+1}{2}} \end{cases} \quad (1.61)$$

with:

$$\begin{cases} p_3 = q_4 = 1 \\ p_{2n+1} > 0 \\ q_{2n+2} > 0 \\ s^3(R_i) < 0 \end{cases}$$

where $\zeta_i^* \in]0, \zeta_i[$, ζ_i is the positive radius of absolute convergence of the Taylor series expansion of $U(.)$ around $E(R_i)$, $m^n(R_i) = E\{[R_i - E(R_i)]^n\}$, $i = [1, 2]$, and $(p_{2n+1} \times q_{2n+2}) = (IR_+^*)^2$.

For any decreasing HARA utility function $U(.)$, there is a strict equivalence between the mean–variance–skewness–*kurtosis* preference ranking and the expected utility preference ordering, since:

$$E[U(R_1)] - E[U(R_2)] = \sum_{n=0}^{\infty} \frac{1}{n!} \{U^{(n)}[E(R_1)] \times m^n(R_1) - U^{(n)}[E(R_2)] \times m^n(R_2)\} > 0$$

$$(1.62)$$

with:

$$\begin{cases} (-1)^n U^{(n)}(R_i) < 0 \\ (-1)^n m^n(R_1) \le (-1)^n m^n(R_2) \end{cases}$$

and:

$$|R_i - E(R_i)| \le \zeta_i^*$$

where $i = [1, 2]$ and $n \in IN^* - \{1\}$.

■

ACKNOWLEDGEMENTS

We are grateful to Chris Adcock, Thierry Chauveau, Eric Jondeau, Thierry Michel and Michael Rockinger for help and encouragement in preparing this work. The content of this chapter engages only its authors and does not necessarily reflect the opinions of their employers.

---

[32] So that, asset 1 with return R_1 is preferred to asset 2 with return R_2 for any investor with mean–variance–skewness–*kurtosis* preferences.

REFERENCES

Adcock, C. (2003) Asset Pricing and Portfolio Selection Based on the Multivariate Skew-Student Distribution, Working Paper, University of Sheffield, 15 pages.

Agarwal, V. and N. Naik (2004) Risks and Portfolio Decisions involving Hedge Funds, *Review of Financial Studies* **17**, 63–98.

Amilon, H. (2001) Comparison of Mean–Variance and Exact Utility Maximisation in Stock Portfolio Selection, Working Paper, Lund University, 15 pages.

Arrow, K. (1970) *Essays in the Theory of Risk Bearing*, North-Holland Publishing Company, Amsterdam-London.

Athayde, G. and R. Flôres (2002) Portfolio Frontier with Higher Moments: the Undiscovered Country, Discussion Paper EPGE-FGV, 42 pages.

Athayde, G. and R. Flôres (2003) Incorporating Skewness and Kurtosis in Portfolio Optimization: A Multidimensional Efficient Set. In: *Advances in Portfolio Construction and Implementation*, S. Satchell and A. Scowcroft (Eds), Butterworth Heinemann, pp. 243–257.

Athayde, G. and R. Flôres (2004) Finding a Maximum Skewness Portfolio: a General Solution to Three-moments Portfolio Choice, *Journal of Economic Dynamics and Control* **28** (7), 1335–1352.

Azzalini, A. and A. Capitanio (2003) Distributions Generated by Perturbation of Symmetry with Emphasis on a Multivariate Skew *t* Distribution, *Journal of Royal Statistical Society series B* **65**, 367–389.

Baker, G. and P. Graves-Morris (1996) *Padé Approximants*, second edition, Cambridge University Press.

Barndorff-Nielsen, O. (1978) Hyperbolic Distributions and Distributions on Hyperbolae, *Scandinavian Journal of Statistics* **5**, 151–157.

Barndorff-Nielsen, O. (1997) Normal Inverse Gaussian Distributions and Stochastic Volatility Modelling, *Scandinavian Journal of Statistics* **24**, 1–13.

Bellalah, M. and F. Selmi (2002) Les fonctions d'utilité et l'avantage informationnel des moments d'ordre supérieurs: application à la couverture d'options, *Finance* **23**, 14–27.

Benishay, H. (1987) A Fourth-degree Polynomial Utility Function and its Implications for Investors' Responses Toward Fourth Moments of the Wealth Distribution, *Journal of Accounting, Auditing and Finance* **2**, 203–238.

Benishay, H. (1989) More Weight to the Friedman–Savage Hypothesis: A Note, *Journal of Accounting, Auditing and Finance* **4**, 518–527.

Benishay, H. (1992) The Pratt–Arrow Requirement in a Fourth Degree Polynomial Utility Function, *Journal of Accounting, Auditing and Finance* **7**, 97–115.

Bera, A. and S. Park (2003) Maximum Entropy Autoregressive Conditional Heteroskedasticity Model, Working Paper, Illinois University, 37 pages.

Bera, A. and G. Premaratne (2001) Modeling Asymmetry and Excess Kurtosis in Stock Return Data, Working Paper, Illinois University, 25 pages.

Berényi, Z. (2001) Accounting for Illiquidity and Non-normality of Returns in the Performance Assessment, Working Paper, University of Munich, 42 pages.

Berényi, Z. (2002) Measuring Hedge Funds' Risks with Moment-based Variance-equivalent Measures, Working Paper, University of Munich, 35 pages.

Berényi, Z. (2004) *Risk and Performance Evaluation with Skewness and Kurtosis for Conventional and Alternative Investments*, Peter Lang Publishing.

Bookstaber, R. and J. McDonald (1987) A General Distribution for Describing Security Price Returns, *Journal of Business* **60** (3), 401–424.

Branco, M., D. Dey and S. Sahu (2003) A New Class of Multivariate Skew Distributions with Applications to Bayesian Regression Models, *Canadian Journal of Statistics* **31**, 129–150.

Brandt, M., A. Goyal, P. Santa-Clara and J. Stroud (2005) A Simulation Approach to Dynamic Portfolio Choice with an Application to Learning about Return Predictability, *Review of Financial Studies* **18**, 831–873.

Brockett, P. and R. Garven (1998) A Reexamination of the Relationship Between Preferences and Moments Ordering by Rational Risk Averse Investors, *Geneva Papers on Risk and Insurance Theory* **23**, 127–137.

Brockett, P. and Y. Kahane (1992) Risk, Return, Skewness and Preference, *Management Science* **38**, 851–866.

Capelle-Blanchard, G., E. Jurczenko and B. Maillet (2001) The Approximate Option Pricing Model: Performances and Dynamic Properties, *Journal of Multinational Financial Management* **11**, 427–444.

Chen, K. (2003) Calibrating the Skewness and Kurtosis Preference of Investors, Working Paper, HEC Lausanne, 31 pages.

Christensen, O. and K. Christensen (2004) *Approximation Theory: from Taylor Polynomials to Wavelets*, Birkhaüser.

Cont, R. (2001) Empirical Properties of Asset Returns: Stylised Facts and Statistical Issues, *Quantitative Finance* **1** (2), 223–236.

Corrado, C. and T. Su (1996a) S&P 500 Index Option Tests of Jarrow and Rudd's Approximate Option Valuation Formula, *Journal of Futures Markets* **16** (6), 611–629.

Corrado, C. and T. Su (1996b) Skewness and Kurtosis in S&P 500 Index Returns Implied by Option Prices, *Journal of Financial Research* **19** (2), 175–192.

Cremers, J., M. Kritzman and S. Page (2004) Portfolio Formation with Higher Moments and Plausible Utility, Working Paper, State Street Associates, 18 pages.

Cremers, J., M. Kritzman and S. Page (2005) Optimal Hedge Fund Allocations: Do Higher Moments Matter?, *Journal of Portfolio Management* **31**, 70–81.

Dittmar, R. (2002) Nonlinear Pricing Kernels, Kurtosis Preference, and Evidence from the Cross-Section of Equity Returns, *Journal of Finance* **57**, 369–403.

Dutta, K. and D. Babbel (2005) Extracting Probabilistic Information from the Prices of Interest Rate Options: Tests of Distributional Assumptions, *Journal of Business* **78**, 841–870.

Ederington, L. (1995) Mean–variance as an Approximation to Expected Utility Maximisation: Semi-Ex-Ante Results. In: *Advances in Financial Economics*, M. Hirschey and M. Marr (Eds), JAI Press, pp. 81–98.

Eriksson, A., L. Forsberg and E. Ghysels (2004) Approximating the Probability Distribution of Functions of Random Variables: A New Approach, Working Paper, Cirano, 22 pages.

Fang, H. and T. Lai (1997) Cokurtosis and Capital Asset Pricing, *Financial Review* **32**, 293–307.

Feigenbaum, J. (2003) Symmetries of the HARA Class, Working Paper, University of Pittsburgh, 29 pages.

Fishburn, P. (1980) Stochastic Dominance and Moments of Distributions, *Mathematics of Operations Research* **5**, 94–100.

Fung, W. and D. Hsieh (1999) Is Mean–variance Analysis Applicable to Hedge Funds?, *Economic Letters* **62**, 53–58.

Gamba, A. and F. Rossi (1997) A Three-moment Based Capital Asset Pricing Model, Working Paper, University of Venice, 16 pages.

Gamba, A. and F. Rossi (1998a) A Three-moment Based Portfolio Selection Model, *Rivista di Matematica per le Scienze Economiche e Sociali* **20**, 25–48.

Gamba, A. and F. Rossi (1998b) Mean–Variance–Skewness Analysis in Portfolio Choice and Capital Markets, *Ricerca Operativa* **28**, 5–46.

Gollier, C. (2004) *The Economics of Risk and Time*, MIT Press.

Gordy, M. (1998) A Generalization of Generalized Beta Distributions, *Finance and Economics Discussion Series* **52**, FED, 28 pages.

Guidolin, M. and A. Timmermann (2005a) Optimal Portfolio Choices under Regime Switching, Skew and Kurtosis Preferences, Working Paper, Federal Reserve Bank of St Louis, 35 pages.

Guidolin, M. and A. Timmermann (2005b) International Asset Allocation under Regime Switching, Skew and Kurtosis Preferences, Working Paper, Federal Reserve Bank of St Louis, 54 pages.

Hamburger, H. (1920) Über eine Erweiterung des Stieljesschen Moment Problems, *Matematische Zeitschrift* **7**, 235–319.

Hanoch, G. and C. Levy (1969) The Efficiency Analysis of Choices Involving Risk, *Review of Economic Studies* **36**, 335–356.

Hanoch, G. and C. Levy (1970) Efficient Portfolio Selection with Quadratic and Cubic Utility, *Journal of Business* **43**, 181–189.

Harvey, C., J. Lietchty, M. Lietchty and P. Müller (2004) Portfolio Selection with Higher Moments, Working Paper, Duke University, 51 pages.

Hasset, M., S. Sears and G. Trennepohl (1985) Asset Preference, Skewness, and the Measurement of Expected Utility, *Journal of Economic Business* **37**, 35–47.

Hausdorff, F. (1921a) Summationsmethoden und Momentfolgen, I, *Matematische Zeitschrift* **9**, 74–109.

Hausdorff, F. (1921b) Summationsmethoden und Momentfolgen, II, *Mathematische Zeitschrift* **9**, 280–299.

Heyde, C. (1963) On a Property of the Lognormal Distribution, *Journal of Royal Statistical Society* **29**, 392–393.

Hlawitschka, W. (1994) The Empirical Nature of Taylor Series Approximations to Expected Utility, *American Economic Review* **84** (3), 713–719.

Horvath, P. and R. Scott (1980) On the Direction of Preference for Moments of Higher Order than the Variance, *Journal of Finance* **35** (4), 915–919.

Hwang, S. and S. Satchell (1999) Modelling Emerging Market Risk Premia using Higher Moments, *International Journal of Finance and Economics* **4** (4), 271–296.

Jarrow, R. and A. Rudd (1982) Approximate Option Valuation for Arbitrary Stochastic Processes, *Journal of Financial Economics* **10**, 347–369.

Jean, W. and B. Helms (1988) Moment Orderings and Stochastic Dominance Tests, *Journal of Busines Finance & Accounting* **15**, 573–583.

Jondeau, E. and M. Rockinger (2002) Entropy Densities with an Application to Autoregressive Conditional Skewness and Kurtosis, *Journal of Econometrics* **106**, 116–142.

Jondeau, E. and M. Rockinger (2003a) Conditional Volatility, Skewness and Kurtosis: Existence, Persistence and Comovements, *Journal of Economic Dynamics and Control* **27** (10), 1699–1737.

Jondeau, E. and M. Rockinger (2003b) How Higher Moments Affect the Allocation of Assets, *Finance Letters* **1** (2), 1–5.

Jondeau, E. and M. Rockinger (2005) Conditional Asset Allocation under Non-Normality: How Costly Is the Mean–Variance Criterion?, Working Paper, HEC Lausanne, 42 pages.

Jondeau, E. and M. Rockinger (2006) Optimal Portfolio Allocation Under Higher Moments, *Journal of the European Financial Management Association* **12**, 29–67.

Jurczenko, E. and B. Maillet (2001) The 3-CAPM: Theoretical Foundations and an Asset Pricing Model Comparison in a Unified Framework. In: *Developments in Forecast Combination and Portfolio Choice*, C. Dunis, A. Timmermann and J. Moody (Eds), John Wiley & Sons, Ltd, Chichester, pp. 239–273.

Jurczenko, E., B. Maillet and B. Negrea (2002a) Skewness and Kurtosis Implied by Option Prices: A Second Comment, FMG Discussion Paper 419, LSE, 32 pages.

Jurczenko, E., B. Maillet and B. Negrea (2002b) Revisited Multi-moment Approximate Option Pricing Models: A General Comparison, FMG Discussion Paper 430, LSE, 85 pages.

Jurczenko, E., B. Maillet and B. Negrea (2004) A Note on Skewness and Kurtosis Adjusted Option Pricing Models under the Martingale Restriction, *Quantitative Finance* **4**, 479–488.

Kendall, A. (1977) *The Advanced Theory of Statistics*, Charles Griffin, London.

Kimball, M. (1990) Precautionary Saving and the Marginal Propensity to Consume, Working Paper 3403, NBER, 16 pages.

Kimball, M. (1993) Standard Risk Aversion, *Econometrica* **61** (3), 589–611.

Kraus, A. and R. Litzenberger (1976) Skewness Preference and the Valuation of Risk Assets, *Journal of Finance* **31**, 1085–1099.

Kraus, A. and R. Litzenberger (1980) On the Distributional Conditions for a Consumption-oriented Three Moment CAPM, *Journal of Finance* **38**, 1381–1391.

Kroll, Y., H. Levy and H. Markowitz (1984) Mean Variance *versus* Direct Utility Maximisation, *Journal of Finance* **39**, 47–61.

Levy, H. (1969) A Utility Function Depending on the First Three Moments, *Journal of Finance* **24**, 715–719.

Levy, H. (1992) Stochastic Dominance and Expected Utility: Survey and Analysis, *Management Science* **38** (4), 555–593.

Levy, H. and H. Markowitz (1979) Approximating Expected Utility by a Function of Mean and Variance, *American Economic Review* **69**, 308–317.

Levy, H., T. Post and P. Vliet (2003) Risk Aversion and Skewness Preference, Working Paper, Erasmus University, 16 pages.

Lhabitant, F. (1997) On the (Ab)use of Expected Utility Approximations for Portfolio Selection and Portfolio Performance, Working Paper, University of Lausanne, 23 pages.

Lin, G. (1997) On the Moment Problems, *Statististical and Probability Letters* **35**, 85–90.

Loistl, O. (1976) The Erroneous Approximation of Expected Utility by Means of a Taylor's Series Expansion: Analytic and Computational Results, *American Economic Review* **66**, 905–910.

Lux, T. (2000) On Moment Condition Failure in German Stock Returns: An Application of Recent Advances in Extreme Value Statistics, *Empirical Economics* **25**, 641–652.

Lux, T. (2001) The Limiting Extremal Behaviour of Speculative Returns: An Analysis of Intra-Daily Data from the Frankfurt Stock Exchange, *Applied Financial Economics* **11**, 299–315.

Markowitz, H. (1952) Portfolio Selection, *Journal of Finance* **7**, 77–91.

Markowitz, H. (1991) Foundations of Portfolio Theory, *Journal of Finance* **46**, 469–477.

McDonald, J. and Y. Xu (1995) A Generalization of the Beta Distribution with Applications, *Journal of Econometrics* **66**, 133–152.

O'Brien, G. (1984) Stochastic Dominance and Moments Inequalities, *Mathematics of Operations Research* **9**, 475–477.

Ortobelli, S. (2001) The Classification of Parametric Choices under Uncertainty: Analysis of the Portfolio Choice Problem, *Theory and Decision* **51**, 297–327.

Ortobelli, S., S. Rachev and E. Schwartz (2000) The Problem of Optimal Asset Allocation with Stable Distributed Returns, Working Paper, UCLA, 50 pages.

Ortobelli, S., I. Huber, S. Rachev and E. Schwartz (2002) Portfolio Choice Theory with non-Gaussian Distributed Returns. In: *Handbook of Heavy Tailed Distributions in Finance*, S. Rachev (Ed.), North Holland, pp. 547–594.

Patton, A. (2001) On the Importance of Skewness and Asymmetric Dependence in Stock Returns for Asset Allocation, Working Paper, UCSD, 67 pages.

Patton, A. (2004) On the Out-of-Sample Importance of Skewness and Asymmetric Dependence for Asset Allocation, *Journal of Financial Econometrics* **2** (1), 130–168.

Pratt, J. (1964) Risk Aversion in the Small and the Large, *Econometrica* **32**, 122–136.

Pulley, L. (1981) A General Mean–Variance Approximation to Expected Utility for Short Holding Periods, *Journal of Financial and Quantitative Analysis* **16** (3), 361–373.

Pulley, L. (1983) Mean–Variance Approximations to Expected Logarithmic Utility, *Operations Research* **31** (4), 685–696.

Rafsnider, G., D. Reid and B. Tew (1992) Rational Mean–Variance Decisions for Subsistence Farmers, *Management Science* **38** (6), 840–845.

Reid, D. and B. Tew (1987) More Evidence on Expected Value–Variance Analysis *versus* Direct Utility Maximisation, *Journal of Financial Research* **10**, 249–258.

Rossi, G. and L. Tibiletti (1996) Higher Order Polynomial Utility Functions: Advantages in their Use, Working Paper, University of Turino, 13 pages.

Rubinstein, M. (1973) The Fundamental Theorem of Parameter-preference Security Valuation, *Journal of Financial and Quantitative Analysis* **8**, 61–69.

Samuelson, P. (1970) The Fundamental Approximation Theorem of Portfolio Analysis in Terms of Means, Variances and Higher Moments, *Review of Economic Studies* **37**, 537–543.

Semenov, A. (2004) High-Order Consumption Moments and Asset Pricing, Working Paper, York University, 38 pages.

Simaan, Y. (1993) Portfolio Selection and Asset Pricing Three Parameter Framework, *Management Science* **5**, 568–577.

Simaan, Y. (1997) What is the Opportunity Cost of Mean–variance Investment Strategies?, *Management Science* **5**, 578–587.

Spanos, A. (1999) *Probability Theory and Statistical Inference*, Cambridge University Press.

Stieltjes, T. (1894) Recherches sur les fractions continues, *Annales de la Faculté des Sciences de Toulouse* **8** (1), 1–22.

Stoyanov, J. (1997) *Counterexamples in Probability*, second edition, John Wiley & Sons, Ltd, Chichester.

Stoyanov, J. (2000) Krein Condition in Probabilistic Moment Problems, *Bernoulli* **6** (5), 939–949.

Tsiang, S. (1972) The Rationale of the Mean–Standard Deviation Analysis, Skewness Preference, and the Demand for Money, *American Economic Review* **62**, 354–371.

Vinod, H. (2001) Non-expected Utility, Stochastic Dominance and New Summary Measures for Risk, *Journal of Quantitative Economics* **17** (1), 1–24.

Vinod, H. (2004) Ranking Mutual Funds Using Unconventional Utility Theory and Stochastic Dominance, *Journal of Empirical Finance* **11**, 353–377.

von Neumann, J. and O. Morgenstern (2004) *Theory of Games and Economic Behaviour*, sixtieth anniversary edition, Princeton University Press.

Weisman, A. (2002) Informationless Investing and Hedge Fund Performance Measurement Bias, *Journal of Portfolio Management* **28** (4), 80–91.

Widder, D. (1946) *The Laplace Transform*, Princeton University Press.

Wu, X. (2003) Calculation of Maximum Entropy Densities with Application to Income Distributions, *Journal of Econometrics* **115**, 347–354.

Xu, Y. (2004) The Effects of Dependence Structure on Portfolio Optimization, Working Paper, University of Miami, 50 pages.

2

On Certain Geometric Aspects of Portfolio
Optimisation with Higher Moments

Gustavo M. de Athayde and Renato G. Flôres Jr

ABSTRACT

In this chapter we discuss geometric properties related to the minimisation of a portfolio kurtosis given its first two odd moments, considering a riskless asset and allowing for short-sales. The findings are generalised for the minimisation of any given even portfolio moment with fixed excess return and skewness, and then for the case in which only excess return is constrained. An example with two risky assets provides a better insight on the problems related to the solutions. The importance of the geometric properties and their use in the higher moments portfolio choice context is highlighted.

2.1 INTRODUCTION

Portfolio optimisation taking into account more than the first two moments has been receiving renewed interest in recent years. Be it on the theoretical side – including its links with the CAPM extensions – or on what relates to econometric tests or updates based on higher conditional moments, works like Adcock and Shutes (1999), Athayde and Flôres (1997, 2003, 2004), Jurczenko and Maillet (2001), Pedersen and Satchell (1998), or Athayde and Flôres (2000), Barone-Adesi (1985), Harvey and Siddique (1999, 2000), Hwang and Satchell (1999) and Pedersen and Satchell (2000), far from exhausting the full list of contributions, pay good witness to the growing awareness of the importance of higher moments in both lines of research.

Since Athayde and Flôres (1997), we have developed a systematic way to treat the key optimisation problems posed to anyone dealing with higher moments in portfolio theory. The approach uses a new notation to represent any moment's tensor related to a multivariate random vector of asset returns, and can be used either in a utility maximising context or, if optimal portfolios are defined, by preference relations. The new notation seemed necessary in order to treat the problem in an absolutely general setting, which means both in the maximum

This chapter was specially prepared as a paper for the *Multi-moment Capital Asset Pricing Models and Related Topics Workshop* held in Paris on April 29, 2002; only some of the references from the November 2002 final version have now been updated.

Multi-moment Asset Allocation and Pricing Models Edited by E. Jurczenko and B. Maillet
© 2006 John Wiley & Sons, Ltd

order, p, of portfolio moments of interest and in the possible patterns of the skewness or higher-order tensors. The latter is crucial as many works generalising the subject consider only the *marginal* higher moments of the returns vector, plainly disregarding any co-moment of the same order. Though the full set of co-moments can quickly become prohibitive – which, besides other issues, may pose serious econometric estimation problems for the applications – and simplifying hypotheses on its pattern will usually be imposed in practice, it is important to have a way to study the general solution to the problem, *irrespective of further assumptions that might be imposed.*

The utility function approach, given its more rigid theoretical constraints and the debates involving any non-normality-implying (utility) function proposed, seems more suitable for theoretical developments related, for instance, to the CAPM. Preference ordering of portfolios, made rigorous by Scott and Horvath (1980), can lead to more interesting results in the strict portfolio optimisation context.

In this chapter, we discuss an interesting geometric structure that arises when optimising an *even* moment subject to *odd* moment constraints. As usual, agents "like" odd moments and "dislike" even ones.

The structure studied – not the only relevant one in the higher moments context – bears important consequences and sheds light on the geometry of efficient portfolio sets in moment space. We believe that its implications have not been fully exploited yet. Moreover, final testing of the gains brought about by using higher moments relies on extensive practical applications of the new results. These, in turn, require proper software tools for solving the nonlinear systems and optimisation problems involved. Better knowledge of the surfaces (or manifolds) related to them may greatly improve the software design.

This chapter is organised as follows. The next section discusses the optimisation of variance, and then kurtosis, given the first and third desired portfolio moments; while Section 2.3 discusses how these results could still be generalised. Section 2.4 outlines, through an example, a few more properties and analyses the sensitivity of certain solutions. The final section concludes by explaining how the results can be useful in a duality context and sets a few lines of further research. The appendix provides a brief explanation of the notation used.

2.2   MINIMAL VARIANCES AND KURTOSES SUBJECT TO THE FIRST TWO ODD MOMENTS

Even moments, being always non-negative, are duly associated with spread, and both variance and kurtosis are used as simple numerical summaries of the dispersion of a set of observations. For fixed portfolio return and skewness, the latter should perhaps be used more in practice as an alternative objective function, given the frequency with which the fat-tailed effect in stock returns has been detected. If we minimise the fourth moment, we will be directly attacking the heavy extremes of the density, the ultimate culprits of the high volatility and uncertainty of returns. Most measures of risk focused on the worst scenarios, like the VaR, would probably be more sensitive to variations in the fourth moment rather than in variance. This sort of behaviour will be further examined in the example in Section 2.4. The material in this section draws on parts of Athayde and Flôres (2004) – where a complete solution to the three-moment portfolio problem is found – and Athayde and Flôres (2003), for the developments related to the kurtosis; proofs omitted here can be found in these papers.

2.2.1   Homothetic properties of the minimum variance set

Minimising the variance, for a given mean return and skewness, amounts to finding the solution to the problem:

$$\text{Min}_\alpha L = \boldsymbol{\alpha}' \mathbf{M}_2 \boldsymbol{\alpha} + \lambda_1 [E(r_p) - (\boldsymbol{\alpha}' \mathbf{M}_1 + (1 - \boldsymbol{\alpha}'[\mathbf{1}]) r_f)] + \lambda_2 (\sigma_{p^3} - \boldsymbol{\alpha}' \mathbf{M}_3 (\boldsymbol{\alpha} \otimes \boldsymbol{\alpha})) \quad (2.1)$$

where $\mathbf{M}_1$, $\mathbf{M}_2$ and $\mathbf{M}_3$ are, respectively, the matrices related to the first, second and third moments' tensors[1], $\boldsymbol{\alpha}$ is the vector of n portfolio weights – where short-sales are allowed, r_f is the riskless rate of return, $[\mathbf{1}]$ stands for an $n \times 1$ vector of 1s, the lambdas are Lagrange multipliers and the two remaining symbols are the α-portfolio (given) mean return and skewness.

Calling

$$\mathbf{x} = \mathbf{M}_1 - [\mathbf{1}] r_f \qquad \text{the vector of mean excess returns, and}$$

$$R = E(r_p) - r_f \qquad \text{the set (excess) portfolio return,}$$

the solution to (2.1) is found by solving the n- equation nonlinear system,

$$\mathbf{M}_2 \boldsymbol{\alpha} = \frac{A_4 R - A_2 \sigma_{p^3}}{A_0 A_4 - (A_2)^2} \mathbf{x} + \frac{A_0 \sigma_{p^3} - A_2 R}{A_0 A_4 - (A_2)^2} \mathbf{M}_3 (\boldsymbol{\alpha} \otimes \boldsymbol{\alpha}) \quad (2.2)$$

where the scalars:

$$A_0 = \mathbf{x}' \mathbf{M}_2^{-1} \mathbf{x}$$

$$A_2 = \mathbf{x}' \mathbf{M}_2^{-1} \mathbf{M}_3 (\boldsymbol{\alpha} \otimes \boldsymbol{\alpha}) \quad (2.3)$$

$$A_4 = (\boldsymbol{\alpha} \otimes \boldsymbol{\alpha})' \mathbf{M}_3 \mathbf{M}_2^{-1} \mathbf{M}_3 (\boldsymbol{\alpha} \otimes \boldsymbol{\alpha})$$

have subscripts corresponding to their degree of homogeneity as (real) functions of the vector $\boldsymbol{\alpha}$. A_0 and A_4, in particular, are positive because the inverse of the covariance matrix is positive definite.

Premultiplying (2.2) by the solutions $\boldsymbol{\alpha}'$, gives the optimal variance(s):

$$\sigma_{p^2} = \frac{A_4 R^2 - 2 A_2 \sigma_{p^3} R + A_0 (\sigma_{p^3})^2}{A_0 A_4 - (A_2)^2} \quad (2.4)$$

an expression where both the numerator and denominator are positive.

The following proposition is fundamental:

Proposition 1   *For a given k, let $\bar{\alpha}$ define the minimum variance portfolio when $R = 1$ and $y_3 = \sqrt[3]{\sigma_{p^3}} = k$, and $\bar{\sigma}_{p^2}$ be the corresponding minimum variance, THEN for all optimal portfolios related to return and skewness pairs (R, σ_{p^3}) such that $\sigma_{p^3} = k^3 R^3$, or $y_3 = kR$, the solution to (2.1) will be $\boldsymbol{\alpha} = \bar{\alpha} R$, with corresponding minimum variance $\sigma_{p^2} = \bar{\sigma}_{p^2} R^2$.*

---

[1] See the appendix for a further explanation of the notation used.

The above result implies that along the direction defined in the returns $\times$ skewness plane by $y_3 = kR$, the optimal variance as a function of the excess return will be a parabola. Taking now the three-dimensional (3D) space where the standard deviation $\sqrt{\sigma_{p^2}} = y_2$ axis is added, in the half-plane formed by a specific direction k in $R \times y_3$ space[2] and the positive part of the standard deviation axis, the optimal portfolio surface will be reduced to the straight line $y_{p^2} = \bar{y}_{p^2} \frac{u}{\sqrt{k^2+1}}$, $u \geq 0$.[3] As $\bar{y}_{p^2}$ differs with k, the angle that this line makes with the standard deviation axis also varies with k.

The proposition then has a far-reaching consequence: the optimal surface in the positive standard deviation (sd) half of 3D space bears a homothetic property from whatever standpoint one assumes. Slicing the surface by a sequence of planes parallel to the two odd-moment axes will generate a sequence of curves starting at the origin and whose expansion ratio will be equal to that of the respective (constant) variance values. Of course, slicing it by planes parallel to the sd and (standardised) skewness axes will produce a sequence of homothetic curves whose expansion ratio will be that of the (excess) returns associated with each plane. Finally, inspection of equation (2.4) easily convinces one that for the last combination, i.e. planes parallel to the sd and mean return axes, the same will apply, as Proposition 1 is also true if the roles of returns and skewness are reversed.

The proposition below is a direct consequence of this important fact.

Proposition 2 *For a given level of y_2 (or R, or y_3), cut the optimal surface with a plane orthogonal to the sd (or returns, or standardised skewness) axis and project the intersection curve in the 'returns $\times$ skewness (or sd $\times$ skewness, or returns $\times$ sd) plane', THEN if they exist, the directions in the $R \times y_3$ (or $y_2 \times y_3$, or $R \times y_2$) half plane related to the highest and lowest value, in each axis, of the curve are invariant with y_2 (or R, or y_3).*

The qualification *if they exist* is important as, especially in the case of cuts parallel to the sd axis, at least part of the curve may go to infinity. For constant variance cuts, it may be shown that closed curves will be produced.[4] Indeed, for this case, the highest and lowest directions are particularly noteworthy, as demonstrated by our next proposition.

Proposition 3 *The direction in the $R \times y_3$ half plane that gives the highest R for all the minimum variance portfolios with the same standard deviation y_2 is unique and related to the celebrated (Markowitz's) capital market line (CML). Moreover, in this direction, the skewness constraint to programme (2.1) is not binding. As regards skewness, although there may be more than one "highest" (and "lowest") direction, the constraint property also applies.*

This means that the unique solution to the minimum variance portfolio, for a given mean return:

$$\alpha = \frac{R}{A_0} \mathbf{M}_2^{-1} \mathbf{x} \tag{2.5}$$

---

[2] We shall, from now on, use the angular coefficient k to name the corresponding line/direction in the first quadrant of the $R \times y_3$ plane.

[3] The variable u stands for the coordinates along the axis defined by the "direction k".

[4] The proof is rather technical to be included in this text.

that defines the famous *capital market line* in mean × variance space, relating the optimal variance to the given R,

$$\sigma_{R^2} = \frac{R^2}{A_0} \tag{2.6}$$

also defines the (unique) direction that will pass through all the points, in each curve, yielding the maximum mean return. In other words, in the $R \times y_3$ half plane, this direction is the geometric locus of all the tangency points between each (projected) curve and a straight line, parallel to the skewness axis, which cuts the mean return axis in the *maximum mean return portfolio value related to the set variance (that defines the cut)*. This last statement is ensured by the well-known duality result in Markowitz world.

Skewnesses – and a k – can also be associated with these optimal portfolios, it being evident that they are independent of the given y_2. It can be proved that the k – the angular coefficient of the line related to the extreme means – will be equal to:

$$k_R = \frac{y_{R^3}}{R} = \frac{\sqrt[3]{\mathbf{w}'\mathbf{M}_3(\mathbf{w} \otimes \mathbf{w})}}{A_0}, \quad \text{where} \quad \mathbf{w} = \mathbf{M}_2^{-1}\mathbf{x} \tag{2.7}$$

Hence, k_R is indeed an invariant and all maximum mean returns for given variances lie in the same direction in mean × skewness space.

Contrary to the previous, mean returns, case, the optimal weights for the skewness extremes are defined implicitly by a nonlinear system like (2.2). When $\sigma_{p^3} = 1$, we have a solution portfolio $\overline{\boldsymbol{\alpha}}_s$ such that:

$$\overline{\boldsymbol{\alpha}}_s = \frac{1}{A_4}\mathbf{M}_2^{-1}\mathbf{M}_3(\overline{\boldsymbol{\alpha}}_s \otimes \overline{\boldsymbol{\alpha}}_s) \tag{2.8}$$

The homothecy implies that $\boldsymbol{\alpha}_s = \overline{\boldsymbol{\alpha}}_s\sqrt[3]{\sigma_{s^3}} = \overline{\boldsymbol{\alpha}}_s y_{s^3}$ is a solution to (2.2), ensuring an optimal variance $\sigma_{s^2} = \overline{\sigma}_{s^2}(y_{s^3})^2$. A corresponding (excess) return and a direction, both independent of the variance level, can be found as:

$$R_s = \overline{R}_s y_{p^3} \qquad k_s = 1/\overline{R}_s \tag{2.9}$$

implying that all these optimal portfolios lie in the same direction.

Combining both results gives a rectangular envelope that circumscribes, in the first quadrant of the mean × skewness plane, the corresponding part of the constant variance curve.

2.2.2   The minimum kurtosis case

The initial step now is minimising kurtosis for a given skewness and expected return:

$$\text{Min}_{\boldsymbol{\alpha}}\, \boldsymbol{\alpha}'\mathbf{M}_4(\boldsymbol{\alpha} \otimes \boldsymbol{\alpha} \otimes \boldsymbol{\alpha}) + \lambda[E(r_p) - (\boldsymbol{\alpha}'\mathbf{M}_1 + (1 - \boldsymbol{\alpha}'[1])r_f)] + \gamma(\sigma_{p^3} - \boldsymbol{\alpha}'\mathbf{M}_3(\boldsymbol{\alpha} \otimes \boldsymbol{\alpha})) \tag{2.10}$$

The first-order conditions are:

$$4\mathbf{M}_4(\boldsymbol{\alpha} \otimes \boldsymbol{\alpha} \otimes \boldsymbol{\alpha}) = \lambda\mathbf{x} + 3\gamma\mathbf{M}_3(\boldsymbol{\alpha} \otimes \boldsymbol{\alpha})$$

$$R = E(r_p) - r_f = \boldsymbol{\alpha}'(\mathbf{M}_1 - r_f[1]) = \boldsymbol{\alpha}'\mathbf{x} \tag{2.11}$$

$$\sigma_{p^3} = \boldsymbol{\alpha}'\mathbf{M}_3(\boldsymbol{\alpha} \otimes \boldsymbol{\alpha})$$

Defining

$$\mathbf{B}_{(-2)} = \mathbf{x}' \left[\mathbf{M}_4 (\boldsymbol{\alpha} \otimes \boldsymbol{\alpha} \otimes \mathbf{I}) \right]^{-1} \mathbf{x}$$

$$\mathbf{B}_0 = \mathbf{x}' \left[\mathbf{M}_4 (\boldsymbol{\alpha} \otimes \boldsymbol{\alpha} \otimes \mathbf{I}) \right]^{-1} \mathbf{M}_3 (\boldsymbol{\alpha} \otimes \boldsymbol{\alpha})$$

$$\mathbf{B}_2 = (\boldsymbol{\alpha} \otimes \boldsymbol{\alpha})' \mathbf{M}_3' \left[\mathbf{M}_4 (\boldsymbol{\alpha} \otimes \boldsymbol{\alpha} \otimes \mathbf{I}) \right]^{-1} \mathbf{M}_3 (\boldsymbol{\alpha} \otimes \boldsymbol{\alpha})$$

with the subscripts chosen according to the degree of homogeneity of the term with respect to the vector $\boldsymbol{\alpha}$, one can find the values of λ and γ and arrive at the nonlinear system that characterises the solution to (2.10):

$$\mathbf{M}_4 (\boldsymbol{\alpha} \otimes \boldsymbol{\alpha} \otimes \boldsymbol{\alpha}) = \frac{\mathbf{B}_2 R - \mathbf{B}_0 \sigma_{p^3}}{\mathbf{B}_{(-2)} \mathbf{B}_2 - (\mathbf{B}_0)^2} \mathbf{x} + \frac{\mathbf{B}_{(-2)} \sigma_{p^3} - \mathbf{B}_0 R}{\mathbf{B}_{(-2)} \mathbf{B}_2 - (\mathbf{B}_0)^2} \mathbf{M}_3 (\boldsymbol{\alpha} \otimes \boldsymbol{\alpha}) \qquad (2.12)$$

The optimal kurtosis will be given by:

$$\sigma_{p^4} = \frac{\mathbf{B}_2 R^2 - 2\mathbf{B}_0 R \sigma_{p^3} + \mathbf{B}_{(-2)} (\sigma_{p^3})^2}{\mathbf{B}_{(-2)} \mathbf{B}_2 - (\mathbf{B}_0)^2} \qquad (2.13)$$

Noticing that $\mathbf{B}_{(-2)}$ and $\mathbf{B}_2$ are positive, because the matrix in their middle is the inverse of a positive definite matrix, it can be proved that both the numerator and the denominator of the expression above are positive.

It is important to highlight the similarities between the pairs of formulas (2.2)–(2.12) and (2.4)–(2.13), as they are at the heart of the similar developments that follow. The first is a key proposition, close to Proposition 1:

Proposition 1* *For a given k, all the minimum kurtosis portfolios related to expected returns, skewness pairs (R, σ_{p^3}) such that $\sigma_{p^3} = k^3 R^3$, or $y_3 = kR$, are given by $\boldsymbol{\alpha} = \overline{\boldsymbol{\alpha}} R$, where $\bar{\alpha}$ defines $\bar{\sigma}_{p^4}$, the (minimum) kurtosis of the optimal portfolio when $R = 1$ and $y_3 = k$. Moreover, the minimum kurtosis for any pair of constraints in the k-line will be $\sigma_{p^4} = \bar{\sigma}_{p^4} R^4$, or $y_{p^4} = \bar{y}_{p^4} \|R\|$.*

The consequence of the above proposition is that exactly the same homothecy applies in 3D space defined by the standardised kurtosis axis and the two odd-moment axes. The results in Proposition 2 are then easily translated to the present context and the following is valid as well:

Proposition 3* *The direction in the $R \times y_3$ half plane that gives the highest R for all the minimum kurtosis portfolios with the same standardised kurtosis y_4 is unique. Moreover, in this direction, the skewness constraint to programme (2.10) is not binding. As regards skewness, there is at least one direction giving the maximum skewness, where the constraint property applies.*

The solution to the problem of minimising kurtosis for a given excess return is:

$$\mathbf{M}_4 (\boldsymbol{\alpha}_R \otimes \boldsymbol{\alpha}_R \otimes \boldsymbol{\alpha}_R) = \frac{R}{\mathbf{B}_{(-2)}} \mathbf{x} \qquad (2.14)$$

which, when $R = 1$, becomes:

$$\mathbf{M}_4(\overline{\boldsymbol{\alpha}}_R \otimes \overline{\boldsymbol{\alpha}}_R \otimes \overline{\boldsymbol{\alpha}}_R) = \frac{1}{\overline{\mathbf{B}}_{(-2)}} \mathbf{x} \qquad (2.15)$$

The systems of weights defined by $\boldsymbol{\alpha}_R = \overline{\boldsymbol{\alpha}}_R R$ are solutions to (2.12); thus, one only needs to find one portfolio $\overline{\boldsymbol{\alpha}}_R$ to generate the whole set of minimum kurtosis portfolios for a given R. The skewness corresponding to $\boldsymbol{\alpha}_R$ is given by:

$$\sigma_{R^3} = \frac{\mathbf{B}_0 R}{\overline{\mathbf{B}}_{(-2)}} = \frac{\mathbf{B}_0}{\overline{\mathbf{B}}_{(-2)}} R^3 \qquad (2.16)$$

so that the angular coefficient

$$k_R = \left(\frac{\mathbf{B}_0}{\overline{\mathbf{B}}_{(-2)}} \right)^{1/3} \qquad (2.17)$$

defines a direction in the expected returns × skewness plane which is the "maximum mean returns line" for a given (minimum) kurtosis.

The "maximum mean returns line" divides the minimum iso-kurtosis curves into two parts; since agents want the highest possible skewness, they will probably work with the upper half of the curve. In contrast to the classical case of minimising variance for a given return, there is no closed form for the portfolio weights $\overline{\boldsymbol{\alpha}}_R$, as can be seen from (2.15). However, it is possible to show that this function is strictly convex in its entire domain, therefore implying that the solution is unique.

The highest/lowest skewness directions, as in the case of variance, will be the ones associated with the solution of the problem of finding the lowest kurtosis subject to a given skewness. Calling these portfolios $\boldsymbol{\alpha}_s$, they are implicitly defined by the system

$$\mathbf{M}_4(\boldsymbol{\alpha}_s \otimes \boldsymbol{\alpha}_s \otimes \boldsymbol{\alpha}_s) = \frac{\sigma_{s^3}}{\mathbf{B}_2} \mathbf{M}_3 [\boldsymbol{\alpha}_s \otimes \boldsymbol{\alpha}_s] \qquad (2.18)$$

the portfolio that solves the problem when $\sigma_{p^3} = 1$ is naturally defined by:

$$\mathbf{M}_4(\overline{\boldsymbol{\alpha}}_s \otimes \overline{\boldsymbol{\alpha}}_s \otimes \overline{\boldsymbol{\alpha}}_s) = \frac{1}{\mathbf{B}_2} \mathbf{M}_3 [\overline{\boldsymbol{\alpha}}_s \otimes \overline{\boldsymbol{\alpha}}_s] \qquad (2.19)$$

It can also easily be verified that the mean return related to the solution of (2.18) is

$$R = \frac{\sigma_{s^3}}{\mathbf{B}_2} \mathbf{B}_0 \qquad (2.20)$$

so that the directions are defined by

$$k_s = \left(\frac{\mathbf{B}_0}{\mathbf{B}_2} \right)^{-1/3} \qquad (2.21)$$

Unfortunately, in this case, there can be more than one solution, and consequently more than one direction with a local maximum skewness for a given level of kurtosis. Notwithstanding this, the projection of each iso-kurtosis curve will also be enveloped, in the first quadrant, by the two axes and two tangent lines parallel to them.

2.3   GENERALISING FOR HIGHER EVEN MOMENTS

We now consider the general case of minimising an even moment given the two first odd moments. The Lagrangian of the problem will be:

$$\boldsymbol{\alpha}'\mathbf{M}_p\boldsymbol{\alpha}^{\otimes(p-1)} + \lambda(R - \boldsymbol{\alpha}'\mathbf{x}) + \gamma(\sigma_{p^3} - \boldsymbol{\alpha}'\mathbf{M}_3\boldsymbol{\alpha}^{\otimes2}) \tag{2.22}$$

giving the first-order conditions:

$$p\mathbf{M}_p\boldsymbol{\alpha}^{\otimes(p-1)} = \lambda\mathbf{x} + 3\gamma\mathbf{M}_3\boldsymbol{\alpha}^{\otimes2}$$

$$R = \boldsymbol{\alpha}'\mathbf{x} \tag{2.23}$$

$$\sigma_{p^3} = \boldsymbol{\alpha}'\mathbf{M}_3\boldsymbol{\alpha}^{\otimes2}$$

Noticing that $\mathbf{M}_p\boldsymbol{\alpha}^{\otimes(p-1)} = \mathbf{M}_p(\boldsymbol{\alpha}^{\otimes(p-2)} \otimes \mathbf{I}_n)\boldsymbol{\alpha}$, and that matrix $\mathbf{M}_p(\boldsymbol{\alpha}^{\otimes(p-2)} \otimes \mathbf{I}_n)$ is symmetric and positive definite, the following system can be formed from (2.23) to give the values of the multipliers:

$$pR = \lambda\mathbf{x}'(\mathbf{M}_p\boldsymbol{\alpha}^{\otimes(p-2)} \otimes \mathbf{I}_n)^{-1}\mathbf{x} + 3\gamma\mathbf{x}'(\mathbf{M}_p\boldsymbol{\alpha}^{\otimes(p-2)} \otimes \mathbf{I}_n)\mathbf{M}_3\boldsymbol{\alpha}^{\otimes2}$$

$$p\sigma_{p^3} = \lambda(\mathbf{M}_3\boldsymbol{\alpha}^{\otimes2})'(\mathbf{M}_p\boldsymbol{\alpha}^{\otimes(p-2)} \otimes \mathbf{I}_n)^{-1}\mathbf{x} + 3\gamma(\mathbf{M}_3\boldsymbol{\alpha}^{\otimes2})'(\mathbf{M}_p\boldsymbol{\alpha}^{\otimes(p-2)} \otimes \mathbf{I}_n)\mathbf{M}_3\boldsymbol{\alpha}^{\otimes2} \tag{2.24}$$

Defining

$$\mathbf{B}_{2-p} = \mathbf{x}'\left[\mathbf{M}_p(\boldsymbol{\alpha}^{\otimes(p-2)} \otimes \mathbf{I}_n)\right]^{-1}\mathbf{x}$$

$$\mathbf{B}_{4-p} = \mathbf{x}'\left[\mathbf{M}_p(\boldsymbol{\alpha}^{\otimes(p-2)} \otimes \mathbf{I}_n)\right]^{-1}\mathbf{M}_3\boldsymbol{\alpha}^{\otimes2}$$

$$\mathbf{B}_{6-p} = (\boldsymbol{\alpha}^{\otimes2})'\mathbf{M}_3'\left[\mathbf{M}_p(\boldsymbol{\alpha}^{\otimes(p-2)} \otimes \mathbf{I}_n)\right]^{-1}\mathbf{M}_3\boldsymbol{\alpha}^{\otimes2}$$

with the subscripts corresponding to the generalised degree of homogeneity with respect to the vector of weights, the final solution comes from the system:

$$(\mathbf{B}_{2-p}\mathbf{B}_{6-p} - \mathbf{B}_{4-p}^2)\mathbf{M}_p\boldsymbol{\alpha}^{\otimes(p-1)} = (\mathbf{B}_{6-p}R - \mathbf{B}_{4-p}\sigma_{p^3})\mathbf{x} + (\mathbf{B}_{4-p}R - \mathbf{B}_{2-p}\sigma_{p^3})\mathbf{M}_3\boldsymbol{\alpha}^{\otimes2} \tag{2.25}$$

the optimal portfolio pth moment being:

$$\sigma_{p^p} = \frac{\mathbf{B}_{6-p}R^2 - 2\mathbf{B}_{4-p}R\sigma_{p^3} + \mathbf{B}_{2-p}(\sigma_{p^3})^2}{\mathbf{B}_{2-p}\mathbf{B}_{6-p} - \mathbf{B}_{4-p^2}} \tag{2.26}$$

Again, the similarities between (2.2)–(2.12)–(2.25) and (2.4)–(2.13)–(2.26) should be stressed.

The following result summarises all the properties of the solutions set.

Theorem 1   *For a given $p = 2, 4, \ldots$, consider in (R, y_3, y_p) space of standardised moments an iso-pth moment curve Γ of solutions to (2.22). THEN:*

i) *the optimal portfolios set is contained in the cone $\{O\} * \Gamma$, where $O = (0, 0, 0)$ is the origin of (R, y_3, y_p) space;*

ii) *the projection of Γ in the $R \times y_3$ plane is a curve: a) symmetric to the origin and b) inscribed in a rectangle whose sides are parallel to the axes; the vertical and horizontal sides correspond, respectively, to the highest (and lowest) R and y_3 values that produce a solution in Γ.*

Proof   (we outline the steps of the proof) For proving i) one first follows steps similar to those in Propositions 1 and 1*, showing that on each line passing through the origin and a general point (R, y_3), the solutions to (2.22) increase linearly either with R – if the solution to $(1, y_3/R)$ is taken as the fundamental one – or with y_3 – if the solution to $(R/y_3, 1)$ is the one fixed. As the origin $O = (0, 0, 0)$ solves (2.22), this is sufficient to demonstrate that any solution will be in the cone. In the case of ii), the symmetry is seen by the fact that reverting to the pair $(-R, -y_3)$ does not change either (2.25) or (2.26). As regards the tangents, a reasoning similar to the ones in the previous section determines the points relative to the highest R and y_3, by symmetry the points of the lowest R and y_3 are obtained and the rectangle can be traced.   ∎

This basic result is important in finding the efficient portfolios set for the three moments at stake. It is easy to convince oneself that not all points in the cone will characterise an efficient portfolio, though, of course, the efficient set will be contained in the cone (see Athayde and Flôres, 2004). Moreover, one could be tempted to derive the following:

(false) **Corollary** If problem (2.22) has a solution THEN the optimal value is unique.

Indeed, by Theorem 1, if (2.22) has a solution then the optimal pth moments must lie in the cone. They will be found in the intersection of a vertical line through the point defined by the given odd moments in the $R \times y_3$ plane and the cone. Simple properties of a cone in finite-dimensional Euclidean spaces ensure that this intersection is unique.

This nice property would mean that the knowledge of the geometric structure of the optimal portfolios set allows a simple and elegant proof of uniqueness. However, such an argument is circular, as the curve Γ used to characterise the cone is supposedly already formed by the minimum pth moments, related to the optimal solutions of (2.25). It is worth reminding ourselves that system (2.25), together with its related cases (2.2) and (2.12), *implicitly* defines the optimal weights, and may as well have more than one solution. These other points either will be local, not global, optima or it might even happen that different optimal vectors $\boldsymbol{\alpha}$ could yield the same optimal pth moment in (2.26). Propositions 1 to 3 (and 1* and 3*) are valid for *any of these solutions* – thus meaning that even different "solution cones" may exist; but Theorem 1 considers, by hypothesis, *the* "optimal cone", and so the corollary is senseless. Unfortunately, at the present stage, we do not have a general, deeper knowledge of the structure of the solutions set. Moreover, the hypothesis also requires the existence of a solution; rigorous conditions for guaranteeing this, as regards system (2.25), are still an open question.

An interesting special case of (2.22) is when only a mean return restriction is imposed, the skewness constraint being disregarded. Without much difficulty one sees that the first-order conditions become:

$$p\mathbf{M}_p\boldsymbol{\alpha}^{\otimes(p-1)} = \lambda\mathbf{x}$$

$$R = \boldsymbol{\alpha}'\mathbf{x} \tag{2.27}$$

So that the optimal weights must solve the system

$$(\mathbf{B}_{2-p})\mathbf{M}_p\boldsymbol{\alpha}^{\otimes(p-1)} = R\mathbf{x} \tag{2.28}$$

and the corresponding pth moment bears the following relationship with the given return:

$$\frac{\sigma_{pp}}{R^2} = (\mathbf{B}_{2-p})^{-1} \tag{2.29}$$

In this case, the homothecy property implies that *only one system needs to be solved*, namely, the one obtained by setting $R=1$ in (2.28).

2.4 FURTHER PROPERTIES AND EXTENSIONS

In order to give a further insight, both on the geometric aspects discussed as well as on the difficulties involved in the solution of system (2.28), we consider the special problem of minimising kurtosis given expected return in the case of two assets and setting to zero all cokurtoses where an asset appears only once. This leaves us with three distinct non-zero elements in the kurtosis tensor, and the $\mathbf{M}_4$ matrix – shown, in the general case, in the appendix – becomes:

$$\begin{bmatrix} \sigma_1 & 0 & 0 & \sigma_{12} & 0 & \sigma_{12} & \sigma_{12} & 0 \\ 0 & \sigma_{12} & \sigma_{12} & 0 & \sigma_{12} & 0 & 0 & \sigma_2 \end{bmatrix}$$

The simplified notation used for the subscripts, suppressing repetition of identical indices, stresses the identical values and should cause no confusion. Notice that, unless the asset distributions are singular, all entries are strictly positive.

Calling $\boldsymbol{\alpha} = (\alpha_1, \alpha_2)'$ the vector of weights, and noticing that:

i) $\mathbf{M}_4\boldsymbol{\alpha}^{\otimes 3} = \begin{bmatrix} \alpha_1^3\sigma_1 + 3\alpha_1\alpha_2^2\sigma_{12} \\ 3\alpha_1^2\alpha_2\sigma_{12} + \alpha_2^3\sigma_2 \end{bmatrix}$

ii) matrix $\left[\mathbf{M}_4(\boldsymbol{\alpha}^{\otimes 2} \otimes \mathbf{I}_2)\right]^{-1}$ will be equal to:

$$\Delta^{-1}\begin{bmatrix} \alpha_1^2\sigma_{12} + \alpha_2^2\sigma_2 & -2\alpha_1\alpha_2\sigma_{12} \\ -2\alpha_1\alpha_2\sigma_{12} & \alpha_1^2\sigma_1 + \alpha_2^2\sigma_{12} \end{bmatrix}$$

where $\Delta = \alpha_1^4\sigma_1\sigma_{12} + \alpha_1^2\alpha_2^2(\sigma_1\sigma_2 - 3\sigma_{12}^2) + \alpha_2^4\sigma_{12}\sigma_2$ is the determinant of the direct matrix, one is ready to build up system (2.28). Of course, as stated in the previous section, only one solution matters, namely that which considers $R=1$. We shall, however, impose the additional assumptions that the marginal kurtoses are equal (i.e., $\sigma_1 = \sigma_2 = \sigma$) and that excess returns for both assets are also equal (to a common value x). With this, we can finally write system (2.30):

$$[\alpha_1^5(\sigma\sigma_{12} + 2\sigma^2) - 4\alpha_1^4\alpha_2\sigma\sigma_{12} + \alpha_1^3\alpha_2^2(3\sigma_{12}^2 + 7\sigma\sigma_{12}) - 12\alpha_1^2\alpha_2^3\sigma_{12}^2 + 3\alpha_1\alpha_2^4\sigma_{12}^2]x$$
$$= \alpha_1^4\sigma\sigma_{12} + \alpha_1^2\alpha_2^2(\sigma^2 - 3\sigma_{12}^2) + \alpha_2^4\sigma\sigma_{12}$$
$$[3\alpha_1^4\alpha_2(2\sigma\sigma_{12} + \sigma_{12}^2) - 12\alpha_1^3\alpha_2^2\sigma_{12}^2 + \alpha_1^2\alpha_2^3(3\sigma_{12}^2 + \sigma\sigma_{12} + 2\sigma^2) - 4\alpha_1\alpha_2^4\sigma\sigma_{12} + \alpha_2^5\sigma\sigma_{12}]x$$
$$= \alpha_1^4\sigma\sigma_{12} + \alpha_1^2\alpha_2^2(\sigma^2 - 3\sigma_{12}^2) + \alpha_2^4\sigma\sigma_{12} \tag{2.30}$$

Given the symmetry of the parameter values, the optimal weights will be identical, it being easy to see that their common value is:

$$\alpha = \frac{1}{2x} \tag{2.31}$$

These weights, however, can be related to either maxima or minima. For the latter, the bordered Hessian sufficient condition[5] amounts, in this case, to checking whether matrix

$$\begin{bmatrix} 12\alpha^2(\sigma + \sigma_{12}) & 24\alpha^2\sigma_{12} & -x \\ 24\alpha^2\sigma_{12} & 12\alpha^2(\sigma + \sigma_{12}) & -x \\ -x & -x & 0 \end{bmatrix} \tag{2.32}$$

has a negative determinant. Replacing α by its value in (2.31), the condition becomes:

$$6(\sigma_{12} - \sigma) < 0 \quad \text{or} \quad \sigma_{12} < \sigma \tag{2.33}$$

The symmetric weights solution produces a minimum *only* if the non-null cokurtosis is smaller than the common marginal kurtosis.

This rather simple example may serve as an illustration of how far intuition can help when considering higher moments, as well as of the impact of simplifications in the higher-moment tensors. The final solution is independent of the marginal kurtoses *and* of the even cokurtosis. Indeed, as the risk measures have a completely symmetric structure as regards the two (risky) assets, the identical weights can be found by direct solution of the excess return constraint. The higher the identical return, obviously the less will be purchased of each risky asset – as the portfolio excess return is *fixed at 1* – and more will be put in the riskless asset.[6]

Given the similar roles played by kurtosis and variance, we could then expect that the same would apply for the identical weights that result when equal marginal variances are used instead of kurtosis. In fact, (2.31) is exactly the solution to (2.5) in this case, the (common) variances and covariances playing no role at all. Moreover, use of the bordered Hessian condition shows that a minimum exists only if

$$\sigma_{12} < \sigma \tag{2.34}$$

Though "identical" to (2.33), (2.34) will always be valid if the assets' covariance is negative, which cannot happen in the case of the even cokurtosis. Indeed, in our simplified kurtosis context, there is no room for diversification.

Absent from (2.31) – in its two versions/solutions – the risk measures do, however, play a role. Beyond determining whether a minimum has been achieved, they explicitly appear in the shadow price of the restrictions, given by the value of the Lagrange multipliers. These are equal to $\lambda = \frac{\sigma + \sigma_{12}}{2x^2}$ in the variance case, and to $\lambda = \frac{\sigma + \sigma_{12}}{2x^2}$ in that of kurtosis.[7] The formal identity of the two values hides different behaviours. Again, in the case of the second moment, a negative covariance may substantially decrease "the cost" of the unit

---

[5] See, for instance, Theorem 9.9, page 202, in Panik (1976).
[6] Asymptotically, all the weight will go to the riskless asset.
[7] The reader should keep in mind that both σ and σ_{12} have different meanings in the two formulas.

return restriction. On the other hand, both (non-negative) kurtoses add up, penalising more heavily an increase in the fixed return.

Summing up, the example shows that the choice to minimise either kurtosis or variance (in this very simple, symmetric case) has, in spite of producing exactly the same solution weights, fairly different implications. Moreover, radical simplifications in the moments tensor may produce rather particular solutions. A small change in the example, like allowing for different marginal kurtoses, would completely alter the above discussion. Informally speaking, introducing higher moments in portfolio choice makes it a "more nonlinear" problem and, consequently, much more sensitive to small changes in the initial conditions.

2.5 CONCLUDING REMARKS

The availability of a general method to treat portfolio choice in a higher-moments context seems an unquestionable advantage. We outlined in the previous sections one such method that allows for a compact, analytical treatment of all formulas involved in the optimisation problem. Thanks to this, powerful geometric insights could be gained.

Nevertheless, the task before anyone interested in the subject is still formidable. A basic existence result and more insights on the solutions set would be welcome. Final characterisation of the efficient portfolios set requires more than the techniques discussed here, duality methods being needed to completely identify the efficient points. We solved this up to the fourth moment, Athayde and Flôres (2003, 2004), but a general method seems possible. Moving from static to dynamic optimisation frameworks generates additional, rather difficult theoretical and computational problems.[8]

Last, but not least, as glimpsed in Section 2.4, the number of different situations in the higher-moments case is extremely large; a great probability existing of senseless or unattractive special formulations. These can only be sorted out through a combination of more theoretical findings with several examples and applied experiments. The notation developed, and its corresponding algebra, may help in designing many of these experiments.

APPENDIX: THE MATRIX NOTATION FOR THE HIGHER-MOMENTS ARRAYS

Dealing with higher moments can easily become algebraically cumbersome. Given an n-dimensional random vector, the set of its pth order moments is, as a mathematical object, a tensor. The second-moment's tensor is the popular $n \times n$ covariance matrix, while that of the third moment can be visualised as an $n \times n \times n$ cube in three-dimensional space. However, the tensor notation, which is so useful in physics, geometry and some areas of statistics (see, for instance, McCullagh, 1987), did not seen appropriate for dealing with the portfolio choice problem. We thus developed a special notation, which allows one to perform all the necessary operations within the realm of matrix calculus. The advantages of this are manifold. Beyond having a synthetic way to treat complicated expressions, the mathematical tools required are standard linear algebra results and, with the help of Euler's theorem – as most real functions involved are homogeneous in the vector of portfolio weights – a differential calculus easily ensues. Moreover, the different formulas and systems arrived at

---

[8] Work in this direction has been initiated with Berç Rustem (Imperial College, London).

are written in a compact and straightforward way, easily translated into formal programming languages.

Before presenting the notation, we remind the reader that, throughout the chapter we deal with *all* the possible p-moments of a given n-dimensional random vector of asset returns. Undoubtedly, the difficulty in manipulating all these values simultaneously has been a deterrent to tackling the problem in its full generality. Thinking of skewness and kurtosis, for instance, the respective three- and four-dimensional "cubes", where several identical values are found, have n^3 and n^4 elements. Of course, in practice, gathering all these values may quickly become a formidable task. Indeed, as an example, the number of *different* kurtoses is, in principle, $\binom{n+3}{4}$, which, in the case of five assets, gives 70 values to be computed. It is, then, very likely that, in each practical problem, either a significant number of co-moments will be set *a priori* to zero or another simplifying assumption will be used, and very seldom will one work with the full set of cross moments. However, as stated in the introduction, the great variety of possible assumptions is an extra argument for a general treatment of the problem.

Our notation transforms the full pth moment's tensor, with n^p elements, into a matrix of order $n \times n^{p-1}$ obtained by slicing all bidimensional $n \times n^{p-2}$ layers defined by fixing one asset and then taking all the moments in which it figures at least once and pasting them, in the same order, sideways. Row i' of the matrix layer, which corresponds to having fixed the ith asset, gives – in a pre-established order – all the moments in which assets i and i' appear at least once. Of course, assets must be ordered once and for all and this order respected in the sequencing of the layers and in the numbering of the rows of each layer. Accordingly, a conformal ordering must be chosen, and thoroughly used, for the combinations (with repetitions) of n elements into groups of p-2 that define the columns of each matrix layer.

In the case of kurtosis, for instance, two indices/variables/coordinates must be held constant. Calling σ_{ijkl} a general (co-) kurtosis, when $n=2$, the resulting 2×8 matrix will be:

$$\begin{bmatrix} \sigma_{1111} & \sigma_{1112} & \sigma_{1121} & \sigma_{1122} & \sigma_{1211} & \sigma_{1212} & \sigma_{1221} & \sigma_{1222} \\ \sigma_{2111} & \sigma_{2112} & \sigma_{2121} & \sigma_{2122} & \sigma_{2211} & \sigma_{2212} & \sigma_{2221} & \sigma_{2222} \end{bmatrix}$$

where, as expected, many entries are identical.

Now suppose that a vector of weights $\alpha \in R^n$ is given, and $M_1, M_2, M_{3, \ldots}$ and M_p stand for the matrices containing the expected (excess) returns, (co)variances, skewnesses ... and p-moments of a random vector of n assets. The mean return, variance, skewness ... and pth moment of the portfolio with these weights will be, respectively: $\alpha' M_1$, $\alpha' M_2 \alpha$, $\alpha' M_3$ $(\alpha \otimes \alpha)$ ... and $\alpha' M_p (\alpha \otimes \alpha \otimes \alpha \ldots \otimes \alpha) \equiv \alpha' M_p \alpha^{\otimes p-1}$ where '$\otimes$' stands for the Kronecker product.

The above expressions provide a clue to the mentioned advantages of the notation. The fact that the tensors were transformed into matrices allows the use of matrix algebra – and differential calculus – in all expressions and derivations, giving way to compact and elegant formulas. It can be seen immediately that, as real functions of α, the four expressions above are homogenous functions of the same degree as the order of the corresponding moment. This means that Euler's theorem can easily be used in the needed derivations.

As an example, the derivative of the portfolio kurtosis with respect to the weights will be:

$$\frac{\partial}{\partial \alpha} [\alpha' M_4 (\alpha \otimes \alpha \otimes \alpha)] = 4 M_4 (\alpha \otimes \alpha \otimes \alpha) = 4 M_4 \alpha^{\otimes 3}$$

ACKNOWLEDGEMENTS

We thank all the participants of the Multi-moment Capital Asset Pricing models and Related Topics workshop for comments and lively related discussions, and particularly Emmanuel Jurczenko and Bertrand Maillet, the workshop organisers on behalf of the *Finance-sur-Seine Association*. All ideas, affirmatives and mistakes are our own.

REFERENCES

Adcock, C. J. and K. Shutes (1999) Portfolio selection based on the multivariate skew-normal distribution. In: *Financial Modelling,* A. Skulimowski (Ed.), Progress and Business Publishers, Krakow.

Athayde, G. M. and R. G. Flôres Jr (1997) *A CAPM with Higher Moments: Theory and Econometrics.* EPGE/Fundação Getulio Vargas, Ensaios Econômicos n° 317, Rio de Janeiro.

Athayde, G. M. and R. G. Flôres Jr (2000) Introducing higher moments in the CAPM: some basic ideas. In: *Advances in Quantitative Asset Management,* C. L. Dunis (Ed.), Kluwer Academic Publishers, Norwell, Mass.

Athayde, G. M. and R. G. Flôres Jr (2003) A journey through an undiscovered country: efficient portfolio sets with four moments. *Forthcoming.*

Athayde, G. M. and R. G. Flôres Jr (2004) Finding a maximum skewness portfolio – a general solution to three-moments portfolio choice, *Journal of Economic Dynamics & Control* **28**, 1335–1352.

Barone-Adesi, G. (1985) Arbitrage equilibrium with skewed asset returns, *Journal of Financial and Quantitative Analysis* **20**, 299–313.

Harvey, C. R. and A. Siddique (1999) Auto-regressive conditional skewness, *Journal of Financial and Quantitative Analysis* **34** (4), 465–487.

Harvey, C. R. and A. Siddique (2000) Conditional skewness in asset pricing tests, *The Journal of Finance* **60**, 1263–1295.

Hwang, S. and S. Satchell (1999) Modelling emerging market risk premia using higher moments, *International Journal of Finance and Economics* **4** (4), 271–296.

Jurczenko, E. and B. Maillet (2001) The 3-CAPM: Theoretical foundations and an asset-pricing model comparison in a unified framework. In: *Developments in Forecast Combination and Portfolio Choice,* C. L. Dunis, A. Timmerman and J. Moody (Eds), John Wiley & Sons, Ltd, Chichester.

McCullagh, P. (1987) *Tensor Methods in Statistics,* Chapman and Hall, London.

Panik, M. J. (1976) *Classical Optimization: Foundations and Extensions,* North-Holland Publishing Company, Amsterdam.

Pedersen, C. S. and S. E. Satchell (1998) An extended family of financial risk measures. *Geneva Papers on Risk and Insurance Theory* **23**, 89–117.

Pedersen, C. S. and S. E. Satchell (2000) Small sample analysis of performance measures in the asymmetric response model, *Journal of Financial and Quantitative Analysis* **35**, 425–450.

Scott, R. and P. A. Horvath (1980) On the direction of preference for moments of higher order than the variance, *The Journal of Finance* **35**, 915–919.

3

Hedge Fund Portfolio Selection with Higher-order Moments: A Nonparametric Mean–Variance–Skewness–*Kurtosis* Efficient Frontier

Emmanuel Jurczenko, Bertrand Maillet and Paul Merlin

ABSTRACT

This chapter proposes a nonparametric optimisation criterion for the static portfolio selection problem in the mean–variance–skewness–*kurtosis* space. Following the work of Briec *et al.* (2004 and 2006), a shortage function is defined, in the four-moment space, that looks simultaneously for improvements in the expected portfolio return, variance, skewness and *kurtosis* directions. This new approach allows us to optimise multiple competing and often conflicting asset allocation objectives within a mean–variance–skewness–*kurtosis* framework. The global optimality is here guaranteed for the resulting optimal portfolios. We also establish a link to a proper indirect four-moment utility function. An empirical application on funds of hedge funds serves to show a three-dimensional representation of the primal nonconvex mean–variance–skewness–*kurtosis* efficient portfolio set and to illustrate the computational tractabilty of the approach.

3.1 INTRODUCTION

The mean–variance decision criterion proposed by Markowitz (1952) is inadequate for allocating wealth when dealing with hedge funds. Not only are hedge fund return distributions asymmetric and leptokurtic, but they also display significant coskewness and co*kurtosis* with the returns of other asset classes, due to the option-like features of alternative investments (see Weisman, 2002; Goetzmann *et al.*, 2004; Agarwal and Naik, 2004 and Davies *et al.*, 2004).

Different approaches have been developed in the financial literature to incorporate the individual preferences for higher-order moments into optimal asset allocation problems, though no single conclusive approach seems to have emerged yet. These approaches can be divided between primal and dual program for determining the mean–variance–skewness–*kurtosis* efficient frontier.

Davies *et al.* (2005) and Berényi (2001 and 2002) use polynomial goal programming (PGP) to determine the set of the mean–variance–skewness–*kurtosis* efficient funds of hedge funds.[1] A shortcoming of this primal approach is that the allocation problem solved in the PGP cannot be related precisely to the expected utility function. In particular, the choice of the parameters used to weight the moment deviations is not related to the parameters of the utility function. Another drawback of the estimation of the four-moment efficient frontier via multi-objective programming is that it is not compliant with the Pareto-optimal definition of an efficient portfolio frontier. Indeed, minimising deviations from the first four moments simultaneously only guarantees a solution close to the mean–variance–skewness–*kurtosis* efficient frontier. Consequently, no portfolio performance measure can be inferred from the exercise. Some primal contributions solve analytically the mean–variance–skewness–*kurtosis* portfolio optimisation problem. For example, Athayde and Flôres (2002), Adcock (2003) and Jurczenko and Maillet in Chapter 6 look for the analytical solution characterising the minimum variance frontier in the mean–variance–skewness–*kurtosis* space, assuming shorting, with the objective of minimising the variance for a given mean, skewness and *kurtosis*. These approaches are, however, partial since they focus mainly on one objective of the mean–variance–skewness–*kurtosis* optimisation program at the cost of the others.[2]

Dual approaches start instead from a particular specification of the indirect mean–variance–skewness–*kurtosis* utility by using a Taylor series expansion of the investors' objective functions to determine the optimal portfolios (see, for instance, Guidolin and Timmermann, 2005; Jondeau and Rockinger, 2003 and 2006 and Jurczenko and Maillet in Chapter 1 of this book.[3] While such approaches have been used extensively in empirical applications to test multi-moment CAPM, they suffer from severe limitations in the context of hedge fund asset allocations. The Taylor series expansion may converge to the expected utility under restrictive conditions only. For some utility functions (such as the exponential one), the expansion converges for all possible levels of return, while for others (e.g. logarithm-power type utility functions), convergence is ensured only over a restricted range that may be problematic for some alternative investments due to the presence of leverage effects. In addition, the truncation of the Taylor series raises several difficulties. In particular, there is generally no rule for selecting the order of truncation. The inclusion of an additional moment does not necessarily improve the quality of the approximation (see Chapter 1). Dual approaches are also hampered by the lack of knowledge of the individual preferences for the first four moments of the portfolio return distribution and suffer from their lack of integration with the primal approaches briefly outlined above. Moreover, since the mean–variance–skewness–*kurtosis* efficient frontier is a nonconvex surface, previous parametric primal and dual approaches can only guarantee local optimal solutions to the portfolio optimisation problems in the four-moment space, not a global one. They inevitably require one to convexify some part of the nonconvex four-moment efficient frontier by using *ad hoc* moment restrictions, separating return distributions or separating utility functions (see Rubinstein, 1973; Ingersoll, 1987 and Athayde and Flôres, 2004). Dual approaches carry, in particular, the risk that certain target portfolios based upon particular specifications of the utility function are infeasible in practice. As the dimensionality of the portfolio

---

[1] For studies of the use of this approach in the mean–variance–skewness portfolio selection case, see Lai (1991), Chunhachinda *et al.* (1997), Wang and Xia (2002), Chang *et al.* (2003) and Sun and Yan (2003).
[2] See also Simaan (1993), Gamba and Rossi (1997, 1998a and 1998b), Pressacco and Stucchi (2000) and Jurczenko and Maillet (2001), for similar optimisation programmes in the mean–variance–skewness space.
[3] See Harvey *et al.* (2004) for the mean–variance–skewness portfolio selection case.

selection problem increases, it then becomes difficult to develop a geometric interpretation of the portfolio efficient frontier and to select the preferred portfolio among the boundary points.

To circumvent these problems, we use a particular distance function – the shortage function – to incorporate investors' preferences for higher moments into the optimal construction of a fund of hedge funds. The shortage function enables us to solve for the multiple conflicting and competing allocation objectives without assuming a detailed knowledge of the preference parameters of the indirect utility function. It integrates the primal and the dual approaches.

The shortage function, first introduced by Luenberger (1995) in production theory, is a distance function that looks simultaneously for reduction in inputs and expansion in outputs, and that is dual to the profit function. It offers a perfect representation of multidimensional choice sets and can position any point relative to the boundary frontier of the choice set. It has been used subsequently by Morey and Morey (1999) and Briec et al. (2004) for gauging the performance of funds in the mean–variance framework, and more recently by Briec et al. (2006) for solving portfolio selection problems involving significant degrees of skewness. In this chapter, we extend the shortage function from the mean–variance–skewness space to the mean–variance–skewness–*kurtosis* one to take into account the aversion to *kurtosis* in addition to individual preferences for expected return, variance and skewness. The shortage function projects any (in)efficient portfolio exactly onto the four-dimensional mean–variance–skewness–*kurtosis* portfolio frontier. It rates portfolio performance by measuring a distance between a portfolio and its optimal projection onto the primal mean–variance–skewness–*kurtosis* efficient frontier. Following the same line of reasoning as Briec et al. (2004 and 2006), we prove that our shortage function achieves a global optimum on the boundary of the nonconvex mean–variance–skewness–*kurtosis* portfolio frontier and establish a duality result between the shortage function and the indirect mean–variance–skewness–*kurtosis* utility function.

Thanks to the global optimality and duality results, the shortage function approach stands out compared to the existing four-moment primal and dual approaches, which only guarantee a local optimal solution to the investor's portfolio optimisation programme. Moreover, our multi-moment portfolio selection approach is more general than the previous ones since we are not assuming the existence of a riskless asset and forbidding short-sales.

The remainder of the chapter is organised as follows. In Section 3.2 we describe the optimal hedge fund portfolio selection program within a four-moment framework. In Section 3.3 we introduce the shortage function, study its axiomatic properties and establish the link between the shortage function and the indirect mean–variance–skewness–*kurtosis* utility function. Section 3.4 describes the data and hedge fund classification and provides illustrative empirical results. Section 3.5 concludes. Proofs are presented separately in the appendix.

3.2 PORTFOLIO SELECTION WITH HIGHER-ORDER MOMENTS

We consider the problem of an investor selecting a portfolio from N risky assets (with $N \geq 4$) in the mean–variance–skewness–*kurtosis* framework (see Chapter 1). We assume that the investor does not have access to a riskless asset, implying that the portfolio weights must sum to one. In addition, we impose a no short-sale portfolio constraint: asset positions must be non-negative. Let $\mathbf{w}_p$ and $\mathbf{E}$ denote respectively the $(N \times 1)$ vector of weights and of expected returns for the N risky assets in the portfolio p; Ω the nonsingular $(N \times N)$ variance–covariance matrix of the risky assets; and Σ and Γ represent respectively the $(N \times N^2)$ skewness–coskewness matrix and the $(N \times N^3)$ *kurtosis–cokurtosis* matrix of the N risky asset returns, defined as (Athayde and Flôres, 2004 and Chapter 2 of this book):

$$
\begin{cases}
\underset{(N \times N^2)}{\Sigma} = (\Sigma_1 \Sigma_2 \cdots \Sigma_N) \\
\underset{(N \times N^3)}{\Gamma} = (\Gamma_{11} \Gamma_{12} \cdots \Gamma_{1N} \,|\, \Gamma_{21} \Gamma_{22} \cdots \Gamma_{2N} \,|\, \ldots \,|\, \Gamma_{N1} \Gamma_{12} \cdots \Gamma_{NN})
\end{cases}
\tag{3.1}
$$

where Σ_k and Γ_{kl} are the $(N \times N)$ associated submatrices of Σ and Γ, with elements (s_{ijk}) and (κ_{ijkl}), with $(i, j, k, l) \in (IN^*)^4$, and the sign $\otimes$ stands for the Kronecker product.[4]

It should be noted that, because of the symmetries, not all the elements of these matrices need to be computed. Only $N(N+1)/2$ elements of the $(N \times N)$ variance–covariance matrix must be computed. Similarly the skewness–coskewness and *kurtosis–cokurtosis* matrices have dimensions $(N \times N^2)$ and $(N \times N^3)$, but only $N(N+1)(N+2)/6$ and $N(N+1)(N+2)(N+3)/24$ elements are independent.[5]

The set of the feasible portfolios $\mathfrak{F}_p$ can be expressed as follows:

$$
\mathfrak{F}_p = \left\{ \mathbf{w}_p \in IR^N : \mathbf{w}_p' \mathbf{1} = 1 \text{ and } \mathbf{w}_p \geq \mathbf{0} \right\}
\tag{3.2}
$$

where $\mathbf{w}_p'$ is the $(1 \times N)$ transposed vector of the investor's holdings of risky assets and $\mathbf{1}$ is the $(N \times 1)$ unitary vector.

The mean, variance, skewness and *kurtosis* of the return of a given portfolio p belonging to $\mathfrak{F}_p$ are respectively given by:

$$
\begin{cases}
E(R_p) = E\left[\sum_{i=1}^{N} (w_{pi} R_i) \right] = \mathbf{w}_p' \mathbf{E} \\[2mm]
\sigma^2(R_p) = E\left\{ \left[R_p - E(R_p) \right]^2 \right\} = \sum_{i=1}^{N} \sum_{j=1}^{N} w_{pi} w_{pj} \sigma_{ij} = \mathbf{w}_p' \Omega \mathbf{w}_p \\[2mm]
s^3(R_p) = E\left\{ \left[R_p - E(R_p) \right]^3 \right\} = \sum_{i=1}^{N} \sum_{j=1}^{N} \sum_{k=1}^{N} w_{pi} w_{pj} w_{pk} s_{ijk} = \mathbf{w}_p' \Sigma (\mathbf{w}_p \otimes \mathbf{w}_p) \\[2mm]
\kappa^4(R_p) = E\left\{ \left[R_p - E(R_p) \right]^4 \right\} = \sum_{i=1}^{N} \sum_{j=1}^{N} \sum_{k=1}^{N} \sum_{l=1}^{N} w_{pi} w_{pj} w_{pk} w_{pl} \kappa_{ijkl} \\[2mm]
\hspace{5cm} = \mathbf{w}_p' \Gamma (\mathbf{w}_p \otimes \mathbf{w}_p \otimes \mathbf{w}_p)
\end{cases}
\tag{3.3}
$$

---

[4] Let $\mathbf{A}$ be an $(n \times p)$ matrix and $\mathbf{B}$ an $(m \times q)$ matrix. The $(mn \times pq)$ matrix $\mathbf{A} \otimes \mathbf{B}$ is called the Kronecker product of $\mathbf{A}$ and $\mathbf{B}$:

$$
\mathbf{A} \otimes \mathbf{B} = \begin{pmatrix}
a_{11}\mathbf{B} & a_{12}\mathbf{B} & \cdots & a_{1N}\mathbf{B} \\
a_{21}\mathbf{B} & a_{22}\mathbf{B} & \cdots & a_{2N}\mathbf{B} \\
\vdots & \vdots & \ddots & \vdots \\
a_{N1}\mathbf{B} & a_{N2}\mathbf{B} & \cdots & a_{NN}\mathbf{B}
\end{pmatrix}
$$

where the sign $\otimes$ stands for the Kronecker product.

[5] For $N = 4$, where these matrices have respectively 16, 64 and 256 terms, ten different elements for the variance–covariance matrix, 20 elements for the skewness–coskewness matrix and 35 elements for the *kurtosis–cokurtosis* matrix are to be computed.

with, $\forall (i, j, k, l) \in [1, \ldots, N]^4$:

$$
\begin{cases}
R_p = \sum_{i=1}^{N} w_{pi} R_i \\
\sigma_{ij} = E\left\{[R_i - E(R_i)][R_j - E(R_j)]\right\} \\
s_{ijk} = E\left\{[R_i - E(R_i)][R_j - E(R_j)][R_k - E(R_k)]\right\} \\
\kappa_{ijkl} = E\left\{[R_i - E(R_i)][R_j - E(R_j)][R_k - E(R_k)][R_l - E(R_l)]\right\}
\end{cases}
$$

where (w_{pi}), (R_i), (σ_{ij}), (s_{ijk}) and (κ_{ijkl}) represent, respectively, the weight of the asset i in the portfolio p, the return on the asset i, the covariance between the returns of asset i and j, the coskewness between the returns of asset i, j and k and the *cokurtosis* between the returns of asset i, j, k and l, with $(i \times j \times k \times l) = (IN^*)^4$.

Following Markowitz (1952) leads to the following disposal representation, denoted $\mathfrak{D}_p$, of the set of the feasible portfolios in the mean–variance–skewness–*kurtosis* space (see Briec *et al.*, 2004 and 2006):

$$
\mathfrak{D}_p = \{m_p : w_p \in \mathfrak{F}_p\} + \left[IR_+ \times (-IR_+) \times IR_+ \times (-IR_+)\right] \tag{3.4}
$$

with:

$$
\mathbf{m}_p = \left[\kappa^4(R_p)\, s^3(R_p)\, \sigma^2(R_p)\, E(R_p)\right]'
$$

where $\mathbf{m}_p$ is the (4×1) vector of the first four moments of the portfolio return p. This disposal representation is necessary to ensure the convexity of the feasible portfolio set in the mean–variance–skewness–*kurtosis* space.

The four-moment (weakly) efficient portfolio frontier is then defined as follows:

$$
\mathfrak{M}_p = \left\{\mathbf{m}_p : \mathbf{m}_q > \mathbf{m}_p \Rightarrow \mathbf{m}_q \notin \mathfrak{D}_p\right\}
$$

The weakly efficient frontier is the set of all the mean, variance, skewness, *kurtosis* quadruplets that are not strictly dominated in the four-dimensional space.

The set of the weakly efficient portfolios in the four-moment case is then given in the simplex as:

$$
\mathfrak{E}_p = \left\{\mathbf{w}_p \in \mathfrak{F}_p : \mathbf{m}_p \in \mathfrak{M}_p\right\} \tag{3.5}
$$

By analogy with production theory (Luenberger, 1995), the next section introduces the shortage function as an indicator of the mean–variance–skewness–*kurtosis* portfolio (in)efficiency.

3.3 THE SHORTAGE FUNCTION AND THE MEAN–VARIANCE–SKEWNESS–*KURTOSIS* EFFICIENT FRONTIER

In production theory, the shortage function measures the distance between some point of the production possibility set and the efficient production frontier (Luenberger, 1995).

The properties of the set of portfolio return moments on which the shortage function is defined have already been discussed in the mean–variance plane by Briec *et al.* (2004) and in the mean–variance–skewness space by Briec *et al.* (2006). It is now possible to extend their definitions to get a portfolio efficiency indicator in the four-moment case.

The shortage function associated with a feasible portfolio p with reference to the direction vector $\mathbf{g}$ in the mean–variance–skewness–*kurtosis* space is the real-valued function $S_{\mathbf{g}}(.)$ defined as:

$$S_{\mathbf{g}}(\mathbf{w}_p) = \sup\{\delta : \mathbf{m}_p + \delta \mathbf{g} \in \mathfrak{D}_p, \mathbf{g} \in IR_+ \times IR_- \times IR_+ \times IR_-\} \tag{3.6}$$

with:

$$\begin{cases} \mathbf{m}_p = \left(\kappa^4(R_p)\, s^3(R_p)\, \sigma^2(R_p)\, E(R_p)\right)' \\ \mathbf{g} = (-g_\kappa + g_s - g_\sigma + g_E)' \end{cases}$$

where $\mathbf{g}$ is the directional vector in the four-moment space.

The use of the shortage function in the mean–variance–skewness–*kurtosis* space can only guarantee weak efficiency for a portfolio, since it does not exclude projections on the vertical and horizontal parts of the frontier allowing for additional improvements. Furthermore, portfolios that are weakly dominated in terms of their expected return, variance, skewness and *kurtosis* are only weakly mean–variance–skewness–*kurtosis* efficient.

The disposal representation of the feasible portfolio set can be used to derive the lower bound of the true unknown four-moment efficient frontier through the computation of the associated portfolio shortage function. Let us consider a specific portfolio $\mathbf{w}_k$ from a sample of P portfolios – or assets – $(\mathbf{w}_p)$, with $p = [1, \ldots, P]$, whose performances need to be evaluated in the four-moment dimensions. The shortage function for this portfolio is then computed by solving the following quartic optimisation program:

$$\mathbf{w}_p^* = \underset{\mathbf{w}_p}{\text{Arg}}\{\text{Max }\delta\}$$

$$\text{s.t.} \begin{cases} E(R_k) + \delta g_E \leq E(R_p) \\ \sigma^2(R_k) - \delta g_\sigma \geq \sigma^2(R_p) \\ s^3(R_k) + \delta g_s \leq s^3(R_p) \\ \kappa^4(R_k) - \delta g_\kappa' \geq \kappa^4(R_p) \\ \mathbf{w}_p' \mathbf{1} = 1 \\ \mathbf{w}_p \geq \mathbf{0} \end{cases} \tag{3.7}$$

where $\mathbf{w}_{p^*}$ is the $(N \times 1)$ efficient portfolio weight vector that maximises the performance, risk, skewness and *kurtosis* relative improvement over the evaluated portfolio in the direction vector $\mathbf{g}$. Using the vectorial notation of the portfolio return higher moments (3.1) and using the first four moments of the evaluated portfolio k in the expression of the direction vector **g**, the nonparametric portfolio optimisation program (3.7) can then be restated as:

$$\mathbf{w}_p^* = \underset{\mathbf{w}_p}{\text{Arg}} \{\text{Max } \delta\}$$

$$\text{s.t.} \begin{cases} E\left(R_k\right) + \delta E\left(R_k\right) \leq \mathbf{w}_p' \mathbf{E} \\ \sigma^2\left(R_k\right) - \delta \sigma^2\left(R_k\right) \geq \mathbf{w}_p' \Omega \, \mathbf{w}_p \\ s^3\left(R_k\right) + \delta s^3\left(R_k\right) \leq \mathbf{w}_p' \Sigma\left(\mathbf{w}_p \otimes \mathbf{w}_p\right) \\ \kappa^4\left(R_k\right) - \delta \kappa^4\left(R_k\right) \geq \mathbf{w}_p' \Gamma\left(\mathbf{w}_p \otimes \mathbf{w}_p \otimes \mathbf{w}_p\right) \\ \mathbf{w}_p' \, \mathbf{1} = 1 \\ \mathbf{w}_p \geq \mathbf{0} \end{cases} \tag{3.8}$$

with:

$$\mathbf{g} = \left[-\kappa^4\left(R_k\right) s^3\left(R_k\right) - \sigma^2\left(R_k\right) E\left(R_k\right)\right]'$$

The optimisation programs (3.7) and (3.8) are special cases of the following standard nonlinear quartic program:

$$\mathbf{z}^* = \underset{\mathbf{z}}{\text{Arg}} \{\text{Min } \mathbf{c}'\mathbf{z}\}$$

$$\text{s.t.} \begin{cases} L_j\left(\mathbf{z}\right) \leq \alpha_j \\ Q_k\left(\mathbf{z}\right) \leq \beta_k \\ C_l\left(\mathbf{z}\right) \leq \gamma_l \\ Q_q^*\left(\mathbf{z}\right) \leq \gamma_q \end{cases} \tag{3.9}$$

where $\mathbf{z} \in IR^p$, $L_j\left(.\right)$ is a linear map for $j = [1, \ldots, J]$, $Q_k\left(.\right)$ is a positive semi-definite quadratic form for k, $k = [1, \ldots, K]$, $C_l\left(.\right)$ is a cubic form for l, $l = [1, \ldots, L]$, and $Q_q^*\left(.\right)$ is a quartic form for q, $q = [1, \ldots, Q]$. In the case of the portfolio optimisation programme (3.8), $p = n$, $J = K = L = Q = 1$. The programme is not a standard convex nonlinear optimisation problem.

Due to the non-convex nature of the optimisation program, we need to state the necessary and sufficient conditions showing that a local optimal solution of (3.8) is also a global optimum (see the appendix).

Despite the nonconvex nature of the mean–variance–skewness–*kurtosis* portfolio selection program, the shortage function maximisation achieves a global optimum for the cubic program. This makes the shortage approach superior to the other primal and dual approaches of the mean–variance–skewness–*kurtosis* efficient set listed in the introduction, since those guarantee only a local optimum solution. To our knowledge, it encompasses also all the existing primal portfolio selection methods with higher-order moments considered in the financial literature. In the next section, we illustrate the shortage function approach in the case of hedge fund selection.

3.4   DATA AND EMPIRICAL RESULTS

Figures 3.1 to 3.8 provide different geometrical representations of a four-moment efficient frontier obtained after the optimisation of hedge funds in 1296 (6^4) directions using our directional distance function approach.

The original data – provided by HFR – consist of monthly net asset values of hedge funds (expressed in EUR) since January 1995. The maximum number of funds in the database is reached in September 2004 (4279 funds were observed). We then delete funds with missing values and normalise fund values to index 100 at the beginning of the final sample. At the end, 20 funds remain – which can be considered a fair number of funds for a fund of hedge funds – and the number of observations considered is 120 (from January 1995 to January 2005) – which can be considered long enough for this kind of application.

Figure 3.1 (3.2) represents the four-moment optimal portfolios in the mean–variance–third moment space (the mean–variance–fourth moment space). The maximisation of the expected return leads, at the optimum, to an increase of the variance – as in the Markowitz case – and the maximisation (minimisation) of the expected return (variance) implies, for hedge funds, also an increase (decrease) in the skewness (fourth moment). That is, while the individual preferences for higher-order moments cause high *kurtosis* and standard deviation

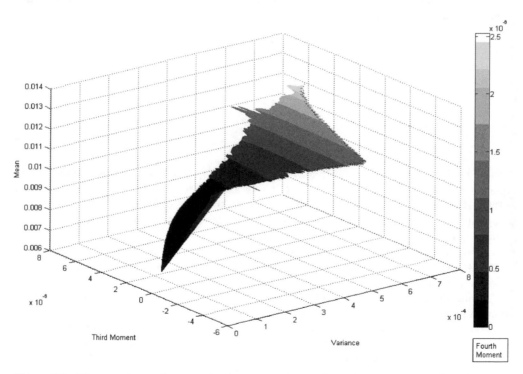

Figure 3.1 Mean–variance–skewness–*kurtosis* constrained efficient frontier in the mean–variance–third moment space. *Source*: HFR, monthly net asset values (1995–2005), computations by the authors. The constrained efficient frontier is obtained after optimisation of 20 hedge funds in 1296 directions. Grey shading represents the level of the fourth noncentral moment.

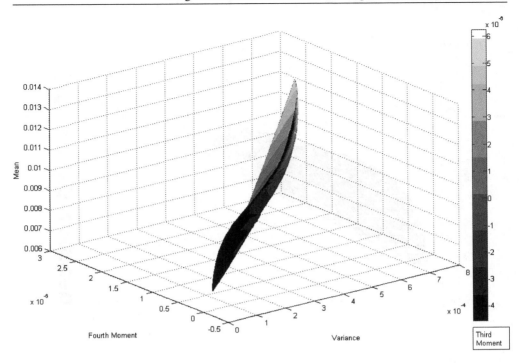

Figure 3.2 Mean–variance–skewness–*kurtosis* constrained efficient frontier in the mean–variance–
fourth moment space. *Source*: HFR, monthly net asset values (1995–2005), computations by the
authors. The constrained efficient frontier is obtained after optimisation of 20 hedge funds in 1296
directions. Grey shading represents the level of the third noncentral moment.

to be traded for higher expected return and skewness, hedge fund returns do not seem
to exhibit the same type of trade-offs between even or odd moments that are typically
observed in the underlying securities markets. These results are confirmed by Figures 3.3 to
3.8, which present the coordinates of the mean–variance–skewness–*kurtosis* efficient portfolios in several moment planes. Indeed, Figure 3.3 shows that mean–variance efficient
portfolios are efficient in terms of *kurtosis*, but not necessarily in terms of skewness. For
instance, given the mean, it is possible to increase the skewness at the cost of the variance. It is, however, not possible to decrease the fourth-order moment when controlling
for variance. Likewise, for intermediate or extreme levels of variance, it is possible to
increase the skewness of an optimal portfolio at the cost of its expected return. These observations contradict the point raised by Davies *et al.* (2004 and 2005) and Andersen and
Sornette (2001), namely that mean–variance optimisers may be nothing more than skewness minimisers and *kurtosis* maximisers. Figures 3.4 and 3.5 document the existence in
the four-moment efficient set of a V-shaped relationship between the third moment and the
mean and the variance, and Figures 3.6 and 3.7 illustrate the existence of a concave and
positive relation between the optimal fourth moment and the expected portfolio return and
variance.[6]

---

[6] Since the properties of the efficient set depend heavily on the technological characteristics of the underlying assets, further
investigations on hedge fund strategies and asset classes are required to assess the generality of our empirical findings.

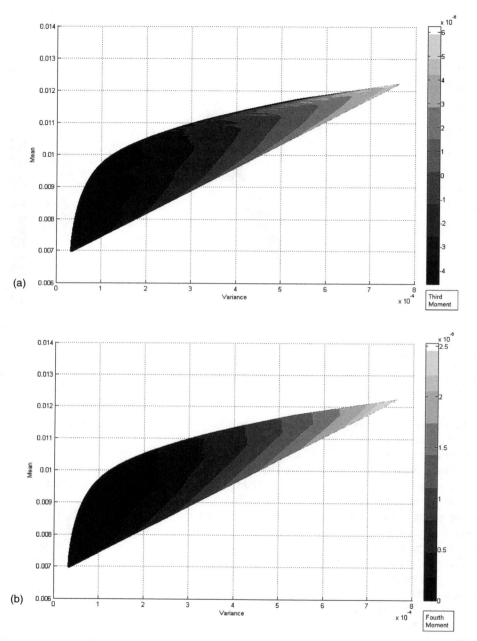

Figure 3.3 Mean–variance–skewness–*kurtosis* constrained efficient frontier in the mean–variance plane. *Source*: HFR, monthly net asset values (1995–2005), computations by the authors. The constrained efficient frontier is obtained after optimisation of 20 hedge funds in 1296 directions. (a) grey shading represents the level of the third noncentral moment; (b) grey shading represents the level of the fourth noncentral moment.

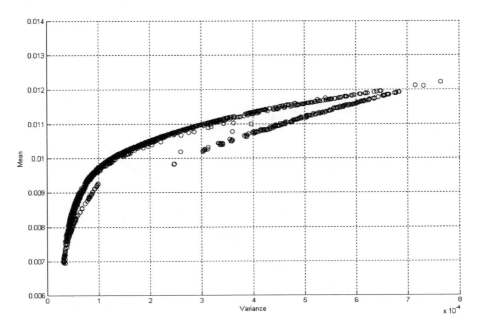

Figure 3.4 Mean–variance–skewness–*kurtosis* constrained efficient portfolios in the mean–variance plane. *Source*: HFR, monthly net asset values (1995–2005), computations by the authors. Optimal points are obtained after optimisation of 20 hedge funds in 1296 directions.

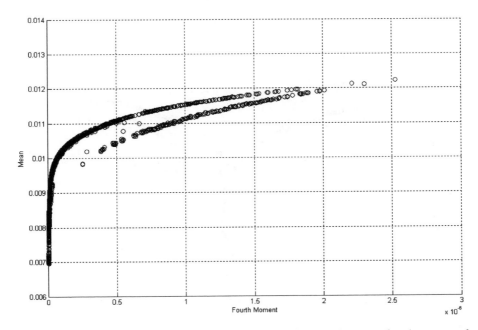

Figure 3.5 Mean–variance–skewness–*kurtosis* efficient portfolios in the mean–fourth moment plane. *Source*: HFR, monthly net asset values (1995–2005), computations by the authors. Optimal points are obtained after optimisation of 20 hedge funds in 1296 directions.

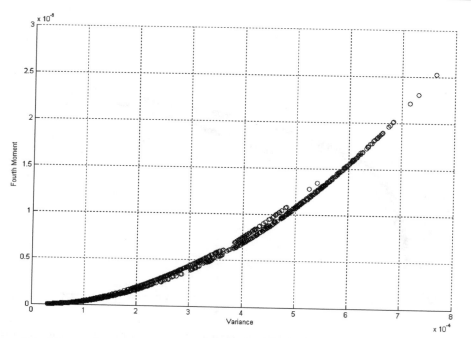

Figure 3.6   Mean–variance–skewness–*kurtosis* efficient portfolios in the variance–fourth moment plane. *Source*: HFR, monthly net asset values (1995–2005), computations by the authors. Optimal points are obtained after optimisation of 20 hedge funds in 1296 directions.

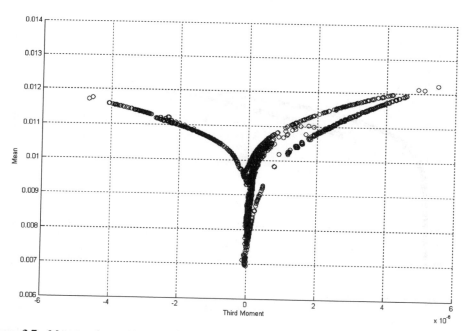

Figure 3.7   Mean–variance–skewness–*kurtosis* constrained efficient portfolios in the mean–third moment plane. *Source*: HFR, monthly net asset values (1995–2005), computations by the authors. Optimal points are obtained after optimisation of 20 hedge funds in 1296 directions.

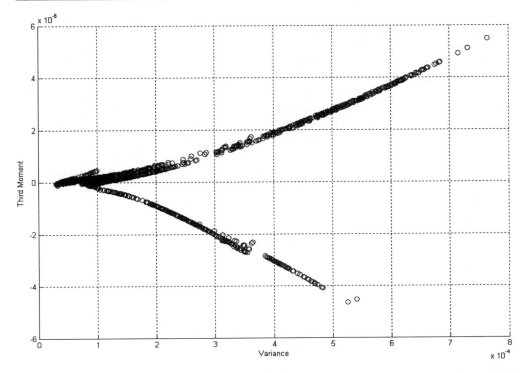

Figure 3.8 Mean–variance–skewness–*kurtosis* constrained efficient portfolios in the variance–third moment plane. *Source*: HFR, monthly net asset values (1995–2005), computations by the authors. Optimal points are obtained after optimisation of 20 hedge funds in 1296 directions.

3.5 CONCLUSION

In this chapter we have introduced a general method for deriving the set of efficient portfolios in the nonconvex mean–variance–skewness–*kurtosis* space, using a shortage optimisation function (see Luenberger, 1995 and Briec *et al.*, 2004 and 2006). The portfolio efficiency is evaluated by looking simultaneously for variance and *kurtosis* contractions and mean and (positive) skewness expansions. This shortage function is linked to an indirect mean–variance–skewness–*kurtosis* utility function. An empirical application on funds of hedge funds provides a three-dimensional representation of the primal nonconvex four-moment efficient portfolio frontier and illustrates the computational tractabilty of the approach.

We approximate the true but unknown mean–variance–skewness–*kurtosis* efficient frontier by a nonparametric portfolio frontier, using an efficiency measure that guarantees global optimality in the four-moment space. In addition, our shortage function can adapt itself to any particular multi-moment asset allocation focusing on return maximisation, skewness maximisation, variance minimisation and *kurtosis* minimisation. Furthermore, dual interpretations are available without imposing any simplifying hypotheses (see Briec *et al.*, 2006). Unfortunately, no global optimal solution can be guaranteed for the indirect mean–variance–skewness–*kurtosis* utility function. These findings indicate that future developments in asset allocation models should probably focus on developing portfolio optimisation methods using moment-based primal, rather than utility-based dual, optimisation approaches.

A natural extension of our framework is the development of a shortage function excluding any projections on the vertical or horizontal parts of the nonconvex feasible portfolio set and optimising the direction vector in the four moment dimensions.

Another extension of our work is the development of a more robust nonparametric multi-moment efficient frontier. This can be done either by working with robust estimators (see Parkinson, 1980; Brys et al., 2004; Kim and White, 2004 and Ledoit and Wolf, 2003, 2004a and 2004b) of the conventional higher-order moments, by using proper statistical inference tools for the nonparametric efficient frontier (see Simar and Wilson, 2000) or by substituting conventional moment definitions by alternative ones such as L-moments (see Hosking, 1990 and Serfling and Xiao, 2005). Finally, it would be of great interest to use our approach to gauge the performance of hedge funds.

APPENDIX

Let the local solution of the following quartic optimisation programme:

$$\mathbf{w}_p^* = \operatorname*{Arg}_{w_p} \{\operatorname{Max} \delta\}$$

$$\text{s.t.} \begin{cases} E(R_k) + \delta g_E \leq E(R_p) \\ \sigma^2(R_k) - \delta g_\sigma \geq \sigma^2(R_p) \\ s^3(R_k) + \delta g_s \leq s^3(R_p) \\ \kappa^4(R_k) - \delta g_\kappa' \geq \kappa^4(R_p) \\ \mathbf{w}_p' \mathbf{1} = 1 \\ \mathbf{w}_p \geq \mathbf{0} \end{cases}$$

where $\mathbf{w}_{p*}$ represents the $(N \times 1)$ efficient portfolio weight vector that maximises the performance, risk, skewness and *kurtosis* improvement with respect to the ones of the evaluated portfolio in the direction vector $\mathbf{g}$ be (δ^*, w_p^*). Then $(\delta^*, \mathbf{w}_p^*)$ is also a global solution of (3.7).

Proof Let us denote:

$$D = \{(\delta, \mathbf{w}_p) \in (IR_+ \times IR^N) : E(R_k) + \delta g_E \leq E(R_p); \tag{3.10}$$
$$\sigma^2(R_k) - \delta g_\sigma \geq \sigma^2(R_p); s^3(R_k) + \delta g_s \leq s^3(R_p); \kappa^4(R_k) - \delta g_\kappa' \geq \kappa^4(R_p)$$
$$\text{with } (\mathbf{w}_p' \mathbf{1}) = 1 \text{ and } \mathbf{w}_p \geq \mathbf{0}\}$$

We have:

$$S_g(\mathbf{w}_p) = \operatorname{Max} \{\delta : (\delta, \mathbf{w}_p) \in D\} \tag{3.11}$$

Assume that the couple $(\delta_1, \mathbf{w}_{p1})$ constitutes a local maximum, but is not a global one. In that case, there exists a couple $(\delta_2, \mathbf{w}_{p2}) \in D$ such that:

$$\delta_2 > \delta_1 \tag{3.12}$$

But since $\mathcal{D}_p$ satisfies the free disposal property, this implies that for all $\delta \in [\delta_1, \delta_2]$, there exists $\mathbf{w}_p \in \mathfrak{F}_p$ such that $(\delta, \mathbf{w}_p) \in D$. Therefore, there does not exist a neighbourhood $V\left[(\delta_1, \mathbf{w}_{p1}), \varepsilon\right]$ where $\varepsilon > 0$, such that $\delta_1 \geq \delta$ for all $(\delta, \mathbf{w}_p) \in V\left[(\delta_1, \mathbf{w}_{p1}), \varepsilon\right]$. Consequently, if (δ^*, w_p^*) is a local maximum, then it is also a global maximum. ∎

ACKNOWLEDGEMENTS

We are grateful to Thierry Chauveau and Thierry Michel for help and encouragement in preparing this work. The content of this chapter engages only its authors and does not necessarily reflect the opinions of their employers.

REFERENCES

Adcock, C. (2003) Asset Pricing and Portfolio Selection Based on the Multivariate Skew-Student Distribution, Working Paper, University of Sheffield, 15 pages.

Agarwal, V. and N. Naik (2004) Risks and Portfolio Decisions Involving Hedge Funds, *Review of Financial Studies* **17**, 63–98.

Andersen, J. and D. Sornette (2001) Have your Cake and Eat it too: Increasing Returns while Lowering Large Risks!, *Journal of Risk Finance* **2**, 70–82.

Athayde, G. and R. Flôres (2002) Portfolio Frontier with Higher Moments: the Undiscovered Country, Discussion Paper EPGE-FGV, 42 pages.

Athayde, G. and R. Flôres (2004) Finding a Maximum Skewness Portfolio: a General Solution to Three-moments Portfolio Choice, *Journal of Economic Dynamics and Control* **28**, 1335–1352.

Berényi, Z. (2001) Performance of Leveraged Asset Funds, Working Paper, University of Munich, 42 pages.

Berényi, Z. (2002) Measuring Hedge Funds' Risks with Moment-based Variance-equivalent Measures, Working Paper, University of Munich, 35 pages.

Briec, W., K. Kerstens and J. Lesourd (2004) Single-Period Markowitz Portfolio Selection, Performance Gauging, and Duality: A Variation on the Luenberger Shortage Function, *Journal of Optimization Theory and Applications* **120**, 1–27.

Briec, W., K. Kerstens and O. Jokung (2006) Mean-Variance-Skewness Portfolio Performance Gauging: A General Shortage Function and Dual Approach, *Management Science forthcoming*, 31 pages.

Brys, G., M. Hubert and A. Struyf (2004) A Robust Measure of Skewness, *Journal of Computational and Graphical Statistics* **13**, 996–1017.

Chang, C., T. Pactwa and A. Prakash (2003) Selecting a Portfolio with Skewness: Recent Evidence from US, European, and Latin American Equity Markets, *Journal of Banking and Finance* **27**, 1375–1390.

Chunhachinda, P., K. Dandapani, K. Hamid and S. Prakash (1997) Portfolio Selection and Skewness: Evidence from International Stock Markets, *Journal of Banking and Finance* **21**, 143–167.

Davies, R., H. Kat and S. Lu (2004) Single Strategy Fund of Hedge Funds, Working Paper, ISMA Center, 27 pages.

Davies, R., H. Kat and S. Lu (2005) Fund of Hedge Funds Portfolio Selection: A Multiple-Objective Approach, Working Paper, ISMA Center, 44 pages.

Gamba, A. and F. Rossi (1997) A Three-moment Based Capital Asset Pricing Model, Working Paper, University of Venice, 16 pages.

Gamba, A. and F. Rossi (1998a) A Three-moment Based Portfolio Selection Model, *Rivista di Matematica per le Scienze Economiche e Sociali* **20**, 25–48.

Gamba, A. and F. Rossi (1998b) Mean-Variance-Skewness Analysis in Portfolio Choice and Capital Markets, *Ricerca Operativa* **28**, Special Issue 1998, 5–46.

Goetzmann, W., J. Ingersoll, M. Spiegel and I. Welch (2004) Sharpening Sharpe Ratios, Working Paper, Yale University, 51 pages.

Guidolin, M. and A. Timmermann (2005) Optimal Portfolio Choices under Regime Switching, Skew and Kurtosis Preferences, Working Paper, Federal Reserve Bank of St Louis, 35 pages.

Harvey, C., J. Lietchty, M. Lietchty and P. Müller (2004) Portfolio Selection with Higher Moments, Working Paper, Duke University, 51 pages.

Hosking, J. (1990) L-moments: Analysis and Estimation, *Journal of the Royal Statistical Society Series B* **52**, 105–124.

Ingersoll, J. (1987) *Theory of Financial Decision Making*, Rowman and Littlefield, Ottowa.

Jondeau, E. and M. Rockinger (2003) How Higher Moments Affect the Allocation of Assets, *Finance Letters* **1** (2), 1–5.

Jondeau, E. and M. Rockinger (2006) Optimal Portfolio Allocation Under Higher Moments, *Journal of the European Financial Management Association* **12**, 29–67.

Jurczenko, E. and B. Maillet (2001) The 3-CAPM: Theoretical Foundations and an Asset Pricing Model Comparison in a Unified Framework. In: *Developments in Forecast Combination and Portfolio Choice*, C. Dunis, A. Timmermann and J. Moody (Eds), John Wiley & Sons, Ltd, Chichester, pp. 239–273.

Kim, T. and H. White (2004) On More Robust Estimation of Skewness and Kurtosis, *Finance Research Letters* **1**, 56–73.

Lai, T. (1991) Portfolio with Skewness: A Multiple-objective Approach, *Review of Quantitative Finance and Accounting* **1**, 293–305.

Ledoit, O. and M. Wolf (2003) Improved Estimation of the Covariance Matrix of Stock Returns with an Application to Portfolio Selection, *Journal of Empirical Finance* **10**, 603–621.

Ledoit, O. and M. Wolf (2004a) A Well-conditioned Estimator for Large-dimensional Covariance Matrices, *Journal of Multivariate Analysis* **88**, 365–411.

Ledoit, O. and M. Wolf (2004b) Honey, I Shrunk the Sample Covariance Matrix, *Journal of Portfolio Management* **30**, 110–119.

Luenberger, D. (1995) *Microeconomic Theory*, McGraw-Hill.

Markowitz, H. (1952) Portfolio Selection, *Journal of Finance* **7**, 77–91.

Morey, M. and R. Morey (1999) Mutual Fund Performance Appraisals: A Multi-horizon Perspective with Endogenous Benchmarking, *Omega International Journal of Management Science* **27**, 241–258.

Parkinson, M. (1980) The Extreme Value Method for Estimating the Variance of the Rate of Return, *Journal of Business* **53**, 61–65.

Pressacco, F. and P. Stucchi (2000) Linearity Properties of a Three-moments Portfolio Model, *Decisions in Economics and Finance* **23**, 133–150.

Rubinstein, M. (1973) The Fundamental Theorem of Parameter-preference Security Valuation, *Journal of Financial and Quantitative Analysis* **8**, 61–69.

Serfling, R. and P. Xiao (2005) Multivariate L-Moments, Working Paper, University of Texas, 33 pages.

Simaan, Y. (1993) Portfolio Selection and Asset Pricing Three Parameter Framework, *Management Science* **5**, 568–577.

Simar, L. and P. Wilson (2000) A General Methodology for Bootstrapping in Non-Parametric Frontier Models, *Journal of Applied Statistics* **27**, 779–802.

Sun, Q. and X. Yan (2003) Skewness Persistence with Optimal Portfolio Selection, *Journal of Banking and Finance* **27**, 1111–1121.

Wang, S. and Y. Xia (2002) *Portfolio Selection and Asset Pricing*, Springer-Verlag.

Weisman, A. (2002) Informationless Investing and Hedge Fund Performance Measurement Bias, *Journal of Portfolio Management* **28** (4), 80–91.

4

Higher-order Moments and Beyond

Luisa Tibiletti

ABSTRACT

As we skip beyond the realms of the normal world, many desirable properties fall short. Specifically, the central moments of linear combinations of random variables do *not* preserve the features of the addenda. For example, not even null-correlated returns preserve the signs of odd central moments as the returns are combined into a portfolio. A mathematical explanation of this counter-intuitive phenomenon is provided. However, using *one-sided higher-order moments* instead of higher-order moments may be a way to overcome these drawbacks. Thanks to the fact that they are coherent risk measures, a number of desirable marginal ordering properties are preserved.

4.1   INTRODUCTION

In recent years, there has been a growing interest in multi-moment capital asset pricing models (see Adcock, 2004; Athayde and Flôres, 2004a; Jondeau and Rockinger, 2003 among others). The widespread use of derivatives in financial business has led to a relaxing of the assumption of normality and, more generally, ellipticality in return distributions. Nevertheless, as we leave behind the "artificial" elliptical world, the second-order moment, i.e. the variance, becomes a questionable tool for measuring large risks. So, the attention of both theorists and practitioners has been focused on higher-order moments as appropriate tools for modelling extremal events (see the seminal papers of Rubinstein, 1973 and Kraus and Litzenberger, 1976 and, more recently, Jurczenko and Maillet, 2001, 2004a, 2004b; Berényi, 2004 and Dittmar, 2002). Unfortunately, outside the elliptical world, many desirable properties fall short. Specifically, the moments of linear combinations of random variables do *not* preserve the features of the addenda. For example, let's consider a risk-averse agent preferring positively skewed portfolios. One might think that adding a positively skewed asset to a positively skewed portfolio makes no change to the final skewness. Unfortunately, this conjecture may turn out to be false. By means of some counter-examples we show that, notwithstanding the addenda being equally skewed, a switching in skewness direction may even occur. The mathematical explanation of this counter-intuitive phenomenon can be given by a thorough insight into the formulas of higher-order moments.

Multi-moment Asset Allocation and Pricing Models   Edited by E. Jurczenko and B. Maillet
© 2006 John Wiley & Sons, Ltd

The aim of this chapter is just to deepen this puzzling problem. Pitfalls in using central moments for making asset selection are outlined. Besides the case of stochastic independence amongst the assets, even the estimation of the sign of the portfolio moments seems to be a challenging task. Moreover, no bounds for them seem to be available.

But a way to overcome these drawbacks may exist. Instead of basing the measures of risk on the familiar pth order moments of the distributions, we suggest using the pth *one-sided order moments*, with any integer $p \geq 2$ (if $p = 2$ the second left-sided moment is the standard semi-deviation). This choice can be supported by the following justifications: 1) insofar as we are looking to control the risk of losses, focusing on the left tail of the return distribution is just a consistent approach, 2) no additional computational efforts are required with respect to those needed for calculating the familiar moments, 3) left-sided moments are compatible with the expected utility theory (Fishburn, 1977), 4) measures of risk based on one-sided moments are coherent measures of risk according to the definition by Artzner *et al.* (1999). Specifically, one-sided moments enjoy a subadditivity property. Thanks to this feature a set of desirable properties can be guaranteed. First of all, we can control not only the sign (which is always nonnegative) but also the magnitude of the one-sided moments of the portfolio (by means of upper bounds). Moreover, if we focus on the standardised one-sided moment of order p, a sharp upper bound of a sum is achievable as the sum of the standardised one-sided pth order moments of the addenda. Nevertheless, the use of one-sided higher-order moments is not drawback-free. One concern is the absence of a closed form for portfolio return risk measures apart from the case of independence (see Section 4.4.1.).

A further point should be stressed. Let $\mathbf{X} = (X_1, \dots X_n)$ and $\mathbf{Y} = (Y_1, \dots, Y_n)$ be two random vectors collecting the returns with the same mean. As $\mathbf{X}$ and $\mathbf{Y}$ have the *same dependence structure*, i.e. a common copula, if $E(X_i)^p \leq E(Y_i)^p$ for all $i = 1, \dots, n$, does it imply that $E\left(\sum_{i=1}^n c_i X_i\right)^p \leq E\left(\sum_{i=1}^n c_i Y_i\right)^p$ for all $c_i \in \Re^+$?

One might expect that for two portfolios with the same dependence structure, the higher the pth order moments of the marginals, the higher the pth order moment of the portfolio. Unfortunately, due to the instability of the moments of linear combination, this conjecture may turn out to be false for *all* $p \geq 2$. On the other hand, sufficient conditions for marginal order preservation can be stated as long as marginal order is given in terms of one-sided higher moments instead of higher moments.

This chapter is organised as follows. In Section 4.2, misinterpretations in using higher-order moments are outlined. Noncoherence in risk measures is explored in Section 4.3. In Section 4.4, one-sided moments are proved to be a way to overcome previous drawbacks. A further problem of marginal ordering preservation under portfolio is examined in Section 4.5. Section 4.6 concludes the chapter.

4.2   HIGHER-ORDER MOMENTS AND SIMPLE ALGEBRA

Let $\mathbf{X} = (X_1, \dots, X_n)$ be a random vector. Suppose $X_i, i = 1, \dots, n$ is the return of the ith financial position. For the sake of notational simplicity, we will deal with *zero-mean* random variables, i.e. $E(X_i) = 0, i = 1, \dots, n$ where $E(.)$ is the expectation operator.[1] Moreover, let moments exist up to the order needed. Let:

$$S = c_1 X_1 + \dots + c_n X_n$$

---

[1] Note that any X can be transformed into the null-mean variable $X - E(X)$.

for any $c_i \in \Re$. The pth order (central) moment, with $p \geq 2$, can easily be worked out by means of the polynomial formula

$$E\left(c_1 X_1 + \cdots + c_n X_n\right)^p = \sum \frac{p!}{p_1! p_2! \cdots p_n!} c_1^{p_1} c_2^{p_2} \cdots c_n^{p_n} E\left(X_1^{p_1} . X_2^{p_2} \cdots X_n^{p_n}\right) \qquad (4.1)$$

$$\text{s.t.} \begin{cases} p_1 + p_2 + \cdots + p_n = p \\ p_i \neq p, \quad i = 1, \ldots, n \end{cases}$$

for all non-negative integers $p_1, p_2, \ldots, p_n$. Straightforward calculations highlight the influence of the pth moment of the marginals over the pth moment of the portfolio:

$$E\left(c_1 X_1 + \cdots + c_n X_n\right)^p = \sum_{i=1}^n c_i^p E\left(X_i^p\right) + \sum \frac{p!}{p_1! p_2! \cdots p_n!} c_1^{p_1} c_2^{p_2} \cdots c_n^{p_n} E\left(X_1^{p_1} . X_2^{p_2} \cdots X_n^{p_n}\right)$$

It is worthwhile noting that the latter addenda are non-null in most cases, and they upgrade in number and in weight as n increases. So that, for large portfolios, co-moments may have the most relevant impact over the pth moment of the portfolio. In conclusion, the portfolio's pth moment may be very far removed from the sum of the asset moments.

Just to prove our point, let's consider the number of addenda in (4.1); it is $C_{n,p}^0 = \binom{n+p-1}{p} = \frac{(n+p-1)!}{p!(n-1)!}$. Let $p=3$. If $n=10$, the number of addenda is $C_{10,3}^0 = 220$, but only 10 (about 4.5 % of all addenda) depend on the marginal third moments, and the remaining 210 on the co-moments. As n increases, the relative weight of the co-moments increases as well. For example, if $n=100$, the number of addenda becomes $C_{100,3}^0 = \frac{(102)!}{3!(99)!} = 171\,700$, where only 100 (about 0.06 % of all addenda) depend on the marginal third moments and the remaining 171 600 on the co-moments.

In Peccati and Tibiletti (1993), an empirical test on the stability in sign of the skewness of a portfolio composed of more than twenty skewed assets was carried out. Analysis of the daily distribution of twenty assets along a stretch of five years showed a persistent positive skewness of portfolio, even though the marginal skewness of the asset was negligible and very unstable. Insight has confirmed our conjecture: the very "gear" in the determination of the skewness of the portfolio was just given by the sum of the co-moments, whereas the relative weight of the marginal skewness of the single assets was negligible.

Next, we give examples to show that the above remarks are well-grounded: the sign of the third moment of the addenda is not preserved under positive linear combination.

Example 1 *Positive linear combinations of variables of equally signed skewness may turn out to be switched in skewness.*

1. First, let us consider two identically distributed binary options:

$$X_1 = \begin{cases} -\frac{1}{3}, & p = \frac{3}{4} \\ 1, & p = \frac{1}{4} \end{cases} \quad \text{and} \quad X_2 = \begin{cases} -\frac{1}{3}, & p = \frac{3}{4} \\ 1, & p = \frac{1}{4} \end{cases}$$

where $\mu_{x_1} = \mu_{x_2} = 0$, $E\left(X_1^3\right) = E\left(X_2^3\right) = +0.22222 > 0$, therefore they are positively skewed. Let the probability matrix be:

	$x_1 = -\frac{1}{3}$	$x_1 = 1$
$x_2 = -\frac{1}{3}$	$p = \frac{1}{2}$	$p = \frac{1}{4}$
$x_2 = 1$	$p = \frac{1}{4}$	$p = 0$

Therefore, the portfolio is:

$$S = c_1 X_1 + c_2 X_2 = \begin{cases} \frac{1}{3}(c_1 + c_2), & p = \frac{1}{2} \\ c_1 - \frac{1}{3}c_2, & p = \frac{1}{4} \\ -\frac{1}{3}c_1 + c_2, & p = \frac{1}{4} \\ c_1 + c_2, & p = 0 \end{cases}$$

It is easy to prove that:

$$if\ c_1 = \frac{3}{4}\ and\ c_2 = \frac{1}{4}\ then\ S = \begin{cases} -\frac{2}{9}, & p = \frac{1}{4} \\ 0, & p = \frac{1}{4} \\ +\frac{1}{3}, & p = \frac{1}{2} \end{cases}\ so\ E\left(S^3\right) = +0.05555 > 0$$

$$if\ c_1 = \frac{1}{2}\ and\ c_2 = \frac{1}{2}\ then\ S = \begin{cases} -\frac{1}{3}, & p = \frac{1}{2} \\ +\frac{1}{3}, & p = \frac{1}{2} \end{cases}\ so\ E\left(S^3\right) = 0$$

In conclusion, just by changing the relative weights of two identically distributed assets in the portfolio, the sign of the third moment of the portfolio is not preserved.

2. *Secondly, let us consider two binary positively skewed options:*

$$X_1 = \begin{cases} -\frac{1}{3}, & p = \frac{3}{4} \\ 1, & p = \frac{1}{4} \end{cases}\ and\ X_2 = \begin{cases} -\frac{3}{4}, & p = \frac{4}{7} \\ 1, & p = \frac{3}{7} \end{cases}$$

where $\mu_{x_1} = \mu_{x_2} = 0$, $E\left(X_1^3\right) = +0.22222 > 0$ *and* $E\left(X_2^3\right) = +0.66964 > 0$. *Let the probability matrix be:*

	$x_1 = -\frac{1}{3}$	$x_1 = 1$
$x_2 = -\frac{3}{4}$	$p = \frac{9}{28}$	$p = \frac{1}{4}$
$x_2 = 1$	$p = \frac{3}{7}$	$p = 0$

So, the portfolio $S = X_1 + X_2 = \begin{cases} -\frac{13}{12}, & p = \frac{9}{28} \\ \frac{1}{4}, & p = \frac{1}{4} \\ \frac{2}{3}, & p = \frac{3}{7} \end{cases}$ *is negatively skewed since* $E\left(S^3\right) = -0.277777652 < 0$

Therefore, adding to X_1 *a more positively skewed asset* X_2, *the final portfolio skewness turns from positive into negative.*

3. *Thirdly, note that:*

$$E\left(c_1 X_1 + c_2 X_2\right)^3 = c_1^3 E\left(X_1^3\right) + c_2^3 E\left(X_2^3\right) + 3c_1^2 c_2 E\left(X_1^2 X_2\right) + 3c_1 c_2^2 E\left(X_1 X_2^2\right)$$

so even if $E\left(X_i^3\right) > 0$, *for* $i = 1, 2$ *and* $E\left(X_1 X_2\right) = 0$, *i.e.* X_1 *and* X_2 *are null-correlated, the overwhelming role played by the coskewness may switch the sign of the portfolio skewness from positive to negative.*

Eventually, a spontaneous question may arise: does a way to control at least the sign of the co-moments exist? Unfortunately, the question seems to be answered in the negative.

Clearly, in some very special cases the sign of the co-moments can be drawn from the sign of the lower-order moments of the addenda. That is the case of stochastic independence.

Theorem 1 *Let* $\mathbf{X} = (X_1, \ldots X_n)$ *be a vector of stochastically independent variables, then:*

$$E\left(c_1 X_1 + \cdots + c_n X_n\right)^p = \sum_{i=1}^{n} c_i^p E\left(X_i^p\right)$$

$$+ \sum \frac{p!}{p_1! p_2! \ldots \cdot p_n!} c_1^{p_1} c_2^{p_2} \ldots \cdot c_n^{p_n} E\left(X_1^{p_1}\right) E\left(X_2^{p_2}\right) \cdots E\left(X_n^{p_1}\right)$$

$$\text{s.t.} \begin{cases} p_1 + p_2 + \cdots + p_n = p \\ p_i \neq p \ i = 1, \ldots, n \end{cases}$$

Proof Let $n = 2$. A necessary and sufficient condition for stochastic independence is the following: X_1 and X_2 are stochastically independent if $E\left(g\left(X_1\right) h\left(X_2\right)\right) = E\left(g\left(X_1\right)\right) E\left(h\left(X_2\right)\right)$ for all Borel-measurable functions g and h, provided that the expectations involved exist. Clearly, power functions are very special Borel-measurable functions. So, for all co-moments it turns out that $E\left(X_1^{p-k} X_2^k\right) = E\left(X_1^{p-k}\right) E\left(X_2^k\right)$ for all $k = 1, \ldots, p - 1$. By induction the desired result follows.

Note that if $E\left(X_i\right) = 0$, the addenda containing at least one $E\left(X_i^{p_i}\right)$ with $p_i = 1$ vanish and the above expression becomes simpler. In conclusion, under stochastic independence the portfolio's pth order moment is given by a combination of kth order moments of the addenda, with $k = 1, \ldots, p$. As the independence assumption is relaxed, stability holds neither in sign nor in magnitude.

4.3 HIGHER MOMENTS: NONCOHERENT RISK MEASURES

At the end of 1998, Artzner *et al.* (1999), for the first time, faced the problem of defining the desirable properties that a risk measure should satisfy. The answer was given through a complete characterisation of such properties via an axiomatic formulation of the concept of *coherent measure of risk*. The question posed is the following: are risk measures based on higher moments coherent risk measures? Unfortunately, the answer is no.

In order to make the chapter self-contained, we now recall these axioms. Fix a probability space (Ω, F, P) and denote by $L^0(\Omega, F, P)$ the set of almost surely finite random variables on that space. Financial risks are represented by a *convex cone* $M \subseteq L^0(\Omega, F, P)$ of random variables. Recall that M is a convex cone if $X_1 \in M$ and $X_2 \in M$ implies that $X_1 + X_2 \in MX_1 \in M$ and $\lambda X_1 \in M$ for every $\lambda > 0$.

Definition 1 *Risk measure. Given some convex cone* M *of random variables, any mapping* $\rho : M \to \Re$ *is called a **risk measure**.*

Following Artzner *et al.* (1999) we list a set of desirable axioms that a risk measure should satisfy.

Axiom 1 (Monotonicity). For all $X_1 \in M$ and $X_2 \in M$, such that $X_1 \le X_2$ as a monotonic risk satisfies $\rho(X_1) \le \rho(X_2)$.

Axiom 2 (Subadditivity). For all $X_1 \in M$ and $X_2 \in M$, a subadditive risk measure satisfies $\rho(X + Y) \le \rho(X) + \rho(Y)$.

Axiom 3 (Positive homogeneity). For all $X \in M$ and $\lambda \ge 0$, a positive homogeneous risk measure satisfies $\rho(\lambda X) = \lambda \rho(X)$.

Axiom 4 (Translation invariance). For all $X \in M$ and $a \in \Re$, a translation-invariant risk measure satisfies $\rho(a + X) = \rho(X) - a$

Axiom 1 says that if a position X_1 is always worth more than X_2, then X_1 cannot be riskier than X_2. Following Artzner *et al.* (1999, p. 209), the rationale behind Axiom 2 can be summarised by the statement "a merger does not create extra risk." Subadditivity reflects the idea that risk can be reduced by diversification, a well-grounded principle in finance and economics. The lack of subadditivity might be an incentive to split up a large portfolio into two smaller ones. That goes against the above-mentioned statement. Axiom 3 is a limit case of subadditivity, representing what happens when there is no diversification effect. With reference to Axiom 3, positive homogeneity asserts that the risk of a position increases in a linear way with the size of the position.

Definition 2 *Coherent risk measure Given a risk measure ρ whose domain includes the convex cone* M, ρ *is called coherent if it satisfies Axioms 1, 2, 3 and 4.*

Surprisingly enough, the second-order central moment (i.e. the variance) – the most common risk measure – falls short in monotonicity, positive homogeneity and translation. Therefore, it is not a coherent risk measure. Standard deviation behaves slightly better since it is positive homogeneous, but it lacks monotonicity and translation. So it is not a coherent risk measure either. In general, higher central moments are not coherent risk measures. Specifically: (1) if p is an even integer, with $p \ge 2$, the pth central moment does not fulfil the monotonicity, positive homogeneity or translation axioms; (2) if p is an odd integer, with $p \ge 3$, the pth central moment is not subadditive. That is the very drawback in using moments as risk measures. In spite of what intuition would suggest, diversification does not guarantee the moment shrinking. In conclusion, odd-order moments do not fulfil the subadditivity, positive homogeneity or translation axioms.

4.4   ONE-SIDED HIGHER MOMENTS

Let us denote $x^- = \min\{x, 0\}$ and $x^+ = \max\{0, x\}$.

Definition 3   *Let ξ be a real-valued random variable. Then:*

$$m_-^p(\xi) = E\left[\{|(\xi - E[\xi])^-|\}^p\right] \quad and \quad m_+^p(\xi) = E\left[\{|(\xi - E[\xi])^+|\}^p\right]$$

are called the left-sided and the right-sided moments of the pth order of ξ, respectively, for $1 \le p < \infty$.

The left-sided moments are loss risk measures. Therefore, they are to be minimised in a problem of portfolio risk allocating. The opposite strategy applies to the right-sided moments.

From here on, we will deal solely with the left-sided moments, since analogous statements can be drawn for the right-sided ones.

Clearly, the one-sided moments are not positive homogeneous measures. This failure can be overcome easily by the following standardised measure:

$$\rho_-^p(\xi) = \sqrt[p]{E[\{|(\xi - E[\xi])^-|\}^p]}$$

which is a *coherent risk measure* (see Fischer, 2003). Moreover, a mean-risk criterion, where the risk is measured by ρ_-^p for $p \in (1, +\infty)$ is coherent with the criterion of the expected utility maximisation (see Fishburn, 1977).

4.4.1   Portfolio left-sided moment bounds

Let us turn back to the higher-moment portfolio problem. The left-sided pth order moment, with $p \geq 2$, of the portfolio can no longer be expressed in a closed form, such as (4.1). That is a drawback. In fact, when using one-sided moments it is no longer possible to obtain analytical expressions of the gradients and the Hessian matrix associated with the investor's portfolio selection problem to derive the expressions and study the general properties of the minimum variance and efficient frontier and to obtain an equilibrium asset pricing relation, as in the traditional higher-order moment case (see Athayde and Flôres, 2003, 2004b). Otherwise, some upper bounds for the standardised left-sided moments can be worked out.

Proposition 1

$$0 \leq E\{|(c_1 X_1 + \cdots + c_n X_n)^-|\}^p \leq \tag{4.2}$$

$$\sum \frac{p!}{p_1! p_2! \cdots \cdot p_n!} |c_1|^{p_1} |c_2|^{p_2} \cdots |c_n|^{p_n} E(\{|(X_1)^-|\}^{p_1} \cdot \{|(X_2)^-|\}^{p_2} \cdots \{|(X_n)^-|\}^{p_n})$$

$$\text{s.t.} \quad p_1 + p_2 + \cdots + p_n = p$$

Proof   Since $|(c_1 X_1 + \cdots + c_n X_n)^-| \leq |(c_1 X_1)^-| + \cdots + |(c_n X_n)^-| = |c_1||(X_1)^-| + \cdots + |c_n||(X_n)^-|$ then:

$$E\{|(c_1 X_1 + \cdots + c_n X_n)^-|\}^p \leq E\{|c_1||(X_1)^-| + \cdots + |c_n||(X_n)^-|\}^p$$

applying the polynomial formula to the right-hand side of (4.2), the desired result comes out.

Proposition 2

$$0 \leq \sqrt[p]{E\{|(c_1 X_1 + \cdots + c_n X_n)^-|\}^p} \leq |c_1|\sqrt[p]{E\{|(X_1)^-|\}^p} + \cdots + |c_n|\sqrt[p]{E\{|(X_n)^-|\}^p}$$

Proof   Thanks to the Minkowski inequality, the stated result follows.

4.4.2   Properties of the upper bound $U^p(S_-)$

On the other hand, if we deal with nonstandardised measures, handling co-moments becomes compulsory. In order to separate the influence of the marginals from the left-sided co-moments, let us re-write the upper bound in the right-hand side of (4.2):

$$U^p(S_-) = \sum_{i=1}^{n} |c_i|^p \, E\{|(X_i)^-|\}^p \tag{4.3}$$

$$+ \sum \frac{p!}{p_1! p_2! \ldots p_n!} |c_1|^{p_1} |c_2|^{p_2} \ldots |c_n|^{p_n} \, E\left(\{|(X_1)^-|\}^{p_1} \cdot \{|(X_2)^-|\}^{p_2} \cdots \{|(X_n)^-|\}^{p_n}\right)$$

$$\text{s.t.} \begin{cases} p_1 + p_2 + \cdots + p_n = p \\ p_i \neq p \; i = 1, \ldots, n \end{cases}$$

Due to the non-negativeness of the latter addendum, we get a *lower bound for* $U^p(S_-)$

$$\sum_{i=1}^{n} c_i^p \, E\{|(X_i)^-|\}^p \leq U^p(S_-)$$

Note that this lower bound is nothing but the weighted sum of the left-sided moments of the marginals. More information is attainable as assumptions on the dependence structure are introduced.

1. *Stochastic independence among the assets.* Since $\varphi(x) = \{|(x)^-|\}^{p_i}, i = 1, \ldots, n$ are Borel-measurable functions, under independence we get

$$E\left(\{|(X_1)^-|\}^{p_1} \cdot \{|(X_2)^-|\}^{p_2} \cdots \{|(X_n)^-|\}^{p_n}\right) = E\{|(X_1)^-|\}^{p_1} \cdot E\{|(X_2)^-|\}^{p_2} \ldots E\{|(X_n)^-|\}^{p_n}$$

Therefore, (4.3) can be re-written as:

$$U^p(S_-) = \sum_{i=1}^{n} |c_i|^p \, E\{|(X_i)^-|\}^p \tag{4.4}$$

$$+ \sum \frac{p!}{p_1! p_2! \ldots p_n!} |c_1|^{p_1} |c_2|^{p_2} \ldots |c_n|^{p_n}$$

$$\times E\{|(X_1)^-|\}^{p_1} \cdot E\{|(X_2)^-|\}^{p_2} \ldots E\{|(X_n)^-|\}^{p_n}$$

Therefore, under independence, the upper bound $U^p(S_-)$ is given by a sum of products of the marginal moments. As soon as the marginals are known, $U^p(S_-)$ can be calculated.

2. *Maximal positive dependence among the assets.* The maximum value of the upper bound $U^p(S_-)$ is reached in the case of maximal positive dependence. Let us denote by $F_1, \ldots, F_n$ the marginal distributions of $X_1, \ldots, X_n$ and let $H(x) = \text{Min}(F_1(x_1), \ldots, F_n(x_n))$ be the upper Fréchet distribution. For any $X = (X_1, \ldots, X_n)$ with marginals $F_1, \ldots, F_n$ the following inequality holds:

$$U^p(S_-) \leq \sum \frac{p!}{p_1! p_2! \ldots p_n!} |c_1|^{p_1} |c_2|^{p_2} \ldots |c_n|^{p_n} \tag{4.5}$$

$$\int \cdots \int_{x_1 + \cdots + x_n \leq 0} \{|x_1|^-\}^{p_1} \cdot \{|x_2|^-\}^{p_2} \ldots \{|x_n|^-\}^{p_n} \, d\text{Min}(F_1(x_1), \ldots, F_n(x_n))$$

3. *Multivariate totally positive dependence (MTP₂) among the assets.* MTP$_2$ is a positive dependence property that has been studied thoroughly in the last twenty years. Many families of distributions have been proven to be MTP$_2$. That is the case for the absolute-value multinormal variables, the multivariate logistic distributions, the negative multivariate distributions among others. Moreover, methods for generating MTP$_2$ distributions are achievable (see Karlin and Rinott, 1980). For MTP$_2$ distributions, $E(g(X)h(X)) \geq E(g(X))E(h(X))$ holds for all Borel-measurable functions g and h, which are simultaneously monotonically increasing or decreasing. Since $\varphi(x) = |x^-|^{p_i}$, $i = 1, \ldots, n$ are just increasing Borel-measurable functions, $U^p(S_-)$ can be bounded from below and above. Specifically, from below by the right-hand side of (4.4) and (4.5), respectively.

4.5 PRESERVATION OF MARGINAL ORDERING UNDER PORTFOLIOS

A further advantage of using one-sided moments concerns the chance to preserve the marginal one-sided moment ordering under portfolios. First, the drawbacks of higher orders are highlighted, then the advantages of using the one-sided moments are shown.

4.5.1 Drawbacks in using higher moments

Let $\mathbf{X} = (X_1, \ldots, X_n)$ and $\mathbf{Y} = (Y_1, \ldots, Y_n)$ be two random vectors collecting the returns, such that $E(X_i) = E(Y_i)$ for all $i = 1, \ldots, n$. As $\mathbf{X}$ and $\mathbf{Y}$ have the *same dependence structure*, i.e. a common copula, if $E(X_i)^p \leq E(Y_i)^p$ for all $i = 1, \ldots, n$, does it imply that $E(\sum_{i=1}^n c_i X_i)^p \leq E(\sum_{i=1}^n c_i Y_i)^p$, for all $c_i \in \Re^+$? (for the definition of copula, see the appendix).

One might expect that for two portfolios with the same dependence structure, the higher the pth order moment of the marginals, the higher the pth order moment of the portfolio. Unfortunately, this conjecture turns out to be false for *all* $p \geq 2$. To the best of our knowledge, the first counter-example was given by Scarsini (1998), where the statement was proved to be false for $p = 2$ and with normal variables. For any other even p, analogous counter-examples can be carried out. If p is odd, then counter-examples are very easy to construct. Consider the following.

Example 2 *Let us consider the case of* $p = 3$. *Let* $\mathbf{X} = (X_1, X_2)$ *be defined as in Example 1, case 2), so* $E(X_1^3) = +0.22222 > 0$ *and* $E(X_2^3) = +0.66964 > 0$. *The portfolio* $S_X = X_1 + X_2$ *is such that* $E(S_X^3) = -0.277777652 < 0$.

Let $\mathbf{Y} = (Y_1, Y_2) = (3X_1, 3X_2)$, *so* $E(Y_i^3) = 3^3 E(X_i^3) > 0$ *and* $E(X_i^3) \leq E(Y_i^3)$ *for* $i = 1, 2$. *Construct the portfolio* $S_Y = Y_1 + Y_2 = 3X_1 + 3X_2$. *Clearly,* S_X *and* S_Y *have the same dependence structure. Since* $E(S_Y^3) = 3^3 E(S_X^3) < 0$, *then* $E(S_X^3) \geq E(S_Y^3)$. *In conclusion, although* $E(X_i^3) \leq E(Y_i^3)$ *for* $i = 1, 2$ *it turns out that* $E(S_X^3) \geq E(S_Y^3)$. *Therefore, a switching in moment ordering results.*

4.5.2 Advantages in using left-sided higher moments

Let's replace the pth order moments by the pth order left-sided moments. The question posed is as follows: as $\mathbf{X}$ and $\mathbf{Y}$ have the *same dependence structure*, i.e. a common copula, if $E\{|(X_i)^-|\}^p \le E\{|(Y_i)^-|\}^p$ for all $i = 1, \ldots, n$, is it true that $E\{|(\sum_{i=1}^n c_i X_i)^-|\}^p \le E\{|(\sum_{i=1}^n c_i Y_i)^-|\}^p$, for all $c_i \in \Re^+$?

Unfortunately, the answer is still negative. Tibiletti (2002) proved that the statement does not hold even for normal variables and $p = 2$ (the semi-variance). But, there is a ray of hope. Left-sided moments are the expected values of convex functions, and some results stemming from multivariate convex ordering are attainable. In any case, further conditions on the dependence structure are compulsory. A list of sufficient conditions for ordering preservation under portfolios is given in Tibiletti (2002). Under independence, the desired left-sided moment ordering is guaranteed.

Theorem 2   Let $\mathbf{X} = (X_1, \ldots, X_n)$ and $\mathbf{Y} = (Y_1, \ldots, Y_n)$ be vectors with independent components. Then, the marginal risk ordering in left-sided moments is preserved under portfolios.

If however, we replace, the assumption of stochastic independence with the assumption of fixed copula, then Theorem 2 is not true any more. Moreover, it is clear that we cannot expect the risk order of the marginals to lead to the one-sided moment order of the portfolios when the components are negatively dependent. The effect of risk hedging may produce a switching in portfolio ordering. A condition of positive dependence is needed. A notion which fits well in this context is that of *conditional increasingness* (CI) proposed by Müller and Scarsini (2001). CI is a weaker condition than *multivariate totally positivity of order 2* (MTP$_2$) investigated by Karlin and Rinott (1980) and stronger than *conditional increasingness in sequence* (CIS). The CI property coupled with convexity in risk measures achieves the desired ordering preservation.

Theorem 3   Let $\mathbf{X} = (X_1, \ldots, X_n)$ and $\mathbf{Y} = (Y_1, \ldots, Y_n)$ be vectors with a common CI copula C. Then, the marginal risk ordering in left-sided moments is preserved under portfolios.

From the mathematical point of view, the CI property is quite a strong condition of positive dependence. But no weaker condition seems to exist. Although copulas are the most elegant tool for studying stochastic events, on the other hand, financial modelling needs to implement algorithms for constructing, step by step, the best-fitting data copula. These algorithms are available for the most popular families of copulas (see Embrechts *et al.*, 2002 and Bouyé *et al.*, 2000). Tibiletti (2002) has checked the CI condition. The required restrictions turn out to be not so restrictive. For example, for elliptical copulas, CI requires the non-negativeness of correlations. For strict Archimedean copulas, which satisfy Lehmann's positive quadrant dependence, CI imposes only a mild additional condition. Marshall–Olkin copulas are always CI.

In conclusion, one-sided moments give a clue to preserving marginal ordering under portfolios.

4.6   CONCLUSION

Higher-order moments fall short in preserving marginal asset properties under portfolios. We have proved that even a positive linear combination of positively skewed null-mean assets may turn out to be negatively skewed. Moreover, as the number of assets in the portfolio grows higher, the control over the magnitude and the sign of the portfolio moments becomes looser. In fact, the portfolio moments are principally driven by the co-moments of the addenda. Higher moments are not coherent measures of risk: that is the real culprit of the above-mentioned drawbacks. One-sided higher-order moments provide a way to overcome the problem. Advantages of these latter measures are: 1) they are a consistent tool for controlling the risk on the left tail of the return distributions. Moreover, if the one-sided moments are replaced by the standardised ones, clear-cut upper bounds are attainable, 2) they do not require additional computational efforts with respect to those needed for the familiar moments, 3) they are compatible with the expected utility theory (Fishburn, 1977), 4) one-sided moments are coherent measures of risk according to Artzner *et al.*'s (1999) definition. On the other hand, a limit on their use exists. No closed form for portfolio return risk measures seems to be available. So, it is no longer possible to obtain analytical expressions of the gradients and the Hessian matrix associated with the investor's portfolio selection problem to derive the expressions of the minimum variance and efficient frontier and to obtain an equilibrium asset pricing relation, as in the traditional higher-order moment case.

APPENDIX

An elegant way to understand how a multivariate distribution is influenced by the dependence structure and the marginals is to use the concept of the *copula*. This notion was introduced by Sklar (1959) (see Schweizer, 1991 for a historical survey). In recent years its use has spread to different fields of insurance and financial modelling. The copula is one of the most useful tools for handling multivariate distributions in the Fréchet class $\Gamma(F_1, \ldots, F_n)$ of joint n-dimensional distribution functions having $F_1, \ldots, F_n$ as univariate marginals. Formally, given a distribution function in $\Gamma(F_1, \ldots, F_n)$, there exists a function $C: [0, 1]^n \rightarrow [0, 1]$, such that, for all $x \in \Re^n$,

$$F(x) = C(F_1(x_1), \ldots, F_n(x_n))$$

The function C is unique on $\Pi_{i=1}^{n} \text{Ran}(F_i)$, the product of the ranges of $F_i, i = 1, \ldots, n$. Therefore if F is continuous, then C is unique and can be constructed as follows:

$$C(u) = F\left(F_1^{-1}(u_1), \ldots, F_n^{-1}(u_n)\right), \quad u \in [0, 1]^n$$

Otherwise, C can be extended to $[0, 1]^n$ in such a way that it is a distribution function with uniform marginals. Any such extension is called the *copula* of F. Most of the multivariate dependence structure properties of F are in the copula, which does not depend on the marginals, and it is often easier to handle than the original F.

REFERENCES

Adcock, C. (2004) Asset Pricing and Portfolio Selection Based on the Multivariate Skew-Student Distribution. In: *Multi-moment Asset Pricing Models*, C. Adcock, E. Jurczenko and B. Maillet (Eds), Springer-Verlag.

Artzner, P., F. Delbaen, J. Eber and D. Heath (1999) Coherent Measures of Risk, *Mathematical Finance* **9**(3), 203–228.

Athayde, G. and R. Flôres (2003) Incorporating Skewness and Kurtosis in Portfolio Optimization: A Multidimensional Efficient set. In *Advances in Portfolio Construction and Implementation*, S. Satchell and A. Scowcroft (Eds), Butterworth-Heinemann Finance, pp. 243–257.

Athayde, G. and R. Flôres (2004a) Finding a Maximum Skewness Portfolio: a General Solution to Three-moments Portfolio Choice, *Journal of Economic Dynamics and Control* **28**(7), 1335–1352.

Athayde, G. and R. Flôres (2004b) On Certain Geometric Aspects of Portfolio Optimisation with Higher Moments. In: *Multimoment Asset Pricing Models*, C. Adcock, E. Jurczenko and B. Maillet (Eds), Springer-Verlag.

Berényi, Z. (2004) Measuring Hedge Funds' Risks with Moment-based Variance-equivalent Measures. In: *Multimoment Asset Pricing Models*, C. Adcock, E. Jurczenko and B. Maillet (Eds), Springer-Verlag.

Bouyé, E., A. Nikeghbali, G. Riboulet and T. Roncalli (2000) Copulas for Finance. A reading Guide and Some Applications. Groupe de Recherche Opérationalle, Crédit Lyonnais, Paris.

Dittmar, R. (2002) Nonlinear Pricing Kernels, Kurtosis Preference, and Evidence from the Cross-Section of Equity Returns, *Journal of Finance* **57**, 369–403.

Embrechts, P., F. Lindskog and A. McNeil (2002) Modelling Dependence with Copulas and Applications to Risk Management. In *Heavy-Tailed Distributions in Finance*, S.T. Rachev (Ed.) North Holland, Amsterdam.

Fischer, T. (2003) Risk capital allocation by coherent risk measures based on one-sided moments, *Insurance: Mathematics and Economics* **32**, 135–146.

Fishburn, P.C. (1977) Mean-Risk Analysis with Risk Associated with Below-Target Returns, *American Economic Review* **67**, 116–126.

Jondeau, E. and M. Rockinger (2003) How Higher Moments Affect the Allocation of Assets, *Finance Letters* **1** (2).

Jurczenko, E. and B. Maillet (2001) The 3-CAPM: Theoretical Foundations and an Asset Pricing Model Comparison in a Unified Framework. In: *Developments in Forecast Combination and Portfolio Choice*, C. Dunis, A. Timmermann and J. Moody (Eds), John Wiley & Sons, Ltd, Chichester, pp. 239–273.

Jurczenko, E. and B. Maillet (2004a) The Theoretical Foundations of Asset Allocation and Pricing Models with High-order Moments. In: *Multi-moment Asset Allocation and Pricing Models*, E. Jurczenko and B. Maillet (Eds), Wiley.

Jurczenko, E. and B. Maillet (2004b) The Four-moment Capital Asset Pricing Model: between Asset Pricing and Asset Allocation. In: *Multi-moment Asset Allocation and Pricing Models*, E. Jurczenko and B. Maillet (Eds), Wiley.

Karlin, S. and Y. Rinott (1980) Classes of orderings of measures and related correlation inequalities, *Journal of Multivariate Analysis* **10**, 467–498.

Kraus, A. and R. Litzenberger (1976) Skewness Preference and the Valuation of Risk Assets, *Journal of Finance* **31**, 1085–1099.

Müller, A. and M. Scarsini (2001) Stochastic comparison of random vectors with common copula, *Mathematics of Operations Research* **26**(4), 723–740.

Peccati, L. and L. Tibiletti (1993) On the asymmetry of stock-return distribution. Presented at the 14th Meeting of the EURO Working Group of Financial Modelling, Mantova, Italy, 25–27 November, 1993.

Rubinstein, M. (1973) The Fundamental Theorem of Parameter-preference Security Valuation, *Journal of Financial and Quantitative Analysis* **8**, 61–69.

Scarsini, M. (1998) Multivariate convex ordering, dependence, and stochastic equality, *Journal of Applied Probability* **35**, 93–103.

Schweizer, B. (1991) Thirty years of copulas. In: *Advances in Probability Distribution with Given Marginals*, G. Dall'Aglio, S. Kotz and G. Salinetti (Eds.), Kluwer, Dordrecht, pp. 13–50.

Tibiletti, L. (2002) The riskier the assets, the riskier the portfolios: pitfalls and misinterpretations. Presented at "Copula Workshop", Kaiserslautern, Germany, November 18–19, 2002. Published in *Capital Markets-Asset,* SSRN journal, downloadable from http://ssrn.com/author=28964.

5

Gram–Charlier Expansions and Portfolio Selection in Non-Gaussian Universes

François Desmoulins-Lebeault

ABSTRACT

Almost all attempts to develop an alternate model to the mean–variance portfolio selection paradigm have failed, due to both technical and theoretical difficulties. In this chapter we try to present all those problems, which are inherent to portfolio selection when asset returns are non-normally distributed. Furthermore, we present in details the Gram–Charlier expansions and their use in a financial context. We show how these expansions are tools that could help explore more easily the complex matter of portfolio selection in a non-Gaussian universe. We show, too, how certain portfolio selection problems can be approximately solved using these expansions when returns are not Gaussian.

5.1 INTRODUCTION

The classical Capital Asset Pricing Model (CAPM) presented by Sharpe (1964) and Lintner (1965), is one of the cornerstones of modern finance and has been thoroughly used and tested. However, during the last few years, it has been somewhat contested. Empirical tests show that, indeed, the betas do not explain entirely the variation of returns over the risky assets' range. A large number of empirical studies show that variables such as the capitalisation, book-to-market ratio, PER, etc. help explain a larger part of return variations (see, for example, works by Fama and French, 1992, 1995, 1996; Chan *et al.*, 1991 and some others).

Different reasons possibly explain the relative empirical failing of the CAPM. A few of them are econometric problems. Indeed, Roll (1977, 1978) and Ross (1977) show that the traditional CAPM is rejected when the portfolio used as the proxy for the market portfolio (which is unobservable) is not mean–variance efficient (i.e. when one can define a portfolio offering the same expected return and smaller variance). Deviation, even of small magnitude, from mean–variance efficiency can make the relationship between betas and returns non-significant.

Moreover, many authors show that incorrectly specified tests and variables make empirical testing of the CAPM difficult. They show that the results are seldom significant (see Amihud *et al.*, 1992 among others).

Multi-moment Asset Allocation and Pricing Models   Edited by E. Jurczenko and B. Maillet
© 2006 John Wiley & Sons, Ltd

However, it seems that the variables employed in multifactorial extensions of the CAPM are only alternate ways to evaluate risk. Firm specific factors are added to variance and covariance in order to explain returns. This shows that the variance–covariance paradigm is not empirically justified. We can note that most of these models stem from the Arbitrage Pricing Theory (Ross, 1976), yet they use the additional variables as measures of risk and not as risk sources. In fact, the central relation of finance could be written as follows: *expected return = risk-free rate + market price of risk × amount of risk*.

The fact that we need to add variables to the traditional CAPM beta indicates that it only measures risk imperfectly. One of the main weaknesses of the CAPM is that its hypotheses are extremely strong. Indeed, we need strong restrictions on either the distribution of returns or the agent's utility functions for the variance–covariance paradigm to be justified. More precisely, the agent's preferences must be established only on the first two moments of the returns' distribution. This can only be the case if returns are distributed according to a law entirely described by its first two moments (such as the normal and lognormal laws) or if the utility function derivatives of order greater than two are all uniformly zero.

We should notice that it is feasible to extend the mean–variance approach to elliptical distributions, yet that is still quite restrictive. The empirical distributions of asset returns are shown to depart significantly from normality. Since the marginal distributions are non-normal, the joint distribution cannot be multivariate Gaussian. Furthermore, even if stock and bond returns were normally distributed, the use of derivative securities and dynamic portfolio strategies implies that the returns on all portfolios cannot be Gaussian. Moreover, there is no economic model allowing us to actually determine the law of risky asset returns, while, despite being difficult, it is nonetheless possible to estimate the moments of their distribution.

It would thus be interesting to extend a CAPM-type analysis to moments of order higher than two. A few attempts in that direction can be found in the literature.

5.2   ATTEMPTS TO EXTEND THE CAPM

In this section we will quickly examine how portfolio theory has been adapted, in the literature, to assets with non-Gaussian returns. Here, it is necessary to mention that, for a very long time, an important number of authors have tried to relax the normality hypothesis from the various financial models where it was present.

In the particular case of the CAPM and portfolio theory, we have mentioned that the normality hypothesis can be expressed either directly, over the distribution of returns or prices, or indirectly through the specification of the agents' utility functions. Hence the existence of two possible ways to extend the CAPM: working on the return distributions, specifically through the use of the moments, or working with agents' preferences. The latter way, which may seem simpler, is the one followed by older articles.

5.2.1   Extensions based on preferences

The more straightforward approach is to make a Taylor expansion on the expected utility up to order three. This, in fact, was the basis of the first attempt to extend the CAPM to higher moments. Moreover, it does not really imply distributional hypotheses for returns and prices. Kraus and Litzenberger (1976) used this approach to establish their model, which takes into account the first three moments of the distribution of returns (expectation, variance and skewness).

These two authors remark that to express preferences on the first three moments of a portfolio's returns, one needs a utility function of the cubic class. Yet, a third-degree polynomial does not have the characteristics expected from a risk-averse agent, such as defined by Arrow (1963, 1971). However, there are utility functions exhibiting these characteristics: power utility functions, logarithmic functions and negative exponential utilities. These utility functions can be expanded easily in Taylor series. If we set the utility function of an investor to $U(.)$, the expected end of period wealth becomes:

$$E\left[U\left(\tilde{W}\right)\right] = U\left(\overline{W}\right) + \frac{U''\left(\overline{W}\right)}{2!}\sigma_W^2 + \frac{U'''\left(\overline{W}\right)}{3!}\xi_W^3 + \cdots$$

In this equation, ξ_W^3 is not really the skewness but the third-order central moment: $E[\tilde{W} - \overline{W}]^3$. This Taylor expansion only converges, in the case of logarithmic and power utility functions, if we have:

$$|\tilde{W} - \overline{W}| \leq \overline{W} \quad P.a.s.$$

The authors then find the equilibrium conditions for individual portfolios. To get from this to a market equilibrium, following a Cass and Stiglitz (1970) type analysis, the condition is for all the agents to have a linear risk tolerance of the type: $-U_k'/U_k'' = a_k + bW_k$ with a "prudence" coefficient, b, identical for every agent.

Under these conditions, and if the market portfolio returns are not symmetric, Kraus and Litzenberger (1976) obtain a market equilibrium condition, quite similar to the CAPM condition. Notice, however, that this condition depends on the form of the utility function assigned to the agents.

For rather a long period, this model has been the only one to deal with portfolio theory in a non-Gaussian universe. Yet, other authors have empirically tested it – primarily Friend and Westerfield (1980), who found that the results did not drastically improve those of the classical CAPM.

The empirical failings of this model probably stem from the fact that to obtain a testable version, one needs to specify a utility function type that is selected from a rather restrictive set. Moreover, the article ignores moments of order higher than three, which may be explained by the fact that at that time, the precise significance of kurtosis was still to be discovered.

Following Kraus and Litzenberger's analysis, Harvey and Siddique (2000) presented a CAPM-type model taking skewness into account. However, while the original model considered the expected return, variances, covariances, skewness and coskewness, and their relationships, to be stable over time, the authors insisted on the fact that skewness is conditional to the available information. Therefore, it is a dated model, the skewness and variance being those of a forthcoming period, thus corresponding to the implicit hypothesis that these parameters are not necessarily intertemporal constants. There is another slight difference, since this model is not based on the expected utility of the end of period wealth but on the intertemporal marginal rate of substitution.

Indeed, in a representative agent economy, the equilibrium condition for an agent to hold a portfolio i of risky assets is that:

$$E[(1 + R_{i,t+1})m_{t+1}|\phi_t] = 1 \tag{5.1}$$

where m_{t+1} is the intertemporal marginal rate of substitution, $R_{i,t+1}$ is the return on portfolio i for the period $[t, t+1]$ and ϕ_t represents the information available on the market at time t.

Using quadratic or logarithmic utility functions in the classical CAPM, or equivalently Gaussian or elliptical distributions, corresponds to the implicit hypothesis that the intertemporal marginal rate of substitution is a linear function of the market rate of return. Therefore, it can be expressed as: $m_{t+1} = a_t + b_t R_{M,t+1}$. By developing the equilibrium condition mentioned above and through aggregation, the classical CAPM equation is then obtained.

Nonetheless, Harvey and Siddique (2000) think that considering the marginal rate of substitution as linear with respect to its observable proxy (the market portfolio rate of return) is not very convincing. Hence their choice to work on nonlinear forms. They proposed to use the simplest of them: a quadratic function. It presents the advantage of being consistent with non-growing absolute risk aversion, one of the fundamental properties defined by Arrow. Supposing that the marginal rate of substitution can be written as follows: $m_{t+1} = a_t + b_t R_{M,t+1} + c_t R^2_{M,t+1}$, the authors explain that, if there exists a conditionally risk-free asset, they obtain the following relationship:

$$E_t(R_{i,t+1}) = \lambda_{1,t} \text{cov}_t(R_{i,t+1}, R_{M,t+1}) + \lambda_{2,t} \text{cov}_t(R_{i,t+1}, R^2_{M,t+1}) \tag{5.2}$$

with

$$\lambda_{1,t} = \frac{\text{var}_t(R^2_{M,t+1})E_t(R_{M,t+1}) - \text{skew}_t(R_{M,t+1})E_t(R^2_{M,t+1})}{\text{var}_t(R^2_{M,t+1})\text{var}_t(R_{M,t+1}) - (\text{skew}_t(R_{M,t+1}))^2}$$

and

$$\lambda_{2,t} = \frac{\text{var}_t(R_{M,t+1})E_t(R^2_{M,t+1}) - \text{skew}_t(R_{M,t+1})E_t(R_{M,t+1})}{\text{var}_t(R^2_{M,t+1})\text{var}_t(R_{M,t+1}) - (\text{skew}_t(R_{M,t+1}))^2}$$

Eventually, the result is quite similar to the equations in Kraus and Litzenberger (1976), the precise hypothesis made on the agents' utility being replaced by the marginal rate of substitution assumption. Both articles present empirical results and, again, they are relatively similar. The results, therefore, are just a little better than those obtained with the classical CAPM. This confirms the fact that with returns being non-normally distributed, a more precise description of their distribution is required to improve our understanding of portfolio theory.

Understanding the way in which distributional properties of risky assets impact portfolio selection appears to be necessary. Therefore, we need to understand the way in which agents react to moments of order higher than two in order to advance further.

Thanks to the works of Arrow (1963, 1971), Pratt (1964), etc. we understand the way in which agents react[1] in the presence of risky assets when risk is measured through the variance. However, Scott and Horvath (1980) bring the beginning of an understanding of agents' preferences in the presence of non-normally distributed assets. Their main result is that if the agents conform to Arrow's definitions, they will exhibit positive preference for even-order moments and aversion to odd-order moments. This is valid for all defined moments of any distribution and stems from the basic characteristics of utilities defined by Arrow.

---

[1] Or, more precisely, the way they *should* react if they were rational, risk-averse, etc.

We have now gained insights on the attitude of risk-averse agents toward all the moments of the distribution of returns. This is a very significant improvement in our knowledge, yet it does not suffice. Indeed, the representative agent will try to maximise the odd moments of his or her portfolio's returns, while limiting the even moments.

The corresponding economic intuition is that the even standardised central moments (which are always positive) of a distribution, measure various forms of dispersion and therefore correspond to uncertainty – avoided by Arrow's agents. On the other hand, odd central moments correspond to various forms of localisation with respect to the mean. Therefore, the agents will try to maximise these odd moments since they prefer more to less.

Nonetheless, this is not enough to build a real portfolio theory when agents express opinions on all moments and when returns do not follow a Gaussian distribution. The problem arising is that we have no idea of the amount of odd moment λ_i required by an agent to maintain his (her) utility when the even moment λ_j is increased by one.

The rate of substitution between mean and variance is obvious in the CAPM as they are the only dimensions of the portfolio problem. However, when the returns are non-Gaussian, there are numerous rates of substitution between moments, and they are unknown and nontrivial to determine for generic utility functions.

However difficult the problem of multi-moment CAPMs appears from the utility point of view, it still attracts lots of attention. Indeed, Harvey and Siddique (1999) review and extend seven versions of asset pricing models with higher moments, including kurtosis. Moreover, using Hansen's (1982) Generalised Method of Moments, they test these models, with two different types of utility function, for various emerging markets. Their research goes even further, as they also study the possible data-generating processes coherent with their results.

Jurczenko and Maillet in Chapter 6 present a complete study of the four moment CAPM and propose a unifying framework for such pricing models. Their work clarifies and extends our knowledge of the subject and poses various signposts for future research, showing the vitality of the utility-based extensions of the CAPM.

5.2.2   Extensions based on return distributions

Another approach can be exploited in order to adapt the CAPM to a world with non-Gaussian risky assets. Indeed, some authors recently tried to extend the classical CAPM relationship by replacing the betas or the variance–covariance matrix by alternate objects taking the non-normality into account. This approach is no longer an extension of preferences but rather an attempt to incorporate more flexible distributional hypotheses into the CAPM. Yet, since both hypotheses are equivalent, these methods are closely related to the ones presented before.

Somewhere between this approach and the preferences-based approach, Leland (1998), basing his model on an article by Rubinstein (1976), finds a relationship relatively similar to the classical CAPM. The main hypothesis is distributional, stating that the returns on the market portfolio are independently and identically distributed. Even if this is a strong hypothesis rejected by many empirical tests, it is clearly better than the general normality hypothesis of the classical CAPM, since the marginal return distributions of all individual securities are not specified.

According to Rubinstein (1976), Brennan (1979) and He and Leland (1993), this distributional hypothesis entails a constraint on the form of the representative agent (and this agent will always exist, as shown by Constantinides, 1982): he will exhibit a power utility function with exponent b. Precise equilibrium conditions, on prices and expected returns, will also follow. By aggregating and transforming the equilibrium conditions, Leland obtains his modified CAPM, which takes the following form:

$$E(r_P) = r_f + B_P \left(E(r_M) - r_f \right) \tag{5.3}$$

where

$$B_P = \frac{\text{cov} \left(r_P, -(1 + r_M)^{-b} \right)}{\text{cov} \left(r_M, -(1 + r_M)^{-b} \right)}$$

and

$$b = \frac{\ln \left(E(1 + r_M) \right) - \ln(1 + r_f)}{\text{var} \left(\ln(1 + r_M) \right)}$$

This model can therefore be considered an extension of the classical theory based on both distributions and preferences. However, we must remark that it does use exactly the same parameters as the classical CAPM. To really incorporate more distributional properties, a different exponent b is needed, which is not coherent with the rest of the model.

In this same direction, but focusing exclusively on the distributions, Sornette *et al.* (1999), propose a highly mathematical approach to the problem. Starting with a hypothesis formulated for the joint distribution of risky asset returns, yet only in the case of symmetric distributions (all odd moments are equal to zero), the authors show how to modify the variance–covariance matrix so as to take into account the fat-tailedness of the returns' distribution.

The key idea is to operate a nonlinear change of variables to transform the returns δx on an asset over period t into a variable $y(\delta x)$ such that y is normally distributed. For unimodal marginal distributions that transformation is always feasible. The change of variable contracts the distribution on its extreme values. To model returns, the authors propose to use a modified Weibull distribution, which fits quite closely empirical data:

$$p(\delta x)d\delta x = d\delta x \frac{1}{2\sqrt{\pi}} \frac{c}{\chi^{c/2}} |\delta x|^{c/2-1} \exp \left(\frac{(\text{sign}(\delta x)|\delta x|^{c/2} - m)^2}{\chi^c} \right) \tag{5.4}$$

If we suppose that the marginal distributions are modified Weibull, the change of variables is as follows: $y = \text{sign}(\delta x)\sqrt{|2(|\delta x|/\chi)^c|}$. If the marginal distributions are different, another, more complex, change of variables is still possible. Then the variance–covariance matrix of the (now Gaussian) y is built. The first really simplifying hypothesis is made at this point. Indeed, the fact that the marginal distributions are normal does not necessarily imply that the joint distribution is a multivariate Gaussian, yet this hypothesis is the one involving the least information.

Therefore, the authors suppose the joint distribution of y to have this form:

$$\hat{P}(\mathbf{y}) = (2\pi)^{-N/2} \det (\mathbf{V})^{-1/2} \exp \left(-\frac{1}{2} \mathbf{y}' \mathbf{V}^{-1} \mathbf{y} \right) \tag{5.5}$$

where N is the number of risky assets and $\mathbf{V}$ is the variance–covariance matrix built for the y.

Starting with this joint distribution, the authors get the real returns' distribution by using the Jacobian of the transform of **x** into **y**. This distribution has the following form:

$$\hat{P}(\mathbf{x}) = \det(\mathbf{V})^{-1/2} \exp\left(-\frac{1}{2}\mathbf{y}'(\mathbf{V}^{-1} - \mathbf{I})\mathbf{y}\right) \prod_{i=1}^{N} P_i(\delta x_i) \tag{5.6}$$

where **V** is, again, the variance–covariance matrix of **y**, and **I** the identity matrix.

Sornette *et al.* (1999) then obtain, using extremely heavy mathematical methods, the expressions of the cumulants of the distribution of a portfolio value variations. Indeed, if the cumulants exist, a distribution can be totally characterised through them:

$$\hat{P}_s(k) = \exp\left(\sum_{m=1}^{+\infty} \frac{c_m}{m!}(ik)^m\right) \tag{5.7}$$

c_m being the mth order cumulant and $i^2 = -1$.

Using their results, the authors show that, in most cases, minimising variance increases kurtosis and that, to use their expression, minimising the smaller risks generally increases the bigger risks: when we reduce the occurrence probability of small losses, it tends to increase the occurrence probability of massive losses.

Another insight provided by this article is that, in the case of risky assets with leptokurtic returns, a precise understanding of the tails' fatness[2] is more important than correlation in determining the distributional properties of portfolios. Thus, it seems that measuring covariances correctly is important, yet the key to a precise understanding of portfolio theory lies in the form of marginal return distributions.

5.3 AN EXAMPLE OF PORTFOLIO OPTIMISATION

We know that before such a description of the portfolio returns' distribution, it is impossible to implement the desired optimisation programme: "Minimise variance, maximise skewness, minimise kurtosis, with the constraint of an expected return of r and with the weights summing to one (all available wealth invested)".

Furthermore, we intuitively know that, for a given expected return, the portfolio minimising the variance is not the portfolio maximising the skewness nor the portfolio minimising the kurtosis, which is confirmed by Sornette *et al.* (1999). Moreover, another question concerns the quantity that should be optimised.

Indeed, minimising the fourth central moment is not equivalent to minimising the kurtosis. In the kurtosis there are interactions with the variance that do not appear in the fourth central moment. It may seem more interesting to work on the kurtosis, since it is "normalised" and thus can be compared between any distribution, yet the fact that the square of variance appears in its denominator implies that, to minimise the kurtosis, one should maximise the variance (the variance and the fourth central moment are always positive).

---

[2] Measured by excess kurtosis, i.e. the difference between the actual kurtosis and 3, the kurtosis of a Gaussian.

Table 5.1   Moments of studied stocks

	Barrick Gold	Bouygues	Canal Plus	Michelin
Mean	−0.00012481	0.00213426	0.00114945	−0.0012201
Variance	0.00101047	0.00075709	0.00059704	0.00072338
μ_3	$1.6277E-05$	$2.3224E-06$	$6.6674E-06$	$7.602E-07$
Skewness	0.50674006	0.11148514	0.4570431	0.03907282
μ_4	$3.8889E-06$	$2.2451E-06$	$2.1695E-06$	$1.5881E-06$
Kurtosis	3.80871934	3.91692329	6.08636384	3.03492233

5.3.1   Portfolio description

In order to understand better the interactions existing between the first four moments of the portfolio returns' distribution and their optimisation, we will examine an example. The portfolio we have selected is quite simple and composed of randomly picked stocks. This portfolio is composed of four stocks from the Paris Bourse: Barrick Gold, Bouygues, Canal Plus and Michelin. We will base our study on the opening prices during 1998, from January 2nd to December 30th. The moments of the empirical distributions are shown in Table 5.1.

These results call for a first comment: there are notable asymmetries in the returns' distribution of all stocks, as measured by skewness. Moreover, the distributions are all more or less leptokurtic. In all cases, it seems difficult to adopt a classical mean–variance approach when the moments of the distributions are departing so much from what they would be if the return distributions were Gaussian.

Therefore, we may logically conclude that we should not use the classical CAPM for the portfolio selection problem when the distributions of returns exhibit moments of order higher than two. Hence, we simulated different portfolios and used numerical methods to realise different optimisations. The results we obtained confirm the remarks of Sornette *et al.* (1999) on the non-existence of a weighting system optimal with regard to all selection parameters.

5.3.2   The various "optimal" portfolios

Before presenting the results, we need to make a remark about the minimisation method we chose. We used a recursive algorithm for three different reasons: first because it is difficult to solve formally for a constrained optimal with standardised central moments of order three and four (the optimisation programmes cannot be expressed in standard matrix form). The second reason is that the number of operations needed for formal resolution is more important than that needed for algorithmic solving, thus implying more rounding errors. We have verified this empirically with the variance minimisation: the algorithmic method leads to a variance slightly inferior to the variance obtained when using the solution weights of the formal programme. The third reason is that, in operational reality, fund managers often find singular "variance–covariance" matrices[3] and thus need to use (complex) pseudo-inversion algorithms.

Let us now look, in Table 5.2, at the structure and characteristics of the equally weighted portfolio, which will be used as a reference, especially for the daily expected returns used in other simulations.

---

[3] This phenomenon can be caused by nonsynchronous estimation of the various parameters. However, most of the time, the matrix obtained is still invertible yet "quasi-singular", as some software terms it, and therefore requires the use of pseudo-inversion, even if theoretically invertible.

Table 5.2   Characteristics of the equally weighted portfolio

	Barrick G.	Bouygues	Canal Plus	Michelin	Portfolio
Mean	−0.0001248	0.00213426	0.00114945	−0.0012201	0.00048469
Variance	0.00101047	0.00075709	0.00059704	0.00072338	0.00027614
μ_3	1.6277E − 05	2.3224E − 06	6.6674E − 06	7.602E − 07	2.798E − 07
Skewness	0.50674006	0.11148514	0.4570431	0.03907282	0.06097394
μ_4	3.8889E − 06	2.2451E − 06	2.1695E − 06	1.5881E − 06	2.6436E − 07
Kurtosis	3.80871934	3.91692329	6.08636384	3.03492233	3.46672267
Weights	0.25	0.25	0.25	0.25	1

Table 5.3   Minimum variance portfolio

	Barrick G.	Bouygues	Canal plus	Michelin	Portfolio
Mean	−0.0001248	0.00213426	0.00114945	−0.0012201	0.00048469
Variance	0.00101047	0.00075709	0.00059704	0.00072338	0.00027421
μ_3	1.6277E − 05	2.3224E − 06	6.6674E − 06	7.602E − 07	2.8144E − 07
Skewness	0.50674006	0.11148514	0.4570431	0.03907282	0.0619805
μ_4	3.8889E − 06	2.2451E − 06	2.1695E − 06	1.5881E − 06	2.6855E − 07
Kurtosis	3.80871934	3.91692329	6.08636384	3.03492233	3.57149574
Weights	0.23883425	0.21880374	0.2993229	0.24303911	1

In these results, we can see already the effects of diversification, which is caused by the co-moments. Note, however, that if the effects of diversification are really positive in the case of variance, which diminishes considerably, and positive in the case of kurtosis, which slightly diminishes (the returns' distribution remains, nonetheless, leptokurtic), they are negative for skewness. Indeed, skewness also diminishes, whereas a risk-averse investor has positive preference for this moment.

5.3.2.1   Variance-optimal portfolio

The portfolio offering the minimum variance, under the constraints of weights summing to 1 and expected return of 0.00048469, is not very different from the equally weighted portfolio. The characteristics of the minimum portfolio are presented in Table 5.3.

Indeed, the variance of this portfolio's returns is slightly inferior to the variance of the equally weighted portfolio. However, the skewness and the kurtosis have increased, as well as the corresponding central moments. We can therefore notice the incompatibility existing between the optimisation of the portfolio returns' variance and higher-order moments, especially kurtosis. It is clear enough that if we diminish the variance, and hence its square, we increase the kurtosis if the fourth central moment does not change; yet diminishing the variance also has an impact on the fourth central moment.

5.3.2.2   Third-moment optimal portfolios

Optimising the skewness and the third central moment is more complex. Indeed, even if there exists a skewness-optimal portfolio (which corresponds to the asset repartition that leads to a maximum skewness, constrained by a mean equal to 0.00048469), it is not possible to

Table 5.4   Maximum skewness portfolio and high μ_3 portfolio

	P_1	P_2
Mean	0.00048469	0.00048469
Variance	0.00356597	6.1908E+12
μ_3	0.00012571	6.3979E+18
Skewness	0.59032752	0.41535074
μ_4	4.7794E−05	1.3928E+26
Kurtosis	3.75851383	3.63412896
Weight Barrick G.	1.79370519	53687091.4
Weight Bouygues	−0.14126442	−42740657.6
Weight Canal plus	0.09031001	35687426.8
Weight Michelin	−0.74275078	−46633859.5

find a portfolio maximising the third central moment. It is indeed possible to let it augment towards infinity, at the cost of a similarly growing variance. We can see, in Table 5.4, the characteristics of the maximum skewness portfolio (portfolio 1) and of a portfolio exhibiting a very high third central moment.

We can immediately remark that optimising the skewness, which is increased by almost a factor of ten, from 0.06 to 0.59, was realised at the expense of all the other unconstrained moments of the distribution. Indeed, the variance also increased by a factor of ten, while the fourth central moment doubled, leading to a kurtosis increasing only slightly. However, we see clearly, thanks to this example and the example given by the extreme values of portfolio P_2 (high central third moment), that optimising the skewness, even if it takes small values, is costly in terms of the other moments studied here.

In addition, we can notice that the weights of the different assets obtained in optimising the skewness are quite extreme and do not respect Lintner's constraint on short-sales, since we have:

$$\sum_{i=1}^{N} |w_i| > 1$$

However, we can obtain a different portfolio of optimal skewness if we include Lintner's constraint to the optimisation programme. The results are less extreme than what we first obtained, yet they still go in the same direction. The maximum skewness is then 0.4719611 with a variance of 0.0006133 and a kurtosis of 3.78059.

5.3.2.3   Fourth-moment optimal portfolios

The fourth-order moments also present some difficulties. Indeed, there is an optimal vector of asset weights in both cases, yet the problem comes from the fact that we have to determine on which of these fourth-order moments investors will express preferences, or, more precisely, aversion. The optimal portfolios with respect to these two moments are not necessarily the same, as we can see from our simulation portfolio in Table 5.5.

We can notice from these results that the portfolio exhibiting the smallest fourth central moment, under complete investment and 0.00048469 mean constraints, is quite similar to the portfolio which, under the same constraints, offers the least variance. It does present slightly less kurtosis and a little more variance, yet the characteristics of both portfolios are similar – a result which is true even with different expected returns.

Table 5.5 Portfolios with minimum kurtosis and minimum μ_4

	P_1	P_2
Mean	0.00048469	0.00048469
Variance	0.00033629	0.0002765
μ_3	6.4614E − 08	2.3888E − 07
Skewness	0.01047765	0.05195433
μ_4	3.6255E − 07	2.6312E − 07
Kurtosis	3.20587965	3.44154742
Weights Barrick G.	0.1297922	0.22890619
Weights Bouygues	0.39529359	0.25557122
Weights Canal plus	0.09988679	0.25186382
Weights Michelin	0.37502741	0.26365877

The portfolio exhibiting the minimum kurtosis, on the other hand, is quite different and further away from the optimal portfolio concerning variance and skewness. We need to be clear that for all moments, the diversification due to the co-moments[4] is really quite an important factor in the determination of the optimal portfolios. Indeed, considering only the kurtosis of the marginal distributions of the asset returns, it could seem logical to place an important weight on the Michelin stock, whose kurtosis is the smallest. In fact, this stock represents a good proportion of the kurtosis-optimal portfolio, yet the Bouygues stock, whose kurtosis is one of the highest, can be found in quite a similar proportion. This stresses the importance of the question about the relative significance of the central moments and the standardised central moments.

We can therefore see how taking into account the moments of order higher than two implies a much more complex portfolio selection problem. Moreover, two portfolios, optimal with respect to different moments, can present, for an investor, the same level of expected utility.

Indeed, in terms of utility, we cannot be certain that a portfolio, optimal with regard to a certain moment of the returns' distribution, will be considered optimal by a given investor. We therefore need to design another approach in order to extend the classical portfolio theory to the case where returns are not distributed normally and investors express their utilities up to the mth moment (m times differentiable functions) or to infinity (infinitely differentiable functions).

5.4 EXTENSION TO ANY FORM OF DISTRIBUTION

As we saw in the literature on CAPM generalised to moments of order higher than two, many problems arise that make it difficult to define a convincing portfolio theory when returns are not normally distributed. Working on preferences might seem interesting, yet too many parameters are undefined and it leads to restrictive models (only fitting one type of utility). More recent studies based on distributions appear promising, but the approaches used up to now present serious flaws.

5.4.1 Obstacles to distribution-based works

All the research based on the distributional properties of returns that we have mentioned is quite promising, yet it presents some disadvantages. Mostly, it is restrictive on the forms of

---

[4] The co-moments and some additional statistics are presented in Appendix A.

the marginal distributions of returns. Indeed, Leland's (1998) hypothesis of identically and independently distributed returns on the market portfolio, entailing a normally distributed market portfolio, is very strong, even if it apparently does not concern marginal distributions of individual stocks.

Similarly, Sornette *et al.* (1999) restrict their work to symmetrical distributions, which may be more than a detail for the most common type of risky assets – stocks. Moreover, the fact that distributions are, thanks to the approximation on transformed returns, elliptical and therefore obey the coherence constraint obtained by Kano (1994), implies that the marginal distributions will be of the same form, even if they can have different parameters. Using heterogenous parameters would add so much mathematical complexity that the authors avoided this case.

However, a very promising work based on the distributional properties of the returns can be found in Athayde and Flôres (2004). Using duality results and a tensor notation, they establish the geometrical properties of the efficient set for investors who have the common preference directions for moments. Their results, even if still limited to the first three moments, provide interesting guidelines for optimising portfolios when higher moments count. Moreover, the notation and methodology employed may well open up new paths of research, even if they cannot be extended yet to any number of moments.

Therefore, we face a real problem in extending the portfolio theory to the case of non-Gaussian returns. It seems clear that working on preferences is useful, but only replaces a strong hypothesis by others.[5] As regards the distribution-based extensions, mathematical complexity eventually entails other strong, unrealistic, hypotheses.

Only empirical data make it possible to work on the marginal distributions of returns. Apparently, there is no economic law forcing them to have a determined form. Moreover, finding out the actual distributions is made difficult by the fact that at least some of the parameters change over time,[6] implying measurement errors and approximations. Therefore, our work should be based on approximate distributions stemming from empirical measures, which are the only premises allowing effective applications of the theory.

5.4.2   Generalised Gram–Charlier expansions

Among the statistical techniques used to approximate densities, the Gram–Charlier expansion is one of the most interesting. This method, which can be generalised to any kind of densities, is based on a given approaching density, and modifies it so that its cumulants correspond to those of the density approximated. We have already seen how, under weak regularity conditions, a distribution can be entirely defined by its cumulants.

Johnson *et al.* (1994) show that Gram–Charlier expansions are among the most efficient approximation methods for an unspecified density. Apparently this cannot be proven, but it can be verified using numerical methods. However, other statistical expansions, like Edgeworth expansions or Hermite polynomials, have been used in a financial context, with a principal focus on the option-pricing theory. These option-pricing methods, and the expansions they are based on, are presented and commented upon by Jurczenko *et al.* (2003), and could permit the proposal of variants to the present research.

---

[5] All agents exhibit the same specific type of utility function, which is not really better than the original CAPM.
[6] It is also possible, and more difficult to model, that the very form of distribution may vary over time, for example in stochastic switching regimes.

In the case of the portfolio selection problem, Gram–Charlier expansions present a very clear advantage over other density approximation methods. These other methods, like using the Pearson family of distributions, the skewed-student t distribution or the entropy density, entail a structurally defined shape for the distribution. For an application, extended to the multivariate case, of one of the most popular of these, the skewed-t, we can refer to Bauwens and Laurent (2002). Using this method, one will find the density closest to the empirical data among a given space of predetermined shapes. This density can indeed, in most cases, be very close to the empirical density. Nevertheless, it is not certain that any of these methods generate a set of densities that is dense in the space of all possible continuous and smooth densities. However, using Weierstrass's approximation theorem, it is clear that, given their polynomial nature, the Gram–Charlier densities of finite order form a countable dense subset of such densities. The main problem with Gram–Charlier approximated densities resides in the fact that the approximation, for a given order and a given approximating density, is really a density only in the neighbourhood of the approximating pdf. This should, however, not be considered profoundly hindering, since we can always select an adapted approximating density, maybe a Pearson density, entropy density or skewed student-t density, thus retaining their advantages and yet increasing their precision.

Moreover, a clear advantage of the use of Gram–Charlier approximation comes from the fact that once the approximating density and the moments of the sample to approximate are known, there is no need to do any extra computation, while other tools require numerical procedures to determine the optimal approximating parameters. In this context, if one, for example, studies a return series which is not too far from normality, for any subperiod, the same expansion can be used, requiring only the adjustment of the sample moments. On the other hand, using other approximation methods requires one to rerun a numerical optimisation for every slightly different subsample.

5.4.2.1   The building of Gram–Charlier expansion series

We will now look at how to obtain this Gram–Charlier expansion, generalised to any kind of approximating distribution. Let $F(s)$ be any probability distribution, called the *true distribution*, and let $A(s)$ be another distribution, called the *approximating distribution*. In the beginning, Gram–Charlier series could only use the standardised normal as approximating distribution (see, for example, Cramer, 1946; Kendall and Stuart, 1977). Jarrow and Rudd (1982) give a generalised version of these expansion series. Capitals will denote cumulative distribution functions, while lower case letters will denote probability density functions. Using the following notation:

$$\alpha_j(F) = \int_{-\infty}^{\infty} s^j f(s)\, ds$$

$$\mu_j(F) = \int_{-\infty}^{\infty} (s - \alpha_1(F))^j f(s)\, ds$$

$$\phi(F, t) = \int_{-\infty}^{\infty} e^{its} f(s)\, ds$$

where $i^2 = -1$, $\alpha_j(F)$ is the jth moment of distribution F, $\mu_j(F)$ is the jth central moment of F and $\phi(F, t)$ is the characteristic function of F.

Let us suppose that $\alpha_j(F)$ exists for all $j \leq n$. As $\alpha_n(F)$ exists, then the first $n-1$ cumulants, $c_j(F)$, exist for $j = 1, \ldots, n-1$ and are defined as:

$$\log \phi(F, t) = \sum_{j=1}^{n-1} c_j(F) \frac{(it)^j}{j!} + o(t^{n-1}) \tag{5.8}$$

The relationship between the moments and the cumulants of a distribution is obtained by developing $\phi(F, t)$ in terms of moments, replacing it in Equation (5.8) and equating the polynomial coefficients. The first four coefficients are therefore:

$$c_1(F) = \alpha_1(F)$$
$$c_2(F) = \mu_2(F)$$
$$c_3(F) = \mu_3(F)$$
$$c_4(F) = \mu_4(F) - 3\mu_2(F)^2$$

Then, the first cumulant is the mean, the second is the variance, the third is a measure of the skewness and the fourth a measure of the excess kurtosis (over the kurtosis of a Gaussian distribution).

Supposing that $\alpha_j(A)$ and $\partial^j A(s)/\partial s^j$ exist for $j \leq m$, m being possibly different from n, and setting $N = \min(n, m)$, then the basic Gram–Charlier expansion is:

$$\log \phi(F, t) = \sum_{j=1}^{N-1} \left(c_j(F) - c_j(A)\right) \frac{(it)^j}{j!} + \sum_{j=1}^{N-1} c_j(A) \frac{(it)^j}{j!} + o(t^{N-1}) \tag{5.9}$$

Moreover, we know that:

$$\sum_{j=1}^{N-1} c_j(A) \frac{(it)^j}{j!} = \log \phi(A, t) + o(t^{N-1})$$

If we substitute the corresponding terms, we find:

$$\log \phi(F, t) = \sum_{j=1}^{N-1} \left(c_j(F) - c_j(A)\right) \frac{(it)^j}{j!} + \log \phi(A, t) + o(t^{N-1}) \tag{5.10}$$

Taking the exponential (a bijective function) of this equation, and remembering that $\exp(o(t^{N-1})) = 1 + o(t^{N-1})$, we get:

$$\phi(F, t) = \exp\left(\sum_{j=1}^{N-1} \left(c_j(F) - c_j(A)\right) \frac{(it)^j}{j!}\right) \phi(A, t) + o(t^{N-1}) \tag{5.11}$$

Since the exponential is an analytical function, it can be developed into an infinite-order polynomial. Therefore, there exist some E_j for $j = 0, \ldots, N-1$ such that we have:

$$\exp\left(\sum_{j=1}^{N-1} \left(c_j(F) - c_j(A)\right) \frac{(it)^j}{j!}\right) = \sum_{j=0}^{N-1} E_j \frac{(it)^j}{j!} + o(t^{N-1}) \tag{5.12}$$

substituting this into Equation (5.11), we obtain:

$$\phi(F, t) = \sum_{j=0}^{N-1} E_j \frac{(it)^j}{j!} \phi(A, t) + o(t^{N-1}) \tag{5.13}$$

Then we take the inverse Fourier transform of (5.13) and use the fact that:

$$f(s) = \frac{1}{2\pi} \int_{-\infty}^{\infty} e^{-its} \phi(F, t)\, ds$$

$$a(s) = \frac{1}{2\pi} \int_{-\infty}^{\infty} e^{-its} \phi(A, t)\, ds$$

$$(-1)^j \frac{\partial^j a(s)}{\partial s^j} = \frac{1}{2\pi} \int_{-\infty}^{\infty} e^{-its} (it)^j \phi(A, t)\, ds$$

thus obtaining:

$$f(s) = a(s) + \sum_{j=0}^{N-1} E_j \frac{(-1)^j}{j!} \frac{\partial^j a(s)}{\partial s^j} + \varepsilon(s, N) \tag{5.14}$$

where

$$\varepsilon(s, N) = \int_{-\infty}^{\infty} \frac{1}{2\pi} e^{-its} o(t^{N-1})\, ds.$$

The error term exists but there are no bounds to it in the form of functions of N. All known results on this error term for different $a(s)$ and $f(s)$ come from numerical analysis. The first four polynomial coefficients being defined as:

$$E_0 = 1$$
$$E_1 = (c_1(F) - c_1(A))$$
$$E_2 = (c_2(F) - c_2(A)) + E_1^2$$
$$E_3 = (c_3(F) - c_3(A)) + 3E_1(c_2(F) - c_2(A)) + E_1^3$$
$$E_4 = (c_4(F) - c_4(A)) + 4E_1(c_3(F) - c_3(A)) + 3(c_2(F) - c_2(A))^2$$
$$+ 6E_1^2(c_2(F) - c_2(A)) + E_1^4$$

we obtain, after having rearranged the terms of (5.14), and with n and $m \geq 5$:

$$f(s) = a(s) + \frac{(c_2(F) - c_2(A))}{2!} \frac{\partial^2 a(s)}{\partial s^2} - \frac{(c_3(F) - c_3(A))}{3!} \frac{\partial^3 a(s)}{\partial s^3} \tag{5.15}$$

$$+ \frac{(c_4(F) - c_4(A)) + 3(c_2(F) - c_2(A))^2}{4!} \frac{\partial^4 a(s)}{\partial s^4} + \varepsilon(s)$$

and $c_1(F) \equiv c_1(A)$ by construction.

5.4.2.2   Gram–Charlier expansions and the distribution of a portfolio's returns

Previous works about Gram–Charlier expansions arrive at this general form and do not further it. However, we need a more specific result in order to use it in a portfolio selection context. In the special case of portfolio management, the time horizon is generally quite long. A large number of empirical studies show that, over a period longer than three months, return distributions tend towards normality. Hence, we justify the use of an approximating distribution, $a(s)$, that is normal. We may therefore write:

$$a(s) = \frac{1}{\sigma\sqrt{2\pi}} e^{-\frac{1}{2}\left(\frac{s-m}{\sigma}\right)^2} \tag{5.16}$$

$$\frac{\partial^2 a(s)}{\partial s^2} = \frac{1}{\sigma\sqrt{2\pi}} e^{-\frac{1}{2}\left(\frac{s-m}{\sigma}\right)^2} \left(\left(\frac{s-m}{\sigma^2}\right)^2 - \frac{1}{\sigma^2}\right)$$

$$\frac{\partial^3 a(s)}{\partial s^3} = \frac{1}{\sigma\sqrt{2\pi}} e^{-\frac{1}{2}\left(\frac{s-m}{\sigma}\right)^2} \left(-\left(\frac{s-m}{\sigma^2}\right)^3 + 3\frac{(s-m)}{\sigma^4}\right)$$

$$\frac{\partial^4 a(s)}{\partial s^4} = \frac{1}{\sigma\sqrt{2\pi}} e^{-\frac{1}{2}\left(\frac{s-m}{\sigma}\right)^2} \left(\left(\frac{s-m}{\sigma^2}\right)^4 - 6\frac{(s-m)^2}{\sigma^6} + \frac{3}{\sigma^4}\right)$$

Moreover, the first four moments of a normal distribution are well known, and remarking that $c_3 = $ skewness $\times \sigma^3$ and $c_4 = \sigma^4$(Kurtosis $- 3$), we obtain the following cumulants:

$$c_1(A) = \alpha_1(A) = m$$

$$c_2(A) = \mu_2(A) = \sigma^2$$

$$c_3(A) = \mu_3(A) = 0$$

$$c_4(A) = \mu_4(A) - 3\mu_2(A)^2 = 0$$

Using these cumulants, we get a Gram–Charlier expansion series with coefficients being the central moments and the mean of the true distribution. A fourth order expansion will thus have this form:

$$f(s) = \frac{1}{\sigma\sqrt{2\pi}} e^{-\frac{1}{2}\left(\frac{s-m}{\sigma}\right)^2} \left\{ 1 - \left(3\frac{(s-m)}{\sigma^4} - \left(\frac{s-m}{\sigma^2}\right)^3\right)\frac{\mu_3(F)}{3!} \right. \tag{5.17}$$

$$\left. + \left(\left(\frac{s-m}{\sigma^2}\right)^4 - 6\frac{(s-m)^2}{\sigma^6} + \frac{3}{\sigma^4}\right)\frac{\mu_4(F) - 3\sigma^4}{4!} \right\} + \varepsilon(s)$$

The above expression allows us to express the probability density function of risky asset returns as a function of the empirical central moments of their distribution. Notice that, by construction, we have $c_1(A) \equiv c_1(F)$ and $c_2(A) \equiv c_2(F)$.

A consequence of our choice of a Gaussian as approximating distribution is that, when empirical skewness and kurtosis are respectively zero and three, the probability density function $f(s)$ will be normal. This is a weak normality hypothesis since a distribution with such skewness and kurtosis is not necessarily a Gaussian. However, the form of return distributions over a medium range justifies the use of this hypothesis.

Moreover, if this assumption seems too inaccurate, the expansion can be constructed on other distributions fitting more precisely the properties empirically detected in the data. The choice of the Gaussian Gram–Charlier expansion in this chapter is but a representative example.

5.4.3   Convergence of the fourth-order Gram–Charlier expansion

The type A Gram–Charlier density is an approximation and thus presents a certain number of mathematical problems. Indeed, we cannot be sure that $f(s) - \varepsilon(s)$ remains a strictly positive function over $\mathbb{R}$, and the integral of this function from $-\infty$ to $+\infty$ may only be approximately equal to 1.

Indeed, for certain values of the parameters, the Gram–Charlier expansion, without error term, can become an object quite different from a probability density function. However, in financial applications, we cannot use the unbounded error term. Hence the need to accurately define the set of parameters (mean, variance, skewness and kurtosis of the true distribution) that make $f(s) - \varepsilon(s)$ a probability density function, that is, strictly positive over $\mathbb{R}$ and with total probability of 1.

First, let us examine the validity of the approximation as regards the integration between $-\infty$ and $+\infty$ of the approximated density $f(s)$ without the error term. Remembering that $a(s)$ is the probability density function of a Gaussian distribution, with mean m and standard deviation σ, we get:

$$\int_{-\infty}^{\infty} (f(s) - \varepsilon(s))\, ds = \int_{-\infty}^{\infty} a(s)\, ds - \frac{\mu_3(F)}{3!} \int_{-\infty}^{\infty} \frac{\partial^3 a(s)}{\partial s^3}\, ds \tag{5.18}$$
$$+ \frac{\mu_4(F) - 3\sigma^4}{4!} \int_{-\infty}^{\infty} \frac{\partial^4 a(s)}{\partial s^4}\, ds$$

if these integrals converge. Moreover, we have:

$$\int_{-\infty}^{\infty} a(s)\, ds = 1$$

$$\int_{-\infty}^{\infty} \frac{\partial^3 a(s)}{\partial s^3}\, ds = \int_{-\infty}^{\infty} a(s) \left(\frac{s-m}{\sigma^2} \right)^3 ds + 3\int_{-\infty}^{\infty} a(s) \frac{s-m}{\sigma^4}\, ds$$
$$= -\frac{1}{\sigma^3} \text{skewness}(A) - 3\frac{m}{\sigma^4} + 3\frac{m}{\sigma^4}$$
$$= 0$$

using the zero skewness property of a Gaussian distribution. Moreover, we have:

$$\int_{-\infty}^{\infty} \frac{\partial^4 a(s)}{\partial s^4}\, ds = \int_{-\infty}^{\infty} a(s) \left(\frac{s-m}{\sigma^2} \right)^4 ds - 6\int_{-\infty}^{\infty} a(s) \frac{(s-m)^2}{\sigma^6}\, ds + \frac{3}{\sigma^4} \int_{-\infty}^{\infty} a(s)\, ds$$
$$= \frac{1}{\sigma^4} \text{kurtosis}(A) - \frac{6}{\sigma^6} \text{var}(A) + \frac{3}{\sigma^4} 1$$
$$= \frac{3}{\sigma^4} - \frac{6\sigma^2}{\sigma^6} + \frac{3}{\sigma^4}$$
$$= 0$$

Therefore, in the case of a Gaussian approximating density $a(s)$, the Gram–Charlier expansion without its error term has at least one of the required properties of a probability density function. Indeed, for all possible values of the mean, variance, skewness and kurtosis of the true distribution, we have:

$$\int_{-\infty}^{\infty} (f(s) - \varepsilon(s))\, ds = 1 \tag{5.19}$$

This property is necessary for our Gram–Charlier expansion to be a probability density function (pdf), yet this property alone is not sufficient. As we mentioned earlier, $f(s) - \varepsilon(s)$ needs also to be strictly positive over $\mathbb{R}$. Clearly, this property cannot be obtained by construction without an error term. As an example, consider a Gram–Charlier expansion of order 4, based on a Gaussian approximating distribution. Taking as parameters of the true distribution a mean of 0.25, a standard deviation of 1, a skewness of -1 and a kurtosis of 7, the expansion is not a pdf. Integrating this function from $-\infty$ to $+\infty$ gives 1, yet the function is negative on certain intervals: from -1.482050808 to -1.052775638 and from 1.982050808 to 2.552775638.

Therefore, a Gaussian-distribution-based Gram–Charlier-expansion cannot be used without the error term for all possible forms of approximated distributions. A more precise analysis may allow us to find the conditions (on the moments of the true distribution) under which this type of Gram–Charlier expansion can be used as pdf without its error term.

When we wrote the functional form of a Gram–Charlier expansion based on a Gaussian approximating distribution, we had a Gaussian probability function times another factor. The former is strictly positive on the real range, by construction,[7] therefore we only have to ensure the positivity of the latter. We obtain the following positivity condition theorem:[8]

Theorem 1 *Let F be any empirical distribution, with mean $\mu = \alpha_1(F)$, standard deviation $\sigma = \mu_2(F)$, skewness $\xi = \mu_3(F)/\sigma^3$ and kurtosis $\kappa = \mu_4(F)/\sigma^4$. Let $G(s)$ be its Gaussian-based Gram–Charlier expansion of order four. Then, $G(s)$ is a probability density function if and only if the polynomial:*

$$P(X) = (\kappa - 3)X^4 + f_1(\kappa, \xi, \sigma, \mu)X^3 + f_2(\kappa, \xi, \sigma, \mu)X^2 \qquad (5.20)$$
$$+ f_3(\kappa, \xi, \sigma, \mu)X + f_4(\kappa, \xi, \sigma, \mu)$$

where

$$f_1(\kappa, \xi, \sigma, \mu) = 4(3\mu - \mu\kappa + \sigma\xi)$$
$$f_2(\kappa, \xi, \sigma, \mu) = 6(\mu^2\kappa - 2\mu\sigma\xi + 3\sigma^2 - \sigma^2\kappa - 3\mu^2)$$
$$f_3(\kappa, \xi, \sigma, \mu) = 4(3\mu^3 - \mu^3\kappa + 3\mu^2\sigma\xi + 3\mu\sigma^2\kappa - 12\mu\sigma^2 - 3\sigma^3\xi)$$
$$f_4(\kappa, \xi, \sigma, \mu) = -3\mu^4 + \mu^4\kappa - 4\mu^3\sigma\xi + 18\mu^2\sigma^2 - 6\mu^2\sigma^2\kappa + 12\mu\sigma^3\xi$$
$$+ 15\sigma^4 + 3\sigma^4\kappa$$

has no real roots.

Using numerical methods, it can be found that a relatively large set of skewness–kurtosis couples can be used that allow the Gram–Charlier expansion (without its error term) to be a pdf. Figure 5.1 shows, approximately, the locus of couples that leads to a pdf for a standard deviation of 0.5, representative of the results obtained for stocks over a year. Notice, however, that the result is almost identical for different standard deviations and means.

---

[7] As a probability density, this function is strictly positive for all possible values of the moments of the true distribution.
[8] A proof is provided in Appendix B.

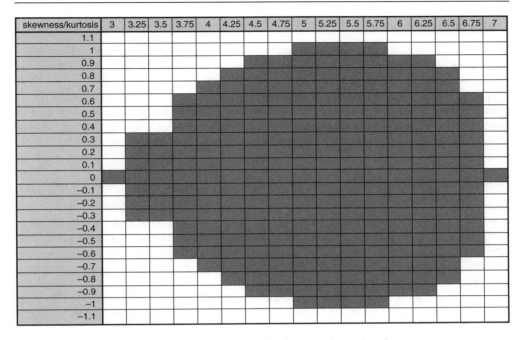

Figure 5.1   Locus of feasible skewness–kurtosis pairs.

This chart of results corresponds to the set of acceptable skewness–kurtosis couples. It is bigger than the one obtained by Rubinstein (1998) for a binomial-distribution-based Edgeworth expansion. The results cover most of the empirical skewness and kurtosis obtained for risky assets' monthly returns. Furthermore, if we accept, for approximation purposes, the use of functions that are slightly negative on short intervals, the locus of acceptable skewness and kurtosis widens quickly. Certain pdfs corresponding to acceptable values (the grey values on the chart giving a true pdf) with a high kurtosis are trimodal – a characteristic often found in stock returns.

However, there are cases when the empirical skewness and kurtosis of the returns distribution are too important for a Gaussian-based Gram–Charlier expansion. These cases are obviously more frequent when the returns are considered on a shorter period of time, and especially for intra-day returns. When the Gaussian-based expansion gives a locally negative function, the solution is the use of another type of approximating distribution, with intrinsic characteristic fitting better to the approximated distribution. In the case of a highly leptokurtic distribution, using a leptokurtic approximating distribution keeps the expansion positive, yet usually makes the functional form of the Gram–Charlier expansion more complicated. In portfolio selection problems, however, this problem arises scarcely, since the horizons are usually close to one year.

The results obtained in this section are quite similar to those of Jondeau and Rockinger (2001), who obtained the locus of skewness and kurtosis which would ensure the positivity of the Gram–Charlier expansion through a different method. However, their method may be more difficult to extend to expansions of an order higher than four. Nevertheless, it allows them also to propose an algorithm controlling the possible negative values of the expansion, thus ensuring that it is a true probability density function.

5.5   THE DISTRIBUTION OF PORTFOLIO RETURNS

We now have a reliable tool that enables us to obtain a good approximate probability density function in an analytical form. We can therefore use a density, built on the basic empirical moments of the returns' distribution, for any risky asset.

However useful that expansion may be, it is not enough to work on the extension of portfolio theory, since we only have a result for univariate distributions. Thus, we need to determine the probability density function of a portfolio composed of many assets, taking diversification on all moments into account.

5.5.1   Feasible approaches

There are two different possibilities for obtaining the density of a portfolio. The first one is to work on a multivariate Gram–Charlier expansion.[9] This approach may initially seem attractive, yet it is far from perfect. Indeed, determining its cumulants is tedious and far from obvious, while, for portfolio management, we only need the distribution of the weighted sum of marginal returns. Trying to determine precisely the approximate joint distribution would therefore be useless and multiply the error sources.

Indeed, the approximation of an unknown joint distribution by a multivariate Gaussian entails more errors than the approximation of an unknown univariate distribution by a normal. This multiplies the possible discrepancies between the true and the estimated distributions, as shown by the information theory theorems presented by Rao (1973). This is because there is a first approximation on the marginal distributions and then a second one on the joint distribution.

The second possible approach to obtaining the approximate portfolio returns' distribution is to base our study on the weighted sum of the risky asset returns. In fact, since we work only on the first four moments, we can suppose that returns are any form of absolutely continuous random variable. In such a case, it is feasible to obtain the expression of the moments of the portfolio distribution as functions of the moments and co-moments of the individual assets' distributions. The Gram–Charlier expansion used in this chapter being of order four, and defined over central moments and the mean, we only need to calculate the mean, the variance, the third central moment and the fourth central moment.

5.5.2   The moments of the portfolio returns' distribution

Let us suppose that the market is composed of N risky assets, their returns being absolutely continuous random variables. Let us suppose that these random variables are initially unknown. It is quite easy to obtain the first four moments of the marginal distribution of each asset return.

Let X_i be the absolutely continuous random variable representing the returns on asset i. Let w_i be the normalised weight of asset i in the total portfolio. Then we have, in all cases:

$$\sum_{i=1}^{N} w_i = 1, \quad \text{with } w_i \in \mathbb{R}, \forall i$$

---

[9] Multivariate Gram–Charlier expansions are theoretically feasible and provide the same good fit as the univariate version. However, the expression for the density is so cumbersome that this expansion is generally avoided.

The expectation being a linear operator, it is well known that the sum of the means will be the mean of the sum. Therefore, the following formula gives us the mean of the portfolio returns' distribution:

$$E\left(\sum_{i=1}^{N} w_i X_i\right) = \sum_{i=1}^{N} w_i E(X_i)$$

The variance of a sum of random variables is also very well known and, if the variances and covariances converge (which is not a problem in our empirical setting), we will have:

$$\text{var}\left(\sum_{i=1}^{N} w_i X_i\right) = \sum_{i=1}^{N} w_i \text{var}(X_i) + 2 \sum_{1 \leq i < j \leq N} w_i w_j \text{cov}(X_i, X_j)$$

In our model we also need the third central moment. This moment, along with the standard deviation, allows us to compute the skewness of the sum distribution. We see that:

$$E\left[\left(\sum_{i=1}^{N} w_i X_i - E\left(\sum_{i=1}^{N} w_i X_i\right)\right)^3\right] = \sum_{i=1}^{N} w_i^3 E\left[(X_i - E(X_i))^3\right] \tag{5.21}$$

$$+ 3 \sum_{i \neq j} w_i^2 w_j E\left[(X_i - E(X_i))^2 (X_j - E(X_j))\right]$$

$$+ 6 \sum_{i < j < k} w_i w_j w_k E\left[(X_i - E(X_i))(X_j - E(X_j))\right.$$

$$\times (X_k - E(X_k))]$$

To calculate the skewness, this third central moment has to be divided by the variance to the power two-thirds. In a similar way, we get the fourth central moment of the distribution[10] of the sum of individual returns as a function of the moments and co-moments of the individual assets' return distributions. Therefore:

$$E\left[\left(\sum_{i=1}^{N} w_i X_i - E\left(\sum_{i=1}^{N} w_i X_i\right)\right)^4\right] = \sum_{i=1}^{N} w_i^4 E\left[(X_i - E(X_i))^4\right] \tag{5.22}$$

$$+ 4 \sum_{i \neq j} w_i^3 w_j E\left[(X_i - E(X_i))^3 (X_j - E(X_j))\right]$$

$$+ 6 \sum_{i < j} w_i^2 w_j^2 E\left[(X_i - E(X_i))^2 (X_j - E(X_j))^2\right]$$

$$+ 12 \sum_{i \neq j \neq k} w_i^2 w_j w_k E\left[(X_i - E(X_i))^2 (X_j - E(X_j))\right.$$

$$\times (X_k - E(X_k))]$$

$$+ 24 \sum_{i < j < k < l} w_i w_j w_k w_l E\left[\prod_{a=i,\dots,l} (X_a - E(X_a))\right]$$

---

[10] The kurtosis is equal to the fourth central moment divided by the squared variance.

This allows us to obtain, when there is dependence between the returns of the assets composing the portfolio, a description of the first four moments that is more complex than the classical mean–variance paradigm. Moreover, there are far more inputs and they are more difficult to handle since it is not possible to use the matrix representation.

We have now built an approximate probability density function of the portfolio returns. The parameters of this function are the first four moments of the assets' marginal distributions of returns and the corresponding co-moments and the weights. Therefore, we have the necessary elements of the optimal portfolio selection problem. This problem consists in finding the optimal wealth repartition between all risky and risk-free assets in the portfolio, in the sense that it maximises the expected utility.

5.5.3 Possible portfolio selection methods

The risky assets' return distributions can be characterised by their moments, and the investors may express their preferences on these moments. Nevertheless, there are interactions between the moments defining a portfolio distribution. The weight attached to each asset can therefore no longer define a unique optimal vector for a given expected return. The set of efficient portfolios is no longer the same for all investors, even if they have utility functions of the same class.

Indeed, in the case of an n moments portfolio selection problem, the portfolios are points in an n-dimensional space. If we consider the subspace of all feasible portfolios, its convex hull surface (in a wider sense than the usual if short-sales are allowed) is the locus of all "efficient" portfolios (the Markowitz frontier in an n-dimensional space). This is because of the complete investment constraint.

This locus of efficient portfolios is a subspace with $n-1$ dimensions. Introducing a riskless asset and looking for convex portfolios reduces, in the classical bidimensional setting, the risky possible portfolio to a subspace of dimension zero, that is, a point, the market portfolio. Hence, multiplicity of the solutions is not a problem. In our n-dimensional setting, however, the market portfolio is no longer unique. It is of dimension $n-2$, as the subset of all tangency points for lines between the riskless asset and the efficient portfolios subspace. Therefore, an infinite number of portfolios are now possible market portfolios. To restrain this to a unique market portfolio, the representative agent's marginal substitution rates between all the moments are to be known.

The problem would be solved if we could restrain ourselves to only one type or class of utility function. Indeed, if we consider that every agent has a CRRA utility function (or any other sort of restricted behaviour) we may solve the optimal portfolio, if not always in closed form. This approach would then take, at least partially, the non-normality of the returns into account. It is quite remarkable, however, that this approach, suggested by Aït-Sahalia and Brandt (2001) and Ang and Bekaert (2002), is a prolongation of the testable version of the Kraus and Litzenberger (1976) theory implemented by Friend and Westerfield (1980), and as such probably only takes into account particular forms of non-normality at particular periods.

We need to know exactly the marginal rates of substitution between all the moments taken into account, or to be able to have a relationship defined between them. This will be necessary to discover an equilibrium portfolio theory in the context of non-Gaussian returns with the least hypotheses. However, even with the marginal rates of substitution between moments, we will need to define methodologies[11] that could effectively be extended to any form of risky asset returns distribution and to any form of preferences. Indeed, some forms of preferences may not be expressible exactly in terms of moments or even partial moments.

5.5.3.1 An extension of the "classical" CAPM

When we examine the formal setting of the CAPM we notice that the optimisation programme is not defined directly for the distribution of returns, but only on its first two moments. Therefore, it may seem logical to extend this type of methodology to assets with non-Gaussian returns.

This would imply that, under the constraint of a given value of the expected returns, we should minimise a function of the moments of order higher than or equal to two on which the agents express their preferences. More specifically, we can suppose that the general form of this function would be of the type:

$$\sum_{i=3}^{m} \eta_i \frac{\mu_i(P)}{\sigma^i(P)} + \eta_2 \sigma^2(P) = \text{objective} \tag{5.23}$$

where P denotes the portfolio returns distribution, $\mu_i(P)$ denotes the central moment of order i, and the η_i are weights originating from the marginal rates of substitution between moments.[12]

This methodology can appear similar in some ways to the Gram–Charlier expansions, since it is based on the use of the moments of the returns' distribution. However, its main weakness comes from its similarity to the "classical" CAPM. Indeed, it is not possible to use all the moments to infinity,[13] and the moments not declared in the objective function are totally excluded from the portfolio selection problem.

That may be an important limit since there is no strong economic reason for the agents not to have preferences on all the existing moments, as we mentioned before. If the agents do not understand precisely the statistical meaning of higher-order moments, they probably will only express a direction of preference (i.e. we know if they have positive preference or aversion towards this moment), yet this has to be taken into account.

Another method of portfolio selection in the presence of higher order moments is presented by Chunhachinda et al. (1997), and was later complemented by Prakash et al. (2003), both with application to international markets. This method is called Polynomial Goal Programming and was originally developed by Tayi and Leonard (1988). It consists, in a first step, of finding separately the optimum portfolio for each of the moments taken into account. In a second step, a "polynomial" function of the discrepancies between these optima and the local realisation, weighted in power forms, is minimised. Both mentioned articles used mean–variance–skewness portfolios. This allowed them to normalise the variances to one and therefore only have to find optima of one type (maxima in this case). However, using this method with other moments of even order may be quite difficult, as there will be simultaneous minimisations and maximisations.

---

[11] The commonality between all the approaches is that, to be able to actually optimise portfolios, we need a scalar risk measure. This risk measure will probably be a functional of the marginal rates of substitution previously evoked.

[12] To derive a market equilibrium relation, these marginal rates of substitution have to be those of the representative agent.

[13] Moreover, the need to use co-moments, whose complexity increases quickly with the order, implies that it is difficult to work with numerous moments.

More to the point, the main limit of such an approach, which quite resembles the one we will advocate, is that the marginal rates of substitution (that determines the power-weights applied to discrepancies) are limited in their number. Indeed, in both articles, substitution is allowed between mean and skewness but not formally between mean and variance or between variance and skewness. However, this method is quite interesting as it is not computationally too intensive and may offer a tool to empirically investigate some of the marginal rates of substitution between moments present in the markets.

5.5.3.2   Possible methodologies based on the distribution shapes

The effects of the diversification between the assets are taken into account in the definition of the probability density function of the portfolio. Since this density is generally not thoroughly known, the method presented before and based on the Gram–Charlier expansion is probably one of the best in this context. We have presented this method at order four since we do not know exactly the significance of the moments of higher order, implying that the agents cannot express more than preference directions on these moments (Scott and Horvath, 1980).

As we mentioned earlier, to work in a really general manner on a distribution, without ignoring some of its characteristics, we need to use its probability density function. However, in the case of risky assets, this density function is unknown and we can only use approximating methods.[14] Indeed, the central point in our methodology is to obtain an expression of the portfolio's returns density conditional on the weights of the assets constituting it. As we believe that the Gram–Charlier expansion is one of the most flexible approaches to obtaining such a density, we propose its use. However, this expansion may present certain difficulties and can be replaced by other methods. For example, its use is limited by the possible negativity. Nevertheless, we consider that the possibility it offers to easily include moments of order greater than four and to use any approximating density[15] with added precision more than balances its limits.

Indeed it is interesting to examine the seminal works in financial economics (Arrow, 1971; Von Neumann and Morgenstern, 1953), which consider that the agents express their preferences over consumption plans. These consumption plans are absolutely continuous random variables. Since the investment portfolios contribute to consumption, examining them through less than their density function could lead to a misunderstanding of their equilibrium prices.

The preferences of the agents being primarily expressed on distributions and not on moments, it is on the risky assets' return distributions, represented by their density functions, that we should work in order to select optimal portfolios. Indeed, most forms of portfolio selection studied to this day are based on the expected utility theory. Expected utility gives us the general possibility to express the choice of the agents, through Taylor expansions of their utility, in terms of moments. This method is well covered in Jurczenko and Maillet (2001). However, some research proves that expected utility theory does not represent faithfully the way investors really express their preferences under uncertainty (see, for example, Allais, 1953; Tversky and Kahneman, 1974; Kahneman and Tversky, 1979). In order to propose a

---

[14] Other than the Gram–Charlier expansions, some methods, generally less accurate, could provide us with such an approximation of the density, like the Edgeworth expansion and the Hermite polynomials. We could also use known distributions, yet we have already seen the many flaws in this method.

[15] The construction of the expansion may sometimes be more complex than with a Gaussian.

portfolio selection method quite robust to the type of preferences agents exhibit, we need to stick to the complete distributions of asset returns as much as we can.

There exist different approaches that could allow us to achieve such a goal. The most promising approach, yet a very complex one, is to minimise the distance between the portfolio returns' density function and an objective density function, corresponding to an ideal portfolio. For a risk-averse agent, this portfolio is obviously the portfolio offering the same expected return μ and no risk. Therefore, we will need to minimise the distance between the portfolio returns' density function and the density function of a random variable degenerated on its mean, a Dirac delta of mean μ.

Moreover, we can easily accommodate the fact that agents express a positive preference on odd-order moments, that is, agents wish a distance to exist between the densities after the mean. To obtain such a result, we can minimise the distance between the real and the ideal densities between minus infinity and the required mean; if the result is more than one portfolio, we select the one exhibiting the most positive asymmetry.

The key problem with this possible method is the definition of the distance minimised. It may initially seem appealing to use a distance based on the classical norm on $\mathcal{L}^2$:

$$d(F, A) = \sqrt{\int_{\mathbb{R}} (f(s) - a(s))^2 \, ds} \tag{5.24}$$

We should note, however, that this distance can, by no means be used for risk-averse agents. Indeed these agents are averse to variance and, *ceteris paribus*, this distance decreases when variance increases, skewness increases and kurtosis decreases.

Therefore, to establish a convincing portfolio theory, it is required that our knowledge of the agents' marginal rates of substitution between moments be paralleled by research on distances coherent with them. When the distribution of returns is a simple Gaussian, we should obviously obtain the classical CAPM as a result of this approach.

A certain number of known distances could probably bring some results, after small modifications, in the context of non-Gaussian portfolio theory. One of them is the Kullback–Leibler distance, also known as relative entropy between the probability measures associated with the actual portfolio distribution and the ideal portfolio distribution. This distance is defined as:

$$\epsilon(Q, P) = \int_{\Omega} \ln\left(\frac{dQ}{dP}\right) dQ \tag{5.25}$$

where dQ/dP is the Radon–Nikodym derivative of Q with respect to P, and Ω is the space on which these probability measures are both defined. The properties of the Kullback–Leibler distance are well known:

$$\epsilon(Q, P) \geq 0$$

$$\epsilon(Q, P) = 0 \Longleftrightarrow P = Q$$

$$\epsilon(Q, P) = \infty \quad \text{if } Q \text{ is not absolutely continuous with respect to } P$$

The first two properties are perfectly adapted to our requirements, yet the third one implies that we define an alternative objective distribution. The probability measure associated with this distribution should be absolutely continuous with respect to the measure associated

with the density defined by the Gram–Charlier expansion used to approximate the portfolio returns' density. The same problem can arise for other measures and distances, since
continuity is often required.

It is therefore necessary to define a probability distribution nearly ideal for a risk-averse
agent. To this purpose, we propose the use of a Gaussian with a standard deviation in the
neighbourhood of zero. Indeed, we can show that it can always be a good approximation of
the Dirac delta at the desired level of precision.

Theorem 2 *Let $U: \mathbb{R} \mapsto \mathbb{R}^+$ be a monotonically increasing utility function, δ_μ be a Dirac
delta with mean μ and $\{\phi_\mu(\sigma)\}_{\sigma \in (0, +\infty)}$ be the family of Gaussian distributions with fixed
mean μ, then:*

$$\forall \varepsilon > 0 \quad \exists \eta \in (0, +\infty) \quad | \quad E[U(\delta_\mu)] - E[U(\phi_\mu(\eta))] < \varepsilon$$

*That is, there's always a σ such that the expected utility of the corresponding Gaussian
distribution is as close as desired to the expected utility of the Dirac delta.*[16]

5.5.3.3 An approximate and simplified methodology

Another methodology we could use is also based on the probability density function. Therefore, it is more general, even if the density is a Gram–Charlier expansion of order four,[17]
than the simple moments-based approaches. Since it will not necessarily be trivial to define
the distances coherent with agents' preferences, a less-refined approach may be useful.

All the characteristics of a distribution cannot be recovered from the description of this
distribution around its mean. Yet, if the density function is taken into account in a large
enough area, it exhibits many of the distribution's moments and their interactions. To obtain
a scalar measure of the risk of a given distribution, while remembering that investors like
positive skewness, we could use the following integral:

$$\text{risk} \approx \int_\alpha^\mu a(s)^\beta \, ds \tag{5.26}$$

In this equation, the parameters $\beta \in \mathbb{R}^*$ and $\alpha \in (-\infty, \mu)$ allow us to give a more or less
important relative influence to the tails of the distribution compared to its central part,
thus reflecting the agents' preferences and marginal rates of substitution between moments.
Since $a(s)$ is always positive (it is a probability density function even if produced by a
Gram–Charlier expansion), complex values are avoided.

Obviously, the critical point is to obtain values for α and β corresponding to the agents'
preferences. Moreover, even in the case of a portfolio with normal returns, the classical
CAPM is not automatically obtained. Yet, this approach is a first way of reaching approximately optimal portfolios under the constraint of a given expected return. Formally solving
the optimisation programme is probably not always possible, and this simpler programme
can allow us to use numerical methods.

---

[16] The proof of this theorem is in Appendix B.
[17] In a Gram–Charlier expansion of order m, the moments of order higher than m exist and have values differing from what they
would be for the approximating Gaussian distribution $a(s)$.

5.6 CONCLUSION

We have examined how different authors have attempted to enlarge the application field of the CAPM to moments of order higher than two. The methods used can be separated into two groups: extensions of the CAPM based on the preferences of the agents and works based on more distributional approaches. The extensions based on utilities are more frequent, yet they present the inconvenience of hiding the fact that the real problem stems from the properties of the returns' distributions. Moreover, distributional hypotheses present the advantage of being fully testable, whereas the hypotheses formulated on the agents' utilities are usually more theoretical and difficult to test.

On the other hand, works based on the study of the returns' distributions are usually too formalised and mathematically complex to really enlighten us on the actual problem of portfolio selection. Furthermore, the work on the portfolio theory based on distributional analysis is generally not overly concerned with agents' preferences, which are nonetheless, central.

However, we have seen how extending portfolio theory to the case of non-normally distributed asset returns implies studying the density function of the returns.[18] Yet, studying the distributions of returns is useless if not accompanied by an accurate description and understanding of how the agents express their preferences on these distributions. This description of the preferences in a context of non-normally distributed returns is complex, since we only know if agents express preference or aversion towards the different moments and have yet to discover how they rank these preferences.

One of the economic preambles to a real extension of the CAPM to a non-Gaussian universe is, therefore, to study the marginal rates of substitution between the different moments of the returns' distributions. Maybe it is feasible to infer these marginal rates of substitution from the variation of returns across the risky asset range, yet this will only unveil the market aggregate values at the specific time of the study.

From another point of view, we have seen that the complexity of the portfolio selection problem in a non-Gaussian universe leads to the questioning of the methodology used until now in portfolio theory. Although we have attempted to submit a few possible ways to explore this problem, important work is still to be undertaken, especially in defining the concept of extended risk.

APPENDIX A: ADDITIONAL STATISTICS FOR THE EXAMPLE PORTFOLIO

A.1 Moments and co-moments

We present the moments and co-moments of the daily return distributions for the assets forming our portfolio. The observations used in establishing these results are from January 2nd, 1998 to December 30th, 1998. First consider the variance–covariance matrix shown in Table 5.6.

Moments and co-moments are more complex when of an order greater than or equal to three. They cannot be represented as easily as they are for order two. Here, we present a

---

[18] To keep our analysis general and realistic enough, we need not restrain the agents' utility functions to any specific class, since such hypotheses cannot be easily verified.

Table 5.6 Variance–covariance matrix

	Barrick Gold	Bouygues	Canal Plus	Michelin
Barrick Gold	0.00101047	$4.9024E-05$	$6.0448E-05$	$4.0928E-05$
Bouygues	$4.9024E-05$	0.00075709	0.00010821	0.00019634
Canal Plus	$6.0448E-05$	0.00010821	0.00059704	0.00020752
Michelin	$4.0928E-05$	0.00019634	0.00020752	0.00072338

Table 5.7 "Skewness–co-skewness" matrix

	Barrick Gold	Bouygues	Canal Plus	Michelin
Barrick Gold	$1.6277E-05$	$7.1291E-07$	$-9.8902E-07$	$-4.6659E-06$
Bouygues	$2.9949E-06$	$2.3224E-06$	$-1.6393E-06$	$-1.7912E-06$
Canal Plus	$-1.4158E-06$	$9.3623E-08$	$6.6674E-06$	$2.6197E-06$
Michelin	$-1.5269E-06$	$-8.166E-07$	$1.1862E-07$	$7.602E-07$

Table 5.8 Third-moment 3×3 dependencies

Barrick Gold	Bouygues	Canal Plus	$-3.0782E-07$
Barrick Gold	Bouygues	Michelin	$3.488E-06$
Barrick Gold	Canal Plus	Michelin	$-7.832E-07$
Bouygues	Canal Plus	Michelin	$-5.978E-07$

matrix of "skewness–co-skewness". In fact, the data presented here are the central moments and co-moments of order three. In Table 5.7, lines correspond to assets i in the expression: $E[(X_i - E(X_i))^2 (X_j - E(X_j))]$.

To finish with the statistical description of the third moments of the assets included in our portfolio, we present, in Table 5.8, the three by three dependency, as given by the expression: $E[(X_i - E(X_i))(X_j - E(X_j))(X_k - E(X_k))]$.

The complete description of the central moment of order four and its related co-moments is even more tedious. We first present, in Table 5.9, the symmetrical co-dependency corresponding to the fourth central moment. On the diagonal are the fourth central moments of the corresponding assets, while the rest are terms given by the expression: $E[(X_i - E(X_i))^2 (X_j - E(X_j))^2]$.

Table 5.10 presents the "matrix" giving the other two by two co-moments of order four. The lines contain the stocks i, and the columns the stocks j, of the expression: $E[(X_i - E(X_i))^3 (X_j - E(X_j))]$.

Table 5.9 Central fourth moments and corresponding symmetrical co-moments

	Barrick Gold	Bouygues	Canal Plus	Michelin
Barrick Gold	$3.8889E-06$	$1.0509E-06$	$5.5628E-07$	$7.571E-07$
Bouygues	$1.0509E-06$	$2.2451E-06$	$4.9715E-07$	$6.4775E-07$
Canal Plus	$5.5628E-07$	$4.9715E-07$	$2.1695E-06$	$6.4028E-07$
Michelin	$7.571E-07$	$6.4775E-07$	$6.4028E-07$	$1.5881E-06$

Table 5.10   Other 2 × 2 fourth-order co-moments

	Barrick Gold	Bouygues	Canal Plus	Michelin
Barrick Gold	x	1.3809E − 07	1.8265E − 07	1.1183E − 07
Bouygues	2.9462E − 08	x	3.462E − 07	5.6403E − 07
Canal Plus	1.6451E − 07	2.0112E − 07	x	8.4691E − 07
Michelin	6.3073E − 08	4.2504E − 07	4.6999E − 07	x

Table 5.11   Fourth-order 3 × 3 co-moments

Barrick Gold	Bouygues	Canal Plus	2.454E − 07
Bouygues	Barrick Gold	Canal Plus	1.2928E − 07
Canal Plus	Barrick Gold	Bouygues	8.7651E − 08
Barrick Gold	Bouygues	Michelin	2.984E − 07
Bouygues	Barrick Gold	Michelin	2.2708E − 08
Michelin	Barrick Gold	Bouygues	−8.8329E − 08
Barrick Gold	Canal Plus	Michelin	2.4999E − 07
Canal Plus	Barrick Gold	Michelin	7.0504E − 08
Michelin	Barrick Gold	Canal Plus	1.5833E − 08
Bouygues	Canal Plus	Michelin	2.2411E − 07
Canal Plus	Bouygues	Michelin	1.4867E − 07
Michelin	Bouygues	Canal Plus	1.4907E − 07

Table 5.11 presents the three by three fourth-order co-moments, as given by the expression:
$E[(X_i − E(X_i))^2 (X_j − E(X_j))(X_k − E(X_k))]$. The stocks named first correspond to asset i in the expression.

Since our portfolio is composed of only four assets, there is only one value for the 4 × 4 fourth-order co-moment, as given by the expression:

$$E(X_i − E(X_i))(X_j − E(X_j))(X_k − E(X_k))(X_l − E(X_l))]$$

In our case, its value is: 3.172767326E − 09

A.2   Statistical tests of normality

There are two main statistical tests for normality. We first present the results of the classical Kolmogorov–Smirnov test, as well as the Lilliefors version, comparing the empirical distribution of our stocks against the Gaussian distributions having the same mean and variance. The results are presented in Table 5.12 (where $\mathcal{L}$ denotes the Lilliefors version, more adapted to Gaussian distributions, but based on the same statistics). Since this test is not specifically aimed at testing the normality of a distribution, we performed it at a quite restrictive 15 % significance level.

To confirm the results obtained with the Kolmogorov–Smirnov and Lilliefors tests, we have used a Jarque–Bera test in Table 5.13. Since this test is specifically designed for testing the normality hypothesis, we can use a low 5 % significance level. Using the test with a more restrictive 10 % significance level does not change the results, since the critical value becomes 4.605170. The only stock for which the test cannot reject the hypothesis of normality is Michelin.

Table 5.12   Results of Kolmogorov–Smirnov tests

	Barrick Gold	Bouygues	Canal Plus	Michelin
K–S statistic	0.06519	0.07611	0.05496	0.04148
p-value	0.236431	0.109125	0.434302	0.780927
Result	not rejected	rejected	not rejected	not rejected

Test at a 15 % significance level, the critical value is 0.071733

$\mathcal{L}$ p-value	0.024467	undefined	0.063699	undefined
$\mathcal{L}$ Result	rejected	rejected	rejected	not rejected

Test at a 15 % significance level, the critical value is 0.048867

Table 5.13   Results of Jarque–Bera tests

	Barrick Gold	Bouygues	Canal Plus	Michelin
J–B statistic	17.3020	9.1644	106.6340	0.0754
p-value	0.000175	0.010233	0	0.963002
Result	rejected	rejected	rejected	not rejected

Test at a 5 % significance level, the critical value is 5.991465

APPENDIX B: PROOFS

B.1   Positivity conditions theorem (Theorem 1)

Let us consider a Gaussian Gram–Charlier expansion of order 4 with our usual notation:

$$f(s) = \frac{1}{\sigma\sqrt{2\pi}} e^{-\frac{1}{2}\left(\frac{s-m}{\sigma}\right)^2} \left\{ 1 - \left(3\frac{(s-m)}{\sigma^4} - \left(\frac{s-m}{\sigma^2}\right)^3 \right) \frac{\mu_3(F)}{3!} \right. \tag{5.27}$$
$$\left. + \left(\left(\frac{s-m}{\sigma^2}\right)^4 - 6\frac{(s-m)^2}{\sigma^6} + \frac{3}{\sigma^4} \right) \frac{\mu_4(F) - 3\sigma^4}{4!} \right\} + \varepsilon(s)$$

We know that:

$$\frac{1}{\sigma\sqrt{2\pi}} e^{-\frac{1}{2}\left(\frac{s-m}{\sigma}\right)^2} > 0 \quad \forall (m, \sigma, s) \in \mathbb{R} \times \mathbb{R}^+ \times \mathbb{R}$$

since it is a probability density function.
   To have $f(s) - \varepsilon(s) > 0$ $\quad \forall s \in \mathbb{R}$ we need to verify that:

$$P(s) = 1 - \left(3\frac{(s-m)}{\sigma^4} - \left(\frac{s-m}{\sigma^2}\right)^3 \right) \frac{\mu_3(F)}{3!} \tag{5.28}$$
$$+ \left(\left(\frac{s-m}{\sigma^2}\right)^4 - 6\frac{(s-m)^2}{\sigma^6} + \frac{3}{\sigma^4} \right) \frac{\mu_4(F) - 3\sigma^4}{4!} > 0$$

Which is equivalent to:

$$P(s) = 1 - \left(3 \frac{(s-\mu)}{\sigma^4} - \left(\frac{s-\mu}{\sigma^2} \right)^3 \right) \frac{\xi \sigma^3}{3!} \tag{5.29}$$

$$+ \left(\left(\frac{s-\mu}{\sigma^2} \right)^4 - 6 \frac{(s-\mu)^2}{\sigma^6} + \frac{3}{\sigma^4} \right) \frac{(\kappa-3)\sigma^4}{4!} > 0$$

where μ denotes the mean, ξ the skewness and κ the kurtosis. Equation (5.29) can be rewritten as a polynomial equation in s:

$$P(s) = \left(-\frac{1}{8\sigma^4} + \frac{\kappa}{24\sigma^4} \right) s^4 + \left(\frac{\xi}{6\sigma^3} - \frac{\mu\kappa}{6\sigma^4} + \frac{\mu}{2\sigma^4} \right) s^3 \tag{5.30}$$

$$+ \left(\frac{\mu^2\kappa}{4\sigma^4} + \frac{3}{4\sigma^2} - \frac{3\mu^2}{4\sigma^4} - \frac{\kappa}{4\sigma^2} - \frac{\xi\mu}{2\sigma^3} \right) s^2$$

Since $24\sigma^4 > 0, \forall \sigma \in \mathbb{R}$, we know that:

$$\text{sign}(P(s)) = \text{sign}(24\sigma^4 P(s)), \forall s \in \mathbb{R}$$

For $f(s) - \epsilon(s) > 0$, it is necessary and sufficient that $24\sigma^4 P(s) > 0, \forall s \in \mathbb{R}$. We easily see that $24\sigma^4 P(\mu) = 15\sigma^4 + 3\sigma^4\kappa$, which is positive for all σ and κ defined as the standard deviation and kurtosis of a probability distribution, respectively.

To have $f(s) - \epsilon(s) > 0$, $\forall s \in \mathbb{R}$, it is therefore necessary and sufficient for polynomial (5.20) in Theorem 1 not to have real roots. ∎

B.2   Approximation of the optimal portfolio density (Theorem 2)

Let us consider a Gaussian density of mean μ and standard deviation σ. For $s \in (-\infty, \mu) \cup (\mu, +\infty)$, we have

$$\lim_{\sigma \to 0} \frac{1}{\sigma\sqrt{2\pi}} e^{-\frac{1}{2}\left(\frac{s-\mu}{\sigma}\right)^2} = 0 \tag{5.31}$$

and for $s = \mu$,

$$\lim_{\sigma \to 0} \frac{1}{\sigma\sqrt{2\pi}} e^{-\frac{1}{2}\left(\frac{\mu-\mu}{\sigma}\right)^2} = \lim_{\sigma \to 0} \frac{1}{\sigma\sqrt{2\pi}} = +\infty \tag{5.32}$$

Moreover, we know that, $\phi_\mu(\sigma)$ being a probability density function, we have:

$$\int_{-\infty}^{+\infty} \frac{1}{\sigma\sqrt{2\pi}} e^{-\frac{1}{2}\left(\frac{\mu-\mu}{\sigma}\right)^2} ds = 1$$

and therefore,

$$\lim_{\sigma \to 0} \int_{-\infty}^{+\infty} \frac{1}{\sigma\sqrt{2\pi}} e^{-\frac{1}{2}\left(\frac{\mu-\mu}{\sigma}\right)^2} ds = 1 \tag{5.33}$$

Since we have (5.31), (5.32) and (5.33), we have shown that:

$$\phi_\mu(\sigma) \xrightarrow[\sigma \to 0]{\text{law}} \delta_\mu$$

As $U(\cdot)$ is monotonically increasing, we have:

$$U(\phi_\mu(\sigma)) \xrightarrow[\sigma \to 0]{\text{law}} U(\delta_\mu)$$

And, from the basic properties of Riemann integrals:

$$\lim_{\sigma \to 0} E[U(\phi_\mu(\sigma))] = E[U(\delta_\mu)]$$

That is:

$$\forall \varepsilon > 0 \quad \exists \eta \in (0, +\infty) \quad | \quad |E[U[\delta_\mu]] - E[U(\phi_\mu(\eta))]| < \varepsilon$$

∎

ACKNOWLEDGEMENTS

Many thanks to the anonymous referee; his helpful comments have greatly improved this chapter I also wish to acknowledge the helpful remarks that participants of the Finance-sur-Seine workshop on multi-moment CAPMs have provided in bettering this chapter. Most prominent among them are Eric Jondeau, who refereed the chapter, and the organisers, Bertrand Maillet and Emmanuel Jurczenko. Their efforts in promoting this area of research are outstanding. More thanks go to Helyette Geman, whose comments and support helped me in getting started on the subject of non-Gaussian portfolio selection.

REFERENCES

Aït-Sahalia, Y. and M. Brandt (2001) Variable Selection for Portfolio Choice, *Journal of Finance* **56**, 1297–1351.

Allais, M. (1953) Le Comportement de l'Homme Rationnel devant le Risque, Critique des Postulats et Axiomes de l'Ecole Américaine, *Econometrica* **21**, 503–546.

Amihud, Y., B. Christensen and H. Mendelson (1992) Further Evidence on the Risk–Return Relationship, Working Paper, New York University.

Ang, A. and G. Bekaert (2002) International Asset Allocation with Time-Varying Correlations, *Review of Financial Studies* **15**, 1137–1187.

Arrow, K. J. (1963) Comment, *Review of Economics and Statistics* **45**, 24–27, (Supplement: February).

Arrow, K. J. (1971) *Essays on the Theory of Risk Bearing*, Markham Publishing Co., New York.

Athayde, G. and R. Flôres Jr (2004) Finding a Maximum Skewness Portfolio – a General Solution to Three-Moments Portfolio Choice, *Journal of Economic Dynamics and Control*, **28** (7), 1335–1352.

Bauwens, L. and S. Laurent (2002) A New Class of Multivariate Skew Densities, with Application to GARCH Model, CORE discussion paper, Université de Liège, Université catholique de Louvain.

Brennan, M. (1979) The Pricing of Contingent Claims in Discrete Time Models, *Journal of Finance* **34**, 53–68.

Cass, D. and J. Stiglitz (1970) The Structure of Investor Preferences and Asset Returns, and Separability in Portfolio Allocation, A Contribution to the Pure Theory of Mutual Funds, *Journal of Economic Theory* **2**, 122–160.

Chan, L., Y. Hamao and J. Lakonishok (1991) Fundamentals and Stock Returns in Japan, *Journal of Finance* **46**, 1739–1764.

Chunhachinda, P., K. Dandapani, S. Hamid and A. J. Prakash (1997) Portfolio Selection and Skewness: Evidence from International Stock Markets, *Journal of Banking and Finance* **21**, 143–167.

Constantinides, G. (1982) Intertemporal Asset Pricing with Heterogeneous Consumers and without Demand Aggregation, *Journal of Business* **55**, 253–268.

Cramer, H. (1946) *Mathematical Methods of Statistics*, Princeton University Press, Princeton.

Fama, E. and K. French (1992) The Cross-Section of Expected Stock Returns, *Journal of Finance* **47**, 427–465.

Fama, E. and K. French (1995) Size and Book to Market Factors in Earnings and Returns, *Journal of Finance* **50**, 131–155.

Fama, E. and K. French (1996) Multifactor Explanations of Asset Pricing Anomalies, *Journal of Finance* **51**, 55–84.

Friend, I. and R. Westerfield (1980) Co-Skewness and Capital Asset Pricing, *Journal of Finance* **35**, 897–913.

Hansen, L. P. (1982) Large Sample Properties of Generalized Method of Moments Estimators, *Econometrica* **50**, 1029–1054.

Harvey, C. and A. Siddique (1999) Autoregressive Conditional Skewness, *Journal of Financial and Quantitative Analysis* **34**, 465–487.

Harvey, C. and A. Siddique (2000) Conditional Skewness in Asset Pricing Tests, *Journal of Finance* **55** 1263–1295.

He, H. and H. Leland (1993) On Equilibrium Asset Price Processes, *Review of Financial Studies* **6**, 593–617.

Jarrow, R. and A. Rudd (1982) Approximate Option Valuation for Arbitrary Stochastic Processes, *Journal of Financial Economics* **10**, 347–369.

Johnson, N., S. Kotz and N. Balakrishnan (1994) *Continuous Univariate Distributions*, 2nd edition, John Wiley & Sons, Inc., New York.

Jondeau, E. and M. Rockinger (2001) Gram–Charlier Densities, *Journal of Economic Dynamics and Control* **25**, 1457–1483.

Jurczenko, E. and B. Maillet (2001) The 3-CAPM: Theoretical Foundations and an Asset Pricing Model Comparison in a Unified Framework. In: *Developments in Forecast Combination and Portfolio Choice*, C. Dunis, A. Timmermann and J. Moody (Eds), John Wiley & Sons, Ltd, Chichester, pp. 239–273.

Jurczenko, E., B. Maillet and B. Negrea (2003) Multi-moment Approximate Option Pricing Models: A General Comparison (Part 1), LSE-FMG working paper.

Kahneman, D. and A. Tversky (1979) Prospect Theory: an Analysis of Decision under Risk, *Econometrica* **47**, 263–291.

Kano, Y. (1994) Consistency Property of Elliptical Probability Density Function, *Journal of Multivariate Analysis* **51**, 139–147.

Kendall, M. and A. Stuart (1977) *The Advanced Theory of Statistics, Vol. 1: Distribution Theory*, 4th edition, MacMillan, New York.

Kraus, A. and R. Litzenberger (1976) Skewness Preference and the Valuation of Risk Assets, *Journal of Finance* **31**, 1085–1100.

Leland, H. (1998) Beyond mean–variance: risk and performance measures for portfolios with nonsymmetric return distributions, Working Paper, University of California, Berkeley.

Lintner, J. (1965) The Valuation of Risk Assets and the Selection of Risky Investments in Stock Portfolios and Capital Budgets, *Review of Economics and Statistics* **47**, 13–37.

Prakash, A., C. Chang and T. Pactwa (2003) Selecting a Portfolio with Skewness: Recent Evidence from US, European, and Latin American Equity Markets, *Journal of Banking and Finance* **27**, 1375–1390.

Pratt, J. (1964) Risk Aversion in the Small and in the Large, *Econometrica* **32**, 122–136.

Rao, C. (1973) *Linear Statistical Inference and its Applications*, 2nd edition, John Wiley & Sons, Inc., New York.

Roll, R. (1977) A Critique of the Asset Pricing Theory's Tests, *Journal of Financial Economics* **4**, 129–176.

Roll, R. (1978) Ambiguity when Performance is Measured by the Securities Market Line, *Journal of Finance* **33**, 1051–1069.

Ross, S. (1976) The Arbitrage Theory of Capital Asset Pricing, *Journal of Economic Theory* **13**, 341–360.

Ross, S. (1977) The Capital Asset Pricing Model, Short Sales Restriction and Related Issues, *Journal of Finance* **32**, 177–183.

Rubinstein, M. (1976) The Valuation of Uncertain Income Streams and the Pricing of Options, *Bell Journal of Economics and Management Science* **7**, 407–425.

Rubinstein, M. (1998) Edgeworth Binomial Trees, *Journal of Derivatives* **5** (Spring), 20–27.

Scott, R. and P. Horvath (1980) On the Direction of Preferences for Moments of Higher Order than the Variance, *Journal of Finance* **35**, 915–919.

Sharpe, W. (1964) Capital Asset Prices: a Theory of Market Equilibrium under Conditions of Risk, *Journal of Finance* **19**, 425–442.

Sornette, D., P. Simonetti and J. Andersen (1999) Nonlinear Covariance Matrix and Portfolio Theory for non-Gaussian Multivariate Distributions, Working Paper, University of California, Los Angeles.

Tayi, G. and P. Leonard (1988) Bank Balance-sheet Management, an Alternative Multi-objective Model, *Journal of the Operational Research Society* **39**, 401–410.

Tversky, A. and D. Kahneman (1974) Judgment under Uncertainty: Heuristics and Biases, *Science* **185**, 1124–1131.

Von Neumann, J. and O. Morgenstern (1953) *Theory of Games and Economic Behavior*, Princeton University Press, Princeton.

─────────── 6 ───────────

The Four-moment Capital Asset Pricing Model: Between Asset Pricing and Asset Allocation

Emmanuel Jurczenko and Bertrand Maillet

ABSTRACT

The purpose of this chapter is to present the four-moment Capital Asset Pricing Model in a unified framework. The traditional CAPM suffers from several restrictive hypotheses. In particular, Gaussianity and a "small" risk are supposed to be valid. Following the seminal article of Rubinstein (1973) and those, more recently, of Fang and Lai (1997), Hwang and Satchell (1999), Adcock (2004 and 2005), Athayde and Flôres (1997 and 2000), Berényi (2001, 2002 and 2004), Christie-David and Chaudhry (2001) and Dittmar (2002), we extend the Sharpe–Lintner–Mossin framework to take into account the asymmetric and leptokurtic characteristics of asset return distributions. Using a two-fund monetary separation theorem, we develop an exact four-moment capital asset pricing relation. We present a similar relation in the more general case of a market without riskless assets. Finally, we put into perspective the link between some multifactor models such as the Sharpe–Lintner–Mossin CAPM, Black's CAPM (1972), the cubic market model, the APT of Ross (1976) and this revisited four-moment CAPM.

6.1 INTRODUCTION

The validity of the Sharpe–Lintner–Mossin Capital Asset Pricing Model (CAPM)[1] has been questioned by several empirical tests. This model remains, nevertheless, one of the most important contributions to modern finance theory, as emphasised by Black (1993) and Jagannathan and Wang (1996) for instance.

This model of the financial market equilibrium is based on several restrictive hypotheses; two of them concern the normality[2] of the asset return distributions and the characteristics of the agent preferences. The latter is necessary to legitimise this formalisation of the investors' optimisation problem in a risky situation, while, in the former, the expected utility function

---

[1] See Sharpe (1964), Lintner (1965) and Mossin (1966).
[2] The CAPM is also suitable for the broader class of elliptical distributions (see Chamberlain, 1983; Owen and Rabinovitch, 1983; Hamada and Valdez, 2004).

Multi-moment Asset Allocation and Pricing Models   Edited by E. Jurczenko and B. Maillet
© 2006 John Wiley & Sons, Ltd

can be expressed as an exact function of the mean and the variance of the investment return distribution.

These hypotheses are subject to two traditional criticisms: the first one is tied to the theoretical foundations of the approach; the second is based on their inadequacy with the stylised facts highlighted in empirical studies. The return normality hypothesis implies, indeed, that the investor can lose more than his initial wealth, and the quadratic utility function does not correspond to the rational agent behavioural characteristics. In particular, it is difficult to accept that a financial asset can be seen generally as an inferior good (Pratt, 1964; Arrow, 1970) and to explain that risk-averse agents would participate in a risky lottery (see Friedman and Savage, 1948; Kahneman and Tversky, 1979; Golec and Tamarkin, 1998). Moreover, the quadratic approximation is usually justified economically by the existence of a "small" absolute risk in the sense of Samuelson (1970), or by a "small" relative risk in the sense of Tsiang (1972). These hypotheses do not correspond to all asset characteristics. The hypothesis of normality of return densities[3] is clearly rejected according to the results of many empirical studies (see, for instance, Fama, 1965 and Mandelbrot, 1997). Most of the empirical asset return distributions are asymmetric and leptokurtic. Limited liability, speculative financial bubbles and incitative schemes induce skewness in financial asset return distributions (Black and Scholes, 1973; Blanchard and Watson, 1982; Goetzman et al., 2004). The skewness is reinforced by the existence of leverage and volatility feedback effects (Black, 1976; Christie and Andrew, 1982; Pindyck, 1984), while the existence of derivatives, active and passive portfolio strategies and the use of short-sale and leverage leads to convex pay-off functions (Bookstaber and Clarke, 1981; Henriksson and Merton, 1981; Davies et al., 2004). Conditional heteroskedasticity, long-term compound return and heterogeneous expectations are also responsible for the skewed and leptokurtic characteristics of asset and portfolio return distributions (Bollerslev, 1986; Fama, 1996; Hong and Stein, 1999 and 2003; Chen et al., 2001).

The relative failures of the traditional CAPM have led several authors to adopt alternative approaches in order to improve the theoretical consistency and empirical performance of the model. Among the main possibilities investigated, the following extensions can be distinguished (without pretence to exhaustibility). Different density probabilities have been substituted for the Gaussian distribution to estimate the CAPM parameters (Harvey and Zhou, 1993). A time-varying version of the CAPM has also been proposed to deal with the autoregressive character of the conditional variance (Bollerslev et al., 1988; Jagannathan and Wang, 1996) or, more generally, with advocated parameter variability. Financial risk measures other than variance[4] have allowed others to develop asset pricing models such as Gini-CAPM (Shalit and Yitzhaki, 1984; Okunev, 1990), Lower-moment CAPM (Nantell et al., 1982; Hwang and Pedersen, 2002), CAPM with asymmetric betas (Ang et al., 2004) and VaR-CAPM (Alexander and Baptista, 2002 and 2003). Multifactor models, based on an arbitrage argument or heuristic considerations, permit authors to improve the explanatory power compared to that of the original model (Fama and French, 1992 and 1995; Carhart, 1997). Finally, the last stream of the literature to be highlighted concerns the use of higher-order moments than the variance in a pricing relation (see, for instance, Rubinstein, 1973;

---

[3] Which can be encompassed by the lognormality hypothesis. Nevertheless, this one has some other drawbacks (see, for instance, Feller, 1971).
[4] For an extended survey of financial risk measures, see Pedersen and Satchell (1998).

Ingersoll, 1975; Kraus and Litzenberger, 1976).[5] The main feature of these models is to obtain, for any risky asset, a linear equilibrium relation between the expected rate of return and higher-order moment systematic risk measures.

Initially developed by Rubinstein (1973), Ingersoll (1975) and Kraus and Litzenberger (1976) to take into account the effects of the unconditional asymmetries on the asset pricing relation, this approach has been extended to the unconditional *kurtosis* by Graddy and Homaifar (1988), Athayde and Flôres (1997 and 2000), Adcock (2003) and Hwang and Satchell (1999)[6] and to the conditional higher-order moments by Harvey and Siddique (2000a and 2000b), Dittmar (2002) and Galagedera *et al.* (2004a and 2004b). The introduction of higher moments in the investors' objective functions can explain some financial anomalies such as individual and institutional portfolio underdiversification (Simkowitz and Beedles, 1978; Conine and Tamarkin, 1981 and 1982; Kane, 1982; Davies *et al.*, 2004 and Mitton and Vorkink, 2004); industry, book-to-market, size or momentum effects (Harvey and Siddique, 2000a and 2001; Dittmar, 2002; Barone-Adesi *et al.*, 2004 and Chapter 9 of this book, and Chung *et al.*, 2006), and the risk-free rate and the equity premium puzzles (Brav *et al.*, 2002; Lim *et al.*, 2004; Semenov, 2004). Departures from normality are also powerful factors in option pricing to explain the volatility smile effect (Jarrow and Rudd, 1982; Corrado and Su, 1996a and 1996b; Jurczenko *et al.*, 2002a, 2002b and 2004).

Even though multi-moment pricing models can handle agent preferences and asset return distributions in a more realistic way than the traditional CAPM, their derivations are not without problems. The four-moment asset pricing models that have been proposed use fourth-order Taylor series expansions of specific HARA utility functions to justify a four-moment-based decision criterion. This means that the asset pricing relations obtained are only valid approximately. Moreover, the aggregation of the individual equilibrium conditions rests on a two-fund monetary separation theorem which restricts the domain of validity of these models to the existence of a risk-free asset and to specific separable quartic or decreasing HARA utility functions (see Chapter 1). In addition, the risk premia of multi-moment models are not generally identified independently of the shape of the utility function considered.

The objective of this chapter is to overcome some of the limits of the multi-moment asset pricing models by combining, in a unified framework, some of the results of Expected Utility Theory, Portfolio Choice Theory and Asset Pricing Theory. Indeed, a unified framework is required in order to obtain a generalisation of the CAPM in a skewed and leptokurtic world, with or without the existence of a riskless asset, where risk-premia can be identified on *a priori* grounds.

When focusing on the theoretical foundations of rational choices, it is possible to justify an exact mean–variance–skewness–*kurtosis* decision criterion and to explain a risky behaviour by a risk-averse agent. But, to our knowledge, no conclusion has yet been applied to portfolio choices and asset pricing relations. When focusing on portfolio choices, one can define a mean–variance–skewness–*kurtosis* efficient frontier with or without a riskless asset, and obtain a linear relation between the expected return on any efficient portfolio and the

---

[5] See also Friend and Westerfield (1980), Sears and Wei (1985 and 1988), Graddy and Homaifar (1988), Lim (1989), Simaan (1993), Nummelin (1997), Fang and Lai (1997), Sánchez-Torres and Sentana (1998), Racine (1998), Faff *et al.* (1998), Adcock and Shutes (2000 and 2001), Athayde and Flôres (1997 and 2000), Berényi (2001, 2002 and 2004), Christie-David and Chaudhry (2001), Hübner and Honhon (2002), Jurczenko and Maillet (2001), Hwang and Satchell (1999), Stutzer (2003), Adcock (2003 and 2004), Polimenis (2002), Harvey and Siddique (2000a and 2000b), Dittmar (2002), Rolph (2003), Galagedera *et al.* (2004a and 2004b), Hung *et al.* (2004), and Chung *et al.* (2006).
[6] See also Fang and Lai (1997), Adcock and Shutes (2000), Christie-David and Chaudhry (2001) and Berényi (2001, 2002 and 2004).

expected return on two specific portfolios (Adcock and Shutes, 2000; Adcock, 2003; Athayde and Flôres, 1997 and 2000). Nevertheless, an explicit characterisation of return densities – or a link between moments – is necessary in order to identify the moment preferences of investors and, consequently, to determine the sign of the risk premia. When focusing on pricing asset relations, these problems can be encompassed, but a two-fund monetary separation theorem is required, entailing restrictive HARA-type preferences and the existence of a riskless asset (Rubinstein, 1973; Kraus and Litzenberger, 1976).

This work benefits from the advantages of all these approaches with very slight distributional hypotheses.[7] Assuming quartic objective functions and adopting a simple vectorial representation of the portfolio skewness and *kurtosis*, we generalise the security market line into a market hyperplane and identify three systematic risk premia independently of the investors' utility specifications. The risk *premium* on any financial asset is, at equilibrium, a linear function of the expected rate of return on four distinct portfolios: the market portfolio, the riskless asset and two orthogonal portfolios.[8] We also study the general properties of the mean–variance–skewness–*kurtosis* efficient frontier with N risky assets. These lead us to extend the four-moment CAPM relation in the absence of a riskless asset, and to make the link between the four-moment CAPM, Black's CAPM (1972), the cubic market model and the APT model of Ross (1976).

This chapter is organised as follows. In Section 6.2 we describe the equilibrium relation in a uniperiodic framework. Using a two-fund monetary separation theorem, we develop an exact four-moment capital asset pricing relation. In Section 6.3 we study the properties of the mean–variance–skewness–*kurtosis* efficient set and generalise the fundamental four-moment CAPM relation when there is no riskless asset traded in the market. Section 6.4 presents the links between the four-moment CAPM and other multifactor models – such as Black's model (1972), the three-moment CAPM of Kraus and Litzenberger (1976), the APT model[9] of Ross (1976) or the cubic market model. Section 6.5 concludes. Proofs of the theorems appear in the appendices.

6.2   THE FOUR-MOMENT CAPITAL ASSET PRICING MODEL

After recalling the main hypotheses of the model, we present the equilibrium relation, using a two-fund monetary separation theorem, following the approach of Rubinstein (1973), Ingersoll (1975) and Graddy and Homaifar (1988). This equilibrium relation is the four-moment CAPM fundamental relation.

6.2.1   Notations and hypotheses

The following hypotheses are assumed. There are N risky assets (with $N \geq 4$) and one riskless asset. The capital market is supposed to be perfect and competitive with no tax. All investors have a von Neumann–Morgenstern utility function, $U_k(.)$, with

---

[7] Our approach required at least the existence of the first four moments and to restrict the range of the portfolio return realisations to the domain of uniform convergence of the investors' utility functions (see Chapter 1 and *infra*).
[8] The first one is characterised by a zero covariance, relative unitary coskewness and zero *cokurtosis* with the market portfolio return; the second one by a zero covariance, zero coskewness and relative unitary *cokurtosis* with the market portfolio return.
[9] Arbitrage Pricing Theory model.

$k = [1, \ldots, K]$, which belongs to the class of utility functions, called D_4, relevant for the fourth-order stochastic dominance,[10] strictly increasing and concave with the gross rate of return of their investments. The K agents hold homogeneous probability beliefs about returns. Each investor is assumed to maximise her expected utility, which can be represented by an indirect utility function, denoted $V_k(.)$, respectively concave and increasing with expected portfolio return, concave and decreasing with variance, concave and increasing with skewness and concave and decreasing with *kurtosis* (see Chapter 1).[11] Asset returns are assumed, moreover, to be linearly independent and to possess finite *kurtosis*.

The expected utility function can then be written as:

$$E\left[U_k\left(R_p\right)\right] = V_k\left[E\left(R_p\right), \sigma^2\left(R_p\right), s^3\left(R_p\right), \kappa^4\left(R_p\right)\right] \tag{6.1}$$

with:

$$V_k^{(1)} = \frac{\partial V_k(.)}{\partial E\left(R_p\right)} > 0, \; V_k^{(2)} = \frac{\partial V_k(.)}{\partial \sigma^2\left(R_p\right)} < 0, \; V_k^{(3)} = \frac{\partial V_k(.)}{\partial s^3\left(R_p\right)} > 0 \text{ and } V_k^{(4)} = \frac{\partial V_k(.)}{\partial \kappa^4\left(R_p\right)} < 0$$

where $R_p = W_F/W_0$ is the gross rate of return of the portfolio held by investor k, with $k \in [1, \ldots, K]$, and W_0 and W_F are the initial and the final wealth of the agent.

Consider an agent investing w_{p_i} of his wealth in the ith risky asset, $i = [1, \ldots, N]$, and w_{p_0} in the riskless asset. The mean, variance, skewness and *kurtosis* of the portfolio return are respectively given by:

$$\begin{cases} E\left(R_p\right) = w_{p_0} R_f + E\left[\sum_{i=1}^{N} w_{pi} R_i\right] \\ \sigma^2\left(R_p\right) = E\left\{\left[R_p - E\left(R_p\right)\right]^2\right\} \\ s^3\left(R_p\right) = E\left\{\left[R_p - E\left(R_p\right)\right]^3\right\} \\ \kappa^4\left(R_p\right) = E\left\{\left[R_p - E\left(R_p\right)\right]^4\right\} \end{cases} \tag{6.2}$$

with:

$$\begin{cases} R_p = w_{p_0} R_f + \sum_{i=1}^{N} w_{pi} R_i \\ \sum_{i=1}^{N} w_{pi} = \left(1 - w_{p_0}\right) \end{cases}$$

where R_i represents the gross rate of return on the risky asset i and R_f is the riskless asset, with $i = [1, \ldots, N]$.

---

[10] Utility functions of class D_4 satisfy the following property (Vinod, 2004):

$$(-1)^i U_k^{(i)}(R) < 0$$

where $U_k^{(i)}(.)$ is the derivative of order i of $U_k(.)$, with $(i \times k) = [1, \ldots, 4] \times [1, \ldots K]$.
[11] Whilst, in general, skewness and *kurtosis* correspond to the standardised third and fourth centred moments, they are used here as the third and fourth centred moments.

Developing terms in (6.2) and using the linear property of the expectation operator, we have:

$$
\begin{cases}
E\left(R_p\right) = w_{p_0} R_f + \sum_{i=1}^{N} w_{pi} E\left(R_i\right) \\[4pt]
\sigma^2\left(R_p\right) = \sum_{i=1}^{N} w_{pi}^2 \sigma_{ii} + \sum_{i=1}^{N}\sum_{j=1,j\neq i}^{N} w_{pi} w_{pj} \sigma_{ij} \\[4pt]
s^3\left(R_p\right) = \sum_{i=1}^{N} w_{pi}^3 s_{iii} + 3\sum_{i=1}^{N}\sum_{j=1,j\neq i}^{N} w_{pi} w_{pj}^2 s_{ijj} \\[4pt]
\qquad + \sum_{i=1}^{N}\sum_{j=1,j\neq i}^{N}\sum_{k=1,k\neq i,k\neq j}^{N} w_{pi} w_{pj} w_{pk} s_{ijk} \\[4pt]
\kappa^4\left(R_p\right) = \sum_{i=1}^{N} w_{pi}^4 \kappa_{iiii} + 4\sum_{i=1}^{N}\sum_{j=1,j\neq i}^{N} w_{pi} w_{pj}^3 \kappa_{ijjj} + 3\sum_{i=1}^{N}\sum_{j=1,j\neq i}^{N} w_{pi}^2 w_{pj}^2 \kappa_{iijj} \\[4pt]
\qquad + 6\sum_{i=1}^{N}\sum_{j=1,j\neq i}^{N}\sum_{k=1,k\neq i,k\neq j}^{N} w_{pi} w_{pj} w_{pk}^2 \kappa_{ijkk} \\[4pt]
\qquad + \sum_{i=1}^{N}\sum_{j=1,j\neq i}^{N}\sum_{k=1,k\neq i,k\neq j}^{N}\sum_{l=1,l\neq i,l\neq j,l\neq k}^{N} w_{pi} w_{pj} w_{pk} w_{pl} \kappa_{ijkl}
\end{cases}
\tag{6.3}
$$

with, $\forall (i, j, k, l) \in [1, \ldots, N]^4$:

$$
\begin{cases}
\sigma_{ij} = E\left\{[R_i - E\left(R_i\right)][R_j - E\left(R_j\right)]\right\} \\[4pt]
s_{ijk} = E\left\{[R_i - E\left(R_i\right)][R_j - E\left(R_j\right)][R_k - E\left(R_k\right)]\right\} \\[4pt]
\kappa_{ijkl} = E\left\{[R_i - E\left(R_i\right)][R_j - E\left(R_j\right)][R_k - E\left(R_k\right)][R_l - E\left(R_l\right)]\right\}
\end{cases}
$$

where $\left(\sigma_{ij}\right)_{i,j}$, $\left(s_{ijk}\right)_{i,j,k}$ and $\left(\kappa_{ijkl}\right)_{i,j,k,l}$ represent, respectively, the covariance between the returns of assets i and j, the coskewness between the returns of assets i, j and k and the *cokurtosis* between the returns of assets i, j, k and l, with $(i \times j \times k \times l) = (IN^*)^4$.

Following Diacogiannis (1994), this system can be written in vectorial notation, by using the bilinearity of the covariance operator, as:[12]

$$
\begin{cases}
E\left(R_p\right) = w_{p_0} R_f + \mathbf{w}_p' \, \mathbf{E} \\[4pt]
\sigma^2\left(R_p\right) = \mathbf{w}_p' \, \mathbf{\Omega} \, \mathbf{w}_p \\[4pt]
s^3\left(R_p\right) = \mathbf{w}_p' \, \mathbf{\Sigma}_p \\[4pt]
\kappa^4\left(R_p\right) = \mathbf{w}_p' \, \mathbf{\Gamma}_p
\end{cases}
\tag{6.4}
$$

with:

$$
\mathbf{w}_p' \mathbf{1} = \left(1 - w_{p_0}\right)
$$

where $\mathbf{w}_p'$ is the $(1 \times N)$ transposed vector of the investor's holdings of risky assets; $\mathbf{w}_p$ is the $(N \times 1)$ vector of the N risky assets in the portfolio p; $\mathbf{E}$ is the $(N \times 1)$ vector of the expected returns of risky assets; $\mathbf{\Omega}$ is the nonsingular $(N \times N)$ variance–covariance matrix of the N risky asset returns; $\mathbf{\Sigma}_p$ is the $(N \times 1)$ vector of coskewness between the asset

---

[12] See Diacogiannis (1994) for the vectorial notation of the skewness of the portfolio return, and Appendix A for a demonstration of the vectorial expression of the skewness and the *kurtosis*.

returns and the portfolio return; $\boldsymbol{\Gamma}_p$ is the $(N \times 1)$ vector of *cokurtosis* between the security returns and the portfolio return and $\mathbf{1}$ is the $(N \times 1)$ unitary vector.

That is, the skewness and the *kurtosis* of the portfolio return can be written, respectively, as a weighted average of the coskewness and the *cokurtosis* between the N risky asset returns and the portfolio return. Each component of the coskewness and the *cokurtosis* vectors between the security returns and the portfolio return, defined as:

$$\begin{cases} \mathrm{Cos}\,(R_i, R_p) = E\left\{[R_i - E\,(R_i)]\,[R_p - E\,(R_p)]^2\right\} \\ \\ \mathrm{Cok}\,(R_i, R_p) = E\left\{[R_i - E\,(R_i)]\,[R_p - E\,(R_p)]^3\right\} \end{cases} \tag{6.5}$$

with $i = [1, \ldots, N]$, can be interpreted as a measure of the covariance between the return of the asset i and the volatility and the skewness of the portfolio p, respectively. This means that an asset that exhibits a positive (negative) coskewness, and a negative (positive) *cokurtosis* with a portfolio, is an asset that tends to perform the best (worst) when the portfolio becomes more volatile and experiences significant losses. It will act as a skewness enhancer (reducer) and a *kurtosis* reducer (enhancer).

Alternatively, the first four moments of the portfolio return may be expressed by using tensor products as follows (Athayde and Flôres, 1997):[13]

$$\begin{cases} E\,(R_p) = w_{p_0} R_f + \mathbf{w}_p' \mathbf{E} \\ \sigma^2\,(R_p) = \mathbf{w}_p' \boldsymbol{\Omega}\, \mathbf{w}_p \\ s^3\,(R_p) = \mathbf{w}_p' \boldsymbol{\Sigma}\,(\mathbf{w}_p \otimes \mathbf{w}_p) \\ \kappa^4\,(R_p) = \mathbf{w}_p' \boldsymbol{\Gamma}\,(\mathbf{w}_p \otimes \mathbf{w}_p \otimes \mathbf{w}_p) \end{cases} \tag{6.6}$$

with:

$$\mathbf{w}_p' \mathbf{1} = (1 - w_{p_0})$$

where $\boldsymbol{\Sigma}$ represents the $(N \times N^2)$ skewness–coskewness matrix and $\boldsymbol{\Gamma}$ is the $(N \times N^3)$ *kurtosis–cokurtosis* matrix of the N risky asset returns, defined as

$$\begin{cases} \underset{(N \times N^2)}{\boldsymbol{\Sigma}} = (\boldsymbol{\Sigma}_1 \boldsymbol{\Sigma}_2 \cdots \boldsymbol{\Sigma}_N) \\ \\ \underset{(N \times N^3)}{\boldsymbol{\Gamma}} = (\boldsymbol{\Gamma}_{11} \boldsymbol{\Gamma}_{12} \cdots \boldsymbol{\Gamma}_{1N} \,|\, \boldsymbol{\Gamma}_{21} \boldsymbol{\Gamma}_{22} \cdots \boldsymbol{\Gamma}_{2N} \,|\ldots|\, \boldsymbol{\Gamma}_{N1} \boldsymbol{\Gamma}_{N2} \cdots \boldsymbol{\Gamma}_{NN}) \end{cases}$$

where $\boldsymbol{\Sigma}_k$ and $\boldsymbol{\Gamma}_{kl}$ are the $(N \times N)$ associated submatrices of $\boldsymbol{\Sigma}$ and $\boldsymbol{\Gamma}$ with elements $(s_{ijk})_{i,j=1,\ldots,N}$ and $(\kappa_{ijkl})_{i,j=1,\ldots,N}$ with $(k \times l) = (IN^*)^2$, and the sign $\otimes$ stands for the Kronecker product.[14]

---

[13] See also Athayde and Flôres, 2002, 2003, 2004 and Chapter 2 of this book.

[14] Let $\mathbf{A}$ be an $(n \times p)$ matrix and $\mathbf{B}$ an $(m \times q)$ matrix. The $(mn \times pq)$ matrix $\mathbf{A} \otimes \mathbf{B}$ is called the Kronecker product of $\mathbf{A}$ and $\mathbf{B}$:

$$\mathbf{A} \otimes \mathbf{B} = \begin{pmatrix} a_{11}\mathbf{B} & a_{12}\mathbf{B} & \cdots & a_{1N}\mathbf{B} \\ a_{21}\mathbf{B} & a_{22}\mathbf{B} & \cdots & a_{2N}\mathbf{B} \\ \vdots & \vdots & \ddots & \vdots \\ a_{N1}\mathbf{B} & a_{N2}\mathbf{B} & \cdots & a_{NN}\mathbf{B} \end{pmatrix}$$

These alternative notations are equivalent to the previous ones, with:

$$\begin{cases} \Sigma_p = \Sigma \left(\mathbf{w}_p \otimes \mathbf{w}_p \right) \\ \Gamma_p = \Gamma \left(\mathbf{w}_p \otimes \mathbf{w}_p \otimes \mathbf{w}_p \right) \end{cases} \qquad (6.7)$$

While the tensor-based approach (6.6) offers the advantage, for asset allocation, of expressing higher-order moments of the portfolio returns as explicit functions of the weight vector (Athayde and Flôres, 1997, 2002, 2003 and 2004; Jondeau and Rockinger, 2003b and 2006; Harvey et al., 2004), the vectorial notation in (6.4) will be preferable for the derivation of multi-moment asset pricing relations, since they require smaller-dimension vectors and are linked directly to the systematic risk measures of skewness and *kurtosis* (see below).

Introducing into the definition of the coskewness and the *cokurtosis* operators – denoted by $\mathrm{Cos}(R_i, R_p)$ and $\mathrm{Cok}(R_i, R_p)$ – the expressions of the variance and the skewness of the portfolio rate of return, we find:

$$\begin{cases} \Sigma_p = E\left[(\mathbf{R} - \mathbf{E}) \left\{ \left[R_p - E\left(R_p \right) \right]^2 - \sigma^2 \left(R_p \right) \right\} \mathbf{1} \right] \\ \Gamma_p = E\left[(\mathbf{R} - \mathbf{E}) \left\{ \left[R_p - E\left(R_p \right) \right]^3 - s^3 \left(R_p \right) \right\} \mathbf{1} \right] \end{cases} \qquad (6.8)$$

The coskewness and the *cokurtosis* between the rate of return on an asset i and the rate of return on a portfolio p give an indication of the asset's ability to protect an investor respectively against unexpected shocks on its portfolio variance and skewness (Racine, 1998).

6.2.2 Aggregation of the individual asset demands and a two-fund monetary separation theorem

In such a framework, the kth agent's portfolio problem can be stated as:

$$\underset{\mathbf{w}_p}{\mathrm{Max}} \left\{ E\left[U_k \left(R_p \right) \right] \right\} = \underset{\mathbf{w}_p}{\mathrm{Max}} \left\{ V_k \left[E\left(R_p \right), \sigma^2 \left(R_p \right), s^3 \left(R_p \right), \kappa^4 \left(R_p \right) \right] \right\} \qquad (6.9)$$

$$\text{s.t.} : \mathbf{w}_p' \mathbf{1} = \left(1 - w_{p_0} \right)$$

where $\mathbf{1}$ is the $(N \times 1)$ unit vector.

The first-order conditions for a *maximum* are:[15]

$$\frac{\partial V_k \left(. \right)}{\partial \mathbf{w}_p} = V_k^{(1)} \left(\mathbf{E} - R_f \mathbf{1} \right) + 2 V_k^{(2)} \Omega \mathbf{w}_p + 3 V_k^{(3)} \Sigma_p + 4 V_k^{(4)} \Gamma_p = \mathbf{0} \qquad (6.10)$$

where $V_k^{(1)}$ is the first derivative of the kth agent's indirect utility function with respect to the portfolio expected rate of return, $V_k^{(i)}$ is the first derivative of the kth investor's objective

---

[15] The first partial derivatives of the portfolio's skewness and *kurtosis* with respect to $\mathbf{w}_p$ are, respectively, equal to (see Appendix B):

$$\begin{cases} \dfrac{\partial s^3 \left(R_p \right)}{\partial \mathbf{w}_p} = 3 \Sigma_p \\[4mm] \dfrac{\partial \kappa^4 \left(R_p \right)}{\partial \mathbf{w}_p} = 4 \Gamma_p \end{cases}$$

function with respect to the ith centred moment of the portfolio return distribution, with $i = [2, 3, 4]$ and $k \in [1, \ldots, K]$; $\Omega \mathbf{w}_p$, Σ_p and Γ_p represent, respectively, the $(N \times 1)$ vectors of covariance, coskewness and *cokurtosis* between the N risky asset returns and the portfolio return.

The first derivatives of the expected utility function (6.10) constitute necessary and sufficient conditions for a *maximum*, since the Hessian matrix of the objective function of the investor is negative definite (see Appendix C).

In order to move from the individual equilibrium conditions to the market equilibrium, it is necessary to introduce a portfolio separation theorem. If agents' probability beliefs are identical, a necessary and sufficient condition to obtain a two-fund monetary separation is that all agents have a hyperbolic absolute risk-aversion utility (HARA) with the same "cautiousness" parameter (Cass and Stiglitz, 1970, pp. 145–147). In this case, the *optimum* risky portfolio's weights are the same as those of the market portfolio m. This condition implies, in the mean–variance–skewness–*kurtosis* case, that all agents must have quartic separable utility functions or hyperbolic decreasing absolute risk-aversion utility functions (see Chapter 1).

Summing demands across all individuals and invoking a two-fund monetary separation theorem, we obtain the following equilibrium relation:

$$\mathbf{E} - R_f \mathbf{1} = \left[-\frac{2V^{(2)}}{V^{(1)}} \right] \Omega \mathbf{w}_m + \left[-\frac{3V^{(3)}}{V^{(1)}} \right] \Sigma_m + \left[-\frac{4V^{(4)}}{V^{(1)}} \right] \Gamma_m \qquad (6.11)$$

with:

$$\mathbf{1}' \mathbf{w}_m = 1$$

where $V^{(1)}$ is the first derivative of the representative agent's indirect utility function with respect to the portfolio expected rate of return; $V^{(i)}$ is the first derivative of the representative investor's objective function with respect to the ith centred moment of the market portfolio return distribution, with $i = [2, 3, 4]$; $\mathbf{1}'$ is the $(1 \times N)$ transposed unitary vector; $\mathbf{w}_m$ is the $(N \times 1)$ vector of the market portfolio N risky asset weights; $\Omega \mathbf{w}_m$, Σ_m and Γ_m represent, respectively, the $(N \times 1)$ vectors of covariance, coskewness and *cokurtosis* between the risky asset returns and the market portfolio return.

When the market portfolio return distribution is asymmetric, rearranging terms in (6.11) yields the following theorem.

Theorem 1 *The four-moment CAPM relation can be written as:*

$$\mathbf{E} - R_f \mathbf{1} = b_1 \boldsymbol{\beta} + b_2 \boldsymbol{\gamma} + b_3 \boldsymbol{\delta} \qquad (6.12)$$

with (using previous notation):

$$\begin{cases} \boldsymbol{\beta} = \left[\sigma^2 (R_m) \right]^{-1} \Omega \mathbf{w}_m \\ \boldsymbol{\gamma} = \left[s^3 (R_m) \right]^{-1} \Sigma_m \\ \boldsymbol{\delta} = \left[\kappa^4 (R_m) \right]^{-1} \Gamma_m \end{cases}$$

and:

$$\begin{cases} b_1 = \theta_2 \sigma^2 (R_m) \\ b_2 = \theta_3 s^3 (R_m) \\ b_3 = \theta_4 \kappa^4 (R_m) \end{cases}$$

where $\theta_2 = -2V^{(2)}/V^{(1)}, \theta_3 = -3V^{(3)}/V^{(1)}$ *and* $\theta_4 = -4V^{(4)}/V^{(1)}$ *are, respectively, a measure of the representative agent's aversion to variance, a measure of his preference for (positive) skewness and a measure of the representative investor's aversion to kurtosis;* $\sigma^2 (R_m) \neq 0, s^3 (R_m) \neq 0, \kappa^4 (R_m) \neq 0$ *and* $\mathbf{w}_m$ *are, respectively, the variance, skewness, kurtosis and the* $(N \times 1)$ *vector of the weights of the market portfolio;* $\boldsymbol{\beta}, \boldsymbol{\gamma}, \boldsymbol{\delta}$ *are, respectively, the* $(N \times 1)$ *relative covariance vector, the* $(N \times 1)$ *relative coskewness vector and the* $(N \times 1)$ *relative cokurtosis vector of specific returns with the market portfolio return.*

Proof   *See previous discussion.*

Thus, for all securities $i, i = [1, \ldots, N]$:

$$E(R_i) - R_f = b_1 \beta_i + b_2 \gamma_i + b_3 \delta_i \tag{6.13}$$

where:

$$\begin{cases} \beta_i = \dfrac{\mathrm{Cov}(R_i, R_m)}{\sigma^2 (R_m)} \\[2mm] \gamma_i = \dfrac{\mathrm{Cos}(R_i, R_m)}{s^3 (R_m)} \\[2mm] \delta_i = \dfrac{\mathrm{Cok}(R_i, R_m)}{\kappa^4 (R_m)} \end{cases}$$

are, respectively, the ith entries, with $i = [1, \ldots, N]$, of the $(N \times 1)$ vectors $\boldsymbol{\beta}, \boldsymbol{\gamma}$ and $\boldsymbol{\delta}$.

The equation (6.12) is equivalent to the one obtained by Graddy and Homaifar (1988). This relation is also similar to the four-moment pricing relation developed by Athayde and Flôres (1997 and 2000), Hwang and Satchell (1999), Christie-David and Chaudhry (2001) and Berényi (2001, 2002 and 2004).[16] The only differences relate to the definition and the theoretical justification of coefficients b_1, b_2 and b_3 (see below), since these authors have considered an indirect utility function that does not depend on the first four centred moments, but upon the mean, the standard deviation, the cube root of the skewness and the quartic root of the *kurtosis*.

At equilibrium, the expected excess return on any security i, with $i = [1, \ldots, N]$, is then a linear function[17] of the parameters β_i, γ_i and δ_i. These parameters yield, respectively,

---

[16] This relation is similar to the one developed by Ingersoll (1975) in the context of an nth order Taylor series expansion. However, Ingersoll (1975) did not determine the sign of the moment preference ordering and the conditions of the aggregation of the individual demands.

[17] If the market portfolio return distribution is not asymmetric, the four-moment CAPM relation (6.12) becomes:

$$\mathbf{E} - R_f \mathbf{1} = \theta_2 \boldsymbol{\Omega} \mathbf{w}_m + \theta_3 \boldsymbol{\Sigma}_m + \theta_4 \boldsymbol{\Gamma}_m$$

where θ_2, θ_3 and θ_4 are defined as previously; $\boldsymbol{\Omega} \mathbf{w}_m, \boldsymbol{\Sigma}_m$ and $\boldsymbol{\Gamma}_m$ are the $(N \times 1)$ covariance vector, the $(N \times 1)$ coskewness vector and the $(N \times 1)$ *cokurtosis* vector of specific returns with the market portfolio return.

measures of marginal contribution of an asset i to the variance of the market portfolio return, the skewness of the market portfolio return and the *kurtosis* of the market portfolio return. The coefficients b_1, b_2 and b_3 can be interpreted as systematic risk market premia. Since investors are assumed to have preferences relevant for the fourth-order stochastic dominance, this implies that b_1 is strictly positive (since θ_2 is positive), b_2 has the opposite sign of $s^3(R_m)$ (since θ_3 is negative) and b_3 is strictly positive (since θ_4 is positive). Investors are thus compensated at equilibrium in terms of expected excess return for bearing the systematic risks linked to the coefficients $\boldsymbol{\beta}, \boldsymbol{\gamma}$ and $\boldsymbol{\delta}$.

When the utility function of the agent is independent of the *kurtosis* (i.e. $b_3 = 0$), Equation (6.12) is reduced to the three-moment CAPM relation developed initially by Kraus and Litzenberger (1976); that is (see Jurczenko and Maillet, 2001):

$$\mathbf{E} - R_f\mathbf{1} = b_1\boldsymbol{\beta} + b_2\boldsymbol{\gamma} \tag{6.14}$$

If the investor is also indifferent to the skewness (i.e. $b_2 = 0$ and $b_3 = 0$), Equation (6.12) collapses to the traditional CAPM relation:

$$\mathbf{E} - R_f\mathbf{1} = b_1\boldsymbol{\beta} \tag{6.15}$$

Following Hwang and Satchell (1999), one can give a theoretical implication for the four-moment CAPM, leading to an alternative interpretation of the coefficients b_1, b_2 and b_3. Since the four-moment CAPM relation is valid for all security returns, it is naturally verified by the market portfolio return; that is:

$$[E(R_m) - R_f] = (b_1 + b_2 + b_3) \tag{6.16}$$

with $\beta_{im} = 1$, $\gamma_{im} = 1$ and $\delta_{im} = 1$, where $E(R_m)$ is the expected gross rate of return on the market portfolio.

Dividing Equation (6.16) by Equation (6.12) yields the following corollary.

Corollary 1   *The four-moment CAPM relation can also be written as:*[18]

$$\mathbf{E} - R_f\mathbf{1} = (\alpha_1\boldsymbol{\beta} + \alpha_2\boldsymbol{\gamma} + \alpha_3\boldsymbol{\delta})[E(R_m) - R_f] \tag{6.17}$$

with:

$$\begin{cases} \boldsymbol{\beta} = [\sigma^2(R_m)]^{-1}\boldsymbol{\Omega}\mathbf{w}_m \\ \boldsymbol{\gamma} = [s^3(R_m)]^{-1}\boldsymbol{\Sigma}_m \\ \boldsymbol{\delta} = [\kappa^4(R_m)]^{-1}\boldsymbol{\Gamma}_m \end{cases}$$

---

[18] This equation is similar to Equation (6.13) in Hwang and Satchell (1999). The only difference is in the definition and the theoretical justification of the parameters α_1, α_2 and α_3 (see above). See also Sears and Wei (1985 and 1988) for a similar formulation in the three-moment case.

and:

$$
\begin{cases}
\alpha_1 = \dfrac{2}{2+3\eta_1+4\eta_2} \\[2ex]
\alpha_2 = \dfrac{3\eta_1}{2+3\eta_1+4\eta_2} \\[2ex]
\alpha_3 = \dfrac{4\eta_2}{2+3\eta_1+4\eta_2} \\[2ex]
\eta_1 = \dfrac{2}{3} \times \dfrac{b_2}{b_1} \\[2ex]
\eta_2 = \dfrac{1}{2} \times \dfrac{b_3}{b_1}
\end{cases}
$$

where b_1, b_2 and b_3 are defined as in (6.12); $\sigma^2(R_m)\neq 0$, $s^3(R_m)\neq 0$ and $\kappa^4(R_m)\neq 0$; and Ωw_m, Σ_m and Γ_m correspond, respectively, to the $(N\times 1)$ vectors of covariance, coskewness and cokurtosis between the risky asset returns and the market portfolio return.

Proof   *See previous discussion.*

Thus, for all securities i, $i=[1,\dots,N]$:

$$
E(R_i) - R_f = [\alpha_1\beta_i + \alpha_2\gamma_i + \alpha_3\delta_i]\,[E(R_m) - R_f] \tag{6.18}
$$

This equation is equivalent to the previous equilibrium relation (6.12) if we recall that, for $j=[1,2,3]$:

$$
b_j = \alpha_j\,[E(R_m) - R_f] \tag{6.19}
$$

Rearranging terms, the four-moment CAPM relation depends only on two parameters η_1 and η_2. Formally, we have:

$$
\mathbf{E} - R_f\mathbf{1} = \left(\frac{1}{2+3\eta_1+4\eta_2}\right)(2\boldsymbol{\beta} + 3\eta_1\boldsymbol{\gamma} + 4\eta_2\boldsymbol{\delta})\,[E(R_m) - R_f] \tag{6.20}
$$

with:

$$
\begin{cases}
\eta_1 = \dfrac{\partial E(R_m)}{\partial s^3(R_m)} \times \left[\dfrac{\partial E(R_m)}{\partial \sigma^2(R_m)}\right]^{-1} \times \dfrac{s^3(R_m)}{\sigma^2(R_m)} \\[3ex]
\eta_2 = \dfrac{\partial E(R_m)}{\partial \kappa^4(R_m)} \times \left[\dfrac{\partial E(R_m)}{\partial \sigma^2(R_m)}\right]^{-1} \times \dfrac{\kappa^4(R_m)}{\sigma^2(R_m)}
\end{cases}
$$

where $\boldsymbol{\beta}$, $\boldsymbol{\gamma}$ and $\boldsymbol{\delta}$ represent, respectively the $(N\times 1)$ relative covariance vector, the $(N\times 1)$ relative coskewness vector and the $(N\times 1)$ relative cokurtosis vector of specific returns with the market portfolio return, with $\sigma^2(R_m)\neq 0$, $s^3(R_m)\neq 0$ and $\kappa^4(R_m)\neq 0$. ·

The coefficients b_1, b_2 and b_3 depend on three elements: the market risk premium $[E(R_m) - R_f]$ and two parameters η_1 and η_2. The last two correspond to elasticities of substitution between the skewness, the *kurtosis* and the variance of the market portfolio return. Since rational investors prefer positive skewness and dislike variance and *kurtosis*, the sign of the parameter η_1, measuring the ratio of b_2 to b_1, must be the opposite of the sign of the market portfolio return skewness. The sign of the parameter η_2, measuring the ratio of b_3 to b_1, must be positive. The coefficients b_2 and b_3, and the parameters η_1 and η_2, constitute two complementary measures of the agent's preference for skewness and *kurtosis*. The coefficients b_2 and b_3 depend on the sign and the size of the market risk premium. Up to a constant, they represent, respectively, the marginal rates of substitution between the skewness and the expected return of the market portfolio (since b_2 depends on θ_3) and between the *kurtosis* and the expected return of the market portfolio (since b_3 depends on θ_4). On the contrary, the parameters η_1 and η_2 are independent of market fluctuations. They highlight the relation between, respectively, the third and second, and the fourth and second centred moments of the market's portfolio return.

In the traditional CAPM framework, the coefficient b_1 corresponds to the market portfolio risk premium, whatever the elementary utility function chosen.[19] In the four-moment CAPM case,[20] using a third and a fourth portfolio in addition to the riskless asset and the market portfolio becomes necessary for identifying the coefficients b_1, b_2 and b_3 independently of the shape of the utility function considered. The following subsection is devoted to the definition of these two additional portfolios. With these portfolios, it is possible to establish the canonical four-moment CAPM relation. Its representation generalises the capital market and the security market lines in the spaces defined respectively by the quadruplets $[E(R_p), \sigma(R_p), s(R_p), \kappa(R_p)]$ and $[E(R_i), \beta_i, \gamma_i, \delta_i]$.[21]

6.2.3 The four-moment CAPM fundamental relation and the security market hyperplane

To obtain the four-moment CAPM fundamental relation, we need to introduce, besides the riskless asset and the market portfolio, two additional specific portfolios, denoted respectively Z_{m1} and Z_{m2}, whose returns have a zero covariance with the market portfolio return.[22]

Following Athayde and Flôres (1997 and 2000) and Berényi (2001, 2002 and 2004), we can identify – as in the traditional CAPM framework – the coefficients b_2 and b_3 independently of the agent preferences by premultiplying Equation (6.12) by the $(N \times 1)$ vectors $\mathbf{w}'_{Z_{m1}}$ and

---

[19] As defined by von Neumann and Morgenstern (2004). Amongst these functions, we consider only the utility functions of the hyperbolic absolute risk-aversion class.

[20] Unless using a logarithmic utility function; see, for example, Hwang and Satchell (1999).

[21] Where:

$$\begin{cases} \sigma(R_p) = \sqrt{\sigma^2(R_p)} \\ s(R_p) = \sqrt[3]{s^3(R_p)} \\ \kappa(R_p) = \sqrt[4]{\kappa^4(R_p)} \end{cases}$$

[22] We suppose that there exist at least two portfolios with the following statistical characteristics (see below).

$\mathbf{w}'_{Z_{m2}}$ that characterise the transpose weight vectors of the uncorrelated portfolios Z_{m1} and Z_{m2}. We get:[23]

$$\begin{cases} b_2 = \left[\dfrac{E\left(R_{Z_{m1}}\right) - R_f}{\gamma_{Z_{m1}}} \right] \\[4mm] b_3 = \left[\dfrac{E\left(R_{Z_{m2}}\right) - R_f}{\delta_{Z_{m2}}} \right] \end{cases} \tag{6.21}$$

where $E\left(R_{Z_{m1}}\right)$ is the expected return of a portfolio Z_{m1}, whose return is uncorrelated with that of the market portfolio and which possesses a zero *cokurtosis* with the market return, i.e.:

$$\begin{cases} \beta_{Z_{m1}} = \dfrac{\mathrm{Cov}\left(R_{Z_{m1}}, R_m\right)}{\sigma^2\left(R_m\right)} = 0 \\[4mm] \gamma_{Z_{m1}} = \dfrac{\mathrm{Cos}\left(R_{Z_{m1}}, R_m\right)}{s^3\left(R_m\right)} \\[4mm] \delta_{Z_{m1}} = \dfrac{\mathrm{Cok}\left(R_{Z_{m1}}, R_m\right)}{\kappa^4\left(R_m\right)} = 0 \end{cases}$$

and $E\left(R_{Z_{m2}}\right)$ is the expected return of a portfolio Z_{m2}, whose return is uncorrelated with the market portfolio and which possesses a zero coskewness with the market return, i.e.:

$$\begin{cases} \beta_{Z_{m2}} = \dfrac{\mathrm{Cov}\left(R_{Z_{m2}}, R_m\right)}{\sigma^2\left(R_m\right)} = 0 \\[4mm] \gamma_{Z_{m2}} = \dfrac{\mathrm{Cos}\left(R_{Z_{m2}}, R_m\right)}{s^3\left(R_m\right)} = 0 \\[4mm] \delta_{Z_{m2}} = \dfrac{\mathrm{Cok}\left(R_{Z_{m2}}, R_m\right)}{\kappa^4\left(R_m\right)} \end{cases}$$

with $\sigma^2\left(R_m\right) \neq 0$, $s^3\left(R_m\right) \neq 0$ and $\kappa^4\left(R_m\right) \neq 0$.

Combining this result with Equation (6.16), we get the following expression for b_1:

$$b_1 = \left[E\left(R_m\right) - R_f\right] - b_2 - b_3 \tag{6.22}$$

The equilibrium equation (6.12) then becomes:

$$\mathbf{E} - R_f \mathbf{1} = \left\{ \left[E\left(R_m\right) - R_f\right] - \left[\frac{E\left(R_{Z_{m1}}\right) - R_f}{\gamma_{Z_{m1}}} \right] - \left[\frac{E\left(R_{Z_{m2}}\right) - R_f}{\delta_{Z_{m2}}} \right] \right\} \boldsymbol{\beta}$$

$$+ \left[\frac{E\left(R_{Z_{m1}}\right) - R_f}{\gamma_{Z_{m1}}} \right] \boldsymbol{\gamma} + \left[\frac{E\left(R_{Z_{m2}}\right) - R_f}{\delta_{Z_{m2}}} \right] \boldsymbol{\delta} \tag{6.23}$$

---

[23] For a similar approach in the mean–variance–skewness framework, see Litzenberger *et al.* (1980), Ingersoll (1987), Simaan (1993), Gamba and Rossi (1997, 1998a and 1998b) and Jurczenko and Maillet (2001).

with:

$$\begin{cases} \boldsymbol{\beta} = \left[\sigma^2\left(R_m\right)\right]^{-1} \boldsymbol{\Omega}\mathbf{w}_m \\ \boldsymbol{\gamma} = \left[s^3\left(R_m\right)\right]^{-1} \boldsymbol{\Sigma}_m \\ \boldsymbol{\delta} = \left[\kappa^4\left(R_m\right)\right]^{-1} \boldsymbol{\Gamma}_m \end{cases}$$

where $\gamma_{Z_{m1}} = \mathrm{Cos}\left(R_{Z_{m1}}, R_m\right)/s^3\left(R_m\right)$ and $\delta_{Z_{m2}} = \mathrm{Cok}\left(R_{Z_{m2}}, R_m\right)/\kappa^4\left(R_m\right)$; $\boldsymbol{\beta}$, $\boldsymbol{\gamma}$, $\boldsymbol{\delta}$ are, respectively, the $(N \times 1)$ relative covariance vector, the $(N \times 1)$ relative coskewness vector and the $(N \times 1)$ relative *cokurtosis* vector of specific returns with the market portfolio return; $\boldsymbol{\Omega}\mathbf{w}_m$, $\boldsymbol{\Sigma}_m$ and $\boldsymbol{\Gamma}_m$ correspond to the vectors of covariance, coskewness and *cokurtosis* between the risky asset returns and the market portfolio return; $\sigma^2\left(R_m\right) \neq 0$, $s^3\left(R_m\right) \neq 0$ and $\kappa^4\left(R_m\right) \neq 0$.

If, following Athayde and Flôres (1997 and 2000) and Berényi (2001, 2002 and 2004), we moreover suppose that it is possible to find – in a large set of feasible portfolios – two portfolios Z_{m1} and Z_{m2} whose relative coskewness and *cokurtosis* with the market portfolio are unitary, i.e. $\gamma_{Z_{m1}} = 1$ and $\delta_{Z_{m2}} = 1$, the relation (6.23) can be simplified as follows:

$$\mathbf{E} - R_f\mathbf{1} = \left\{\left[E\left(R_m\right) - E\left(R_{Z_{m1}}\right)\right] - \left[E\left(R_{Z_{m2}}\right) - R_f\right]\right\} \boldsymbol{\beta} + \left[E\left(R_{Z_{m1}}\right) - R_f\right] \boldsymbol{\gamma} \qquad (6.24)$$
$$+ \left[E\left(R_{Z_{m2}}\right) - R_f\right] \boldsymbol{\delta}$$

These relations lead to the following theorem.

Theorem 2 *When a riskless asset exists, the risk premium of an asset is given by the equation:*

$$\mathbf{E} - R_f\mathbf{1} = \left[E\left(R_m\right) - R_f\right] \boldsymbol{\beta} + \left[E\left(R_{Z_{m1}}\right) - R_f\right]\left(\boldsymbol{\gamma} - \boldsymbol{\beta}\right) \qquad (6.25)$$
$$+ \left[E\left(R_{Z_{m2}}\right) - R_f\right]\left(\boldsymbol{\delta} - \boldsymbol{\beta}\right)$$

with (using previous notation):

$$\begin{cases} \boldsymbol{\beta} = \left[\sigma^2\left(R_m\right)\right]^{-1} \boldsymbol{\Omega}\,\mathbf{w}_m \\ \boldsymbol{\gamma} = \left[s^3\left(R_m\right)\right]^{-1} \boldsymbol{\Sigma}_m \\ \boldsymbol{\delta} = \left[\kappa^4\left(R_m\right)\right]^{-1} \boldsymbol{\Gamma}_m \end{cases}$$

where $E\left(R_{Z_{m1}}\right)$ is the expected rate of return on the portfolio Z_{m1} with zero covariance with the market portfolio, unitary relative coskewness and zero relative cokurtosis (i.e. $\beta_{Z_{m1}} = \delta_{Z_{m1}}, \delta_{Z_{m1}} = 0$ and $\gamma_{Z_{m1}} = 1$); $E\left(R_{Z_{m2}}\right)$ is the expected return of the portfolio Z_{m2} with a zero covariance with the market portfolio, a zero relative coskewness and a unitary relative cokurtosis (i.e. $\beta_{Z_{m2}} = \gamma_{Z_{m2}}, \gamma_{Z_{m2}} = 0$ and $\delta_{Z_{m2}} = 1$); $\boldsymbol{\beta}, \boldsymbol{\gamma}, \boldsymbol{\delta}$ are, respectively, the $(N \times 1)$ relative covariance vector, the $(N \times 1)$ relative coskewness vector and the $(N \times 1)$ relative cokurtosis vector of specific returns with the market portfolio return; $\sigma^2\left(R_m\right) \neq 0$, $s^3\left(R_m\right) \neq 0$ and $\kappa^4\left(R_m\right) \neq 0$.

Proof   *See previous discussion.*

The relation is thus, for any security i, $i = [1, \ldots, N]$:

$$E(R_i) - R_f = [E(R_m) - R_f]\beta_i + [E(R_{Z_{m1}}) - R_f](\gamma_i - \beta_i) \qquad (6.26)$$
$$+ [E(R_{Z_{m2}}) - R_f](\delta_i - \beta_i)$$

where:

$$\begin{cases} \beta_i = \dfrac{\text{Cov}(R_i, R_m)}{\sigma^2(R_m)} \\[2mm] \gamma_i = \dfrac{\text{Cos}(R_i, R_m)}{s^3(R_m)} \\[2mm] \delta_i = \dfrac{\text{Cok}(R_i, R_m)}{\kappa^4(R_m)} \end{cases}$$

are, respectively, the ith entries, with $i = [1, \ldots, N]$, of the $(N \times 1)$ vectors $\boldsymbol{\beta}$, $\boldsymbol{\gamma}$ and $\boldsymbol{\delta}$.

This relation differs from those of Athayde and Flôres (1997 and 2000) and Berényi (2001, 2002 and 2004) since we use an objective function that depends explicitly on the first four moments of portfolio returns and not on the nth roots of their moments.

Nevertheless, the validity of (6.25) depends crucially on the existence and uniqueness of two uncorrelated portfolios Z_{m1} and Z_{m2}. When this condition is fulfilled (see Appendix D), we note that, without imposing any supplementary assumptions about return distributions, it is possible to sign – on *a priori* grounds – the risk market premia associated with the market variance, the skewness and the *kurtosis*; that is:

$$\begin{cases} [E(R_m) - E(R_{Z_{m1}})] - [E(R_{Z_{m2}}) - R_f] > 0 \\[2mm] \text{sign}\,[E(R_{Z_{m1}}) - R_f] = -\text{sign}\,[s^3(R_m)] \\[2mm] [E(R_{Z_{m2}}) - R_f] > 0 \end{cases} \qquad (6.27)$$

Such a result might not be obtainable under more general assumptions concerning investors' preferences, due to the absence of orthogonality between higher moments (see, for instance, Adcock, 2003).

Under this form, the four-moment CAPM is a direct generalisation of the Sharpe–Lintner–Mossin model.[24] It differs from the mean–variance model by the term:

$$[E(R_{Z_{m1}}) - R_f](\gamma_i - \beta_i) + [E(R_{Z_{m2}}) - R_f](\delta_i - \beta_i) \qquad (6.28)$$

If this term is positive, the traditional CAPM relation underestimates the risk premium, which confirms Kraus and Litzenberger's intuition[25] that taking into account higher-order centred moments than the first two might explain some of the CAPM anomalies.

---

[24] In order to take into account the leptokurtic characteristic of asset return distributions, Rachev and Mittnik (2000) propose a generalisation of the Sharpe–Lintner CAPM under the hypothesis of a symmetric joint stable return distribution.
[25] See Kraus and Litzenberger (1976), pp. 1085–1086.

If, for some equities i, $\gamma_i = 0$ and $\delta_i = 0$ (i.e. the coskewness and the *cokurtosis* of asset i's return with that of the market portfolio m are null), with $i = [1, \ldots, N]$, Equation (6.25) differs from the two-moment CAPM, since the risk premia $[E(R_{Z_{m1}}) - R_f]$ and $[E(R_{Z_{m2}}) - R_f]$ are, by definition, non-null. This happens because skewness and *kurtosis* are valued by economic agents.

The four-moment CAPM collapses to the Sharpe–Lintner–Mossin model under skewed and leptokurtic return distributions if and only if: 1) $[E(R_{Z_{m1}}) - R_f] = 0$ and $[E(R_{Z_{m2}}) - R_f] = 0$ or 2) if $\gamma_i = \beta_i$ and $\delta_i = \beta_i$, with $i = [1, \ldots, N]$. The first condition is met when all the agents are indifferent to non-null (positive) return skewness and *kurtosis*. The second one is satisfied for securities i whose sensitivities to the variance, skewness and *kurtosis* of the market portfolio return are equal. Thus, the prices of a subset of assets – those for which $\gamma_i = \beta_i$ and $\delta_i = \beta_i$ – may be evaluated correctly by the CAPM, even if this relation does not hold for all assets.

From (6.26), we can represent the four-moment CAPM relation in the space $[E(R_i), \beta_i, \gamma_i, \delta_i]$. When the four-moment CAPM relation is satisfied, all the expected asset returns must theoretically lie on a hyperplane of dimension three. This plane corresponds to a "security market hyperplane" and is defined in IR^4 by the following vectors: $(E(R_m), 1, 1, 1)$, $(E(R_{Z_{m1}}), 0, 1, 0)$, $(E(R_{Z_{m2}}), 0, 0, 1)$ and $(R_f, 0, 0, 0)$.

The *optimal* portfolios set can be equally represented in the space $[E(R_p), \sigma(R_p), s(R_p), \kappa(R_p)]$ by a generalised "capital market line", defined by the characteristics of the riskless asset, a zero-beta unitary-gamma zero-delta portfolio, a zero-beta zero-gamma unitary-delta portfolio and those of the market portfolio. Using the definitions of the covariance, coskewness and *cokurtosis* operators, $\mathrm{Cov}(.)$, $\mathrm{Cos}(.)$ and $\mathrm{Cok}(.)$, the four-moment CAPM relation can be written, for any portfolio p, as:

$$E(R_p) - R_f = \{[E(R_m) - E(R_{Z_{m1}})] - [E(R_{Z_{m2}}) - R_f]\} \frac{\sigma(R_p)}{\sigma(R_m)} \rho_{p,m} \qquad (6.29)$$

$$+ [E(R_{Z_{m1}}) - R_f] \frac{s(R_p)}{s(R_m)} s_{p,m} + [E(R_{Z_{m2}}) - R_f] \frac{\kappa(R_p)}{\kappa(R_m)} \zeta_{p,m}$$

where $\sigma(R_p)$, $s(R_p)$ and $\kappa(R_p)$ are, respectively, the standard deviation, the cube root of the skewness and the quartic root of the *kurtosis* of portfolio p's return; $\rho_{p,m}$, $s_{p,m}$ and $\zeta_{p,m}$ are respectively, the coefficients of correlation, coskewness and *cokurtosis* between the portfolio p's return and the market portfolio return, that is:

$$\begin{cases} \rho_{p,m} = \dfrac{\mathrm{Cov}(R_p, R_m)}{\sigma(R_p)\,\sigma(R_m)} \\[4mm] s_{p,m} = \dfrac{\mathrm{Cos}(R_p, R_m)}{s(R_p)\,s^2(R_m)} \\[4mm] \zeta_{p,m} = \dfrac{\mathrm{Cok}(R_p, R_m)}{\kappa(R_p)\,\kappa^3(R_m)} \end{cases}$$

Using a two-fund monetary separation theorem (see Section 6.2.2), we deduce that the expected return of any *optimal* portfolio p must, at equilibrium, satisfy the following relation:

$$E(R_p) - R_f = \left\{ \left[E(R_m) - E(R_{Z_{m1}}) \right] - \left[E(R_{Z_{m2}}) - R_f \right] \right\} \frac{\sigma(R_p)}{\sigma(R_m)} \qquad (6.30)$$

$$+ \left[E(R_{Z_{m1}}) - R_f \right] \frac{s(R_p)}{s(R_m)} + \left[E(R_{Z_{m2}}) - R_f \right] \frac{\kappa(R_p)}{\kappa(R_m)}$$

with:

$$\begin{cases} \sigma(R_p) = w_{pm} \sigma(R_m) \\ s(R_p) = w_{pm} s(R_m) \\ \kappa(R_p) = w_{pm} \kappa(R_m) \end{cases}$$

where w_{pm}, with $0 \le w_{pm} \le 1$, is the proportion of the agent's wealth invested in the market portfolio. The optimal portfolio set can thus be represented in the space $[E(R_p), \sigma(R_p), s(R_p), \kappa(R_p)]$ by a line that we call the generalised "capital market line".

A linear relation between the expected rate of return on any risky asset i and the expected excess return on the market portfolio and the expected excess return on a zero-beta portfolio is highlighted in Black's model (1972). But here, we consider a financial market with a riskless asset and two uncorrelated risky portfolios with the market portfolio, Z_{m1} and Z_{m2}, whose returns are multiplied, respectively, by the specific asset constants $(\gamma_i - \beta_i)$ and $(\delta_i - \beta_i)$. Equation (6.25) is equally compatible with a multifactor arbitrage pricing model.[26] The four-moment CAPM allows pre-identification of the risk factors as the market portfolio and two specific portfolios Z_{m1} and Z_{m2}. All the asset pricing relations established previously assume the existence of a riskless asset. The study of the general properties of the efficient frontier in the space $[E(R_p), \sigma^2(R_p), s^3(R_p), \kappa^4(R_p)]$ generalises the approach in the N risky assets case.

6.3   AN N RISKY ASSET FOUR-MOMENT CAPM EXTENSION

The aggregation of the individual equilibrium conditions, given by the maximisation of a mean–variance–skewness–*kurtosis* preference function leads to the fundamental four-moment CAPM relation. The use of a two-fund monetary separation theorem is, however, necessary to obtain such a result, restricting the domain of validity of the four-moment CAPM to the existence of a riskless asset and to separable quartic or HARA utility functions.

In the following subsection, we adopt the approach of the portfolio choice theory with N risky assets, developed by Markowitz (1952) and generalised by Athayde and Flôres (1997, 2002, 2003 and 2004) in the mean–variance–skewness and/or *kurtosis* case with a riskless asset.[27] In this framework, each investor selects the portfolio minimising the variance of her portfolio return for a given mean, skewness and *kurtosis*. Then, we can obtain a characterisation of the mean–variance–skewness–*kurtosis* efficient frontier with N

---

[26] In Section 6.4, we study the links between the four-moment CAPM and the APT of Ross (1976).
[27] See also Adcock and Shutes (2000 and 2001) and Adcock (2003 and 2004).

risky assets (see Section 6.3.1). The hypothesis of a *Pareto-optimal* equilibrium allocation leads to the generalisation of the four-moment CAPM relation in the absence of a riskless asset (see Section 6.3.2).

6.3.1 General properties of the mean–variance–skewness–*kurtosis* efficient set

The general hypotheses assumed are the same as before; specifically, there are N risky assets (with $N \geq 4$) and K agents. The investors' preferences are represented by an indirect utility function, denoted $V_k(.)$, with $k = [1, \ldots, K]$, concave and increasing with odd portfolio return moments and concave and decreasing with even portfolio return moments. The K agents hold homogeneous probability beliefs and asset returns are linearly independent.

In this case, the portfolio choice problem with N risky assets of an investor k reads:

$$\underset{\mathbf{w}_p}{\text{Max}} \left\{ V_k \left[E\left(R_p\right), \sigma^2\left(R_p\right), s^3\left(R_p\right), \kappa^4\left(R_p\right) \right] \right\} \tag{6.31}$$

$$\text{s.t.}: \mathbf{w}'_p \mathbf{1} = 1$$

with:

$$\begin{cases} E\left(R_p\right) = \mathbf{w}'_p \mathbf{E} \\ \sigma^2\left(R_p\right) = \mathbf{w}'_p \mathbf{\Omega} \mathbf{w}_p \\ s^3\left(R_p\right) = \mathbf{w}'_p \mathbf{\Sigma}_p \\ \kappa^4\left(R_p\right) = \mathbf{w}'_p \mathbf{\Gamma}_p \end{cases}$$

and:

$$(-1)^i V_k^{(i)} < 0$$

with $i = [1, \ldots, 4]$ and $k = [1, \ldots, K]$.

As agents have a preference for the expected return and (positive) skewness, and an aversion to the variance and the *kurtosis*, the optimisation program (6.31) can be reformulated as follows:[28]

$$\underset{\mathbf{w}_p}{\text{Min}} \left\{ \frac{1}{2} \mathbf{w}'_p \mathbf{\Omega} \mathbf{w}_p \right\} \tag{6.32}$$

$$\text{s.t.} \begin{cases} \mathbf{w}'_p \mathbf{E} = \mu_p \\ \mathbf{w}'_p \mathbf{1} = 1 \\ \mathbf{w}'_p \mathbf{\Sigma}_p = s_p^3 \\ \mathbf{w}'_p \mathbf{\Gamma}_p = \kappa_p^4 \end{cases}$$

---

[28] See also Simaan (1993), Gamba and Rossi (1997, 1998a and 1998b), Pressacco and Stucchi (2000), Jurczenko and Maillet (2001) and Harvey *et al.* (2004) for similar optimisation program in the mean–variance–skewness space.

where μ_p, s_p^3 and κ_p^4 represent, respectively, the level of expected return, skewness and *kurtosis* wished by investor k.

The set of optimal portfolios p, corresponding to the different triplets of coordinates $\left[\mu_p, s_p^3, \kappa_p^4\right]$, characterises the mean–variance–skewness–*kurtosis* efficient set. By definition, it corresponds to the set of the portfolios minimising, respectively, the variance (or *kurtosis*) – for some level of mean, skewness and *kurtosis* (or variance) – and maximising, at the same time, respectively, the mean (or skewness) – for some given level of variance, skewness (or mean) and *kurtosis*.

This optimisation program is, nevertheless, not unique. For instance, Berényi (2001 and 2002), Davies *et al.* (2005) and Jurczenko *et al.* in Chapter 3 of this book propose to introduce simultaneously the higher-order moments into the portfolio choice decision, using, respectively, a polynomial goal programming (PGP) approach[29] and a multi-objective optimisation programme based on a microeconomic directional distance function.[30]

Assuming that the values reached by the constraints in (6.32) are already known, the resolution of the investor's portfolio choice problem leads to the following general theorem.

Theorem 3   *The vector of asset weights of any mean–variance–skewness–kurtosis efficient portfolio p can be written as a linear combination of those of four distinct funds defined by:*

$$\mathbf{w}_{a_1} = \frac{\mathbf{\Omega}^{-1}\mathbf{E}}{\mathbf{1}'\mathbf{\Omega}^{-1}\mathbf{E}}; \; \mathbf{w}_{a_2} = \frac{\mathbf{\Omega}^{-1}\mathbf{1}}{\mathbf{1}'\mathbf{\Omega}^{-1}\mathbf{1}}; \; \mathbf{w}_{a_3} = \frac{\mathbf{\Omega}^{-1}\mathbf{\Sigma}_p}{\mathbf{1}'\,\mathbf{\Omega}^{-1}\mathbf{\Sigma}_p} \text{ and } \mathbf{w}_{a_4} = \frac{\mathbf{\Omega}^{-1}\mathbf{\Gamma}_p}{\mathbf{1}'\mathbf{\Omega}^{-1}\mathbf{\Gamma}_p} \quad (6.33)$$

Proof   *See Appendix E.*

Corollary 2   *If there exists a riskless asset, every efficient portfolio weight vector can be expressed as a linear combination of those of the riskless asset and of the three distinct funds defined by:*

$$\mathbf{w}_{a_5} = \frac{\mathbf{\Omega}^{-1}\left(\mathbf{E} - R_f\,\mathbf{1}\right)}{\mathbf{1}'\mathbf{\Omega}^{-1}\left(\mathbf{E} - R_f\,\mathbf{1}\right)}, \; \mathbf{w}_{a_6} = \frac{\mathbf{\Omega}^{-1}\mathbf{\Sigma}_p}{\mathbf{1}'\,\mathbf{\Omega}^{-1}\mathbf{\Sigma}_p} \text{ and } \mathbf{w}_{a_7} = \frac{\mathbf{\Omega}^{-1}\mathbf{\Gamma}_p}{\mathbf{1}'\mathbf{\Omega}^{-1}\mathbf{\Gamma}_p} \quad (6.34)$$

Proof   *See Appendix F.*

Compared to the mean–variance analysis, the introduction of the third and fourth centred moments has the effect of changing the structure of the efficient set: it is no longer determined by two, but rather by four, portfolios.[31] The first two are common to all investors and correspond to the two mutual funds generating the traditional mean–variance

---

[29] For studies of the use of this approach in the mean–variance–skewness portfolio selection case, see Lai (1991), Chunhachinda *et al.* (1997), Chang *et al.* (2003) and Sun and Yan (2003).

[30] For studies of the use of this approach in the mean–variance–skewness portfolio selection case, see Joro and Na (2001) and Briec *et al.* (2006).

[31] We can notice here, that $\mathbf{w}_{a_3}$ (or $\mathbf{w}_{a_6}$) differs from the third portfolio used by Simaan (1993) in the mean–variance–skewness case since $\mathbf{w}_{a_3}$ (or $\mathbf{w}_{a_6}$) depends on the agent preferences.

efficient frontier. We remark that $\mathbf{w}_{a_2}$ is the global *minimum* variance portfolio in the mean–variance plane.[32] The third portfolio $\mathbf{w}_{a_3}$ (or $\mathbf{w}_{a_6}$ if there is a riskless asset) and the fourth portfolio $\mathbf{w}_{a_4}$ (or $\mathbf{w}_{a_7}$ if there is a riskless asset) are specific to each investor. They represent, respectively, the portfolio that, for a given variance, maximises (minimises) the skewness and minimises the *kurtosis*. Consequently, the mean–variance–skewness–*kurtosis* efficient set includes the mean–variance efficient set, since it is generated by $\mathbf{w}_{a_1}$ and by $\mathbf{w}_{a_2}$ (or by the riskless asset and $\mathbf{w}_{a_5}$ if there is a riskless asset). Since investors have demands depending upon their preferences, it is clear that the standard portfolio separation result is generally not verified when return densities are asymmetric and leptokurtic.

Another characterisation of the mean–variance–skewness–*kurtosis* efficient frontier can be obtained as follows.

Theorem 4   *A necessary condition for a portfolio p to belong to the mean–variance–skewness–kurtosis efficient set is – except for portfolios that belong to the minimum variance set in the variance–skewness–kurtosis space[33] – that there exist three portfolios uncorrelated with p, denoted Z_{p0}, Z_{p1} and Z_{p2}, such that:*

$$\mathbf{E} - E\left(R_{Z_{p0}}\right)\mathbf{1} = \left\{\left[E\left(R_p\right) - E\left(R_{Z_{p1}}\right)\right] - \left[E\left(R_{Z_{p2}}\right) - E\left(R_{Z_{p0}}\right)\right]\right\}\mathbf{\Omega}\,\mathbf{w}_p\left[\sigma^2\left(R_p\right)\right]^{-1}$$
$$+ \left[E\left(R_{Z_{p1}}\right) - E\left(R_{Z_{p0}}\right)\right]\mathbf{\Sigma}_p\left[s^3\left(R_p\right)\right]^{-1} \tag{6.35}$$
$$+ \left[E\left(R_{Z_{p2}}\right) - E\left(R_{Z_{p0}}\right)\right]\mathbf{\Gamma}_p\left[\kappa^4\left(R_p\right)\right]^{-1}$$

where $E\left(R_{Z_{p0}}\right)$ represents the expected return on a portfolio whose return is zero-correlated and has a zero coskewness and a zero cokurtosis with the return of the portfolio p; $E\left(R_{Z_{p1}}\right)$ represents the expected return on a portfolio whose return is zero-correlated with the portfolio p and has a coskewness equal to the skewness of that portfolio return and a zero cokurtosis with it; $E\left(R_{Z_{p2}}\right)$ represents the expected return on a portfolio whose return is zero-correlated with the portfolio p and has a zero coskewness with it and a cokurtosis equal to the kurtosis of that portfolio return; $\mathbf{\Omega}\,\mathbf{w}_p$, $\mathbf{\Sigma}_p$, $\mathbf{\Gamma}_p$ are the $(N \times 1)$ vectors of covariance, coskewness and cokurtosis between the risky asset returns and the portfolio p return; $\sigma^2\left(R_p\right) \neq 0$, $s^3\left(R_p\right) \neq 0$ and $\kappa^4\left(R_p\right) \neq 0$.

Proof   *See Appendix G.*

---

[32] We verify that the mean and variance of the portfolio defined by the weights vector $\mathbf{w}_{a_2}$ are:

$$\begin{cases} E\left(R_{a_2}\right) = a/c \\ \sigma^2\left(R_{a_2}\right) = 1/c \end{cases}$$

where $a = \mathbf{E}'\mathbf{\Omega}^{-1}\mathbf{1}$ and $c = \mathbf{1}'\mathbf{\Omega}^{-1}\mathbf{1}$.

[33] That is, portfolios that are solutions to the program of an investor minimising the variance of its investment for some given level of skewness and *kurtosis*.

For any security i, $i=[1, \ldots, N]$, we can write:

$$E(R_i) - E\left(R_{Z_{p0}}\right) = \left\{\left[E(R_p) - E\left(R_{Z_{p1}}\right)\right] - \left[E\left(R_{Z_{p2}}\right) - E\left(R_{Z_{p0}}\right)\right]\right\} \frac{\mathrm{Cov}(R_i, R_p)}{\sigma^2(R_p)}$$

$$+ \left[E\left(R_{Z_{p1}}\right) - E\left(R_{Z_{p0}}\right)\right] \frac{\mathrm{Cos}(R_i, R_p)}{m^3(R_p)} \qquad (6.36)$$

$$+ \left[E\left(R_{Z_{p2}}\right) - E\left(R_{Z_{p0}}\right)\right] \frac{\mathrm{Cok}(R_i, R_p)}{\kappa^4(R_p)}$$

where $\mathrm{Cov}(R_i, R_p)$, $\mathrm{Cos}(R_i, R_p)$ and $\mathrm{Cok}(R_i, R_p)$ are, respectively, the ith entries, for $i=[1, \ldots, N]$, of the $(N \times 1)$ vectors $\Omega\, \mathbf{w}_p$, Σ_p and Γ_p.

This relation states that a portfolio p is mean–variance–skewness–*kurtosis* efficient if its return is such that every single expected asset return on asset i, for $i=[1, \ldots, N]$, can be expressed as a linear combination of the covariance, the coskewness and the *cokurtosis* of its rate of return with the efficient portfolio p return. The terms Π_1, Π_2 and Π_3 defined as:

$$\begin{cases} \Pi_1 = \left\{\left[E(R_p) - E\left(R_{Z_{p1}}\right)\right] - \left[E\left(R_{Z_{p2}}\right) - E\left(R_{Z_{p0}}\right)\right]\right\} \\ \Pi_2 = \left[E\left(R_{Z_{p1}}\right) - E\left(R_{Z_{p0}}\right)\right] \\ \Pi_3 = \left[E\left(R_{Z_{p2}}\right) - E\left(R_{Z_{p0}}\right)\right] \end{cases} \qquad (6.37)$$

can be interpreted as subjective risk premia of variance, skewness and *kurtosis*.

The fact that investors dislike variance and *kurtosis* and have a preference for (positive) skewness implies that:

$$\begin{cases} \Pi_1 > 0 \\ \mathrm{sign}(\Pi_2) = -\mathrm{sign}\left[s^3(R_p)\right] \\ \Pi_3 > 0 \end{cases} \qquad (6.38)$$

Once these properties are stated, one can develop a four-moment CAPM relation when there is no riskless asset. To achieve this goal, it is sufficient to identify a specific mean–variance–skewness–*kurtosis* efficient portfolio: the market portfolio.

6.3.2   A zero-beta zero-gamma zero-delta four-moment CAPM

If agents have homogenous probability beliefs and the market portfolio return distribution is skewed, a necessary and sufficient condition to obtain, from (6.35), an N risky asset four-moment CAPM relation, is that there exists a Pareto-optimal equilibrium allocation.[34] Under this last hypothesis, the mean–variance–skewness–*kurtosis* efficient set is convex

---

[34] This last hypothesis has also been considered by Simaan (1993) in order to develop a 3-CAPM asset pricing relation with N risky assets.

(see Ingersoll, 1987, pp. 194–195). Since rational investors must choose efficient portfolios, this implies that the market portfolio – which is a convex combination of individual portfolios – must, at equilibrium, be a mean–variance–skewness–kurtosis efficient portfolio. The main result is then that the expected return on any risky security i, with $i = [1, \ldots, N]$, can be expressed as a linear function of its covariance, coskewness and *cokurtosis* with the market portfolio return.

Theorem 5   *In the absence of a riskless asset, the asset risk premia of a Pareto-optimal equilibrium are given by:*

$$\mathbf{E} - E\left(R_{Z_{m0}}\right)\mathbf{1} = \left\{\left[E\left(R_m\right) - E\left(R_{Z_{m1}}\right)\right] - \left[E\left(R_{Z_{m2}}\right) - E\left(R_{Z_{m0}}\right)\right]\right\}\boldsymbol{\beta}$$
$$+ \left[E\left(R_{Z_{m1}}\right) - E\left(R_{Z_{m0}}\right)\right]\boldsymbol{\gamma} + \left[E\left(R_{Z_{m2}}\right) - E\left(R_{Z_{m0}}\right)\right]\boldsymbol{\delta} \qquad (6.39)$$

with:

$$\begin{cases} \boldsymbol{\beta} = \left[\sigma^2\left(R_m\right)\right]^{-1}\boldsymbol{\Omega}\mathbf{w}_m \\ \boldsymbol{\gamma} = \left[s^3\left(R_m\right)\right]^{-1}\boldsymbol{\Sigma}_m \\ \boldsymbol{\delta} = \left[\kappa^4\left(R_m\right)\right]^{-1}\boldsymbol{\Gamma}_m \end{cases}$$

where $E\left(R_{Z_{m0}}\right)$ represents the expected return on a portfolio whose return is zero-correlated and has a zero coskewness, zero cokurtosis with the return of the market portfolio m; $E\left(R_{Z_{m1}}\right)$ represents the expected return on a portfolio whose return is zero-correlated with the market portfolio m and has a coskewness equal to the skewness of the market portfolio and a zero cokurtosis with it; $E\left(R_{Z_{m2}}\right)$ represents the expected return on a portfolio whose return is zero-correlated with the market portfolio m and has a zero coskewness with it and a cokurtosis equal to the kurtosis of the market portfolio; $\boldsymbol{\Omega}\mathbf{w}_m$, $\boldsymbol{\Sigma}_m$, $\boldsymbol{\Gamma}_m$ are the $(N \times 1)$ vectors of covariance, coskewness and cokurtosis between the risky asset returns and the market portfolio return; $\sigma^2\left(R_m\right) \neq 0$, $s^3\left(R_m\right) \neq 0$ and $\kappa^4\left(R_m\right) \neq 0$.

Proof   *See Appendix H.*

Thus, for any security i, $i = [1, \ldots, N]$:

$$E\left(R_i\right) - E\left(R_{Z_{m0}}\right) = \left\{\left[E\left(R_m\right) - E\left(R_{Z_{m1}}\right)\right] - \left[E\left(R_{Z_{m2}}\right) - E\left(R_{Z_{m0}}\right)\right]\right\}\beta_i \qquad (6.40)$$
$$+ \left[E\left(R_{Z_{m1}}\right) - E\left(R_{Z_{m0}}\right)\right]\gamma_i + \left[E\left(R_{Z_{m2}}\right) - E\left(R_{Z_{m0}}\right)\right]\delta_i$$

where:

$$\begin{cases} \beta_i = \dfrac{\text{Cov}\left(R_i, R_m\right)}{\sigma^2\left(R_m\right)} \\[2mm] \gamma_i = \dfrac{\text{Cos}\left(R_i, R_m\right)}{s^3\left(R_m\right)} \\[2mm] \delta_i = \dfrac{\text{Cok}\left(R_i, R_m\right)}{\kappa^4\left(R_m\right)} \end{cases}$$

are, respectively, the ith entries, for $i = [1, \ldots, N]$, of the $(N \times 1)$ vectors $\boldsymbol{\beta}$, $\boldsymbol{\gamma}$ and $\boldsymbol{\delta}$.

We remark that:

$$\begin{cases} \left[E\left(R_m\right) - E\left(R_{Z_{m1}}\right) \right] - \left[E\left(R_{Z_{m2}}\right) - E\left(R_{Z_{m0}}\right) \right] > 0 \\ \text{sign} \left[E\left(R_{Z_{m1}}\right) - E\left(R_{Z_{m0}}\right) \right] = -\text{sign} \left[s^3 \left(R_m\right) \right] \\ \left[E\left(R_{Z_{m2}}\right) - E\left(R_{Z_{m0}}\right) \right] > 0 \end{cases} \tag{6.41}$$

This equation is the four-moment CAPM relation with N risky assets. As for the fundamental four-moment CAPM relation (6.25), the risk premium on any financial asset i must be equal at equilibrium to the sum of three risk premia: one market premium proportional to the beta of the asset corresponding to the premium placed by the market on the systematic risk of variance; a premium on a zero-beta unitary-gamma zero-delta portfolio, proportional to the gamma of the asset representing the risk premium placed by the market on the systematic risk of skewness and a premium on a zero-beta zero-gamma unitary-delta portfolio, proportional to the delta of the asset representing the risk premium placed by the market on the systematic risk of *kurtosis*.

Introducing the risk premium on the market portfolio into Equation (6.39), we can rewrite it as:

$$\begin{aligned} \mathbf{E} - E\left(R_{Z_{m0}}\right) \mathbf{1} = & \left[E\left(R_m\right) - E\left(R_{Z_{m0}}\right) \right] \boldsymbol{\beta} \\ & + \left[E\left(R_{Z_{m1}}\right) - E\left(R_{Z_{m0}}\right) \right] (\boldsymbol{\gamma} - \boldsymbol{\beta}) \\ & + \left[E\left(R_{Z_{m2}}\right) - E\left(R_{Z_{m0}}\right) \right] (\boldsymbol{\delta} - \boldsymbol{\beta}) \end{aligned} \tag{6.42}$$

Thus, for any security i, $i = [1, \ldots, N]$:

$$\begin{aligned} E\left(R_i\right) - E\left(R_{Z_{m0}}\right) = & \left[E\left(R_m\right) - E\left(R_{Z_{m0}}\right) \right] \beta_i \\ & + \left[E\left(R_{Z_{m1}}\right) - E\left(R_{Z_{m0}}\right) \right] (\gamma_i - \beta_i) \\ & + \left[E\left(R_{Z_{m2}}\right) - E\left(R_{Z_{m0}}\right) \right] (\delta_i - \beta_i) \end{aligned} \tag{6.43}$$

where:

$$\begin{cases} \beta_i = \dfrac{\text{Cov}\left(R_i, R_m\right)}{\sigma^2\left(R_m\right)} \\ \gamma_i = \dfrac{\text{Cos}\left(R_i, R_m\right)}{s^3\left(R_m\right)} \\ \delta_i = \dfrac{\text{Cok}\left(R_i, R_m\right)}{\kappa^4\left(R_m\right)} \end{cases}$$

are, respectively, the ith entries, for $i = [1, \ldots, N]$, of the $(N \times 1)$ vectors $\boldsymbol{\beta}$, $\boldsymbol{\gamma}$ and $\boldsymbol{\delta}$.

Under this presentation, the N risky assets four-moment CAPM version is a direct extension of Black's zero-beta CAPM (1972) when the expected rate of return of the zero-beta zero-gamma zero-delta portfolio corresponds to that of the zero-beta portfolio in the mean–variance case. Indeed, unless the portfolio Z_{m0} belongs to the *minimum* variance frontier in the mean–variance plane, the pricing relation that we obtain in (6.39), when $\left[E\left(R_{Z_{m1}}\right) - E\left(R_{Z_{m0}}\right)\right] = 0$ and $\left[E\left(R_{Z_{m2}}\right) - E\left(R_{Z_{m0}}\right)\right] = 0$ or when $\gamma_i = \beta_i$ and $\delta_i = \beta_i$ with $i = [1, \ldots, N]$, does not have any reason to be equal to Black's model (1972).

If a riskless asset exists, its return replaces $E\left(R_{Z_{m0}}\right)$ in the equilibrium relation and we are back to the fundamental relation with a riskless asset derived in Section 6.2.

6.4   THE FOUR-MOMENT CAPM, THE CUBIC MARKET MODEL AND THE ARBITRAGE ASSET PRICING MODEL

When asset return distributions are asymmetric and leptokurtic, the data-generating process is governed by three risk factors determining investor portfolio holdings. Such risk factors lead, for any risky asset, to three specific risk premia, which are associated, respectively, with the variance, the skewness and the *kurtosis* of the market portfolio return probability distribution.

Following the approaches of Kraus and Litzenberger (1976) and Barone-Adesi (1985) in the mean–variance–skewness case, and generalised in the four-moment framework by Fang and Lai (1997), Hwang and Satchell (1999) and Galagedera *et al.* (2004a), it is possible to link the main multifactor models with the four-moment CAPM when there exists a riskless asset. In the next subsections, we focus on the cubic market model (see Section 6.4.1.) and on the APT model (see Section 6.4.2.).

6.4.1   The cubic market model and the four-moment CAPM

Fang and Lai (1997), Hwang and Satchell (1999) and Galagedera *et al.* (2004a) use the cubic market model as a consistent data-generating process (DGP) for the four-moment CAPM. The cubic market model assumes that the excess return on any security is generated by the following nonlinear factor model:

$$\begin{cases} \mathbf{R} - R_f \mathbf{1} = \boldsymbol{\alpha}_0 + \left(R_m - R_f\right)\boldsymbol{\alpha}_1 + \left[R_m - E\left(R_m\right)\right]^2 \boldsymbol{\alpha}_2 \\ \qquad\qquad + \left[R_m - E\left(R_m\right)\right]^3 \boldsymbol{\alpha}_3 + \boldsymbol{\varepsilon} \\ E(\boldsymbol{\varepsilon}) = \mathbf{0} \\ E(\boldsymbol{\varepsilon}|R_m, R_m^2, R_m^3) = \mathbf{0} \end{cases} \qquad (6.44)$$

where $\mathbf{R}$ is the $(N \times 1)$ vector of the returns of risky assets; $\boldsymbol{\alpha}_0$ is the $(N \times 1)$ vector of asset return intercepts of the data-generating process (6.44); $\boldsymbol{\alpha}_1$, $\boldsymbol{\alpha}_2$ and $\boldsymbol{\alpha}_3$ are, respectively, the $(N \times 1)$ vector of asset return sensitivities with the return, the squared and the cubed market portfolio return and $\boldsymbol{\varepsilon}$ is the $(N \times 1)$ vector of asset return disturbances.

Provided the sixth centred moment of the market portfolio exists, it is possible to link the coefficients $\boldsymbol{\alpha}_1$, $\boldsymbol{\alpha}_2$ and $\boldsymbol{\alpha}_3$ of the cubic market model with the parameters $\boldsymbol{\beta}$, $\boldsymbol{\gamma}$ and

$\boldsymbol{\delta}$ of the four-moment CAPM. Subtracting Equation (6.44) from its expected value, and using the definition of the relative risk measures $\boldsymbol{\beta}$, $\boldsymbol{\gamma}$ and $\boldsymbol{\delta}$, yields the following result (see Appendix I):

$$
\begin{cases}
\boldsymbol{\beta} = \boldsymbol{\alpha}_1 + \left[\dfrac{s^3\,(R_m)}{\sigma^2\,(R_m)}\right]\boldsymbol{\alpha}_2 + \left[\dfrac{\kappa^4\,(R_m)}{\sigma^2\,(R_m)}\right]\boldsymbol{\alpha}_3 \\[4mm]
\boldsymbol{\gamma} = \boldsymbol{\alpha}_1 + \left\{\dfrac{\kappa^4\,(R_m) - \left[\sigma^2\,(R_m)\right]^2}{s^3\,(R_m)}\right\}\boldsymbol{\alpha}_2 + \left\{\dfrac{\xi^5\,(R_m) - \sigma^2\,(R_m)\,s^3\,(R_m)}{s^3\,(R_m)}\right\}\boldsymbol{\alpha}_3 \\[4mm]
\boldsymbol{\delta} = \boldsymbol{\alpha}_1 + \left\{\dfrac{\xi^5\,(R_m) - \sigma^2\,(R_m)\,s^3\,(R_m)}{\kappa^4\,(R_m)}\right\}\boldsymbol{\alpha}_2 + \left\{\dfrac{\psi^6\,(R_m) - \left[s^3\,(R_m)\right]^2}{\kappa^4\,(R_m)}\right\}\boldsymbol{\alpha}_3
\end{cases}
\tag{6.45}
$$

where $\sigma^2\,(R_m) \neq 0$, $s^3\,(R_m) \neq 0$ and $\kappa^4\,(R_m) \neq 0$ are defined as before and $\xi^5\,(R_m)$ and $\psi^6\,(R_m)$ represent, respectively, the fifth and sixth centred moments of the market portfolio return probability distribution.

Thus, for any security i, $i = [1, \ldots, N]$:

$$
\begin{cases}
\beta_i = \alpha_{1i} + \alpha_{2i}\left[\dfrac{s^3\,(R_m)}{\sigma^2\,(R_m)}\right] + \alpha_{3i}\left[\dfrac{\kappa^4\,(R_m)}{\sigma^2\,(R_m)}\right] \\[4mm]
\gamma_i = \alpha_{1i} + \alpha_{2i}\left\{\dfrac{\kappa^4\,(R_m) - \left[\sigma^2\,(R_m)\right]^2}{s^3\,(R_m)}\right\} + \alpha_{3i}\left\{\dfrac{\xi^5\,(R_m) - \sigma^2\,(R_m)\,s^3\,(R_m)}{s^3\,(R_m)}\right\} \\[4mm]
\delta_i = \alpha_{1i} + \alpha_{2i}\left\{\dfrac{\xi^5\,(R_m) - \sigma^2\,(R_m)\,s^3\,(R_m)}{\kappa^4\,(R_m)}\right\} + \alpha_{3i}\left\{\dfrac{\psi^6\,(R_m) - \left[s^3\,(R_m)\right]^2}{\kappa^4\,(R_m)}\right\}
\end{cases}
\tag{6.46}
$$

where $\beta_i = \mathrm{Cov}\,(R_i, R_m)\,/\sigma^2\,(R_m)$, $\gamma_i = \mathrm{Cos}\,(R_i, R_m)\,/s^3\,(R_m)$ and $\delta_i = \mathrm{Cok}\,(R_i, R_m)\,/\kappa^4\,(R_m)$; α_{1i}, α_{2i} and α_{3i} are, respectively, the ith entries, with $i = [1, \ldots, N]$, of the $(N \times 1)$ vectors $\boldsymbol{\beta}$, $\boldsymbol{\gamma}$, $\boldsymbol{\delta}$, $\boldsymbol{\alpha}_1$, $\boldsymbol{\alpha}_2$ and $\boldsymbol{\alpha}_3$; and $\sigma^2\,(R_m) \neq 0$, $s^3\,(R_m) \neq 0$ and $\kappa^4\,(R_m) \neq 0$.

These equations provide, moreover, some insights on the nature of the relations that exist between the cubic market model and the four-moment CAPM. For example, if we find for an asset i, with $i = [1, \ldots, N]$, that the weights on the coefficients α_{2i} and α_{3i} are equal, then we have $\beta_i = \gamma_i$ and $\beta_i = \delta_i$. Following the same line of reasoning, if two out of three coefficients of the cubic market model α_{1i}, α_{2i} and α_{3i} are identical for all risky assets, then β_i, γ_i and δ_i are perfectly collinear.

Note that when the market model is quadratic (i.e. $\alpha_3 = 0$), we have the following relation between the coefficients of the data-generating process and the systematic risk measures of the four-moment CAPM:

$$
\left\{
\begin{aligned}
\beta &= \alpha_1 + \left[\frac{s^3(R_m)}{\sigma^2(R_m)} \right] \alpha_2 \\[2ex]
\gamma &= \alpha_1 + \left\{ \frac{\kappa^4(R_m) - [\sigma^2(R_m)]^2}{s^3(R_m)} \right\} \alpha_2 \\[2ex]
\delta &= \left\{ \left[\frac{\kappa^4(R_m) - [\sigma^2(R_m)]^2}{s^3(R_m)} - \frac{\xi^5(R_m) - \sigma^2(R_m)s^3(R_m)}{\kappa^4(R_m)} \right] \middle/ \right. \\[2ex]
&\qquad \times \left[\frac{\kappa^4(R_m) - \sigma^2(R_m)}{s^3(R_m)} - \frac{s^3(R_m)}{\sigma^2(R_m)} \right] \right\} \beta \\[2ex]
&\qquad + \left\{ \left[\frac{\xi^5(R_m) - \sigma^2(R_m)s^3(R_m)}{\kappa^4(R_m)} - \frac{s^3(R_m)}{\sigma^2(R_m)} \right] \middle/ \left[\frac{\kappa^4(R_m) - \sigma^2(R_m)}{s^3(R_m)} - \frac{s^3(R_m)}{\sigma^2(R_m)} \right] \right\} \gamma
\end{aligned}
\right.
$$

$$(6.47)$$

In such a case, the 3-CAPM, rather than the 4-CAPM, must be used, otherwise the systematic risk measures of *kurtosis* will be collinear with the systematic risk measures of variance and skewness for all the assets.[35]

When the data-generating process is a linear function of the market return (i.e. $\alpha_2 = 0$ and $\alpha_3 = 0$), we then have:

$$
\left\{
\begin{aligned}
\beta &= \gamma \\
\beta &= \delta \\
\beta &= \alpha_1
\end{aligned}
\right.
\qquad (6.48)
$$

In this case, the two-moment CAPM, rather than the three or four-moment CAPM, must be used, otherwise the systematic risk measures in the four-moment CAPM are perfectly collinear with each other.

Under certain parameter restrictions, the cubic market model (6.44) is then consistent with the four-moment CAPM.[36]

6.4.2   The arbitrage pricing model and the four-moment CAPM

In the same way, it is also possible to link the four-moment CAPM with the Arbitrage Pricing Theory model of Ross (1976).

---

[35] For a complete discussion of the use of the quadratic market model within the three-moment framework see Kraus and Litzenberger (1976), Barone-Adesi (1985), Brooks and Faff (1998), Jurczenko and Maillet (2001) and Barone-Adesi *et al.* (2004).

[36] Since pay-offs on derivatives can be expressed as a polynomial function of the market portfolio return, the cubic market model is also consistent with a piecewise linear market model involving selected options on the market portfolio as additional risk factors (see Glosten and Jagannathan, 1994; Mitchell and Pulvino, 2001; Agarwal and Naik, 2004).

Consider first the following cubic market model:[37]

$$
\begin{cases}
\mathbf{R} = \boldsymbol{\alpha}_0^* + R_m \boldsymbol{\alpha}_1^* + v_m^2 \boldsymbol{\alpha}_2^* + v_m^3 \boldsymbol{\alpha}_3^* + \boldsymbol{\varepsilon}^* \\
\mathrm{Cov}(R_m, v_m^2) = 0 \\
\mathrm{Cov}(R_m, v_m^3) = 0 \\
\mathrm{Cov}(v_m^2, v_m^3) = 0 \\
E(\boldsymbol{\varepsilon}) = \mathbf{0} \\
E(\boldsymbol{\varepsilon} | R_m, v_m^2, v_m^3) = \mathbf{0} \\
E(\boldsymbol{\varepsilon}\boldsymbol{\varepsilon}') = \mathbf{D}_{\boldsymbol{\varepsilon}}
\end{cases}
\tag{6.49}
$$

where $\mathbf{R}$ is the $(N \times 1)$ vector of asset returns; $\boldsymbol{\alpha}_0^*$ is the $(N \times 1)$ vector of asset return intercepts of the factor model (6.49); $\boldsymbol{\alpha}_1^*$, $\boldsymbol{\alpha}_2^*$ and $\boldsymbol{\alpha}_3^*$ are, respectively, the $(N \times 1)$ vectors of asset return sensitivities with the market portfolio return, with the squared market portfolio return component that is independent of the market portfolio return, denoted v_m^2, and with the cubed market portfolio return component that is independent of the market portfolio return and of the squared market portfolio return, denoted v_m^3; $\boldsymbol{\varepsilon}^*$ is the $(N \times 1)$ vector of asset return disturbances and $\mathbf{D}_{\boldsymbol{\varepsilon}^*}$ is the $(N \times N)$ diagonal variance–covariance matrix of asset return disturbances associated with the cubic market model (6.49).

If Equation (6.49) represents the true DGP of the asset returns, then, under the standard assumptions of the Arbitrage Pricing Theory, the expected rate of returns on all the securities must satisfy asymptotically the following equality:[38]

$$
\mathbf{E} - R_f \mathbf{1} = \boldsymbol{\alpha}_1^* \left[E(R_1) - R_f \right] + \boldsymbol{\alpha}_2^* \left[E(R_2) - R_f \right] + \boldsymbol{\alpha}_3^* \left[E(R_3) - R_f \right]
\tag{6.50}
$$

where $E(R_1)$, $E(R_2)$ and $E(R_3)$ are, respectively, the expected rates of return on three well-diversified portfolios perfectly correlated with the risk factors R_m, v_m^2 and v_m^3.

Using the statistical properties of the market portfolio, it is possible to identify the expected rate of return on the first portfolio, $E(R_1)$, as:

$$
\left[E(R_1) - R_f \right] = \left[E(R_m) - R_f \right]
\tag{6.51}
$$

with $\alpha_{1m}^* = 1$, $\alpha_{2m}^* = 0$ and $\alpha_{3m}^* = 0$.

It is hardly possible to give a similar definition for the two other systematic risk premia of the three-factor arbitrage pricing model (6.50). Following the approaches developed by Barone-Adesi (1985) and Barone-Adesi *et al.* (2004) in the mean–variance–skewness

---

[37] This formulation is equivalent to (6.44) with:

$$
\boldsymbol{\alpha}_0^* = \boldsymbol{\alpha}_0 + R_f (1 - \boldsymbol{\alpha}_1^*) + \left\{ [R_m - E(R_m)]^2 - v_m^2 \right\} \boldsymbol{\alpha}_2^*
$$
$$
+ \left\{ [R_m - E(R_m)]^3 - v_m^3 \right\} \boldsymbol{\alpha}_2^*
$$

[38] To write (6.50) as an exact pricing relation in an infinite economy, we suppose that the conditions of Theorem 5 in Ingersoll (1987), p. 184, are met. That is, the systematic risk factors are pervasive and the market portfolio is a well-diversified portfolio, i.e. it contains a large number of assets with relative weights of order $(1/N)$.

framework, it can be shown, however, that the arbitrage pricing model (6.50) implies an upper bound for the expected rate of return on the second portfolio, $E(R_2)$, that is (see Appendix J):

$$E(R_2) < E(v_m^2) \tag{6.52}$$

Substituting (6.51) into (6.50) leads to the following asymptotic arbitrage asset pricing relation:

$$\mathbf{E} - R_f \mathbf{1} = \boldsymbol{\alpha}_1^* \left[E(R_m) - R_f \right] + \boldsymbol{\alpha}_2^* \left[E(R_2) - R_f \right] + \boldsymbol{\alpha}_3^* \left[E(R_3) - R_f \right] \tag{6.53}$$

This relation indicates that the expected excess return on a security is, at equilibrium, a linear function of three different risk premia: the first corresponds to the market portfolio risk premium, $\left[E(R_m) - R_f \right]$; the second relies on the excess return of a portfolio whose return is perfectly correlated with the squared market portfolio return and is independent of the market portfolio return, $\left[E(R_2) - R_f \right]$; and the third relies on the excess return of a portfolio whose return is perfectly correlated with the cubed market portfolio return and is independent of the market return and of the squared market portfolio return, $\left[E(R_3) - R_f \right]$.

Taking the expected value of Equation (6.49) and setting the resulting equation equal to Equation (6.53), yields:

$$\begin{aligned} \alpha_0^* + E(R_m) \alpha_1^* + E(v_m^2) \alpha_2^* + E(v_m^3) \alpha_3^* = \\ R_f \mathbf{1} + \left[E(R_m) - R_f \right] \alpha_1^* + \left[E(R_2) - R_f \right] \alpha_2^* + \left[E(R_3) - R_f \right] \alpha_3^* \end{aligned} \tag{6.54}$$

Rearranging terms gives:

$$\alpha_0^* = R_f (1 - \alpha_1^*) + \phi \alpha_2^* + \varphi \alpha_3^* \tag{6.55}$$

with:

$$\begin{cases} \phi = \left[E(R_2) - R_f \right] - E(v_m^2) \\ \varphi = \left[E(R_3) - R_f \right] - E(v_m^3) \end{cases}$$

The three-factor APT model (6.53) leads one to restrict the asset return intercepts of the cubic market model (6.49) to a nonlinear combination of the asset return sensitivity coefficients with the market portfolio return and its orthogonalised components v_m^2 and v_m^3.

It is then possible to test, as in the traditional CAPM case, the four-moment CAPM with this restriction, or, more precisely, the three-factor APT version consistent with the four-moment CAPM. Indeed, rewriting the four-moment asset pricing relation (6.25) for the portfolio whose return is v_m^2, leads to:

$$\begin{aligned} E(v_m^2) - R_f = \left[E(R_m) - E(R_{Z_{m1}}) - E(R_{Z_{m2}}) + R_f \right] \beta_{v_m^2} \\ + \left[E(R_{Z_{m1}}) - R_f \right] \gamma_{v_m^2} + \left[E(R_{Z_{m2}}) - R_f \right] \delta_{v_m^2} \end{aligned} \tag{6.56}$$

with:

$$\begin{cases} \beta_{v_m^2} = \dfrac{\mathrm{Cov}\left(v_m^2, R_m\right)}{\sigma^2(R_m)} \\[2mm] \gamma_{v_m^2} = \dfrac{\mathrm{Cos}\left(v_m^2, R_m\right)}{s^3(R_m)} \\[2mm] \delta_{v_m^2} = \dfrac{\mathrm{Cok}\left(v_m^2, R_m\right)}{\kappa^4(R_m)} \end{cases}$$

Since R_2 is perfectly correlated with ν_m^2 and $E\left(R_2\right) < E\left(\nu_m^2\right)$, we can write the four-moment CAPM relation (6.25) and the quadratic market model restriction (6.52) as:

$$\left[E\left(R_2\right) - R_f\right] < \left[E\left(R_m\right) - E\left(R_{Z_{m1}}\right) - E\left(R_{Z_{m2}}\right) + R_f\right]\beta_{\nu_m^2}$$
$$+ \left[E\left(R_{Z_{m1}}\right) - R_f\right]\gamma_{\nu_m^2} + \left[E\left(R_{Z_{m2}}\right) - R_f\right]\delta_{\nu_m^2}$$

(6.57)

Moreover, since, by definition, the portfolio whose returns are given by ν_m^2 has a market beta equal to zero, we obtain:

$$\pi_1 = \left[E\left(R_{Z_{m1}}\right) - R_f\right]\gamma_{\nu_m^2} - \left[E\left(R_{Z_{m2}}\right) - R_f\right]\delta_{\nu_m^2}$$

(6.58)

The market value of π_1 (which is negative) gives an upper bound for the risk premium of the second common risk factor of the cubic market model (6.49), i.e. $\left[E\left(R_2\right) - R_f\right]$.

The restrictions (6.52), (6.55) and (6.58) differ from the ones obtained by Barone-Adesi (1985) and Barone-Adesi *et al.* (2004) in the mean–variance–skewness case since they assumed that the market portfolio return is linearly independent from its square.[39] Moreover, these restrictions are not applicable to the third risky portfolio, whose return is perfectly correlated with the cubed market portfolio return component ν_m^3. So, we have no supplementary indications concerning the risk premium associated with the third common risk factor of the cubic market model (6.49).

6.5 CONCLUSION

In this chapter we develop the theoretical foundations and restrictions for multi-moment capital asset pricing models. We first recall the main necessary hypotheses for an equilibrium asset-valuation relation when asset return distributions are asymmetric and leptokurtic. Investors are here supposed to be rational and aiming to maximise an objective function depending on the first four moments of their portfolio return distribution. We then use a two-fund monetary separation theorem to obtain an exact asset pricing relation independent of the functional of the investors' preference, called the four-moment CAPM fundamental relation. This approach leads simultaneously to the generalisation of a security market line into a security market hyperplane and to the identification – on *a priori* grounds – of the market risk premia and their signs. In this model, specific asset returns are a function of the market portfolio return but the relation is no longer linear as in the CAPM framework; it is, rather, a cubic one.

We also use the portfolio choice theory to investigate the general properties of the mean–variance–skewness–*kurtosis* efficient set. While no general mutual fund separation theorem seems to exist when centred moments higher than the second one are considered in the investor's optimisation program, we found that, under certain conditions, it is possible to generalise the fundamental four-moment CAPM relation when no riskless asset exists. Finally, we make the link between different multifactor models of asset returns – such as Black's model (1972), the three-moment CAPM, the cubic market model or the APT model of Ross (1976) – and the four-moment CAPM. All these relations appear to be different because of specific constraints on the implicit parameters.

---

[39] Which reduces to assuming that the market portfolio return has a zero mean and is normally distributed (Favre and Galeano, 2002).

The multi-moment CAPM relations having been presented, an obvious extension of our framework consists in the simplification of the mathematics of the mean–variance–skewness–*kurtosis* efficient frontier in order to prove the existence and the unicity of the three (two) uncorrelated portfolios considered in the pricing relation when no (one) riskless asset exists. This can be done either by imposing some heuristic restrictions on the higher-order moments of the portfolio returns (see Athayde and Flôres, 2002, 2003, 2004 and Chapter 2 of this Book) or by restricting the joint asset return distribution to a skew-elliptical multivariate separating distribution (see Ross, 1978; Ingersoll 1987; Ortobelli *et al.*, 2000).

Another extension of our work is the development of conditional versions of the Capital Asset Pricing Model in a non-elliptical uniperiodic or multiperiodic setting. A time-varying modelisation of a four-moment CAPM model can be achieved by using a regime-switching process (see Ang and Beckaert, 2002; Guidolin and Timmermann, 2005a and 2005b), a GARCH-model specification with a multivariate skewed student-*t* distribution for asset returns (see Bauwens and Laurent, 2002; Branco *et al.*, 2003 and Adcock, 2003), a conditional portfolio return specification with a Hansen's skewed-*t* univariate distribution (see Jondeau and Rockinger, 2003a), a Gram–Charlier Type A statistical series expansion (see Bera and Premaratne, 2001) or a conditional asymmetric copula with (non) elliptical marginal distributions (see Patton, 2001 and 2004, and Chapter 8 of this book).

Finally, it would be of great interest to test the information content of the different asset-pricing restrictions obtained in the mean–variance–skewness–*kurtosis* framework by using robust estimators[40] of realised higher-moment systematic risk measures (see Andersen *et al.*, 2001; Bollerslev and Zhang, 2003; Beine *et al.*, 2004) on individual stocks or by using hedge fund databases (see Favre and Ranaldo, 2004; Berényi, 2002 and 2004). It would also be interesting to investigate the relative performance of the 4-CAPM with respect to alternative asset pricing models that can take into account the skewness and the fat-tailedness of the asset return distributions (see Ang *et al.*, 2004, and Chapters 4 and 7 of this book). Another potential extension would consist in the derivation and test of higher-order moment performance measures (see Stephens and Proffitt, 1991; Chunhachinda *et al.*, 1994; Berényi, 2001, 2002 and 2004). All these extensions are left to future works.

APPENDIX A

Following Diacogiannis (1994), the skewness and the *kurtosis* of the portfolio return can be written, respectively, as a weighted average of the coskewness and the *cokurtosis* between the N risky asset returns and the portfolio return; that is, in the vectorial case:

$$\begin{cases} s^3 \left(R_p \right) = \mathbf{w}'_p \mathbf{\Sigma}_p \\ \kappa^4 \left(R_p \right) = \mathbf{w}'_p \mathbf{\Gamma}_p \end{cases}$$

where $\mathbf{w}'_p$ is the $(1 \times N)$ transposed vector of the investor's holdings of risky assets; $\mathbf{w}_p$ is the $(N \times 1)$ vector of the N risky assets in the portfolio p; $\mathbf{E}$ is the $(N \times 1)$ vector of the expected returns of risky assets; $\mathbf{\Sigma}_p$ is the $(N \times 1)$ vector of coskewness between the asset returns and the portfolio return and $\mathbf{\Gamma}_p$ is the $(N \times 1)$ vector of *cokurtosis* between the security returns and the portfolio return.

---

[40] Such as extreme value – range based – (see Parkinson, 1980; Garman and Klass, 1980; Kunitomo, 1992; Yang and Zhang, 2000), non-parametric (see Kim and White, 2004) or shrinkage estimators (see Ledoit and Wolf, 2003, 2004a and 2004b).

Proof   The coskewness and the *cokurtosis* between the returns on a security i and a portfolio p return are given by:

$$\begin{cases} \text{Cos}\,(R_i,\,R_p) = E\left\{[R_i - E\,(R_i)]\,[R_p - E\,(R_p)]^2\right\} \\ \text{Cok}\,(R_i,\,R_p) = E\left\{[R_i - E\,(R_i)]\,[R_p - E\,(R_p)]^3\right\} \end{cases} \qquad (6.59)$$

$\forall i,\ i = [1, \ldots, N]$.

Developing the square and the cube in (6.59) and rearranging terms, we have:

$$\begin{cases} \text{Cos}\,(R_i,\,R_p) = E\,(R_i\,R_p^2) - E\,(R_i)\ E\,(R_p^2) \\ \qquad\qquad - 2\,E\,(R_p)\,[E\,(R_iR_p) - E\,(R_i)\,E\,(R_p)] \\ \text{Cok}\,(R_i,\,R_p) = E\,(R_i\,R_p^3) - E\,(R_i)\,E\,(R_p^3) \\ \qquad\qquad - 3\,E\,(R_p)\,[E\,(R_i\,R_p^2) - E\,(R_i)\,E\,(R_p^2)] \\ \qquad\qquad + 3\,[E\,(R_p)]^2\,[E\,(R_i\,R_p) - E\,(R_i)\,E\,(R_p)] \end{cases} \qquad (6.60)$$

This is equivalent to:

$$\begin{cases} \text{Cos}\,(R_i,\,R_p) = \text{Cov}\,(R_i,\,R_p^2) - 2\,E\,(R_p)\,\text{Cov}\,(R_i,\,R_p) \\ \text{Cok}\,(R_i,\,R_p) = \text{Cov}\,(R_i,\,R_p^3) - 3\,E\,(R_p)\,\text{Cov}\,(R_i,\,R_p^2) + 3\,[E\,(R_p)]^2\,\text{Cov}\,(R_i,\,R_p) \end{cases} \qquad (6.61)$$

The skewness and the *kurtosis* of the rate of return on a portfolio p are given by:

$$\begin{cases} s^3\,(R_p) = E\,(R_p^3) - 3\,E\,(R_p^2)\,E\,(R_p) + 2\,[E\,(R_p)]^3 \\ \kappa^4\,(R_p) = E\,(R_p^4) - 4\,E\,(R_p^3)\,E\,(R_p) + 6\,E\,(R_p^2)\,[E\,(R_p)]^2 - 3\,[E\,(R_p)]^4 \end{cases} \qquad (6.62)$$

Using the definition of variance and the bilinear property of the covariance operator, the system of equations (6.62) can be simplified to:

$$\begin{cases} s^3\,(R_p) = \text{Cov}\,(R_p,\,R_p^2) - 2\,E\,(R_p)\,\sigma^2\,(R_p) \\ \kappa^4\,(R_p) = \text{Cov}\,(R_p,\,R_p^3) - 3\,E\,(R_p)\,\text{Cov}\,(R_p,\,R_p^2) + 3\,[E\,(R_p)]^2\,\sigma^2\,(R_p) \end{cases} \qquad (6.63)$$

Rearranging terms in (6.63) leads to:

$$\begin{cases} s^3\,(R_p) = \sum_{i=1}^{N} w_{pi}\,[\text{Cov}\,(R_i,\,R_p^2) - 2\,E\,(R_p)\,\text{Cov}\,(R_i,\,R_p)] \\ \kappa^4\,(R_p) = \sum_{i=1}^{N} w_{pi}\,\{\text{Cov}\,(R_i,\,R_p^3) - 3\,E\,(R_p)\,\text{Cov}\,(R_i,\,R_p^2) \\ \qquad\qquad + 3\,E\,[(R_p)]^2\,\text{Cov}\,(R_i,\,R_p)\} \end{cases} \qquad (6.64)$$

with:

$$\begin{cases} R_p = w_{p_0} R_f + \sum_{l=1}^{N} w_{pi} R_i \\ \sum_{i=1}^{N} w_{pi} = 1 \end{cases}$$

where w_{p_i} is the weight of the ith risky asset in the portfolio, with $i = [1, \ldots, N]$.

From (6.61) we find:

$$\begin{cases} s^3 (R_p) = \sum_{i=1}^{N} w_{pi} \, Cos (R_i, R_p) \\ \kappa^4 (R_p) = \sum_{i=1}^{N} w_{pi} \, Cok (R_i, R_p) \end{cases} \tag{6.65}$$

That is, in the vectorial case:

$$\begin{cases} s^3 (R_p) = \mathbf{w}'_p \, \mathbf{\Sigma}_p \\ \kappa^4 (R_p) = \mathbf{w}'_p \, \mathbf{\Gamma}_p \end{cases} \tag{6.66}$$

where $\mathbf{w}'_p$ is the $(1 \times N)$ vector of portfolio weights on a portfolio p; $\mathbf{\Sigma}_p$ is the $(N \times 1)$ vector of coskewness between the returns of N risky assets and the portfolio return; and $\mathbf{\Gamma}_p$ is the $(N \times 1)$ vector of *cokurtosis* between the returns of N risky assets and the portfolio return. ∎

APPENDIX B

The first derivatives of the skewness and of the *kurtosis* of the return portfolio with respect to $\mathbf{w}_p$, are, respectively, equal to three times the coskewness vector and four times the *cokurtosis* vector, that is:

$$\begin{cases} \dfrac{\partial s^3 (R_p)}{\partial \mathbf{w}_p} = 3 \mathbf{\Sigma}_p \\ \dfrac{\partial \kappa^4 (R_p)}{\partial \mathbf{w}_p} = 4 \mathbf{\Gamma}_p \end{cases} \tag{6.67}$$

where $\Omega \, \mathbf{w}_p$, $\mathbf{\Sigma}_p$ and $\mathbf{\Gamma}_p$ represent, respectively, the $(N \times 1)$ vectors of covariance, coskewness and *cokurtosis* between the risky asset returns and the portfolio p return.

Proof The nth centred moment of the return of a portfolio p is given by:

$$m^n (R_p) = E \left\{ [R_p - E (R_p)]^n \right\}$$
$$= E \left\{ \left[\sum_{i=1}^{N} w_{pi} (R_i - E (R_i)) \right]^n \right\} \tag{6.68}$$

Taking the first partial derivative of the nth centred moment of the portfolio return distribution with respect to w_{pi}, the ith entry of the $(N \times \mathbf{1})$ vector $\mathbf{w}_p$, yields:

$$\frac{\partial m^n (R_p)}{\partial w_{pi}} = n E \left\{ [R_i - E(R_i)][R_p - E(R_p)]^{(n-1)} \right\} = n C_n (R_i, R_p) \tag{6.69}$$

where $C_n (R_i, R_p)$ is the co-moment of nth order between the rate of return on the asset i and the rate of return on the portfolio p, with $i = [1, \ldots, N]$.

This last equation leads, in the vectorial case, to:

$$\frac{\partial m^n (R_p)}{\partial \mathbf{w}_p} = \begin{pmatrix} \dfrac{\partial m^n (R_p)}{\partial w_{p1}} \\ \vdots \\ \dfrac{\partial m^n (R_p)}{\partial w_{pN}} \end{pmatrix} = \begin{pmatrix} n C_n (R_1, R_p) \\ \vdots \\ n C_n (R_N, R_p) \end{pmatrix} = n \mathbf{C}_{np} \tag{6.70}$$

For $n = 3$ we obtain:

$$\frac{\partial s^3 (R_p)}{\partial \mathbf{w}_p} = \begin{pmatrix} \dfrac{\partial s^3 (R_p)}{\partial w_{p1}} \\ \vdots \\ \dfrac{\partial s^3 (R_p)}{\partial w_{pN}} \end{pmatrix} = \begin{pmatrix} 3 \operatorname{Cos} (R_1, R_p) \\ \vdots \\ 3 \operatorname{Cos} (R_N, R_p) \end{pmatrix} = 3 \mathbf{\Sigma}_p \tag{6.71}$$

For $n = 4$, we have:

$$\frac{\partial \kappa^4 (R_p)}{\partial \mathbf{w}_p} = \begin{pmatrix} \dfrac{\partial \kappa^4 (R_p)}{\partial w_{p1}} \\ \vdots \\ \dfrac{\partial \kappa^4 (R_p)}{\partial w_{pN}} \end{pmatrix} = \begin{pmatrix} 4 \operatorname{Cok} (R_1, R_p) \\ \vdots \\ 4 \operatorname{Cok} (R_N, R_p) \end{pmatrix} = 4 \mathbf{\Gamma}_p \tag{6.72}$$

APPENDIX C

The first-order conditions of the agent's portfolio problem are sufficient for a *maximum*, since the Hessian matrix of the expected utility function is negative definite.

Proof The second partial derivative of the expected utility of an investor k with respect to w_{pi} and w_{pj}, yields:

$$\frac{\partial^2 E[U_k (R_p)]}{\partial w_{pi} \partial w_{pj}} = E\left[U_k^{(2)} (R_p) R_i R_j \right] \tag{6.73}$$

with $(i, j) = [1, \ldots, N]^2$ and $k \in [1, \ldots, K]$.

The $(N \times N)$ Hessian matrix $\mathbf{H}_k$ of the expected utility function is then given by:

$$
\underset{(N \times N)}{\mathbf{H}_k} = E \left[U_k^{(2)} (R_p) \begin{pmatrix} R_1^2 & R_1 R_2 & \cdots & R_1 R_N \\ R_1 R_2 & R_2^2 & \cdots & R_2 R_N \\ \vdots & \vdots & \ddots & \vdots \\ R_1 R_N & R_2 R_N & \cdots & R_N^2 \end{pmatrix} \right] \tag{6.74}
$$

Premultiplying (6.74) by $\mathbf{w}_p'$ and postmultiplying it by $\mathbf{w}_p$ leads to the following quadratic form:

$$
\begin{aligned}
Q_k &= \mathbf{w}_p' \mathbf{H}_k \mathbf{w}_p \\
&= \sum_{i=1}^{N} \sum_{j=1}^{N} w_{pi} w_{pj} \, E \left[U_k^{(2)} (R_p) \, R_i R_j \right] \\
&= E \left[U_k^{(2)} (R_p) \left(\sum_{i=1}^{N} w_{pi} R_i \right)^2 \right]
\end{aligned} \tag{6.75}
$$

which is negative $\forall \mathbf{w}_p \neq \mathbf{0}$, with $\mathbf{w}_p \in IR^N$, since, by definition, investors are risk averse, i.e.: $U_k^{(2)} (R_p) < 0, \forall k \in [1, \ldots, K]$.

The Hessian matrix is then negative definite and the concavity condition is met.   ∎

APPENDIX D

On the existence and unicity of the portfolios Z_{p0}, Z_{p1} and Z_{p2}, we have to consider that they may not exist or be unique, since their definitions lead to systems that are generally underdetermined. We illustrate this point with the portfolio Z_{p0} – with weights $\mathbf{w}_{Z_{p0}}$ – which is zero-correlated, zero-coskewed and has a zero *cokurtosis* with the mean–variance–skewness–*kurtosis* efficient portfolio p; that is:

$$
\begin{cases}
\mathbf{w}_{Z_{p0}} \mathbf{\Omega} \mathbf{w}_p = 0 \\
\mathbf{w}_{Z_{p0}} \mathbf{\Sigma} \mathbf{w}_p^2 = 0 \\
\mathbf{w}_{Z_{p0}} \mathbf{\Gamma} \mathbf{w}_p^3 = 0
\end{cases} \tag{6.76}
$$

where $\mathbf{w}_p^2 = \mathbf{w}_p \odot \mathbf{w}_p$ and $\mathbf{w}_p^3 = \mathbf{w}_p \odot \mathbf{w}_p \odot \mathbf{w}_p$ (with $\odot$ being the Hanada element-by-element product). Matrices $\boldsymbol{\Omega}$, $\boldsymbol{\Sigma}$ and $\boldsymbol{\Gamma}$ are the covariance, the coskewness and *cokurtosis* matrices:

$$
\begin{cases}
\boldsymbol{\Omega} = \mathbf{R}'\mathbf{R} \\[6pt]
\boldsymbol{\Sigma} = \mathbf{R}'\mathbf{R} \odot \mathbf{R} \\[6pt]
\boldsymbol{\Gamma} = \mathbf{R}'\mathbf{R} \odot \mathbf{R} \odot \mathbf{R}
\end{cases}
\tag{6.77}
$$

where $\mathbf{R}'$ is the matrix of centred time-series of returns $r_{i,t}$ on the N assets i of the economy. These matrices are then composed with the following elements:

$$
\begin{cases}
\boldsymbol{\Omega}_{[i,j]} = \hat{\sigma}_{ij} = \dfrac{1}{T}\sum_{t=1}^{T}\left(r_{i,t}\, r_{j,t}\right) \\[14pt]
\boldsymbol{\Sigma}_{[i,j]} = \hat{\sigma}_{ijj} = \dfrac{1}{T}\sum_{t=1}^{T}\left(r_{i,t}\, r_{j,t}\, r_{j,t}\right) \\[14pt]
\boldsymbol{\Gamma}_{[i,j]} = \hat{\sigma}_{ijjj} = \dfrac{1}{T}\sum_{t=1}^{T}\left(r_{i,t}\, r_{j,t}\, r_{j,t}\, r_{j,t}\right)
\end{cases}
\tag{6.78}
$$

Weights $w_{Z_{p0i}}$ of the portfolio Z_{p0} are linked with the weights w_{pj} of the efficient portfolio p in the following way:

$$
\begin{cases}
\dfrac{1}{T}\sum_{t=1}^{T}\sum_{i=1}^{N}\sum_{j=1}^{N}\left[\left(w_{Z_{p0i}} r_{i,t}\right)\left(w_{pj}r_{j,t}\right)\right] = 0 \\[14pt]
\dfrac{1}{T}\sum_{t=1}^{T}\sum_{i=1}^{N}\sum_{j=1}^{N}\left[\left(w_{Z_{p0i}} r_{i,t}\right)\left(w_{pj}r_{j,t}\right)^2\right] = 0 \\[14pt]
\dfrac{1}{T}\sum_{t=1}^{T}\sum_{i=1}^{N}\sum_{j=1}^{N}\left[\left(w_{Z_{p0i}} r_{i,t}\right)\left(w_{pj}r_{j,t}\right)^3\right] = 0
\end{cases}
\tag{6.79}
$$

If we first assume the simplest case in a 4-CAPM framework with $N = 3$ for the sake of simplicity, we get the following system:

$$
S_3\left(\mathbf{w}_{Z_{p0}}, \mathbf{w}_p\right):
\begin{cases}
w_{Z_{p01}}\left(\mathbf{a}_{11}\mathbf{w}_p'\right) + w_{Z_{p02}}\left(\mathbf{a}_{12}\mathbf{w}_p'\right) + w_{Z_{p03}}\left(\mathbf{a}_{13}\mathbf{w}_p'\right) = 0 \\[8pt]
w_{Z_{p01}}\left(\mathbf{a}_{21}\mathbf{w}_p^{20}\right) + w_{Z_{p02}}\left(\mathbf{a}_{22}\mathbf{w}_p^{20}\right) + w_{Z_{p03}}\left(\mathbf{a}_{23}\mathbf{w}_p^{20}\right) = 0 \\[8pt]
w_{Z_{p01}}\left(\mathbf{a}_{31}\mathbf{w}_p^{30}\right) + w_{Z_{p02}}\left(\mathbf{a}_{32}\mathbf{w}_p^{30}\right) + w_{Z_{p03}}\left(\mathbf{a}_{33}\mathbf{w}_p^{30}\right) = 0
\end{cases}
\tag{6.80}
$$

where $\mathbf{a}_{kj}$ are line vectors of cross-products of returns, whose l-elements are: $\mathbf{a}_{kj}[l] = \sum_{t=1}^{T}[r_{l,t}\, r_{j,t}]$. In this case, the link between Z_{p0} and p can be denoted by $\mathbf{w}_{Z_{p0S_3}(\mathbf{w}_p,\mathbf{w}_{Z_{p0}})}$. and reads – after a straightforward calculus:

$$\mathbf{w}_{Z_{p0S_3}(\mathbf{w}_p,\mathbf{w}_{Z_{p0}})} : \tag{6.81}$$

$$
\begin{cases}
\begin{aligned}
w_{Z_{p01}} =\ & -\frac{(a_{12}w'_p)\left[(a_{23}w_p^{20})+\left[(a_{13}w'_p)/(a_{11}w'_p)\right]\right]}{(a_{11}w'_p)\left[(a_{22}w_p^{20})-\left[(a_{12}w'_p)/(a_{11}w'_p)\right]\right]}\\
&\times\left[\frac{(a_{12}w'_p)(a_{33}w_p^{30})}{(a_{11}w'_p)}\frac{\left[(a_{23}w_p^{20})(a_{12}w'_p)+(a_{13}w'_p)\right]}{\left[(a_{23}w_p^{20})(a_{12}w'_p)-(a_{12}w'_p)\right]}\right]\\
&\times\left[\frac{\left[(a_{33}w_p^{30})\left[(a_{23}w_p^{20})(a_{12}w'_p)-(a_{12}w'_p)\right]-(a_{32}w_p^{30})\left[(a_{23}w_p^{20})(a_{12}w'_p)+(a_{13}w'_p)\right]\right]}{\left[(a_{23}w_p^{20})(a_{12}w'_p)-(a_{12}w'_p)\right]}\right]^{-1}\\
&-\left[\frac{(a_{13}w'_p)(a_{12}w'_p)(a_{33}w_p^{30})}{(a_{11}w'_p)^2}\frac{\left[(a_{23}w_p^{20})(a_{12}w'_p)+(a_{13}w'_p)\right]}{\left[(a_{23}w_p^{20})(a_{12}w'_p)-(a_{12}w'_p)\right]}\right]\\
&\times\left[\frac{\left[(a_{33}w_p^{30})\left[(a_{23}w_p^{20})(a_{12}w'_p)-(a_{12}w'_p)\right]-(a_{32}w_p^{30})\left[(a_{23}w_p^{20})(a_{12}w'_p)+(a_{13}w'_p)\right]\right]}{\left[(a_{23}w_p^{20})(a_{12}w'_p)-(a_{12}w'_p)\right]}\right]^{-1}\\[2mm]
w_{Z_{p02}} =\ & -\frac{\left[(a_{23}w_p^{20})+\left[(a_{13}w'_p)/(a_{11}w'_p)\right]\right]}{\left[(a_{22}w_p^{20})-\left[(a_{12}w'_p)/(a_{11}w'_p)\right]\right]}\\
&\times\left[\frac{(a_{12}w'_p)(a_{33}w_p^{30})}{(a_{11}w'_p)}\frac{\left[(a_{23}w_p^{20})(a_{12}w'_p)+(a_{13}w'_p)\right]}{\left[(a_{23}w_p^{20})(a_{12}w'_p)-(a_{12}w'_p)\right]}\right]\\
&\times\left[\frac{\left[(a_{33}w_p^{30})\left[(a_{23}w_p^{20})(a_{12}w'_p)-(a_{12}w'_p)\right]-(a_{32}w_p^{30})\left[(a_{23}w_p^{20})(a_{12}w'_p)+(a_{13}w'_p)\right]\right]}{\left[(a_{23}w_p^{20})(a_{12}w'_p)-(a_{12}w'_p)\right]}\right]^{-1}\\[2mm]
w_{Z_{p03}} =\ & \left[\frac{(a_{12}w'_p)(a_{33}w_p^{30})}{(a_{11}w'_p)}\frac{\left[(a_{23}w_p^{20})(a_{12}w'_p)+(a_{13}w'_p)\right]}{\left[(a_{23}w_p^{20})(a_{12}w'_p)-(a_{12}w'_p)\right]}\right]\\
&\times\left[\frac{\left[(a_{33}w_p^{30})\left[(a_{23}w_p^{20})(a_{12}w'_p)-(a_{12}w'_p)\right]-(a_{32}w_p^{30})\left[(a_{23}w_p^{20})(a_{12}w'_p)+(a_{13}w'_p)\right]\right]}{\left[(a_{23}w_p^{20})(a_{12}w'_p)-(a_{12}w'_p)\right]}\right]^{-1}
\end{aligned}
\end{cases}
$$

The system is then just identified in this simplified case and that guarantees the emergence of an analytical solution.

In the general case with $N \geq 4$ and when considering portfolios p, Z_{p0}, Z_{p1} and Z_{p2} altogether, we need at least $4N$ conditions (4 specific portfolios times N asset weights) implying cross-terms of degree 3 or less. A natural idea would be to impose some further restrictions on the interrelations between portfolios p, Z_{p0}, Z_{p1} and Z_{p2}. In particular, since we are here in the skewed and leptokurtic world, we may require these different portfolio returns to be truly independent (in the sense of the covariance, the coskewness and the *cokurtosis* orthogonality). We thus have:

$$\left(\mathbf{w}_p, \mathbf{w}_{Z_{p0}}, \mathbf{w}_{Z_{p1}}, \mathbf{w}_{Z_{p2}}\right) = \left\{\mathbf{w}_{P_{S_N}\left(\mathbf{w}_p \cdot \mathbf{w}_{Z_{p0}}\right)} \cap \mathbf{w}_{P_{S_N}\left(\mathbf{w}_p \cdot \mathbf{w}_{Z_{p1}}\right)} \cap \mathbf{w}_{P_{S_N}\left(\mathbf{w}_p \cdot \mathbf{w}_{Z_{p2}}\right)} \cap \ldots \cap \mathbf{w}_{Z_{p2S_N}\left(\mathbf{w}_{Z_{p2}} \cdot \mathbf{w}_{Z_{p1}}\right)}\right\}$$

$$(6.82)$$

where $S_N(.)$ is the generalisation – to N assets and to portfolios p, Z_{p0}, Z_{p1} and Z_{p2} – of the previous $S_3\left(\mathbf{w}_p, \mathbf{w}_{Z_{p0}}\right)$ system for three assets and two portfolios. That implies 36 conditions ($2 \times 3 \times 3!$); adding a possible 16 arbitrary conditions (on the given moments of these portfolios), we can easily access a total of 52 conditions. That is clearly insufficient for a realistic developed financial market, but might be sufficient for asset allocation purposes.

Nevertheless, unicity – and more importantly the existence – of these desired portfolios Z_{p0}, Z_{p1} and Z_{p2}, is also an empirical question and is under the scope of this chapter. Indeed, first, we cannot guarantee – with given real financial asset characteristics – the existence of such portfolios on the market. One may guess, however, that the variety of tradable asset features has to be large enough for such portfolios to exist. Second, the dimension of the global system to be solved when $N \geq 4$ is too high for attaining a feasible analytical solution (one might think about the polynomial goal program approach or genetic algorithms to approach a satisfying solution). According to the results by Athayde and Flôres (1997 and 2000) and Berényi (2001 and 2002), who find reasonable market premia, we suppose in the following the existence of these portfolios and try to assess further asset pricing relations that are compatible with our simple set of hypotheses.

APPENDIX E

When return densities are asymmetric and leptokurtic, the vector of relative asset weights of any efficient portfolio p can be expressed as a linear combination of those of the following four distinct funds:

$$\mathbf{w}_{a_1} = \frac{\Omega^{-1}\mathbf{E}}{\mathbf{1}^0\Omega^{-1}\mathbf{E}}, \quad \mathbf{w}_{a_2} = \frac{\Omega^{-1}\mathbf{1}}{\mathbf{1}^0\Omega^{-1}\mathbf{1}}, \quad \mathbf{w}_{a_3} = \frac{\Omega^{-1}\Sigma_p}{\mathbf{1}^0\Omega^{-1}\Sigma_p} \quad \text{and} \quad \mathbf{w}_{a_4} = \frac{\Omega^{-1}\Gamma_p}{\mathbf{1}^0\Omega^{-1}\Gamma_p}$$

where $\mathbf{E}$ is the ($N \times 1$) vector of the expected returns of risky assets; $\mathbf{1}$ is the ($N \times 1$) unit vector; Ω is the nonsingular ($N \times N$) variance–covariance matrix of the N risky asset returns; Σ_p is the ($N \times 1$) vector of coskewness between the asset returns and the portfolio p return; and Γ_p is the ($N \times 1$) vector of *cokurtosis* between securities and portfolio p returns.

Proof The solution of the investor's portfolio selection program is given by solving the following Lagrangian:

$$\mathcal{L} = \frac{1}{2}\mathbf{w}'_p\Omega\,\mathbf{w}_p + \lambda_1\left[\mu_p - \mathbf{w}'_p\mathbf{E}\right] + \lambda_2\left[1 - \mathbf{w}'_p\mathbf{1}\right] \qquad (6.83)$$

$$+ \frac{\lambda_3}{3}\left[s_p^3 - \mathbf{w}'_p\Sigma_p\right] + \frac{\lambda_4}{4}\left[\kappa_p^4 - \mathbf{w}'_p\Gamma_p\right]$$

where λ_1, λ_2, λ_3 and λ_4 are the Lagrange coefficients and μ_p, s_p^3, κ_p^4 represent the levels of expected return, skewness and *kurtosis* fixed by the investor considered.

The first-order conditions are:

$$\begin{cases} \dfrac{\partial \mathscr{L}}{\partial \mathbf{w}_p} = \mathbf{\Omega}\mathbf{w}_p - \lambda_1 \mathbf{E} - \lambda_2 \mathbf{1} - \lambda_3 \mathbf{\Sigma}_p - \lambda_4 \mathbf{\Gamma}_p = 0 \\[2mm] \dfrac{\partial \mathscr{L}}{\partial \lambda_1} = \mu_p - \mathbf{w}_p' \mathbf{E} = 0 \\[2mm] \dfrac{\partial \mathscr{L}}{\partial \lambda_2} = 1 - \mathbf{w}_p' \mathbf{1} = 0 \\[2mm] \dfrac{\partial \mathscr{L}}{\partial \lambda_3} = s_p^3 - \mathbf{w}_p' \mathbf{\Sigma}_p = 0 \\[2mm] \dfrac{\partial \mathscr{L}}{\partial \lambda_4} = \kappa_p^4 - \mathbf{w}_p' \mathbf{\Gamma}_p = 0 \end{cases} \tag{6.84}$$

Premultiplying the first equation of the system (6.84) by the inverse matrix $\mathbf{\Omega}^{-1}$ and rearranging yields:

$$\mathbf{w}_p = \lambda_1 \mathbf{\Omega}^{-1}\mathbf{E} + \lambda_2 \mathbf{\Omega}^{-1}\mathbf{1} + \lambda_3 \mathbf{\Omega}^{-1}\mathbf{\Sigma}_p + \lambda_4 \mathbf{\Omega}^{-1}\mathbf{\Gamma}_p \tag{6.85}$$

that is:

$$\mathbf{w}_p = \delta_1 \frac{\mathbf{\Omega}^{-1}\mathbf{E}}{\mathbf{1}^0\,\mathbf{\Omega}^{-1}\mathbf{E}} + \delta_2 \frac{\mathbf{\Omega}^{-1}\mathbf{1}}{\mathbf{1}^0\,\mathbf{\Omega}^{-1}\mathbf{1}} + \delta_3 \frac{\mathbf{\Omega}^{-1}\mathbf{\Sigma}_p}{\mathbf{1}^0\mathbf{\Omega}^{-1}\mathbf{\Sigma}_p} + \delta_4 \frac{\mathbf{\Omega}^{-1}\mathbf{\Gamma}_p}{\mathbf{1}^0\,\mathbf{\Omega}^{-1}\mathbf{\Gamma}_p} \tag{6.86}$$

with:

$$\begin{cases} \delta_1 = \lambda_1\, \mathbf{1}^0 \mathbf{\Omega}^{-1}\mathbf{E} \\[1mm] \delta_2 = \lambda_2\, \mathbf{1}^0 \mathbf{\Omega}^{-1}\mathbf{1} \\[1mm] \delta_3 = \lambda_3\, \mathbf{1}^0 \mathbf{\Omega}^{-1}\mathbf{\Sigma}_p \\[1mm] \delta_4 = \lambda_4\, \mathbf{1}^0\, \mathbf{\Omega}^{-1}\mathbf{\Gamma}_p \end{cases}$$

and:

$$\delta_1 + \delta_2 + \delta_3 + \delta_4 = 1$$

■

APPENDIX F

When a riskless asset exists, the vector of asset weights of any mean–variance–skewness–*kurtosis* efficient portfolio can be represented by a linear combination of those of the riskless asset and of the three following distinct risky funds:

$$\mathbf{w}_{a_5} = \frac{\mathbf{\Omega}^{-1}\left(\mathbf{E} - R_f \mathbf{1}\right)}{\mathbf{1}^0\mathbf{\Omega}^{-1}\left(\mathbf{E} - R_f \mathbf{1}\right)}, \quad \mathbf{w}_{a_6} = \frac{\mathbf{\Omega}^{-1}\mathbf{\Sigma}_p}{\mathbf{1}^0\,\mathbf{\Omega}^{-1}\mathbf{\Sigma}_p} \text{ and } \mathbf{w}_{a_7} = \frac{\mathbf{\Omega}^{-1}\mathbf{\Gamma}_p}{\mathbf{1}^0\,\mathbf{\Omega}^{-1}\mathbf{\Gamma}_p}$$

where R_f is the risk-free rate; $\mathbf{E}$ is the $(N \times 1)$ vector of the expected return of risky assets; $\mathbf{1}$ is the $(N \times 1)$ unit vector; and $\mathbf{\Omega w}_p$, $\mathbf{\Sigma}_p$, $\mathbf{\Gamma}_p$ are, respectively, the $(N \times 1)$ vectors of covariance, coskewness and *cokurtosis* between the risky asset returns and the portfolio p return.

Proof   If we introduce a riskless asset, the investor's programme becomes:

$$\underset{\mathbf{w}_p}{\text{Min}} \left\{ \frac{1}{2} \mathbf{w}'_p \mathbf{\Omega} \, \mathbf{w}_p \right\} \tag{6.87}$$

$$\text{s.t.} \begin{cases} \mathbf{w}'_p \mathbf{E} + \left(1 - \mathbf{w}'_p \mathbf{1}\right) R_f = \mu_p \\ \mathbf{w}'_p \mathbf{\Sigma}_p = s^3_p \\ \mathbf{w}'_p \mathbf{\Gamma}_p = \kappa^4_p \end{cases}$$

where μ_p, s^3_p, κ^4_p are the levels of expected return, skewness and *kurtosis* fixed by the investor considered.

Using the same approach as previously, we obtain:

$$\mathbf{w}_p = \lambda'_1 \mathbf{\Omega}^{-1} \left(\mathbf{E} - R_f \mathbf{1}\right) + \lambda'_2 \mathbf{\Omega}^{-1} \mathbf{\Sigma}_p + \lambda'_3 \mathbf{\Omega}^{-1} \mathbf{\Gamma}_p \tag{6.88}$$

where λ'_1, λ'_2 and λ'_3 are the Lagrange coefficients.
That is:

$$\mathbf{w}_p = \delta_5 \frac{\mathbf{\Omega}^{-1} \left(\mathbf{E} - R_f \mathbf{1}\right)}{\mathbf{1}^0 \, \mathbf{\Omega}^{-1} \left(\mathbf{E} - R_f \mathbf{1}\right)} + \delta_6 \frac{\mathbf{\Omega}^{-1} \mathbf{\Sigma}_p}{\mathbf{1}^0 \, \mathbf{\Omega}^{-1} \mathbf{\Sigma}_p} + \delta_7 \frac{\mathbf{\Omega}^{-1} \mathbf{\Gamma}_p}{\mathbf{1}^0 \, \mathbf{\Omega}^{-1} \mathbf{\Gamma}_p} \tag{6.89}$$

with:

$$\begin{cases} \delta_5 = \lambda'_1 \, \mathbf{1}^0 \, \mathbf{\Omega}^{-1} \left(\mathbf{E} - R_f \mathbf{1}\right) \\ \delta_6 = \lambda'_2 \, \mathbf{1}^0 \, \mathbf{\Omega}^{-1} \mathbf{\Sigma}_p \\ \delta_7 = \lambda'_3 \, \mathbf{1}^0 \, \mathbf{\Omega}^{-1} \mathbf{\Gamma}_p \end{cases}$$

and:

$$w_{a_8} = 1 - \mathbf{w}'_p \mathbf{1} = 1 - \delta_5 - \delta_6 - \delta_7$$

APPENDIX G

In the absence of a riskless asset, the four-moment CAPM relation is written as:

$$\mathbf{E} - E\left(R_{Z_{p0}}\right) \mathbf{1} = \left\{ \left[E\left(R_p\right) - E\left(R_{Z_{p1}}\right)\right] - \left[E\left(R_{Z_{p2}}\right) - E\left(R_{Z_{p0}}\right)\right] \right\} \mathbf{\Omega} \, \mathbf{w}_p \left[\sigma^2\left(R_p\right)\right]^{-1}$$

$$+ \left[E\left(R_{Z_{p1}}\right) - E\left(R_{Z_{p0}}\right)\right] \mathbf{\Sigma}_p \left[s^3\left(R_p\right)\right]^{-1}$$

$$+ \left[E\left(R_{Z_{p2}}\right) - E\left(R_{Z_{p0}}\right)\right] \mathbf{\Gamma}_p \left[\kappa^4\left(R_p\right)\right]^{-1}$$

where $E(R_{Z_{p0}})$ represents the expected return on a portfolio whose return is zero-correlated and has a zero coskewness and a zero *cokurtosis* with the return of the portfolio p; $E(R_{Z_{p1}})$ represents the expected return on a portfolio whose return is zero-correlated with the portfolio p and has a coskewness equal to the skewness of that portfolio return and a *zero cokurtosis* with it; $E(R_{Z_{p2}})$ represents the expected return on a portfolio whose return is zero-correlated with the portfolio p and has a zero coskewness with it and a *cokurtosis* equal to the *kurtosis* of that portfolio return; $\Omega \mathbf{w}_p$, Σ_p, Γ_p are the $(N \times 1)$ vectors of covariance, coskewness and *cokurtosis* between the risky asset returns and the portfolio p return; and $\sigma^2(R_p) \neq 0$, $s^3(R_p) \neq 0$ and $\kappa^4(R_p) \neq 0$.

Proof   The $(N \times 1)$ vector of the covariances between the return of a portfolio p and the returns of the N risky assets is $\Omega \mathbf{w}_p$. Consequently, using the first equation of the system (6.84) we obtain:

$$\Omega \mathbf{w}_p = \lambda_1 \mathbf{E} + \lambda_2 \mathbf{1} + \lambda_3 \Sigma_p + \lambda_3 \Gamma_p \tag{6.90}$$

which can be rewritten, if we assume that $\lambda_1 \neq 0$ (i.e. the expected return constraint is binding), as:

$$\mathbf{E} = \theta_{p_1} \Omega \mathbf{w}_p + \theta_{p_2} \mathbf{1} + \theta_{p_3} \Sigma_p + \theta_{p_4} \Gamma_p \tag{6.91}$$

where:

$$\begin{cases} \theta_{p_1} = (\lambda_1)^{-1} \\[2mm] \theta_{p_2} = -\left(\dfrac{\lambda_2}{\lambda_1}\right) \\[2mm] \theta_{p_3} = -\left(\dfrac{\lambda_3}{\lambda_1}\right) \\[2mm] \theta_{p_4} = -\left(\dfrac{\lambda_4}{\lambda_1}\right) \end{cases}$$

To determine the values of the parameters θ_{p_1}, θ_{p_2}, θ_{p_3} and θ_{p_4}, we premultiply (6.91) by the transpose vectors $\mathbf{w}'_p$, $\mathbf{w}'_{Z_{p0}}$, $\mathbf{w}'_{Z_{p1}}$ and $\mathbf{w}'_{Z_{p2}}$, denoting respectively the $(1 \times N)$ vector of portfolio weights for the efficient portfolio p, the $(1 \times N)$ vector of portfolio weights for a portfolio Z_{p0} whose return is uncorrelated with the return of the portfolio p and which possesses a zero coskewness and zero *cokurtosis* with it, the $(1 \times N)$ vector of portfolio weights for a portfolio Z_{p1} whose return is uncorrelated with the return of that portfolio p and which possesses a unitary relative coskewness and a zero *cokurtosis* with it and the $(1 \times N)$ vector of portfolio weights for a portfolio Z_{p2} whose return is uncorrelated with the return of that portfolio p and which possesses a zero coskewness and a unitary relative *cokurtosis* with it.[41]

---

[41] That is:

$$\begin{cases} \mathrm{Cos}\left(R_p, R_{Z_{p1}}\right) = s^3(R_p) \\[2mm] \mathrm{Cok}\left(R_p, R_{Z_{p2}}\right) = \kappa^4(R_p) \end{cases}$$

We thus obtain:

$$
\begin{cases}
E\left(R_p\right) = \theta_{p_1} \sigma^2\left(R_p\right) + \theta_{p_2} + \theta_{p_3} s^3\left(R_p\right) + \theta_{p_4} \kappa^4\left(R_p\right) \\
E\left(R_{Z_{p0}}\right) = \theta_{p_2} \\
E\left(R_{Z_{p1}}\right) = \theta_{p_2} + \theta_{p_3} s^3\left(R_p\right) \\
E\left(R_{Z_{p2}}\right) = \theta_{p_2} + \theta_{p_4} \kappa^4\left(R_p\right)
\end{cases}
\tag{6.92}
$$

The resolution of this system for θ_{p_1}, θ_{p_2}, θ_{p_3} and θ_{p_4} gives:

$$
\begin{cases}
\theta_{p_1} = \left\{ \dfrac{\left[E\left(R_p\right) - E\left(R_{Z_{p1}}\right)\right] - \left[E\left(R_{Z_{p2}}\right) - E\left(R_{Z_{p0}}\right)\right]}{\sigma^2\left(R_p\right)} \right\} \\[2mm]
\theta_{p_2} = E\left(R_{Z_0}\right) \\[2mm]
\theta_{p_3} = \dfrac{\left[E\left(R_{Z_{p1}}\right) - E\left(R_{Z_{p0}}\right)\right]}{s^3\left(R_p\right)} \\[2mm]
\theta_{p_4} = \dfrac{\left[E\left(R_{Z_{p2}}\right) - E\left(R_{Z_{p0}}\right)\right]}{\kappa^4\left(R_p\right)}
\end{cases}
\tag{6.93}
$$

with $\sigma^2\left(R_p\right) \neq 0$, $s^3\left(R_p\right) \neq 0$ and $\kappa^4\left(R_p\right) \neq 0$.
Substituting these values into Equation (6.91) leads to the desired result.

APPENDIX H

In the absence of a riskless asset, the asset risk premia of a Pareto-optimal equilibrium are given by the equation:

$$
\mathbf{E} - E\left(R_{Z_{m0}}\right)\mathbf{1} = \left\{\left[E\left(R_m\right) - E\left(R_{Z_{m1}}\right)\right] - \left[E\left(R_{Z_{m2}}\right) - E\left(R_{Z_{m0}}\right)\right]\right\}\boldsymbol{\beta}
$$
$$
+ \left[E\left(R_{Z_{m1}}\right) - E\left(R_{Z_{m0}}\right)\right]\boldsymbol{\gamma} + \left[E\left(R_{Z_{m2}}\right) - E\left(R_{Z_{m0}}\right)\right]\boldsymbol{\delta}
$$

with:

$$
\begin{cases}
\boldsymbol{\beta} = \left[\sigma^2\left(R_m\right)\right]^{-1}\boldsymbol{\Omega}\mathbf{w}_m \\
\boldsymbol{\gamma} = \left[s^3\left(R_m\right)\right]^{-1}\boldsymbol{\Sigma}_m \\
\boldsymbol{\delta} = \left[\kappa^4\left(R_m\right)\right]^{-1}\boldsymbol{\Gamma}_m
\end{cases}
$$

where $E\left(R_{Z_{m0}}\right)$ represents the expected return on a portfolio whose return is zero-correlated and has a zero coskewness zero *cokurtosis* with the return of the market portfolio; $E\left(R_{Z_{m1}}\right)$ represents the expected return on a portfolio whose return is zero-correlated with the market portfolio and has a coskewness equal to the skewness of the market portfolio and a zero *cokurtosis* with it; $E\left(R_{Z_{m2}}\right)$ represents the expected return on a portfolio whose return is zero-correlated with the market portfolio m and has a zero coskewness with it and a *cokurtosis* equal to the *kurtosis* of the market portfolio; Ωw_m, Σ_m, Γ_m are the $(N \times 1)$ vectors of covariance, coskewness and *cokurtosis* between the risky asset returns and the market portfolio return; and $\sigma^2\left(R_m\right) \neq 0$, $s^3\left(R_m\right) \neq 0$ and $\kappa^4\left(R_m\right) \neq 0$.

Proof The study of the properties of the mean–variance–skewness–*kurtosis* frontier showed that any efficient portfolio p – that does not belong to the variance–skewness–*kurtosis* efficient set – must satisfy the following equality:

$$
\mathbf{E} - E\left(R_{Z_{p0}}\right)\mathbf{1} = \left\{\left[E\left(R_p\right) - E\left(R_{Z_{p1}}\right)\right] - \left[E\left(R_{Z_{p2}}\right) - E\left(R_{Z_{p0}}\right)\right]\right\} \Omega\, w_p\left[\sigma^2\left(R_p\right)\right]^{-1}
$$

$$
+ \left[E\left(R_{Z_{p1}}\right) - E\left(R_{Z_{p0}}\right)\right]\Sigma_p\left[s^3\left(R_p\right)\right]^{-1}
$$

$$
+ \left[E\left(R_{Z_{p2}}\right) - E\left(R_{Z_{p0}}\right)\right]\Gamma_p\left[\kappa^4\left(R_p\right)\right]^{-1}
$$

$$
\tag{6.94}
$$

where $E\left(R_p\right)$ is the expected return on the efficient portfolio p and $E(R_{Z_{p0}})$, $E(R_{Z_{p1}})$ and $E(R_{Z_{p2}})$ are the expected return on uncorrelated portfolios with portfolio p, characterised respectively by a zero coskewness and a zero *cokurtosis* with it, a unitary relative coskewness and a zero *cokurtosis* with the portfolio p and a zero coskewness and a unitary relative *cokurtosis* with the efficient portfolio considered; and $\sigma^2\left(R_p\right) \neq 0$, $s^3\left(R_p\right) \neq 0$ and $\kappa^4\left(R_p\right) \neq 0$.

Previously, we have established that when there exists a Pareto-optimal equilibrium allocation, the market portfolio must be a mean–variance–skewness–*kurtosis* efficient portfolio. Consequently, to obtain the relation (6.94), it is sufficient to show that the market portfolio does not belong to the minimum variance frontier in the variance–skewness–*kurtosis* space. This condition is always satisfied, unless we assume that all traded assets possess the same expected return, which is in contradiction to our hypothesis of nonredundancy of the securities. ∎

APPENDIX I

If the asset returns conform to the cubic market model, the systematic risk measures of the fourth-moment CAPM are a linear combination of the coefficients of the cubic DGP.

Proof Consider the cubic market model:

$$
\begin{cases}
\mathbf{R} - R_f\mathbf{1} = \alpha_0 + \left(R_m - R_f\right)\alpha_1 + \left[R_m - E\left(R_m\right)\right]^2 \alpha_2 + \left[R_m - E\left(R_m\right)\right]^3 \alpha_3 + \varepsilon \\
E(\varepsilon) = 0 \\
E(\varepsilon | R_m, R_m^2, R_m^3) = 0
\end{cases}
\tag{6.95}
$$

where $\mathbf{R}$ is the $(N \times 1)$ vector of the returns of risky assets; α_0 is the $(N \times 1)$ vector of asset return intercepts; α_1, α_2 and α_3 are, respectively, the $(N \times 1)$ vectors of asset return sensitivities with the market portfolio return, the squared and the cubed market portfolio return and ε is the $(N \times 1)$ vector of asset return disturbances.

Subtracting from (6.95) its expected value gives:

$$\mathbf{R} - \mathbf{E} = [R_m - E(R_m)]\,\alpha_1$$
$$+ \left\{[R_m - E(R_m)]^2 - \sigma^2(R_m)\right\}\alpha_2 \tag{6.96}$$
$$+ \left\{[R_m - E(R_m)]^3 - s^3(R_m)\right\}\alpha_3 + \varepsilon$$

Provided that the sixth centred moment of the market portfolio return exists, we obtain, using the definition of the relative risk measures $\boldsymbol{\beta}$, $\boldsymbol{\gamma}$ and $\boldsymbol{\delta}$, the desired results; that is:

$$\begin{cases} \boldsymbol{\beta} = \alpha_1 + \left[\dfrac{s^3(R_m)}{\sigma^2(R_m)}\right]\alpha_2 + \left[\dfrac{\kappa^4(R_m)}{\sigma^2(R_m)}\right]\alpha_3 \\[2mm] \boldsymbol{\gamma} = \alpha_1 + \left\{\dfrac{\kappa^4(R_m) - [\sigma^2(R_m)]^2}{s^3(R_m)}\right\}\alpha_2 + \left\{\dfrac{\xi^5(R_m) - \sigma^2(R_m)\,s^3(R_m)}{s^3(R_m)}\right\}\alpha_3 \\[2mm] \boldsymbol{\delta} = \alpha_1 + \left\{\dfrac{\xi^5(R_m) - \sigma^2(R_m)\,s^3(R_m)}{\kappa^4(R_m)}\right\}\alpha_2 + \left\{\dfrac{\psi^6(R_m) - [s^3(R_m)]^2}{\kappa^4(R_m)}\right\}\alpha_3 \end{cases} \tag{6.97}$$

with:

$$\begin{cases} \boldsymbol{\beta} = [\sigma^2(R_m)]^{-1}\,E\left\{[R_m - E(R_m)](\mathbf{R} - \mathbf{E})\right\} \\[2mm] \boldsymbol{\gamma} = [s^3(R_m)]^{-1}\,E\left\{[R_m - E(R_m)]^2(\mathbf{R} - \mathbf{E})\right\} \\[2mm] \boldsymbol{\delta} = [\kappa^4(R_m)]^{-1}\,E\left\{[R_m - E(R_m)]^3(\mathbf{R} - \mathbf{E})\right\} \end{cases}$$

where $\xi^5(R_m)$ and $\psi^6(R_m)$ represent, respectively, the fifth and sixth centred moments of the market portfolio returns.

APPENDIX J

When asset returns conform to the cubic market model (6.49), and standard APT hypotheses are met, the expected return on a large diversified portfolio perfectly correlated with the squared market portfolio return component ν_m^2 which is independent of the market portfolio return, denoted $E(R_2)$, must verify the following inequality:

$$E(R_2) < E(\nu_m^2)$$

Proof   Consider an arbitrage (with zero net investment) well-diversified portfolio a with:

$$\begin{cases} \alpha_{1a}^* = 0 \\[1mm] \alpha_{2a}^* = 1 \\[1mm] \alpha_{3a}^* = 0 \end{cases} \tag{6.98}$$

From the Arbitrage Pricing Theory, we have:

$$E(R_a) = E(R_2) \tag{6.99}$$

Due to the perfect correlation of the well-diversified portfolio a with the second risk factor v_m^2 of the cubic market model (6.95), it is possible to express the return of this portfolio as:

$$R_a \simeq \alpha_{0a}^* + v_m^2 \tag{6.100}$$

Taking the conditional expected value of expression (6.100) yields:

$$E\left(R_a \mid v_m^2\right) = \alpha_{0a}^* + v_m^2 \tag{6.101}$$

Taking the expected value of expression (6.101), we obtain:

$$E\left[E\left(R_a \mid v_m^2\right)\right] = E(R_a) = \alpha_{0a}^* + E\left(v_m^2\right) \tag{6.102}$$

That is, using (6.99):

$$\alpha_{0a}^* = E(R_2) - E\left(v_m^2\right) \tag{6.103}$$

Substituting this expression into Equation (6.100), we obtain:

$$R_a \simeq \left[E(R_2) - E\left(v_m^2\right)\right] + v_m^2 \tag{6.104}$$

When the condition $E(R_2) < E\left(v_m^2\right)$ does not hold, asset returns are always non-negative and no market equilibrium is possible. ∎

ACKNOWLEDGEMENTS

We are grateful to Chris Adcock, Giovanni Barone-Adesi, Thierry Chauveau, Campbell Harvey, Eric Jondeau, Thierry Michel, Ser-huang Poon, Michael Rockinger, Stephen Satchell and Alan Timmermann for help and encouragement in preparing this work. The content of this chapter engages only its authors and does not necessarily reflect the opinions of their employers.

REFERENCES

Adcock, C. (2003) Asset Pricing and Portfolio Selection Based on the Multivariate Skew-Student Distribution, Working Paper, University of Sheffield, 15 pages.

Adcock, C. (2004) Capital Asset Pricing for UK Stocks under the Multivariate Skew-Normal Distribution. In: *Skew-Elliptical Distributions and their Applications: A Journey beyond Normality*, M. Genton (Ed.) Chapman & Hall/CRC Press, pp. 191–204.

Adcock, C. (2005) Exploiting Skewness to Build an Optimal Hedge Fund with a Currency Overlay, *European Journal of Finance* 11, 445–462.

Adcock, C. and K. Shutes (2000) Fat Tails and The Capital Asset Pricing Model. In: *Advances in Quantitative Asset Management*, C. Dunis (Ed.) Kluwer.

Adcock, C. and K. Shutes (2001) Portfolio Selection Based on the Multivariate Skew Normal Distribution, Working Paper, *Financial Modelling*, A. Skulimowski (Ed.), Krakow, 9 pages.

Agarwal, V. and N. Naik (2004) Risks and Portfolio Decisions Involving Hedge Funds, *Review of Financial Studies* **17**, 63–98.

Alexander, G. and A. Baptista (2002) Economic Implications of Using a Mean-VaR Model for Portfolio Selection: A Comparison with Mean–Variance Analysis, *Journal of Economic Dynamics and Control* **26**, 1159–1193.

Alexander, G. and A. Baptista (2003) Portfolio Performance Evaluation Using Value-at-Risk, *Journal of Portfolio Management* **29**, 93–102.

Andersen, T., T. Bollerslev, F. Diebold and H. Ebens (2001) The Distribution of Stock Return Volatility, *Journal of Financial Economics* **61**, 43–76.

Ang, A. and G. Beckaert (2002) International Asset Allocation with Regime Shifts, *Review of Financial Studies* **15**, 1137–1187.

Ang, A., J. Chen and X. Xing (2004) Downside Risk, Working Paper, University of Columbia, 43 pages.

Arrow, K. (1970) *Essays in the Theory of Risk Bearing*, North-Holland Publishing Company, Amsterdam–London.

Athayde, G. and R. Flôres (1997) A CAPM with Higher Moments: Theory and Econometrics, Discussion Paper EPGE-FGV, 23 pages.

Athayde, G. and R. Flôres (2000) Introducing Higher Moments in the CAPM: Some Basic Ideas. In: *Advances in Quantitative Asset Management*, C. Dunis (Ed.), Kluwer, 23 pages.

Athayde, G. and R. Flôres (2002) Portfolio Frontier with Higher Moments: The Undiscovered Country, Discussion Paper EPGE-FGV, 42 pages.

Athayde, G. and R. Flôres (2003) Incorporating Skewness and Kurtosis in Portfolio Optimization: A Multidimensional Efficient Set. In: *Advances in Portfolio Construction and Implementation*, S. Satchell and A. Scowcroft (Eds), Butterworth Heinemann, pp. 243–257.

Athayde, G. and R. Flôres (2004) Finding a Maximum Skewness Portfolio: a General Solution to Three-moments Portfolio Choice, *Journal of Economic Dynamics and Control* **28**, 1335–1352.

Barone-Adesi, G. (1985) Arbitrage Equilibrium with Skewed Asset Returns, *Journal of Financial and Quantitative Analysis* **20**, 299–311.

Barone-Adesi, G., P. Gagliardini and G. Urga (2004) Testing Asset Pricing Models with Coskewness, Working Paper, *Journal of Business and Economic Statistics* **22**, 474–485.

Bauwens, L. and S. Laurent (2002) A New Class of Multivariate Skew Densities with Application to GARCH Models, CORE Discussion Paper 20, University of Louvain, 35 pages.

Beine, M., S. Laurent and F. Palm (2004) Central Bank Forex Interventions Assessed Using Realized Moments, CORE Discussion Paper 1, University of Louvain, 39 pages.

Bera, A. and G. Premaratne (2001) Modeling Asymmetry and Excess Kurtosis in Stock Return Data, Working Paper, Illinois University, 25 pages.

Berényi, Z. (2001) Performance of Leveraged Asset Funds, Working Paper, University of Munich, 42 pages.

Berényi, Z. (2002) Measuring Hedge Funds' Risks with Moment-based Variance-equivalent Measures, Working Paper, University of Munich, 35 pages.

Berényi, Z. (2004) *Risk and Performance Evaluation with Skewness and Kurtosis for Conventional and Alternative Investments*, Peter Lang Publishing.

Black, F. (1972) Capital Market Equilibrium with Restricted Borrowing, *Journal of Business* **7**, 444–454.

Black, F. (1976) Studies of Stock Price Volatility Changes, *Proceedings of the 1976 meeting of the Business and Economic Statistics Section*, American Statistical Association, pp. 177–181.

Black, F. (1993) Beta and Return, *Journal of Portfolio Management*, Fall 1993, 8–18.

Black, F. and M. Scholes (1973) The Pricing of Options and Corporate Liabilities, *Journal of Political Economy* **81**, 637–654.

Blanchard, O. and M. Watson (1982) Bubbles, Rational Expectations and Financial Markets. In: *Crises in Economic and Financial Structure*, P. Wachtel (Ed.), Lexington Books, pp. 295–315.

Bollerslev, T. (1986) Generalized AutoRegressive Conditional Heteroskedasticity, *Journal of Econometrics* **31**, 307–327.

Bollerslev, T. and B. Zhang (2003) Measuring and Modeling Systematic Risk in Factor Pricing Models Using High-frequency Data, *Journal of Empirical Finance* **10**, 533–558.

Bollerslev, T., R. Engle and J. Wooldridge (1988) A Capital Asset Pricing Model with Time-varying Covariances, *Journal of Political Economy* **96**, 116–131.

Bookstaber, R. and R. Clarke (1981) Options Can Alter Portfolio Return Distributions, *Journal of Portfolio Management* **7**, 63–70.

Branco, M., D. Dey and S. Sahu (2003) A New Class of Multivariate Skew Distributions with Applications to Bayesian Regression Models, *Canadian Journal of Statistics* **31**, 129–150.

Brav, A., G. Constantinides and C. Géczy (2002) Asset Pricing with Heterogeneous Consumers and Limited Participation: Empirical Evidence, *Journal of Political Economy* **110**, 793–824.

Briec, W., K. Kerstens and O. Jokung (2006) Mean–Variance–Skewness Portfolio Performance Gauging: A General Shortage Function and Dual Approach, *Management Science forthcoming*.

Brooks, R. and R. Faff (1998) A Test of a Two-factor APT based on the Quadratic Market Model: International Evidence, *Studies in Economics and Econometrics* **22**, 65–76.

Carhart, M. (1997) On Persistence in Mutual Fund Performance, *Journal of Finance* **52**, 57–82.

Cass, D. and J. Stiglitz (1970) The Structure of Investor Preferences and Asset Returns, and Separability in Portfolio Allocation: A Contribution to the Pure Theory of Mutual Funds, *Journal of Economic Theory* **2**, 122–160.

Chamberlain, G. (1983) A Characterization of the Distributions that Imply Mean–Variance Utility Functions, *Journal of Economic Theory* **29**, 185–201.

Chang, C., T. Pactwa and A. Prakash (2003) Selecting a Portfolio with Skewness: Recent Evidence from US, European, and Latin American Equity Markets, *Journal of Banking and Finance* **27**, 1375–1390.

Chen, J., H. Hong and J. Stein (2001) Forecasting Crashes: Trading Volume, Past Returns and Conditional Skewness in Stock Prices, *Journal of Financial Economics* **61**, 345–381.

Christie, A. and A. Andrew (1982) The Stochastic Behavior of Common Stock Variances: Value, Leverage, and Interest Rate Effects, *Journal of Financial Economics* **23**, 407–432.

Christie-David, R. and M. Chaudhry (2001) Coskewness and Cokurtosis in Futures Markets, *Journal of Empirical Finance* **8**, 55–81.

Chung, P., H. Johnson and M. Schill (2006) Asset Pricing When Returns are Nonnormal: Fama–French Factors *vs* Higher-Order Systematic Co-Moments, *Journal of Business* **79**.

Chunhachinda, P., K. Dandapani, K. Hamid and S. Prakash (1994) Efficacy of Portfolio Performance Measures: An Evaluation, *Quarterly Journal of Business and Economics* **33**, 74–87.

Chunhachinda, P., K. Dandapani, K. Hamid and S. Prakash (1997) Portfolio Selection and Skewness: Evidence from International Stock Markets, *Journal of Banking and Finance* **21**, 143–167.

Conine, T. and M. Tamarkin (1981) On Diversification Given Asymmetry in Returns, *Journal of Finance* **36**, 1143–1155.

Conine, T. and M. Tamarkin (1982) On Diversification Given Asymmetry in Returns: Erratum, *Journal of Finance* **37**, 1101.

Corrado, C. and T. Su (1996a) S&P 500 Index Option Tests of Jarrow and Rudd's Approximate Option Valuation Formula, *Journal of Futures Markets* **16**, 611–629.

Corrado, C. and T. Su (1996b) Skewness and Kurtosis in S&P 500 Index Returns Implied by Option Prices, *Journal of Financial Research* **19**, 175–192.

Davies, R., H. Kat and S. Lu (2004) Single Strategy Fund of Hedge Funds, Working Paper, ISMA Center, 27 pages.

Davies, R., H. Kat and S. Lu (2005) Fund of Hedge Funds Portfolio Selection: A Multiple-Objective Approach, Working Paper, ISMA Center, 34 pages.

Diacogiannis, G. (1994) Three-parameter Asset Pricing, *Managerial and Decision Economics* **15**, 149–158.

Dittmar, R. (2002) Nonlinear Pricing Kernels, Kurtosis Preference, and Evidence from the Cross-Section of Equity Returns, *Journal of Finance* **57**, 369–403.

Faff, R., Y. Ho and L. Zhang (1998) A GMM Test of the Three-moment CAPM in Australian Equity Markets, *Asia Pacific Journal of Finance* **1**, 45–60.

Fama, E. (1965) The Behavior of Stock Prices, *Journal of Business* **38**, 34–105.

Fama, E. (1996) Discounting under Uncertainty, *Journal of Business* **69**, 415–428.

Fama, E. and K. French (1992) The Cross-section of Expected Stock Returns, *Journal of Finance* **47**, 427–465.

Fama, E. and K. French (1995) Size and Book-to-Market Factors in Earnings and Returns, *Journal of Finance* **50**, 131–155.

Fang, H. and T. Lai (1997) Co-kurtosis and Capital Asset Pricing, *Financial Review* **32**, 293–307.

Favre, L. and J. Galeano (2002) An Analysis of Hedge Fund Performance Using Loess Fit Regression, *Journal of Alternative Investments*, Spring, 8–24.

Favre, L. and A. Ranaldo (2004) How to Price Hedge Funds: From Two- to Four-Moment CAPM, Working Paper, UBS, 18 pages.

Feller, W. (1971) *An Introduction to Probability Theory and its Applications*, Volume II, John Wiley & Sons, Inc., New York.

Friedman, M. and L. Savage (1948) The Utility Analysis of Choices Involving Risk, *Journal of Political Economy* **56**, 279–304.

Friend, I. and R. Westerfield (1980) Co-skewness and Capital Asset Pricing, *Journal of Finance* **35**, 897–913.

Galagedera, D., D. Henry and P. Silvapulle (2004a) Empirical Evidence on the Conditional Relation Between Higher-order Systematic Co-Moments and Security Returns, *Quarterly Journal of Business and Economics* **42**, 121–137.

Galagedera, D. and E. Maharaj (2004b) Wavelet Timescales and Conditional Relationship between Higher Order Systematic Co-moments and Portfolio Returns: Evidence in Australian Data, Working Paper, Monash University, 30 pages.

Gamba, A. and F. Rossi (1997) A Three-moment Based Capital Asset Pricing Model, Working Paper, University of Venice, 16 pages.

Gamba, A. and F. Rossi (1998a) A Three-moment Based Portfolio Selection Model, *Rivista di Matematica per le Scienze Economiche e Sociali* **20**, 25–48.

Gamba, A. and F. Rossi (1998b) Mean–Variance–Skewness Analysis in Portfolio Choice and Capital Markets, *Ricerca Operativa* **28**, Special Issue 1998, 5–46.

Garman, M. and M. Klass (1980) On the Estimation of Security Price Volatilities from Historical Data, *Journal of Business* **53**, 67–78.

Glosten, L. and R. Jagannathan (1994) A Contingent Claim Approach to Performance Evaluation, *Journal of Empirical Finance* **1**, 133–160.

Goetzmann, W., J. Ingersoll, M. Spiegel and I. Welch (2004) Sharpening Sharpe Ratios, Working Paper, Yale University, 51 pages.

Golec, J. and M. Tamarkin (1998) Bettors Love Skewness, not Risk, at the Horse Track, *Journal of Political Economy* **106**, 205–225.

Graddy, D. and G. Homaifar (1988) Equity Yields in Models Considering Higher Moments of the Return Distribution, *Applied Economics* **20**, 325–334.

Guidolin, M. and A. Timmermann (2005a) Optimal Portfolio Choices under Regime Switching, Skew and Kurtosis Preferences, Working Paper, Federal Reserve Bank of St Louis, 35 pages.

Guidolin, M. and A. Timmermann (2005b) International Asset Allocation under Regime Switching, Skew and Kurtosis Preferences, Working Paper, Federal Reserve Bank of St Louis, 54 pages.

Hamada, M. and E. Valdez (2004) CAPM and Option Pricing with Elliptical Distributions, Working Paper, University of Sydney, 32 pages.

Harvey, C. and S. Siddique (2000a) Conditional Skewness in Asset Pricing Tests, *Journal of Finance* **54**, 1263–1296.

Harvey, C. and S. Siddique (2000b) Time-Varying Conditional Skewness and the Market Risk Premium, *Research in Banking and Finance* **1**, 25–58.

Harvey, C. and S. Siddique (2001) The Cross-Section of Expected Risk Exposure, Working Paper, Duke University, 31 pages.

Harvey, C. and G. Zhou (1993) International Asset Pricing with Alternative Distributional Specifications, *Journal of Empirical Finance* **1**, 107–131.

Harvey, C., J. Lietchty, M. Lietchty and P. Müller (2004) Portfolio Selection with Higher Moments, Working Paper, Duke University, 51 pages.

Henriksson, R. and R. Merton (1981) On Market Timing and Investment Performance. II. Statistical Procedures for Evaluating Forecasting Skills, *Journal of Business* **54**, 513–533.

Hong, H. and J. Stein (1999) A Unified Theory of Underreaction, Momentum Trading and Overreaction in Asset Markets, *Journal of Finance* **6**, 2143–2184.

Hong, H. and J. Stein (2003) Differences of Opinion, Short-Sales Constraints, and Market Crashes, *Review of Financial Studies* **16**, 487–525.

Hübner, G. and D. Honhon (2002) Equilibrium Asset Pricing with Nonparametric Horizon Risk, Working Paper, University of Liège, 26 pages.

Hung, D., M. Shackleton and X. Xu (2004) CAPM, Higher Co-moment and Factor Models of UK Stock Returns, *Journal of Business Finance and Accounting* **31**, 87–112.

Hwang, S. and C. Pedersen (2002) Best Practice Risk Measurement in Emerging Markets: Empirical Test of Asymmetric Alternatives to CAPM, Working Paper, CASS University, 35 pages.

Hwang, S. and S. Satchell (1999) Modelling Emerging Market Risk Premia Using Higher Moments, *International Journal of Finance and Economics* **4**, 271–296.

Ingersoll, J. (1975) Multidimensional Security Pricing, *Journal of Financial and Quantitative Analysis* **10**, 785–798.

Ingersoll, J. (1987) *Theory of Financial Decision Making*, Rowman & Littlefield, Totowa.

Jagannathan, R. and Z. Wang (1996) The Conditional CAPM and the Cross-section of Expected Returns, *Journal of Finance* **51**, 3–53.

Jarrow, R. and A. Rudd (1982) Approximate Option Valuation for Arbitrary Stochastic Processes, *Journal of Financial Economics* **10**, 347–369.

Jondeau, E. and M. Rockinger (2003a) Conditional Volatility, Skewness and Kurtosis: Existence, Persistence and Comovements, *Journal of Economic Dynamics and Control* **27** (10), 1699–1737.

Jondeau, E. and M. Rockinger (2003b) How Higher Moments Affect the Allocation of Assets, *Finance Letters* **1** (2), 1–5.

Jondeau, E. and M. Rockinger (2006) Optimal Portfolio Allocation Under Higher Moments, *Journal of the European Financial Management Association* **12**, 29–67.

Joro, T. and P. Na (2001) Portfolio Performance Evaluation in Mean–Variance–Skewness Framework, Working Paper, University of Alberta, 22 pages.

Jurczenko, E. and B. Maillet (2001) The 3-CAPM: Theoretical Foundations and an Asset Pricing Model Comparison in a Unified Framework. In: *Developments in Forecast Combination and Portfolio Choice*, C. Dunis, A. Timmermann and J. Moody (Eds), John Wiley & Sons, Ltd, Chichester, pp. 239–273.

Jurczenko, E., B. Maillet and B. Negrea (2002a) Skewness and Kurtosis Implied by Option Prices: A Second Comment, FMG Discussion Paper 419, LSE, 32 pages.

Jurczenko, E., B. Maillet and B. Negrea (2002b) Revisited Multi-moment Approximate Option Pricing Models: A General Comparison, FMG Discussion Paper 430, LSE, 85 pages.

Jurczenko, E., B. Maillet and B. Negrea (2004) A Note on Skewness and Kurtosis Adjusted Option Pricing Models under the Martingale Restriction, *Quantitative Finance* **4**, 479–488.

Kahneman, D. and A. Tversky (1979) Prospect Theory: An Analysis of Decision under Risk, *Econometrica* **47**, 263–291.

Kane, A. (1982) Skewness Preference and Portfolio Choice, *Journal of Financial and Quantitative Analysis* **17**, 15–25.

Kim, T. and H. White (2004) On More Robust Estimation of Skewness and Kurtosis, *Finance Research Letters* **1**, 56–73.

Kraus, A. and R. Litzenberger (1976) Skewness Preference and the Valuation of Risk Assets, *Journal of Finance* **31**, 1085–1099.

Kunitomo, N. (1992) Improving the Parkinson Method of Estimating Security Price Volatilities, *Journal of Business* **65**, 295–302.

Lai, T. (1991) Portfolio with Skewness: A Multiple-objective Approach, *Review of Quantitative Finance and Accounting* **1**, 293–305.

Ledoit, O. and M. Wolf (2003) Improved Estimation of the Covariance Matrix of Stock Returns with an Application to Portfolio Selection, *Journal of Empirical Finance* **10**, 603–621.

Ledoit, O. and M. Wolf (2004a) A Well-conditioned Estimator for Large-dimensional Covariance Matrices, *Journal of Multivariate Analysis* **88**, 365–411.

Ledoit, O. and M. Wolf (2004b) Honey, I Shrunk the Sample Covariance Matrix, *Journal of Portfolio Management* **30**, 110–119.

Lim, K. (1989) A New Test of the Three-moment Capital Asset Pricing Model, *Journal of Financial and Quantitative Analysis* **24**, 205–216.

Lim, G., E. Maasoumi and V. Martin (2004) Discounting the Equity Premium Puzzle, Working Paper, University of Melbourne, 48 pages.

Lintner, J. (1965) The Valuation of Risk Assets and the Selection of Risky Investments in Stock Portfolios and Capital Budgets, *Review of Economics and Statistics* **13**, 13–37.

Litzenberger, K., K. Ramaswamy and H. Sosin (1980) On the CAPM Approach to the Estimation of A Public Utility's Cost of Equity Capital, *Journal of Finance* **35**, 369–383.

Mandelbrot, B. (1997) *Fractals and Scaling in Finance*, Springer-Verlag, New York.

Markowitz, H. (1952) Portfolio Selection, *Journal of Finance* **7**, 77–91.

Mitchell, M. and T. Pulvino (2001) Characteristics of Risk and Return in Risk Arbitrage, *Journal of Finance* **56**, 2135–2175.

Mitton, T. and K. Vorkink (2004) Equilibrium Underdiversification and the Preference for Skewness, Working Paper, Marriot School of Management, 45 pages.

Mossin, J. (1966) Equilibrium in a Capital Market, *Econometrica* **34**, 768–783.

Nantell, T., B. Price and K. Price (1982) Variance and Lower Partial Moments Measures of Systematic Risk: Some Analytical and Empirical Results, *Journal of Finance* **37**, 843–855.

Nummelin, K. (1997) Global Coskewness and the Pricing of Finnish Stocks: Empirical Tests, *Journal of International Financial Markets, Institutions and Money* **7**, 137–155.

Okunev, J. (1990) An Alternative Measure of Mutual Fund Performance, *Journal of Business, Finance and Accounting* **17**, 247–264.

Ortobelli, S., S. Rachev and E. Schwartz (2000) The Problem of Optimal Asset Allocation with Stable Distributed Returns, Working Paper, UCLA, 50 pages.

Owen, J. and R. Rabinovitch (1983) On the Class of Elliptical Distributions and their Applications to the Theory of Portfolio Choice, *Journal of Finance* **38**, 745–752.

Parkinson, M. (1980) The Extreme Value Method for Estimating the Variance of the Rate of Return, *Journal of Business* **53**, 61–65.

Patton, A. (2001) On the Importance of Skewness and Asymmetric Dependence in Stock Returns for Asset Allocation, Working Paper, UCSD, 67 pages.

Patton, A. (2004) On the Out-of-Sample Importance of Skewness and Asymmetric Dependence for Asset Allocation, *Journal of Financial Econometrics* **2**, 130–168.

Pedersen, C. and S. Satchell (1998) An Extended Family of Financial Risk Measures, *Geneva Papers on Risk and Insurance Theory* **23**, 89–117.

Pindyck, R. (1984) Risk, Inflation, and the Stock Market, *American Economic Review* **74**, 335–352.

Polimenis, V. (2002) The Distributional CAPM: Connecting Risk Premia to Return Distributions, Working Paper, University of California, 67 pages.

Pratt, J. (1964) Risk Aversion in the Small and the Large, *Econometrica* **32**, 122–136.

Pressacco, F. and P. Stucchi (2000) Linearity Properties of a Three-moments Portfolio Model, *Decisions in Economics and Finance* **23**, 133–150.

Rachev, S. and S. Mittnik (2000) *Stable Paretian Models in Finance Series*, John Wiley & Sons, Ltd, Chichester.

Racine, M. (1998) Hedging Volatility Shocks to the Canada Opportunity Set, *Journal of Business and Economics* **37**, 59–79.

Rolph, D. (2003) Co-skewness, Firm-Level Equity Returns and Financial Leverage, Working Paper, University of Washington, 36 pages.

Ross, S. (1976) The Arbitrage Theory of Capital Asset Pricing Theory, *Journal of Economic Theory* **13**, 341–360.

Ross, S. (1978) Mutual Fund Separation in Financial Theory: The Separation Distributions, *Journal of Economic Theory* **17**, 254–286.

Rubinstein, M. (1973) The Fundamental Theorem of Parameter-preference Security Valuation, *Journal of Financial and Quantitative Analysis* **8**, 61–69.

Samuelson, P. (1970) The Fundamental Approximation Theorem of Portfolio Analysis in Terms of Means, Variances and Higher Moments, *Review of Economic Studies* **37**, 537–543.

Sánchez-Torres, P. and E. Sentana (1998) Mean–Variance–Skewness Analysis: An Application to Risk Premia in the Spanish Stock Market, *Investigaciones Económicas* **22**, 5–17.

Sears, R. and K. Wei (1985) Asset Pricing, Higher Moments, and the Market Risk Premium: A Note, *Journal of Finance* **40**, 1251–1253.

Sears, R. and K. Wei (1988) The Structure of Skewness Preferences in Asset Pricing Models with Higher Moments: An Empirical Test, *Financial Review* **23**, 25–38.

Semenov, A. (2004) High-Order Consumption Moments and Asset Pricing, Working Paper, York University, 38 pages.

Shalit, H. and S. Yitzhaki (1984) Mean-Gini, Portfolio Theory, and the Pricing of Risky Assets, *Journal of Finance* **39**, 1449–1468.

Sharpe, W. (1964) Capital Asset Prices: A Theory of Market Equilibrium under Conditions of Risk, *Journal of Finance* **19**, 425–442.

Simaan, Y. (1993) Portfolio Selection and Asset Pricing Three Parameter Framework, *Management Science* **5**, 568–577.

Simkowitz, M. and W. Beedles (1978) Diversification in a Three- moment World, *Journal of Financial and Quantitative Analysis* **13**, 927–941.

Stephens, A. and D. Profitt (1991) Performance Measurement when Return Distributions are Nonsymmetric, *Quarterly Journal of Business and Economics* **30**, 23–41.

Stutzer, M. (2003) Portfolio Choice with Endogenous Utility: A Large Deviations Approach, *Journal of Econometrics* **116**, 365–386.

Sun, Q. and X. Yan (2003) Skewness Persistence with Optimal Portfolio Selection, *Journal of Banking and Finance* **27**, 1111–1121.

Tsiang, S. (1972) The Rationale of the Mean–Standard Deviation Analysis, Skewness Preference, and the Demand for Money, *American Economic Review* **62**, 354–371.

Vinod, H. (2004) Ranking Mutual Funds Using Unconventional Utility Theory and Stochastic Dominance, *Journal of Empirical Finance* **11**, 353–377.

von Neumann, J. and O. Morgenstern (2004) *Theory of Games and Economic Behaviour*, Sixtieth Anniversary Edition, Princeton University Press, Princeton.

Yang, D. and Q. Zhang (2000) Drift Independent Volatility Estimation Based on High, Low, Open, and Close Prices, *Journal of Business* **73**, 477–492.

7

Multi-moment Method for Portfolio Management: Generalised Capital Asset Pricing Model in Homogeneous and Heterogeneous Markets

Yannick Malevergne and Didier Sornette

ABSTRACT

We introduce a new set of consistent measures of risk, in terms of the semi-invariants of probability density functions (pdf). The main interest of this new class of risk measures is to provide a flexible tool allowing the final user to put more emphasis on the particular size of risk to which he is more sensitive. Some typical and well-known examples of such risk measures are the centred moments and the cumulants of the portfolio distribution of returns. We then derive generalised efficient frontiers based on these novel measures of risk and present the generalised CAPM, both in the cases of homogeneous and heterogeneous markets.

7.1 INTRODUCTION

The Capital Asset Pricing Model (CAPM) is still the most widely used approach to relative asset valuation, although its empirical roots have been found weaker and weaker in recent years. This asset-valuation model describing the relationship between expected risk and expected return for marketable assets is strongly entangled with the Mean–Variance Portfolio Model. Indeed both of them rely, to a large extent, on the description of the probability density function (pdf) of asset returns in terms of Gaussian functions. The mean–variance description is thus at the basis of Markowitz's portfolio theory (Markowitz, 1959) and of the CAPM (Sharpe, 1964).

In general, the determination of the risks and returns associated with a given portfolio comprising N assets is completely embedded in the knowledge of their multivariate distribution of returns. Indeed, the dependence between random variables is completely described by their joint distribution. This remark entails the two major problems of portfolio theory: 1) determining the multivariate distribution function of asset returns; 2) deriving from it useful measures of portfolio risks and using them to analyse and optimise portfolios. In the present chapter, we will focus mainly on the second problem.

The variance (or volatility) of portfolio returns provides the simplest way to quantify its fluctuations and is at the basis of Markowitz's portfolio selection theory. Nonetheless, the variance of a portfolio offers only a limited quantification of incurred risks (in terms of fluctuations), as the empirical distributions of returns have "fat tails" (Lux, 1996; Gopikrishnan et al., 1998; Malevergne et al., 2005 among many others) and the dependences between assets are only imperfectly accounted for by the covariance matrix (Litterman and Winkelmann, 1998). It is thus essential to extend portfolio theory and the CAPM to tackle these empirical facts.

The value-at-risk (Jorion, 1997) and many other measures of risk (Artzner et al., 1997, 1999; Sornette, 1998; Bouchaud et al., 1998; Sornette et al., 2000b) have been developed to account for the larger moves allowed by non-Gaussian distributions and nonlinear correlations, but they mainly allow for the assessment of down-side risks. Here, we consider both-sides risk and define general measures of fluctuation. This is the first goal of this chapter. Indeed, we characterise the minimum set of properties a fluctuation measure must fulfil. In particular, we show that any absolute central moments and some cumulants satisfy these requirements, as does any combination of these quantities. Moreover, the weights involved in these combinations can be interpreted in terms of the portfolio manager's aversion to large fluctuations.

Once the definition of the fluctuation measures has been given, it is possible to classify the assets and portfolios using, for instance, a risk-adjustment method (Sharpe, 1994; Dowd, 2000) and to develop a portfolio selection and optimisation approach. This is the second goal of this chapter.

Then, a new model of market equilibrium can be derived, which generalises the usual Capital Asset Pricing Model (CAPM). This is the third goal of our chapter. This improvement is necessary since, although the use of the CAPM is still widespread, its empirical justification has been found less and less convincing in recent years (Lim, 1989; Harvey and Siddique, 2000; Fama and French, 2004).

The chapter is organised as follows. Section 7.2 presents a new set of consistent measures of risk, in terms of the semi-invariants of pdfs, such as the centred moments and the cumulants of the portfolio distribution of returns, for example. Section 7.3 derives the generalised efficient frontiers based on these novel measures of risk. Cases with and without risk-free assets are analysed. Section 7.4 offers a generalisation of the Sharpe ratio and thus provides new tools to classify assets with respect to their risk-adjusted performance. In particular, we show that this classification may depend on the chosen risk measure. Section 7.5 presents the generalised CAPM based on these new measures of risk, both in the cases of homogeneous and heterogeneous agents. Section 7.6 concludes.

Before proceeding with the presentation of our results, we set the notation to derive the basic problem addressed in this chapter, namely the study of the distribution of the sum of weighted random variables with arbitrary marginal distributions and dependence. Consider a portfolio with n_i shares of asset i of price $p_i(0)$ at time $t = 0$ whose initial wealth is

$$W(0) = \sum_{i=1}^{N} n_i p_i(0) \qquad (7.1)$$

A time τ later, the wealth has become $W(\tau) = \sum_{i=1}^{N} n_i p_i(\tau)$ and the wealth variation is

$$\delta_\tau W \equiv W(\tau) - W(0) = \sum_{i=1}^{N} n_i p_i(0) \frac{p_i(\tau) - p_i(0)}{p_i(0)} = W(0) \sum_{i=1}^{N} w_i r_i(t, \tau) \qquad (7.2)$$

where

$$w_i = \frac{n_i p_i(0)}{\sum_{j=1}^{N} n_j p_j(0)} \tag{7.3}$$

is the fraction in capital invested in the ith asset at time 0 and the return $r_i(t, \tau)$ between time $t - \tau$ and t of asset i is defined as:

$$r_i(t, \tau) = \frac{p_i(t) - p_i(t - \tau)}{p_i(t - \tau)} \tag{7.4}$$

The definition (7.4) justifies us in writing the return S_τ of the portfolio over a time interval τ as the weighted sum of the returns $r_i(\tau)$ of the assets $i = 1, \ldots, N$ over the time interval τ

$$S_\tau = \frac{\delta_\tau W}{W(0)} = \sum_{i=1}^{N} w_i r_i(\tau) \tag{7.5}$$

We shall thus consider asset returns as the fundamental variables (denoted x_i or X_i). We shall consider a single timescale, τ, which can be chosen arbitrarily, say equal to one day. We shall thus drop the dependence on τ, understanding implicitly that all our results hold for returns estimated over the time step τ.

7.2   MEASURING LARGE RISKS OF A PORTFOLIO

The question of how to assess risk is recurrent in finance (and in many other fields) and has not yet received a general solution. Since the middle of the twentieth century, several paths have been explored. The pioneering work by von Neumann and Morgenstern (1947) has given birth to the mathematical definition of the expected utility function, which provides interesting insights on the behaviour of a rational economic agent and formalises the concept of risk aversion. Based upon the properties of the utility function, Rothschild and Stiglitz (1970, 1971) have attempted to define the notion of increasing risk. But, as revealed by Allais (1953, 1990), empirical investigation has proven that the postulates chosen by von Neumann and Morgenstern (1947) are actually often violated. Many generalisations have been proposed for curing the so-called Allais's Paradox, but up to now, no generally accepted procedure has been found in this way.

Recently, a theory by Artzner *et al.* (1997, 1999), and its generalisation by Föllmer and Schied (2002, 2003), have appeared. Based on a series of postulates that are quite natural, this theory allows one to build coherent (convex) measures of risk. In fact, this theory seems well-adapted to the assessment of the needed economic capital, that is, of the fraction of capital a company must keep as risk-free assets in order to face its commitments and thus avoid ruin. However, for the purpose of quantifying the fluctuations of the asset returns and of developing a theory of portfolios, this approach does not seem to be the most operational. Here, we shall rather revisit Markowitz's (1959) approach to investigate how its extension to higher-order moments or cumulants, and any combination of these quantities, can be used operationally to account for large risks.

7.2.1   Why do higher moments allow us to assess larger risks?

In principle, the complete description of the fluctuations of an asset at a given timescale is given by the knowledge of the probability density function (pdf) of its returns. The pdf encompasses all the risk dimensions associated with this asset. Unfortunately, it is impossible to classify or order the risks described by the entire pdf, except in special cases where the concept of stochastic dominance applies. Therefore, the whole pdf cannot provide an adequate measure of risk, embodied by a single variable. In order to perform a selection among a basket of assets and construct optimal portfolios, one needs measures given as real numbers, not functions, which can be ordered according to the natural ordering of real numbers on a line.

In this vein, Markowitz (1959) has proposed to summarise the risk of an asset by the variance of its pdf of returns (or, equivalently, by the corresponding standard deviation). It is clear that this description of risk is fully satisfying only for assets with Gaussian pdfs. In any other case, the variance generally provides a very poor estimate of the real risk. Indeed, it is a well-established empirical fact that the pdfs of asset returns have fat tails (Lux, 1996; Pagan, 1996; Gopikrishnan et al., 1998; Malevergne et al., 2005), so that the Gaussian approximation underestimates significantly the large price movements frequently observed on stock markets. Consequently, the variance cannot be taken as a suitable measure of risk, since it only accounts for the smallest contributions to the fluctuations of the asset returns.

The variance of the return X of an asset involves its second moment $E[X^2]$ and, more precisely, is equal to its second centred moment (or moment about the mean) $E\left[(X - E[X])^2\right]$. Thus, the weight of a given fluctuation X in the definition of the variance of the returns is proportional to its square. Due to the decay of the pdf of X for large X bounded from above by $\sim 1/|X|^{1+\alpha}$ with $\alpha > 2$, the largest fluctuations do not contribute significantly to this expectation. To increase their contributions, and in this way to account for the largest fluctuations, it is natural to invoke higher-order moments of order $n > 2$. The larger n becomes, the larger is the contribution of the rare and large returns in the tail of the pdf. This phenomenon is demonstrated in Figure 7.1, where we can observe the evolution of the quantity $x^n \cdot P(x)$ for $n = 1, 2$ and 4, where $P(x)$, in this example, is the standard exponential distribution e^{-x}. The expectation $E[X^n]$ is then simply represented geometrically as being equal to the area below the curve $x^n \cdot P(x)$. These curves provide an intuitive illustration of the fact that the main contributions to the moment $E[X^n]$ of order n come from values of X in the vicinity of the maximum of $x^n \cdot P(x)$, which increases quickly with the order n of the moment we consider, and makes the tail of the pdf of the returns X even fatter. For the exponential distribution chosen to construct Figure 7.1, the value of x corresponding to the maximum of $x^n \cdot P(x)$ is exactly equal to n. Thus, increasing the order of the moment allows one to sample larger fluctuations of the asset prices.

7.2.2   Quantifying the fluctuations of an asset

Let us now examine what should be the properties that consistent measures of risk adapted to the portfolio problem must satisfy in order to best quantify the asset price fluctuations. Let us consider an asset denoted X, and let $\mathcal{G}$ be the set of all the risky assets available on the market. Its profit and loss distribution is the distribution of $\delta X = X(\tau) - X(0)$, while the return distribution is given by the distribution of $\frac{X(\tau) - X(0)}{X(0)}$. The risk measures will be defined for the profit and loss distribution and then shown to be equivalent to another definition applied to the return distribution.

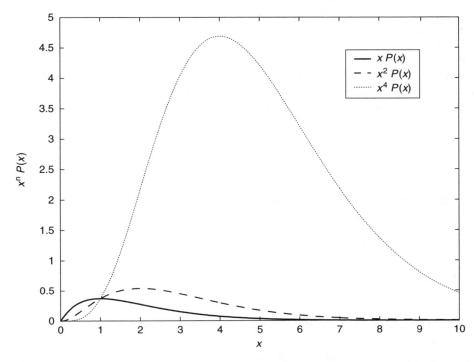

Figure 7.1 The function $x^n \cdot e^{-x}$ for $n = 1, 2$ and 4. The figure shows the typical size of the fluctuations involved in the moment of order n.

Our first requirement is that the risk measure $\rho(\cdot)$, which is a functional on $\mathcal{G}$, should always remain positive.

Axiom 1

$$\forall X \in \mathcal{G}, \quad \rho(\delta X) \geq 0$$

where the equality holds if and only if X is certain.[1] Let us now add to this asset a given amount a invested in the risk-free asset whose return is μ_0 (with, therefore, no randomness in its price trajectory) and define the new asset $Y = X + a$. Since a is nonrandom, the fluctuations of X and Y are the same. Thus, it is desirable that ρ enjoys the property of *translational invariance*, whatever the asset X and the nonrandom coefficient a may be, as in Axiom 2.

Axiom 2

$$\forall X \in \mathcal{G}, \forall a \in \mathbb{R}, \quad \rho(\delta X + \mu \cdot a) = \rho(\delta X)$$

We also require that our risk measure increases with the quantity of assets held in the portfolio. *A priori*, one should expect that the risk of a position is proportional to its size. Indeed, the fluctuations associated with the variable $2 \cdot X$, say, are naturally twice as large

---

[1] We say that X is *certain* if $X(\omega) = a$, for some $a \in \mathbb{R}$, for all $\omega \in \Omega$ such that $\mathbb{P}(\omega) \neq 0$, where $\mathbb{P}$ denotes a probability measure on $(\Omega, \mathcal{F})$ and $\mathcal{F}$ is an σ-algebra so that $(\Omega, \mathcal{F}, \mathbb{P})$ is a usual probability space.

as the fluctuations of X. This is true as long as we can consider that a large position can be cleared as easily as a smaller one. This is obviously not true, due to the limited liquidity of real markets. Thus, a large position in a given asset is more risky than the sum of the risks associated with the many smaller positions that add up to the large position. To account for this point, we assume that ρ depends on the size of the position in the same manner for all assets. This assumption is slightly restrictive but not unrealistic for companies with comparable properties in terms of market capitalisation or sector of activity (Farmer and Lillo, 2004). This requirement leads to Axiom 3.

Axiom 3

$$\forall X \in \mathcal{G}, \forall \lambda \in \mathbb{R}_+, \quad \rho(\lambda \cdot \delta X) = f(\lambda) \cdot \rho(\delta X)$$

where the function $f : \mathbb{R}_+ \longrightarrow \mathbb{R}_+$ is increasing and convex to account for liquidity risk. In fact, it is straightforward to show[2] that the only functions satisfying this axiom are the functions $f_\alpha(\lambda) = \lambda^\alpha$ with $\alpha \geq 1$, so that Axiom 3 can be reformulated in terms of positive homogeneity of degree α to give Axiom 4.

Axiom 4

$$\forall X \in \mathcal{G}, \forall \lambda \in \mathbb{R}_+, \quad \rho(\lambda \cdot \delta X) = \lambda^\alpha \cdot \rho(\delta X) \tag{7.6}$$

Note that the case of liquid markets is recovered by $\alpha = 1$, for which the risk is directly proportional to the size of the position.

These axioms, which define our risk measures for profit and loss, can easily be extended to the returns of the assets. Indeed, the return is nothing but the profit and loss divided by the initial value $X(0)$ of the asset. One can thus easily check that the risk defined on the profit and loss distribution is $[X(0)]^\alpha$ times the risk defined on the return distribution. From here on, we will only consider this later definition and, to simplify the notation, since we will only consider the returns and not the profit and loss, the notation X will be used to denote the asset price and its return as well.

We can remark that the risk measures ρ enjoying the two properties defined by Axioms 2 and 4 are known as the *semi-invariants* of the distribution of the profit and loss/returns of X (see Stuart and Ord, 1994, pp. 86–87). Among the large family of semi-invariants, we can cite the well-known centred moments and cumulants of X.

7.2.3 Examples

The set of risk measures obeying Axioms 1–4 is huge, since it includes all the homogeneous functionals of $(X - E[X])$, for instance. The centred moments (or moments about the mean) and the cumulants are two well-known classes of semi-invariants. Then, a given value of α can be seen as nothing but a specific choice of the order n of the centred moments or of the cumulants. In this case, our risk measures defined via these semi-invariants fulfil the two following conditions:

$$\rho(X + \mu) = \rho(X) \tag{7.7}$$

$$\rho(\lambda \cdot X) = \lambda^n \cdot \rho(X) \tag{7.8}$$

---

[2] Using the trick $\rho(\lambda_1 \lambda_2 \cdot \delta X) = f(\lambda_1) \cdot \rho(\lambda_2 \cdot \delta X) = f(\lambda_1) \cdot f(\lambda_2) \cdot \rho(\delta X) = f(\lambda_1 \cdot \lambda_2) \cdot \rho(\delta X)$ leading to $f(\lambda_1 \cdot \lambda_2) = f(\lambda_1) \cdot f(\lambda_2)$. The unique increasing convex solution of this functional equation is $f_\alpha(\lambda) = \lambda^\alpha$ with $\alpha \geq 1$.

In order to satisfy the positivity condition (Axiom 1), one needs to restrict the set of values taken by n. By construction, the centred moments of even order are always positive while the odd-order centred moments can be negative. In addition, a vanishing value of an odd-order moment does not mean that the random variable – or risk – $X \in \mathcal{G}$ is certain in the sense of footnote 1, since, for instance, any symmetric random variable has vanishing odd-order moments. Thus, only the even-order centred moments seem acceptable risk measures. However, this restrictive constraint can be relaxed by first recalling that, given any homogeneous function $f(\cdot)$ of order p, the function $f(\cdot)^q$ is also homogeneous of order $p \cdot q$. This allows one to decouple the order of the moments considered, which quantifies the impact of the large fluctuations, from the influence of the size of the positions held, measured by the degree of homogeneity of the measure ρ. Thus, considering any even-order centred moments, we can build a risk measure $\rho(X) = E\left[(X - E[X])^{2n}\right]^{\alpha/2n}$, which accounts for the fluctuations measured by the centred moment of order $2n$ but with a degree of homogeneity equal to α.

A further generalisation is possible for odd-order moments. Indeed, the *absolute* centred moments satisfy Axioms 1–4 for any odd or even order. So, we can even go one step further and use non-integer order absolute centred moments, and define the more general risk measure

$$\rho(X) = E\left[|X - E[X]|^{\gamma}\right]^{\alpha/\gamma} \tag{7.9}$$

where γ denotes any positive real number.

These sets of risk measures are very interesting since, due to the Minkowski inequality, they are convex for any α and γ larger than 1:

$$\rho(u \cdot X + (1 - u) \cdot Y) \leq u \cdot \rho(X) + (1 - u) \cdot \rho(Y) + \forall u \; \varepsilon[0, 1] \tag{7.10}$$

which ensures that aggregating two risky assets leads to diversifying their risk. In fact, in the special case $\gamma = 1$, these measures enjoy the stronger subadditivity property.

Finally, we should stress that any discrete or continuous (positive) sum of these risk measures, with the same degree of homogeneity, is again a risk measure. This allows us to define "spectral measures of fluctuations" in the spirit of Acerbi (2002):

$$\rho(X) = \int d\gamma \, \phi(\gamma) E\left[|X - E[X]|^{\gamma}\right]^{\alpha/\gamma} \tag{7.11}$$

where ϕ is a positive real-valued function defined on any subinterval of $[1, \infty)$ such that the integral in (7.11) remains finite. It is interesting to restrict oneself to the functions ϕ whose integral sums up to one: $\int d\gamma \, \phi(\gamma) = 1$, which is always possible, up to a renormalisation. Indeed, in such a case, $\phi(\gamma)$ represents the relative weight attributed to the fluctuations measured by a given moment order. Thus, the function ϕ can be considered as a measure of the risk aversion of the risk manager with respect to large fluctuations.

The situation is not so clear for the cumulants, since the even-order cumulants, as well as the odd-order ones, can be negative (even if, for a large class of distributions, even-order cumulants remain positive, especially for fat-tailed distributions – even though there are simple but somewhat artificial counter-examples). In addition, cumulants suffer from another problem with respect to the positivity axiom. As for odd-order centred moments, they can vanish even when the random variable is not certain. Just think of the cumulants of the Gaussian law. All but the first two (which represent the mean and the variance) are equal to zero. Thus, the strict formulation of the positivity axiom cannot be fulfilled by the cumulants. Should we thus reject them as useful measures of risk? It is important to emphasise that the cumulants enjoy a property that can be considered as a natural requirement for a risk measure. It can be desirable that the risk associated with a portfolio made of independent assets is exactly the sum of the risk associated with each individual asset. Thus, given N independent assets $\{X_1, \ldots, X_N\}$, and the portfolio $S_N = X_1 + \cdots + X_N$, we would like to have

$$\rho(S_N) = \rho(X_1) + \cdots + \rho(X_N) \tag{7.12}$$

This property is verified for all cumulants, while it is not true for centred moments. In addition, as seen from their definition in terms of the characteristic function

$$E\left[e^{ik \cdot X}\right] = \exp\left(\sum_{n=1}^{+\infty} \frac{(ik)^n}{n!} C_n\right) \tag{7.13}$$

cumulants C_n of order larger than 2 quantify deviations from the Gaussian law, and thus measure large risks beyond the variance (equal to the second-order cumulant). Finally, cumulants – seen as risk measures – have an interesting interpretation in terms of investors' behaviour, which will be discussed in Section 7.4.1.

To summarise, centred moments of even order possess all the minimal properties required for a suitable portfolio risk measure. Cumulants only partially fulfil these requirements, but have an additional advantage compared with centred moments; that is, they fulfil condition (7.12). For these reasons, we think it is interesting to consider both the centred moments and the cumulants in risk analysis and decision making. As a final remark, let us stress that the variance, originally used in Markowitz's portfolio theory (Markowitz, 1959), is nothing but the second centred moment, also equal to the second-order cumulant (the three first cumulants and centred moments are equal). Therefore, a portfolio theory based on the centred moments or on the cumulants automatically contains Markowitz's theory as a special case, and thus offers a natural generalisation encompassing large risks of this masterpiece of financial science. It also embodies several other generalisations where homogeneous measures of risk are considered, as, for instance, in Hwang and Satchell (1999).

7.3 THE GENERALISED EFFICIENT FRONTIER AND SOME OF ITS PROPERTIES

We now address the problem of the portfolio selection and optimisation, based on the risk measures introduced in the previous section. As we have already seen, there is a large choice of relevant risk measures from which the portfolio manager is free to choose as a function of his own aversion to small versus large risks. A strong risk aversion to large risks will lead him to choose a risk measure that puts the emphasis on large fluctuations. The simplest examples of such risk measures are provided by the high-order centred moments or cumulants. Obviously, the utility function of the fund manager plays a central role in his choice of risk measure. The relation between the central moments and the utility function has already been underlined by several authors, such as Rubinstein (1973) and Jurczenko and Maillet (2006), who have shown that an economic agent with a quartic utility function is naturally sensitive to the first four moments of his expected wealth distribution. But, as stressed before, we do not wish to consider the expected utility formalism, since our goal in this chapter is not to study the underlying behaviour leading to the choice of any specific risk measure.

The choice of risk a measure also depends upon the time horizon of investment. Indeed, as the timescale increases, the distribution of asset returns progressively converges to the Gaussian pdf (Campbell *et al.*, 1997), so that only the variance remains relevant for very long-term investment horizons. However, for shorter time horizons, say for portfolios rebalanced on weekly, daily or intra-day timescales, choosing a risk measure putting the emphasis on large fluctuations, such as the centred moments μ_6 or μ_8 or the cumulants C_6 or C_8 (or of larger orders), may be necessary to account for the "wild" price fluctuations usually observed for such short timescales.

Our present approach uses a single timescale over which the returns are estimated, and is thus restricted to portfolio selection with a fixed investment horizon. Extensions to a portfolio analysis and optimisation in terms of high-order moments and cumulants performed simultaneously over different timescales can be found in Muzy *et al.* (2001).

7.3.1 Efficient frontier without a risk-free asset

Let us consider N risky assets, denoted by $X_1, \cdots, X_N$. Our goal is to find the best possible allocation, given a set of constraints. The portfolio optimisation generalising the approach of Sornette *et al.* (2000a) and Andersen and Sornette (2001) corresponds to accounting for large fluctuations of the assets through the risk measures introduced above in the presence of a constraint on the return as well as the "no short-sells" constraint:

$$
\begin{cases}
\inf_{w_i \in [0,1]} \rho_\alpha(\{w_i\}) \\
\sum_{i \geq 1} w_i = 1 \\
\sum_{i \geq 1} w_i \mu(i) = \mu \\
w_i \geq 0, \quad \forall i > 0
\end{cases}
\tag{7.14}
$$

where w_i is the weight of X_i and $\mu(i)$ its expected return. In all the subsequent text, the subscript α in ρ_α will refer to the degree of homogeneity of the risk measure.

This problem cannot be solved analytically (except in the Markowitz case where the risk measure is given by the variance). We need to perform numerical calculations to obtain the shape of the efficient frontier. Nonetheless, when the ρ_αs denote the centred moments or any convex risk measure, we can assert that this optimisation problem is a convex optimisation problem and that it admits one and only one solution, which can be determined easily by standard numerical relaxation or gradient methods.

As an example, we have represented, in Figure 7.2, the mean-ρ_α efficient frontier for a portfolio made of seventeen assets (see Appendix A for details) in the plane $(\mu, \rho_\alpha^{1/\alpha})$, where ρ_α represents the centred moments $\mu_{n=\alpha}$ of order $n = 2, 4, 6$ and 8. The efficient frontier is concave, as expected from the nature of the optimisation problem (7.14). For a given value of the expected return μ, we observe that the amount of risk measured by $\mu_n^{1/n}$ increases with n, so that there is an additional price to pay for earning more: not only does the μ_2-risk increase, as expected according to Markowitz's theory, but the large risks increase faster – the more so the larger n is. This means that, in this example, the large risks increase more rapidly than the small risks, as the required return increases. This is an important empirical result that has obvious implications for portfolio selection and risk assessment. For instance, let us consider an efficient portfolio whose expected (daily) return

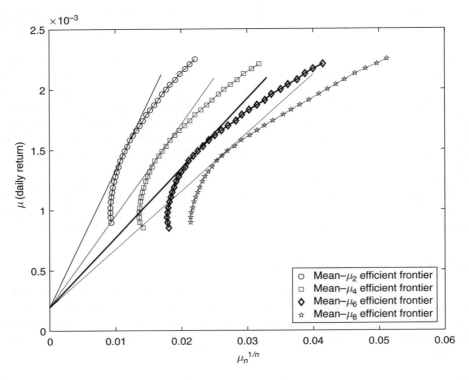

Figure 7.2 The generalised efficient frontier for a portfolio made of seventeen risky assets. The optimisation problem is solved numerically, using a genetic algorithm, with risk measures given respectively by the centred moments μ_2, μ_4, μ_6 and μ_8. The straight lines are the efficient frontiers when we add to these assets a risk-free asset whose interest rate is set to 5 % a year.

Table 7.1 The risk measured by $\mu_n^{1/n}$ for $n = 2, 4, 6, 8$, for a given value of the expected (daily) return μ

μ	$\mu_2^{1/2}$	$\mu_4^{1/4}$	$\mu_6^{1/6}$	$\mu_8^{1/8}$
0.10%	0.92%	1.36%	1.79%	2.15%
0.12%	0.96%	1.43%	1.89%	2.28%
0.14%	1.05%	1.56%	2.06%	2.47%
0.16%	1.22%	1.83%	2.42%	2.91%
0.18%	1.47%	2.21%	2.92%	3.55%
0.20%	1.77%	2.65%	3.51%	4.22%

equals 0.12 %, which gives an annualised return equal to 30 %. We can see in Table 7.1 that the typical fluctuations around the expected return are about twice as large when measured by μ_6 compared with μ_2, and that they are 1.5 times larger when measured with μ_8 compared with μ_4.

7.3.2   Efficient frontier with a risk-free asset

Let us now assume the existence of a risk-free asset X_0. The optimisation problem with the same set of constraints as previously – except for the no short-sells constraints – can be written as:

$$
\begin{cases}
\inf_{w_i \in [0,1]} \rho_\alpha(\{w_i\}) \\
\sum_{i \geq 0} w_i = 1 \\
\sum_{i \geq 0} w_i \mu(i) = \mu
\end{cases}
\tag{7.15}
$$

This optimisation problem can be solved exactly. Indeed, due to the existence of a risk-free asset, the normalisation condition $\sum w_i = 1$ is not constraining, since one can always adjust, by lending or borrowing money, the fraction w_0 to a value satisfying the normalisation condition. Thus, as shown in Appendix B, the efficient frontier is a straight line in the plane $(\mu, \rho_\alpha^{1/\alpha})$, with positive slope and whose intercept is given by the value of the risk-free interest rate:

$$
\mu = \mu_0 + \xi \cdot \rho_\alpha^{1/\alpha}
\tag{7.16}
$$

where ξ is a coefficient given explicitly below. This result is very natural when ρ_α denotes the variance, since it is then nothing but Markowitz's (1959) result. But in addition, it shows that the mean–variance result can be generalised to every mean-ρ_α optimal portfolio.

In Figure 7.3 we present the results given by numerical simulations. The set of assets is the same as before and the risk-free interest rate has been set to 5 % a year. The optimisation

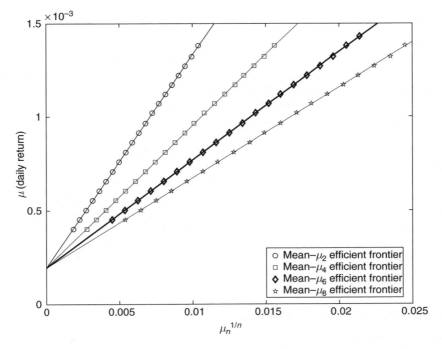

Figure 7.3   The generalised efficient frontier for a portfolio made of seventeen risky assets and a risk-free asset whose interest rate is set to 5 % a year. The optimisation problem is solved numerically, using a genetic algorithm, with risk measures given by the centred moments μ_2, μ_4, μ_6 and μ_8.

procedure has been performed using a genetic algorithm on the risk measure given by the centred moments μ_2, μ_4, μ_6 and μ_8. As expected, we observe four increasing straight lines, whose slopes monotonically decay with the order of the centred moment under consideration. Below, we will discuss this property in greater detail.

7.3.3   Two-fund separation theorem

The two-fund separation theorem is a well-known result associated with mean–variance efficient portfolios. It results from the concavity of the Markowitz efficient frontier for portfolios made of risky assets only. It states that, if the investors can choose between a set of risky assets and a risk-free asset, they invest a fraction w_0 of their wealth in the risk-free asset and the fraction $1 - w_0$ in a portfolio composed only of risky assets. This risky portfolio is the same for all the investors and the fraction w_0 of wealth invested in the risk-free asset only depends on the risk aversion of the investor or on the amount of economic capital an institution must keep aside due to the legal requirements ensuring its solvency at a given confidence level. We shall see that this result can be generalised to any mean-ρ_α efficient portfolio.

Indeed, it can be shown (see Appendix B) that the weights of the optimal portfolios that are solutions of (7.15) are given by:

$$w_0^* = w_0 \tag{7.17}$$

$$w_i^* = (1 - w_0) \cdot \tilde{w}_i, \quad i \geq 1 \tag{7.18}$$

where the $\tilde{w}_i$s are constants such that $\sum_i \tilde{w}_i = 1$ and whose expressions are given in Appendix B. Thus, denoting by Π the portfolio made only of risky assets whose weights are the $\tilde{w}_i$s, the optimal portfolios are the linear combination of the risk-free asset, with weight w_0, and of the portfolio Π, with weight $1 - w_0$. This result generalises the mean–variance two-fund theorem to any mean-ρ_α efficient portfolio.

To check this prediction numerically, Figure 7.4 represents the five largest weights of assets in the portfolios previously investigated as a function of the weight of the risk-free asset, for the four risk measures given by the centred moments μ_2, μ_4, μ_6 and μ_8. One can observe decaying straight lines that intercept the horizontal axis at $w_0 = 1$, as predicted by Equations (7.17–7.18).

In Figure 7.2, the straight lines representing the efficient portfolios with a risk-free asset are also depicted. They are tangential to the efficient frontiers without risk-free assets. This is natural since the efficient portfolios with the risk-free asset are the weighted sum of the risk-free asset and the optimal portfolio Π only made of risky assets. Since Π also belongs to the efficient frontier without risk-free assets, the optimum is reached when the straight line describing the efficient frontier with a risk-free asset and the (concave) curve of the efficient frontier without risk-free assets are tangential.

7.3.4   Influence of the risk-free interest rate

Figure 7.3 has shown that the slope of the efficient frontier (with a risk-free asset) decreases when the order n of the centred moment used to measure risk increases. This is an important qualitative property of the risk measures offered by the centred moments, as this means that higher and higher large risks are sampled under increasing imposed return.

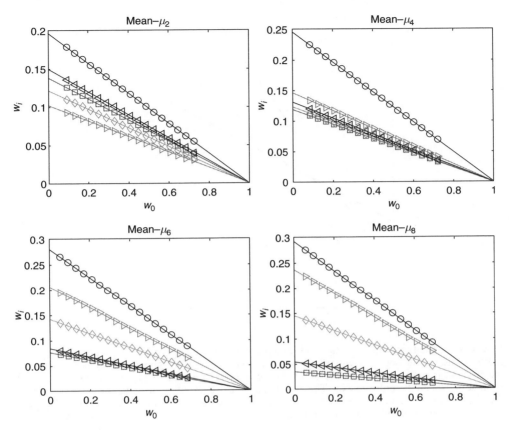

Figure 7.4 Dependence of the five largest weights of risky assets in the efficient portfolios found in Figure 7.3 as a function of the weight w_0 invested in the risk-free asset, for the four risk measures given by the centred moments μ_2, μ_4, μ_6 and μ_8. The same symbols always represent the same asset.

Is it possible that the largest risks captured by the high-order centred moments could increase at a slower rate than the small risks embodied in the low-order centred moments? For instance, is it possible for the slope of the mean-μ_6 efficient frontier to be larger than the slope of the mean-μ_4 frontier? This is an important question as it conditions the relative costs in terms of the panel of risks under increasing specified returns. To address this question, consider Figure 7.2. Changing the value of the risk-free interest rate amounts to moving the intercept of the straight lines along the ordinate axis so as to keep them tangential to the efficient frontiers without risk-free assets. Therefore, it is easy to see that, in the situation depicted in Figure 7.2, the slope of the four straight lines will always decay with the order of the centred moment.

In order to observe an inversion in the order of the slopes, it is necessary and sufficient that the efficient frontiers without risk-free assets cross each other. This assertion is proved by visual inspection of Figure 7.5. Can we observe such crossing of efficient frontiers? In the most general case of risk measure, nothing forbids this occurrence. Nonetheless, we think that this kind of behaviour is not realistic in a financial context since, as mentioned above, it

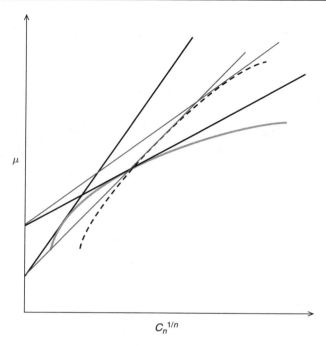

Figure 7.5 The black and grey thick curves represent two efficient frontiers for a portfolio without a risk-free interest rate obtained with two measures of risk. The dark and grey thin straight lines represent the efficient frontiers in the presence of a risk-free asset, whose value is given by the intercept of the straight lines with the ordinate axis. This illustrates the existence of an inversion of the dependence of the slope of the efficient frontier with a risk-free asset as a function of the order n of the measures of risk, which can occur only when the efficient frontiers without a risk-free asset cross each other.

would mean that the large risks could increase at a slower rate than the small risks, implying an irrational behaviour of the economic agents.

7.4   CLASSIFICATION OF THE ASSETS AND OF PORTFOLIOS

Let us consider two assets or portfolios X_1 and X_2 with different expected returns $\mu(1), \mu(2)$ and different levels of risk measured by $\rho_\alpha(X_1)$ and $\rho_\alpha(X_2)$. An important question is then to be able to compare these two assets or portfolios. The most general way to perform such a comparison is to refer to decision theory and to calculate the utility of each of them. But, as already stated, the utility function of an agent is generally not known, so that other approaches have to be developed. The simplest solution is to consider that the couple (expected return, risk measure) fully characterises the behaviour of the economic agent and thus provides a sufficiently good approximation for her utility function.

In Markowitz's (1959) world, for instance, the preferences of the agents are summarised by the two first moments of the distribution of asset returns. Thus, as shown by Sharpe (1966, 1994), a simple way to synthesise these two parameters, in order to get a measure of the performance of the assets or portfolios, is to build the ratio of the expected return μ (minus the risk-free interest rate) over the standard deviation σ:

$$S = \frac{\mu - \mu_0}{\sigma} \qquad (7.19)$$

which is the so-called Sharpe ratio and simply represents the amount of expected return per unit of risk, measured by the standard deviation. It is an increasing function of the expected return and a decreasing function of the level of risk, which is natural for risk-averse or prudential agents.

7.4.1 The risk-adjustment approach

This approach can be generalised to any type of risk measure (see, for instance, Dowd, 2000) and thus allows for the comparison of assets whose risks are not well accounted for by the variance (or the standard deviation). Indeed, instead of considering the variance, which only accounts for small risks, one can build the ratio of the expected return over any risk measure. In fact, looking at Equation (7.58) in Appendix B, the expression

$$\frac{\mu - \mu_0}{\rho_\alpha(X)^{1/\alpha}} \qquad (7.20)$$

naturally arises and is constant for every efficient portfolio. In this expression, α denotes the coefficient of homogeneity of the risk measure. It is nothing but a simple generalisation of the usual Sharpe ratio. Indeed, when ρ_α is given by the variance σ^2, the expression above recovers the Sharpe ratio. Thus, once the portfolio manager has chosen her measure of fluctuation ρ_α, she can build a consistent risk-adjusted performance measure, as shown by (7.20).

As just stated, these generalised Sharpe ratios are constant for every efficient portfolio. In fact, they are not only constant but also maximum for every efficient portfolio, so that looking for the portfolio with maximum generalised Sharpe ratio yields the same optimal portfolios as those found with the whole optimisation programme solved in the previous section.

As an illustration, Table 7.2 gives the risk-adjusted performance of the set of seventeen assets already studied, for several risk measures. We have considered the three first even-order centred moments (columns 2 to 4) and the three first even-order cumulants (columns 2, 5 and 6) as fluctuation measures. Obviously the second-order centred moment and the second-order cumulant are the same, and again give the usual Sharpe ratio (7.19). The assets have been sorted with respect to their Sharpe ratios.

The first point to note is that the rank of an asset in terms of risk-adjusted performance strongly depends on the risk measure under consideration. The case of MCI Worldcom is very striking in this respect. Indeed, according to the usual Sharpe ratio, it appears in 12th position with a value larger than 0.04, while according to the other measures, it is the last asset of our selection with a value lower than 0.02.

The second interesting point is that, for a given asset, the generalised Sharpe ratio is always a decreasing function of the order of the considered centred moment. This is not particular to our set of assets since we can prove that, $\forall p > q$,

$$(E[|X|^p])^{1/p} \geq (E[|X|^q])^{1/q} \qquad (7.21)$$

Table 7.2   The values of the generalised Sharpe ratios for the set of seventeen assets listed in the first column. The assets are ranked with respect to their Sharpe ratios, given in the second column. The third and fourth columns give the generalised Sharpe ratio calculated with respect to the fourth and sixth centred moments μ_4 and μ_6, while the fifth and sixth columns give the generalised Sharpe ratio calculated with respect to the fourth and sixth cumulants C_4 and C_6

	$\dfrac{\mu}{\mu_2^{1/2}}$	$\dfrac{\mu}{\mu_4^{1/4}}$	$\dfrac{\mu}{\mu_6^{1/6}}$	$\dfrac{\mu}{C_4^{1/4}}$	$\dfrac{\mu}{C_6^{1/6}}$
Wal-Mart	0.0821	0.0555	0.0424	0.0710	0.0557
EMC	0.0801	0.0552	0.0430	0.0730	0.0612
Intel	0.0737	0.0512	0.0397	0.0694	0.0532
Hewlett Packard	0.0724	0.0472	0.0354	0.0575	0.0439
IBM	0.0705	0.0465	0.0346	0.0574	0.0421
Merck	0.0628	0.0415	0.0292	0.0513	0.0331
Procter & Gamble	0.0590	0.0399	0.0314	0.0510	0.0521
General Motors	0.0586	0.0362	0.0247	0.0418	0.0269
SBC Communication	0.0584	0.0386	0.0270	0.0477	0.0302
General Electric	0.0569	0.0334	0.0233	0.0373	0.0258
Applied Material	0.0525	0.0357	0.0269	0.0462	0.0338
MCI WorldCom	0.0441	0.0173	0.0096	0.0176	0.0098
Medtronic	0.0432	0.0278	0.0202	0.0333	0.0237
Coca-Cola	0.0430	0.0278	0.0207	0.0335	0.0252
Exxon-Mobil	0.0410	0.0256	0.0178	0.0299	0.0197
Texas Instruments	0.0324	0.0224	0.0171	0.0301	0.0218
Pfizer	0.0298	0.0184	0.0131	0.0213	0.0148

so that

$$\forall p > q, \qquad \frac{\mu - \mu_0}{(E[|X|^p])^{1/p}} \le \frac{\mu - \mu_0}{(E[|X|^q])^{1/q}} \tag{7.22}$$

On the contrary, when the cumulants are used as risk measures, the generalised Sharpe ratios are not monotonically decreasing, as shown by Procter & Gamble for instance. This can be surprising in view of our previous remark that the larger the order of the moments involved in a risk measure, the larger the fluctuations it is accounting for. Extrapolating this property to cumulants, it would mean that Procter & Gamble presents less large risks according to C_6 than according to C_4, while according to the centred moments, the reverse evolution is observed.

Thus, the question of the coherence of the cumulants as measures of fluctuation may arise. And if we accept that such measures are coherent, what are the implications on the preferences of the agents employing such measures? To answer this question, it is informative to express the cumulants as a function of the moments. For instance, let us consider the fourth-order cumulant

$$C_4 = \mu_4 - 3 \cdot \mu_2^{\,2} \tag{7.23}$$

$$= \mu_4 - 3 \cdot C_2^{\,2} \tag{7.24}$$

An agent assessing the fluctuations of an asset with respect to C_4 presents aversion for the fluctuations quantified by the fourth central moment μ_4 – since C_4 increases with μ_4 – but is attracted by the fluctuations measured by the variance – since C_4 decreases with μ_2. This behaviour is not irrational since it remains globally risk-averse. Indeed, it depicts an agent who tries to avoid the larger risks but is ready to accept the smallest ones.

This kind of behaviour is characteristic of any agent using the cumulants as risk measures. It thus allows us to understand why Procter & Gamble is more attractive for an agent sensitive to C_6 than for an agent sensitive to C_4. From the expression of C_6, we remark that the agent sensitive to this cumulant is risk-averse with respect to the fluctuations measured by μ_6 and μ_2, but is a risk-seeker with respect to the fluctuations measured by μ_4 and μ_3. Then, in this particular case, the later ones compensate the former ones.

It also allows us to understand from a behavioural stand-point why it is possible to "have your cake and eat it too" in the sense of Andersen and Sornette (2001); that is, why, when the cumulants are chosen as risk measures, it may be possible to increase the expected return of a portfolio while lowering its large risks, or in other words, why its generalised Sharpe ratio may increase when one considers larger cumulants to measure its risks.

7.4.2 Marginal risk of an asset within a portfolio

Another important question that arises is the contribution of a given asset to the risk of the whole portfolio. Indeed, it is crucial to know whether the risk is homogeneously shared by all the assets of the portfolio or if it is only held by a few of them. The quality of the diversification is then at stake. Moreover, this also allows for the sensitivity analysis of the risk of the portfolio with respect to small changes in its composition,[3] which is of practical interest since it can prevent us from recalculating the whole risk of the portfolio after a small readjustment of its composition.

Due to the homogeneity property of the fluctuation measures and to Euler's theorem for homogeneous functions, we can write

$$\rho(\{w_1, \dots, w_N\}) = \frac{1}{\alpha} \sum_{i=1}^{N} w_i \cdot \frac{\partial \rho}{\partial w_i} \qquad (7.25)$$

provided the risk measure ρ is differentiable, which will be assumed henceforth. In this expression, the coefficient α again denotes the degree of homogeneity of the risk measure ρ.

This relation simply shows that the amount of risk brought by one unit of the asset i in the portfolio is given by the first derivative of the risk of the portfolio with respect to the weight w_i of this asset. Thus, $\alpha^{-1} \cdot \frac{\partial \rho}{\partial w_i}$ represents the marginal amount of risk of asset i in the portfolio. It is then easy to check that, in a portfolio with minimum risk, irrespective of the expected return, the weight of each asset is such that the marginal risks of the assets in the portfolio are equal.

7.5   A NEW EQUILIBRIUM MODEL FOR ASSET PRICES

Using the portfolio selection method explained in the two previous sections, we now present an equilibrium model generalising the original Capital Asset Pricing Model developed by Sharpe (1964), Lintner (1965) and Mossin (1966). Many generalisations have already been

---

[3] See Gouriéroux *et al.* (2000) and Scaillet (2004) for a sensitivity analysis of the value-at-risk and the expected shortfall.

proposed to account for the fat-tailedness of the asset return distributions, which led to the multi-moment CAPM. For instance, Rubinstein (1973), Kraus and Litzenberger (1976), Lim (1989) and Harvey and Siddique (2000) have underlined and tested the role of the asymmetry in the risk premium by accounting for the skewness of the distribution of returns. More recently, Fang and Lai (1997) and Hwang and Satchell (1999) have introduced a four-moment CAPM to take into account the leptokurtic behaviour of the asset return distributions. Many other extensions have been presented, such as the VaR-CAPM (see Alexander and Baptista, 2002) or the distributional-CAPM by Polimenis (2002). All these generalisations become more and more complicated and not do not necessarily provide more accurate prediction of the expected returns.

Here, we will assume that the relevant risk measure is given by any measure of fluctuation previously presented that obeys Axioms 1–4 of Section 7.2. We will also relax the usual assumption of a homogeneous market to give to the economic agents the choice of their own risk measure: some of them may choose a risk measure that puts the emphasis on small fluctuations, while others may prefer those that account for the large ones. We will show that, in such a heterogeneous market, an equilibrium can still be reached and that the excess returns of individual stocks remain proportional to the market excess return.

For this, we need the following assumptions about the market:

- H1: We consider a one-period market, such that all the positions held at the beginning of a period are cleared at the end of the same period.
- H2: The market is perfect, i.e., there are no transaction costs or taxes, the market is efficient and the investors can lend and borrow at the same risk-free rate μ_0.

We will now add another assumption that specifies the behaviour of the agents acting on the market, which will lead us to make the distinction between homogeneous and heterogeneous markets.

7.5.1   Equilibrium in a homogeneous market

The market is said to be homogeneous if all the agents acting on this market aim to fulfil the same objective. This means that:

- H3-1: all the agents want to maximise the expected return of their portfolio at the end of the period under a given constraint of measured risk, using the same measure of risks ρ_α for all of them.

In the special case where ρ_α denotes the variance, all the agents follow a Markowitz optimisation procedure, which leads to the CAPM equilibrium, as proved by Sharpe (1964). When ρ_α represents the centred moments, we will be led to the market equilibrium described by Rubinstein (1973). Thus, this approach allows for a generalisation of the most popular asset pricing in equilibrium market models.

When all the agents have the same risk function ρ_α, whatever α may be, we can assert that they all have a fraction of their capital invested in the same portfolio Π, the composition of which is given in Appendix B, and the remainder in the risk-free asset. The amount of capital invested in the risky fund only depends on their risk aversion or on the legal margin requirement they have to fulfil.

Let us now assume that the market is at equilibrium, i.e., supply equals demand. In such a case, since the optimal portfolios can be any linear combinations of the risk-free asset and of the risky portfolio Π, it is straightforward to show (see Appendix C) that the market portfolio, made of all traded assets in proportion to their market capitalisation, is nothing but the risky portfolio Π. Thus, as shown in Appendix D, we can state that, whatever the risk measure ρ_α chosen by the agents to perform their optimisation, the excess return of any asset over the risk-free interest rate is proportional to the excess return of the market portfolio Π over the risk-free interest rate:

$$\mu(i) - \mu_0 = \beta_\alpha^i \cdot (\mu_\Pi - \mu_0) \tag{7.26}$$

where

$$\beta_\alpha^i = \left. \frac{\partial \ln \left(\rho_\alpha^{\frac{1}{\alpha}} \right)}{\partial w_i} \right|_{w_1^*, \ldots, w_N^*} \tag{7.27}$$

where $w_1^*, \ldots, w_N^*$ are defined in Appendix D. When ρ_α denotes the variance, we recover the usual β^i given by the mean–variance approach:

$$\beta^i = \frac{\text{Cov}(X_i, \Pi)}{\text{Var}(\Pi)} \tag{7.28}$$

Thus, the relations (7.26) and (7.27) generalise the usual CAPM formula, showing that the specific choice of the risk measure is not very important, as long as it follows Axioms 1–4 characterising the fluctuations of the distribution of asset returns.

7.5.2   Equilibrium in a heterogeneous market

Does this result hold in the more realistic situation of a heterogeneous market? A market will be said to be heterogeneous if the agents seek to fulfil different objectives. We thus consider the following assumption:

- H3-2: There exist N agents. Each agent n is characterised by her choice of a risk measure $\rho_\alpha(n)$ so that she invests only in the mean-$\rho_\alpha(n)$ efficient portfolio.

According to this hypothesis, an agent n invests a fraction of her wealth in the risk-free asset and the remainder in Π_n, the mean-$\rho_\alpha(n)$ efficient portfolio only made of risky assets. The fraction of wealth invested in the risky fund depends on the risk aversion of each agent, which may vary from one agent to another.

The composition of the market portfolio for such a heterogeneous market is derived in Appendix C. We find that the market portfolio Π is nothing but the weighted sum of the mean-$\rho_\alpha(n)$ optimal portfolios Π_n:

$$\Pi = \sum_{n=1}^{N} \gamma_n \Pi_n \tag{7.29}$$

where γ_n is the fraction of the total wealth invested in the fund Π_n by the nth agent.

Appendix D demonstrates that, for every asset i and for any mean-$\rho_\alpha(n)$ efficient portfolio Π_n, for all n, the following equation holds:

$$\mu(i) - \mu_0 = \beta_n^i \cdot (\mu_{\Pi_n} - \mu_0) \tag{7.30}$$

Multiplying these equations by γ_n/β_n^i, we get

$$\frac{\gamma_n}{\beta_n^i} \cdot (\mu(i) - \mu_0) = \gamma_n \cdot (\mu_{\Pi_n} - \mu_0) \tag{7.31}$$

for all n, and summing over the different agents, we obtain

$$\left(\sum_n \frac{\gamma_n}{\beta_n^i} \right) \cdot (\mu(i) - \mu_0) = \left(\sum_n \gamma_n \cdot \mu_{\Pi_n} \right) - \mu_0 \tag{7.32}$$

so that

$$\mu(i) - \mu_0 = \beta^i \cdot (\mu_\Pi - \mu_0) \tag{7.33}$$

with

$$\beta^i = \left(\sum_n \frac{\gamma_n}{\beta_n^i} \right)^{-1} \tag{7.34}$$

This allows us to conclude that, even in a heterogeneous market, the expected excess return of each individual stock is directly proportional to the expected excess return of the market portfolio, showing that the homogeneity of the market is not a key property necessary for observing a linear relationship between individual excess asset returns and the market excess return.

7.6   CONCLUSION

We have introduced three axioms that define a consistent set of risk measures, in the spirit of Artzner *et al.* (1997, 1999). Contrary to the risk measures of Artzner *et al.*, our consistent risk measures may account for both-side risks and not only for down-side risks. Thus, they supplement the notion of coherent measures of risk and are well adapted to the problem of portfolio risk assessment and optimisation. We have shown that these risk measures, which contain centred moments (and cumulants with some restriction) as particular examples, generalise them significantly. We have presented a generalisation of previous generalisations of the efficient frontiers and of the CAPM based on these risk measures in the cases of homogeneous and heterogeneous agents.

APPENDIX A: DESCRIPTION OF THE DATASET

We have considered a set of seventeen assets traded on the New York Stock Exchange: Applied Material, Coca-Cola, EMC, Exxon-Mobil, General Electric, General Motors, Hewlett Packard, IBM, Intel, MCI WorldCom, Medtronic, Merck, Pfizer, Procter & Gamble, SBC Communication, Texas Instruments, Wal-Mart. These assets have been chosen since they are among the largest capitalisations of the NYSE at the time of writing.

   The dataset comes from the Center for Research in Security Prices (CRSP) database and covers the time interval from the end of January 1995 to the end of December 2000,

Table 7.3 The main statistical features of the daily returns of the set of seventeen assets studied here over the time interval from the end of January 1995 to the end of December 2000

	Mean (10^{-3})	Variance (10^{-3})	Skewness	Kurtosis	min	max
Applied Material	2.11	1.62	0.41	4.68	−14%	21%
Coca-Cola	0.81	0.36	0.13	5.71	−11%	10%
EMC	2.76	1.13	0.23	4.79	−18%	15%
Exxon-Mobil	0.92	0.25	0.30	5.26	−7%	11%
General Electric	1.38	0.30	0.08	4.46	−7%	8%
General Motors	0.64	0.39	0.12	4.35	−11%	8%
Hewlett Packard	1.17	0.81	0.16	6.58	−14%	21%
IBM	1.32	0.54	0.08	8.43	−16%	13%
Intel	1.71	0.85	−0.31	6.88	−22%	14%
MCI WorldCom	0.87	0.85	−0.18	6.88	−20%	13%
Medtronic	1.70	0.55	0.23	5.52	−12%	12%
Merck	1.32	0.35	0.18	5.29	−9%	10%
Pfizer	1.57	0.46	0.01	4.28	−10%	10%
Procter & Gamble	0.90	0.41	−2.57	42.75	−31%	10%
SBC Communication	0.86	0.39	0.06	5.86	−13%	9%
Texas Instruments	2.20	1.23	0.50	5.26	−12%	24%
Wal-Mart	1.35	0.52	0.16	4.79	−10%	9%

which represents exactly 1500 trading days. The main statistical features of the companies composing the dataset are presented in Table 7.3. Note the high kurtosis of each distribution of returns, as well as the large values of the observed minimum and maximum returns compared with the standard deviations, that clearly underlines the non-Gaussian behaviour of these assets.

APPENDIX B: GENERALISED EFFICIENT FRONTIER AND TWO-FUND SEPARATION THEOREM

Let us consider a set of N risky assets $X_1, \ldots, X_N$ and a risk-free asset X_0. The problem is to find the optimal allocation of these assets in the following sense:

$$\begin{cases} \inf_{w_i \in [0,1]} \rho_\alpha(\{w_i\}) \\ \sum_{i \geq 0} w_i = 1 \\ \sum_{i \geq 0} w_i \mu(i) = \mu \end{cases} \tag{7.35}$$

In other words, we search for the portfolio $\mathcal{P}$ with minimum risk as measured by any risk measure ρ_α obeying Axioms 1–4 of Section 7.2 for a given amount of expected return μ and normalised weights w_i. Short-sells are forbidden except for the risk-free asset, which can be lent and borrowed at the same interest rate μ_0. Thus, the weights w_i are assumed positive for all $i \geq 1$.

B.1   Case of independent assets when the risk is measured by the cumulants

To start with a simple example, let us assume that the risky assets are independent and that we choose to measure the risk with the cumulants of their distributions of returns. The case when the assets are dependent and/or when the risk is measured by any ρ_α will be considered later. Since the assets are assumed independent, the cumulant of order n of the pdf of returns of the portfolio is simply given by

$$C_n = \sum_{i=1}^{N} w_i^n C_n(i) \tag{7.36}$$

where $C_n(i)$ denotes the marginal nth order cumulant of the pdf of returns of the asset i. In order to solve this problem, let us introduce the Lagrangian

$$\mathcal{L} = C_n - \lambda_1 \left(\sum_{i=0}^{N} w_i \mu(i) - \mu \right) - \lambda_2 \left(\sum_{i=0}^{N} w_i - 1 \right) \tag{7.37}$$

where λ_1 and λ_2 are two Lagrange multipliers. Differentiating with respect to w_0 yields

$$\lambda_2 = \mu_0 \lambda_1 \tag{7.38}$$

which, by substitution in Equation (7.37), gives

$$\mathcal{L} = C_n - \lambda_1 \left(\sum_{i=1}^{N} w_i(\mu(i) - \mu_0) - (\mu - \mu_0) \right) \tag{7.39}$$

Let us now differentiate $\mathcal{L}$ with respect to w_i, $i \geq 1$. We obtain

$$n\, w_i^{*n-1} C_n(i) - \lambda_1 (\mu(i) - \mu_0) = 0 \tag{7.40}$$

so that

$$w_i^* = \lambda_1^{\frac{1}{n-1}} \left(\frac{\mu(i) - \mu_0}{n\, C_n(i)} \right)^{\frac{1}{n-1}} \tag{7.41}$$

Applying the normalisation constraint yields

$$w_0 + \lambda_1^{\frac{1}{n-1}} \sum_{i=1}^{N} \left(\frac{\mu(i) - \mu_0}{n\, C_n(i)} \right)^{\frac{1}{n-1}} = 1 \tag{7.42}$$

thus

$$\lambda_1^{\frac{1}{n-1}} = \frac{1 - w_0}{\sum_{i=1}^{N} \left(\frac{\mu(i) - \mu_0}{n\, C_n(i)} \right)^{\frac{1}{n-1}}} \tag{7.43}$$

and finally

$$w_i^* = (1 - w_0) \frac{\left(\frac{\mu(i) - \mu_0}{C_n(i)} \right)^{\frac{1}{n-1}}}{\sum_{i=1}^{N} \left(\frac{\mu(i) - \mu_0}{C_n(i)} \right)^{\frac{1}{n-1}}} \tag{7.44}$$

Let us now define the portfolio Π exclusively made of risky assets with weights

$$\tilde{w}_i = \frac{\left(\frac{\mu(i)-\mu_0}{C_n(i)}\right)^{\frac{1}{n-1}}}{\sum_{i=1}^{N}\left(\frac{\mu(i)-\mu_0}{C_n(i)}\right)^{\frac{1}{n-1}}}, \quad i \geq 1 \tag{7.45}$$

The optimal portfolio $\mathcal{P}$ can be split into two funds: the risk-free asset whose weight is w_0 and a risky fund Π with weight $(1 - w_0)$. The expected return of the portfolio $\mathcal{P}$ is thus

$$\mu = w_0\mu_0 + (1 - w_0)\mu_\Pi \tag{7.46}$$

where μ_Π denotes the expected return of portfolio Π:

$$\mu_\Pi = \frac{\sum_{i=1}^{N}\mu(i)\left(\frac{\mu(i)-\mu_0}{C_n(i)}\right)^{\frac{1}{n-1}}}{\sum_{i=1}^{N}\left(\frac{\mu(i)-\mu_0}{C_n(i)}\right)^{\frac{1}{n-1}}} \tag{7.47}$$

The risk associated with $\mathcal{P}$ and measured by the cumulant C_n of order n is

$$C_n = (1 - w_0)^n \frac{\sum_{i=1}^{N}C_n(i)\left(\frac{\mu(i)-\mu_0}{C_n(i)}\right)^{\frac{n}{n-1}}}{\left[\sum_{i=1}^{N}\left(\frac{\mu(i)-\mu_0}{C_n(i)}\right)^{\frac{1}{n-1}}\right]^n} \tag{7.48}$$

Putting together the last three equations allows us to obtain the equation of the efficient frontier:

$$\mu = \mu_0 + \left[\sum \frac{(\mu(i)-\mu_0)^{\frac{n}{n-1}}}{C_n(i)^{\frac{1}{n-1}}}\right]^{\frac{n-1}{n}} \cdot C_n^{\frac{1}{n}} \tag{7.49}$$

which is a straight line in the plane $(C_n^{1/n}, \mu)$.

B.2 General case

Let us now consider the more realistic case when the risky assets are dependent and/or when the risk is measured by any risk measure ρ_α obeying Axioms 1–4 presented in Section 7.2, where α denotes the degree of homogeneity of ρ_α. Equation (7.39) always holds (with C_n replaced by ρ_α), and the differentiation with respect to w_i, $i \geq 1$, yields the set of equations:

$$\frac{\partial \rho_\alpha}{\partial w_i}(w_1^*, \ldots, w_N^*) = \lambda_1(\mu(i) - \mu_0), \quad i \in \{1, \ldots, N\} \tag{7.50}$$

Since $\rho_\alpha(w_1, \ldots, w_N)$ is a homogeneous function of order α, its first-order derivative with respect to w_i is also a homogeneous function of order $\alpha - 1$. Using this homogeneity property allows us to write

$$\lambda_1^{-1}\frac{\partial \rho_\alpha}{\partial w_i}(w_1^*, \ldots, w_N^*) = (\mu(i) - \mu_0), \quad i \in \{1, \ldots, N\} \tag{7.51}$$

$$\frac{\partial \rho_\alpha}{\partial w_i}\left(\lambda_1^{-\frac{1}{\alpha-1}}w_1^*, \ldots, \lambda_1^{-\frac{1}{\alpha-1}}w_N^*\right) = (\mu(i) - \mu_0), \quad i \in \{1, \ldots, N\} \tag{7.52}$$

Denoting by $\{\hat{w}_1, \ldots, \hat{w}_N\}$ the solution of

$$\frac{\partial \rho_\alpha}{\partial w_i}(\hat{w}_1, \ldots, \hat{w}_N) = (\mu(i) - \mu_0), \quad i \in \{1, \cdots, N\} \tag{7.53}$$

this shows that the optimal weights are

$$w_i^* = \lambda_1^{\frac{1}{\alpha-1}} \hat{w}_i \tag{7.54}$$

Now, performing the same calculation as in the case of independent risky assets, the efficient portfolio $\mathcal{P}$ can be realised by investing a weight w_0 of the initial wealth in the risk-free asset and the weight $(1 - w_0)$ in the risky fund Π, whose weights are given by

$$\tilde{w}_i = \frac{\hat{w}_i}{\sum_{i=1}^{N} \hat{w}_i} \tag{7.55}$$

Therefore, the expected return of every efficient portfolio is

$$\mu = w_0 \cdot \mu_0 + (1 - w_0) \cdot \mu_\Pi \tag{7.56}$$

where μ_Π denotes the expected return of the market portfolio Π, while the risk, measured by ρ_α, is

$$\rho_\alpha = (1 - w_0)^\alpha \rho_\alpha(\Pi) \tag{7.57}$$

so that

$$\mu = \mu_0 + \frac{\mu_\Pi - \mu_0}{\rho_\alpha(\Pi)^{1/\alpha}} \rho_\alpha^{1/\alpha} \tag{7.58}$$

This expression is the natural generalisation of the relation obtained by Markowitz (1959) for mean–variance efficient portfolios.

APPENDIX C: COMPOSITION OF THE MARKET PORTFOLIO

In this appendix we derive the relationship between the composition of the market portfolio and the composition of the optimal portfolio Π obtained by the minimisation of the risks measured by $\rho_\alpha(n)$.

C.1   Homogeneous case

We first consider a homogeneous market, peopled with agents choosing their optimal portfolio with respect to the same risk measure ρ_α. A given agent p invests a fraction $w_0(p)$ of his wealth $W(p)$ in the risk-free asset and a fraction $1 - w_0(p)$ in the optimal portfolio Π. Therefore, the total demand D_i of asset i is the sum of the demand $D_i(p)$ over all agents p in asset i:

$$D_i = \sum_p D_i(p) \tag{7.59}$$

$$= \sum_p W(p) \cdot (1 - w_0(p)) \cdot \tilde{w}_i \tag{7.60}$$

$$= \tilde{w}_i \cdot \sum_p W(p) \cdot (1 - w_0(p)) \tag{7.61}$$

where the $\tilde{w}_i$s are given by (7.55). The aggregated demand D over all assets is

$$D = \sum_i D_i \tag{7.62}$$

$$= \sum_i \tilde{w}_i \cdot \sum_p W(p) \cdot (1 - w_0(p)) \tag{7.63}$$

$$= \sum_p W(p) \cdot (1 - w_0(p)) \tag{7.64}$$

By definition, the weight of asset i, denoted by w_i^m, in the market portfolio equals the ratio of its capitalisation (the supply S_i of asset i) over the total capitalisation of the market $S = \sum_i S_i$. At equilibrium, demand equals supply, so that

$$w_i^m = \frac{S_i}{S} = \frac{D_i}{D} = \tilde{w}_i \tag{7.65}$$

Thus, at equilibrium, the optimal portfolio Π is the market portfolio.

C.2   Heterogeneous case

We now consider a heterogeneous market, defined such that the agents choose their optimal portfolio with respect to different risk measures. Some of them choose the usual mean–variance optimal portfolios, others prefer any mean-ρ_α efficient portfolio, and so on. Let us denote by Π_n the mean-$\rho_\alpha(n)$ optimal portfolio made only of risky assets. Let ϕ_n be the fraction of agents who choose the mean-$\rho_\alpha(n)$ efficient portfolios. By normalisation, $\sum_n \phi_n = 1$. The demand $D_i(n)$ of asset i from the agents optimising with respect to $\rho_\alpha(n)$ is

$$D_i(n) = \sum_{p \in \mathcal{S}_n} W(p) \cdot (1 - w_0(p)) \cdot \tilde{w}_i(n) \tag{7.66}$$

$$= \tilde{w}_i(n) \sum_{p \in \mathcal{S}_n} W(p) \cdot (1 - w_0(p)) \tag{7.67}$$

where $\mathcal{S}_n$ denotes the set of agents, among all the agents, who follow the optimisation strategy with respect to $\rho_\alpha(n)$. Thus, the total demand of asset i is

$$D_i = \sum_n \mathcal{N} \phi_n \cdot D_i(n) \tag{7.68}$$

$$= \mathcal{N} \sum_n \phi_n \cdot \tilde{w}_i(n) \sum_{p \in \mathcal{S}_n} W(p) \cdot (1 - w_0(p)) \tag{7.69}$$

where $\mathcal{N}$ is the total number of agents. This finally yields the total demand D for all assets and for all agents

$$D = \sum_i D_i \tag{7.70}$$

$$= \mathcal{N} \sum_i \sum_n \phi_n \cdot \tilde{w}_i(n) \sum_{p \in \mathcal{S}_n} W(p) \cdot (1 - w_0(p)) \tag{7.71}$$

$$= \mathcal{N} \sum_n \phi_n \sum_{p \in \mathcal{S}_n} W(p) \cdot (1 - w_0(p)) \tag{7.72}$$

since $\sum_i \tilde{w}_i(n) = 1$, for every n. Thus, setting

$$\gamma_n = \frac{\phi_n \sum_{p \in \mathcal{S}_n} W(p) \cdot (1 - w_0(p))}{\sum_n \phi_n \sum_{p \in \mathcal{S}_n} W(p) \cdot (1 - w_0(p))} \tag{7.73}$$

the market portfolio is the weighted sum of the mean-$\rho_\alpha(n)$ optimal portfolios Π_n:

$$w_i^m = \frac{S_i}{S} = \frac{D_i}{D} = \sum_n \gamma_n \cdot \tilde{w}_i(n) \tag{7.74}$$

APPENDIX D: GENERALISED CAPITAL ASSET PRICING MODEL

Our proof of the generalised Capital Asset Pricing Model is similar to the usual demonstration of the CAPM. Let us consider an efficient portfolio $\mathcal{P}$. It necessarily satisfies Equation (7.50) in Appendix B:

$$\frac{\partial \rho_\alpha}{\partial w_i}(w_1^*, \ldots, w_N^*) = \lambda_1(\mu(i) - \mu_0), \quad i \in \{1, \ldots, N\} \tag{7.75}$$

Let us now choose any portfolio $\mathcal{R}$ made only of risky assets and let us denote by $w_i(\mathcal{R})$ its weights. We can thus write

$$\sum_{i=1}^{N} w_i(\mathcal{R}) \cdot \frac{\partial \rho_\alpha}{\partial w_i}(w_1^*, \ldots, w_N^*) = \lambda_1 \sum_{i=1}^{N} w_i(\mathcal{R}) \cdot (\mu(i) - \mu_0) \tag{7.76}$$

$$= \lambda_1(\mu_\mathcal{R} - \mu_0) \tag{7.77}$$

We can apply this last relation to the market portfolio Π, because it is only composed of risky assets (as proved in Appendix B). This leads to $w_i(\mathcal{R}) = w_i^*$ and $\mu_\mathcal{R} = \mu_\Pi$, so that

$$\sum_{i=1}^{N} w_i^* \cdot \frac{\partial \rho_\alpha}{\partial w_i}(w_1^*, \ldots, w_N^*) = \lambda_1(\mu_\Pi - \mu_0) \tag{7.78}$$

which, by the homogeneity of the risk measures ρ_α, yields

$$\alpha \cdot \rho_\alpha(w_1^*, \ldots, w_N^*) = \lambda_1(\mu_\Pi - \mu_0) \tag{7.79}$$

Substituting Equation (7.75) into (7.79) allows us to obtain

$$\mu_j - \mu_0 = \beta_\alpha^j \cdot (\mu_\Pi - \mu_0) \tag{7.80}$$

where

$$\beta_\alpha^j = \frac{\partial \left(\ln \rho_\alpha^{\frac{1}{\alpha}} \right)}{\partial w_j} \tag{7.81}$$

calculated at the point $\{w_1^*, \ldots, w_N^*\}$. Expression (7.79) with (7.81) provides our CAPM, generalised with respect to the risk measures ρ_α.

In the case where ρ_α denotes the variance, the second-order centred moment is equal to the second-order cumulant and reads

$$C_2 = w_1^* \cdot \mathrm{Var}[X_1] + 2w_1^* w_2^* \cdot \mathrm{Cov}(X_1, X_2) + w_2^* \cdot \mathrm{Var}[X_2] \tag{7.82}$$

$$= \mathrm{Var}[\Pi] \tag{7.83}$$

Since

$$\frac{1}{2} \cdot \frac{\partial C_2}{\partial w_1} = w_1^* \cdot \mathrm{Var}[X_1] + w_2^* \cdot \mathrm{Cov}(X_1, X_2) \tag{7.84}$$

$$= \mathrm{Cov}(X_1, \Pi) \tag{7.85}$$

we find

$$\beta = \frac{\mathrm{Cov}(X_1, X_\Pi)}{\mathrm{Var}[X_\Pi]} \tag{7.86}$$

which is the standard result of the CAPM derived from the mean–variance theory.

ACKNOWLEDGEMENTS

We acknowledge helpful discussions and exchanges with J.V. Andersen, J.P. Laurent and V. Pisarenko. We are grateful to participants of the workshop on *Multi-moment Capital Asset Pricing Models and Related Topics*, ESCP-EAP European School of Management, Paris, April, 19, 2002, and in particular to Philippe Spieser, for their comments. This work was partially supported by the James S. McDonnell Foundation 21st century scientist award/studying complex system.

REFERENCES

Acerbi, C. (2002) Spectral measures of risk: A coherent representation of subjective risk aversion, *Journal of Banking and Finance* **26**, 1505–1518.

Alexander, G.J. and A.M. Baptista (2002) Economic implications of using a mean-VaR model for portfolio selection: A comparison with mean–variance analysis, *Journal of Economic Dynamics and Control* **26**, 1159–1193.

Allais, M. (1953) Le comportement de l'homme rationel devant le risque, critique des postulat de l'école américaine, *Econometrica* **21**, 503–546.

Allais, M. (1990) Allais Paradox. In: *The new Palgrave: Utility and probability*, J. Eatwell, M. Milgate and P. Newman (Eds), Macmillan, pp. 3–9.

Andersen, J.V. and D. Sornette (2001) Have your cake and eat it too: increasing returns while lowering large risks! *Journal of Risk Finance* **2**, 70–82.

Artzner, P., F. Delbaen, J.M. Eber and D. Heath (1997) Thinking coherently, *Risk* **10**, 68–71.

Artzner, P., F. Delbaen, J.M. Eber and D. Heath (1999) Coherent measures of risk, *Mathematical Finance* **9**, 203–228.

Bouchaud, J.-P., D. Sornette, C. Walter and J.-P. Aguilar (1998) Taming large events: Optimal portfolio theory for strongly fluctuating assets, *International Journal of Theoretical and Applied Finance* **1**, 25–41.

Campbell, J.Y., A.W. Lo and A.C. MacKinlay (1997) *The econometrics of financial markets*, Princeton University Press, Princeton.

Dowd, K. (2000) Adjusting for risk: An improved Sharpe ratio, *International Review of Economics and Finance* **9**, 209–222.

Fama, E.F. and K.R. French (2004) The CAPM: Theory and evidence, *Journal of Economic Perspectives* **18**, 25–46.

Fang, H. and T. Lai (1997) Co-kurtosis and capital asset pricing, *Financial Review* **32**, 293–307.

Farmer, J.D. and Lillo, F. (2004) On the origin of power-law tails in price fluctuations, *Quantitative Finance* **4**, 11–15.

Föllmer, H. and A. Schied (2002) Convex measures of risk and trading constraints, *Finance and Stochastics* **6**, 429–447.

Föllmer, H. and A. Schied (2003) Robust preferences and convex measures of risk. In: *Advances in Finance and Stochastics, Essays in Honour of Dieter Sondermann*, K. Sandmann and P.J. Schonbucher (Eds), Springer Verlag.

Gopikrishnan, P., M. Meyer, L.A. Nunes Amaral and H.E. Stanley (1998) Inverse cubic law for the distribution of stock price variations, *European Physical Journal B* **3**, 139–140.

Gouriéroux, C., J.P. Laurent and O. Scaillet (2000) Sensitivity Analysis of Values at Risk, *Journal of Empirical Finance* **7**, 225–245.

Harvey, C.R. and A. Siddique (2000) Conditional skewness in asset pricing tests, *Journal of Finance* **55**, 1263–1295.

Hwang, S. and S. Satchell (1999) Modelling emerging market risk premia using higher moments, *International Journal of Finance and Economics* **4**, 271–296.

Jorion, P. (1997) *Value-at-Risk: The New Benchmark for Controlling Derivatives Risk*, Irwin Publishing, Chicago.

Jurczenko, E. and B. Maillet (2006) The 4-moment CAPM: In between Asset Pricing and Asset Allocation. In: *Multi-moment Asset Allocation and Pricing Models*, E. Jurczenko and B. Maillet (Eds), Wiley, Chapter 6.

Kraus, A. and R. Litzenberger (1976) Skewness preference and the valuation of risk assets, *Journal of Finance* **31**, 1085–1099.

Lim, K.G. (1989) A new test for the three-moment capital asset pricing model, *Journal of Financial and Quantitative Analysis* **24**, 205–216.

Lintner, J. (1965) The valuation of risk assets and the selection of risky investments in stock portfolios and capital budgets, *Review of Economics and Statistics* **47**, 13–37.

Litterman, R. and K. Winkelmann (1998) *Estimating covariance matrices*, Risk Management Series, Goldman Sachs.

Lux, T. (1996) The stable Paretian hypothesis and the frequency of large returns: an examination of major German stocks, *Applied Financial Economics* **6**, 463–475.

Malevergne, Y., V.F. Pisarenko and D. Sornette (2005) Empirical distributions of stock returns: Exponential or power-like? *Quantitative Finance* **5**, 379–401.

Markowitz, H. (1959) *Portfolio selection: Efficient diversification of investments*, John Wiley & Sons, Inc., New York.

Mossin, J. (1966) Equilibrium in a capital market, *Econometrica* **34**, 768–783.

Muzy, J.-F., D. Sornette, J. Delour and A. Arneodo (2001) Multifractal Returns and Hierarchical Portfolio Theory, *Quantitative Finance* **1**, 131–148.

Pagan, A. (1996) The Econometrics of Financial Markets, *Journal of Empirical Finance* **3**, 15–102.

Polimenis, V. (2002) The distributional CAPM: Connecting risk premia to return distributions. Working Paper.

Rothschild, M. and J.E. Stiglitz (1970) Increasing risk I: A definition, *Journal of Economic Theory* **2**, 225–243.

Rothschild, M. and J.E. Stiglitz (1971) Increasing risk II: Its economic consequences, *Journal of Economic Theory* **3**, 66–84.

Rubinstein, M. (1973) The fundamental theorem of parameter-preference security valuation, *Journal of Financial and Quantitative Analysis* **8**, 61–69.

Scaillet, O. (2004) Nonparametric estimation and sensitivity analysis of expected shortfall, *Mathematical Finance* **14**, 115–129.

Sharpe, N.F. (1964) Capital asset prices: A theory of market equilibrium under conditions of risk, *Journal of Finance* **19**, 425–442.

Sharpe, W.F. (1966) Mutual fund performance, *Journal of Business* **39**, 119–138.

Sharpe, W.F. (1994) The Sharpe ratio, *Journal of Portfolio Management* **21**(1), 49–58.

Sornette, D. (1998) Large deviations and portfolio optimization, *Physica A* **256**, 251–283.

Sornette, D., J. V. Andersen and P. Simonetti (2000a) Portfolio Theory for "Fat Tails", *International Journal of Theoretical and Applied Finance* **3**(3), 523–535.

Sornette, D., P. Simonetti and J.V. Andersen (2000b) ϕ^q-field theory for portfolio optimization: "fat-tails" and non-linear correlations, *Physics Reports* **335**(2), 19–92.

Stuart, A. and J.K. Ord (1994) Kendall's advanced theory of statistics, 6th edition, Edward Arnold, London and Halsted Press, New York.

von Neumann, J. and O. Morgenstern (1947) *Theory of Games and Economic Behavior*, Princeton University Press, Princeton.

8

Modelling the Dynamics of Conditional Dependency Between Financial Series

Eric Jondeau and Michael Rockinger

ABSTRACT

In this chapter we develop a new methodology to measure conditional dependency between daily stock-market returns, which are known to be driven by complicated marginal distributions. For this purpose we use copula functions, which are a convenient tool for joining marginal distributions. The marginal model is a GARCH-type model with time-varying skewness and kurtosis. Then, we model the dynamics of the dependency parameter of the copula as a function of predetermined variables. We provide evidence that our model fits the data quite well. We establish that the dependency parameter is both large and persistent between European markets. Our methodology has many potential applications, such as VaR measurement and portfolio allocation in non-Gaussian environments.

8.1 INTRODUCTION

This chapter presents a new methodology, based on the so-called "copula" functions, to measure conditional dependency. These functions provide an interesting tool for joining complicated marginal distributions. The insight of this research is that the dependency parameter can easily be rendered conditional and time-varying. Here, we use this methodology to investigate the dynamics of the dependency parameter between daily returns for major stock markets.

Many univariate models exist to express returns; however, given the focus of this work, we draw on recent advances in the modelling of conditional returns that allow second, third and fourth moments to vary over time. We therefore consider a univariate model for each stock index, join these models via a copula into a multivariate framework and then estimate the dynamics of the dependency parameter. Let's relate these three building blocks to the existing literature. First, our univariate model builds on the so-called skewed student-t distribution, first presented in Hansen's (1994) seminal paper. This distribution is able to capture both asymmetry and fat-tailedness through parameters that can easily be rendered conditional.

Multi-moment Asset Allocation and Pricing Models Edited by E. Jurczenko and B. Maillet
© 2006 John Wiley & Sons, Ltd

This yields time-varying higher moments.[1] This model, therefore, extends Engle's (1982) ARCH and Bollerslev's (1986) GARCH model. In an extension to Hansen (1994), Jondeau and Rockinger (2003a, 2003b) determine the expression of skewness and kurtosis of the skewed student-t distribution, compute the domain of definition for these parameters, which ensures definiteness of the distribution, and show how the cumulative distribution function (cdf) and its inverse can be computed. They also discuss how the parameters of the skewed student-t distribution should be parametrised. A number of studies consider alternative skewed student-t distributions; recent work is by Adcock (2002) and Lambert and Laurent (2002). Other recent contributions also render higher moments time-varying. For instance, Harvey and Siddique (1999) model the conditional skewness with a noncentral student-t distribution, while Brooks, Burke and Persand (2005) model the conditional kurtosis with a standard student-t distribution. Premaratne and Bera (2000) and Rockinger and Jondeau (2002) achieve time variation in skewness and kurtosis by using the Pearsonian densities and the entropy density, respectively.

Second, copulas are introduced to capture the dependency structure between two complicated marginal distributions. Such an approach is particularly fruitful in situations where multivariate normality does not hold. Copulas are mathematical objects used previously in statistics (see Riboulet, Roncalli and Bouyé, 2000). In recent financial applications, copulas have been used to model default, e.g. Tibiletti (1995), Li (2000), Lindskog (2000) and Embrechts, Lindskog and McNeil (2003). Other empirical applications are by Malevergne and Sornette (2003) and Denuit and Scaillet (2004).[2] Some recent papers focus on multivariate skewed distributions, and in particular on the skewed student-t distribution (Azzalini and Capitanio, 2003; Bauwens and Laurent, 2005 and Sahu, Dey and Branco, 2003). Yet, it should be noted that, since their estimation is, in general, very easy to implement, copulas allow one to deal with more general marginal dynamic models. In addition, most copula functions introduce explicitly a dependency parameter that can be conditioned easily.

Third, we apply our framework to investigate the dynamics of the dependency parameter. In a multivariate GARCH framework, Hamao, Masulis and Ng (1990), Susmel and Engle (1994) and Bekaert and Harvey (1995) have measured the interdependence of returns and volatilities across stock markets. More specifically, Longin and Solnik (1995) have tested the hypothesis of a constant conditional correlation between a large number of stock markets. They found that correlation generally increases in periods of high volatility of the US market. In addition, in such a context, tests of a constant correlation have been proposed by Bera and Kim (2002) and Tse (2000). In this chapter we follow recent advances in the modelling of correlation, as proposed by Kroner and Ng (1998), Engle and Sheppard (2001) and Tse and Tsui (2002). These authors propose multivariate GARCH models with dynamic conditional covariances or correlations. We propose a similar approach for the dependency parameter of the copula function.

The remainder of the chapter is organised as follows. In Section 8.2 we present our univariate model, which allows volatility, skewness and kurtosis to vary over time. In Section 8.3 we introduce copula functions and describe the copulas investigated in this chapter. Section 8.4 is devoted to the modelling of the dependency parameter. In Section 8.5 we describe the data and discuss our results. Our study investigates daily returns of five

---

[1] Higher moments refer to the third and fourth moments.

[2] Hwang and Salmon (2002) use copulas in performance measurement to focus on extreme events. Copulas have also been used to model extreme values (Embrechts, McNeil and Straumann, 1999) or to price contingent claims (Rosenberg, 2003). Gagliardini and Gouriéroux (2002) develop a new theory, involving copulas, to model dependency between trading durations.

major stock markets from January 1980 to December 1999. We also provide evidence that, for European market pairs, dependency is very strongly persistent. Section 8.6 contains a conclusion and guidelines for further research. Our model is very general and the idea of capturing conditional dependency within the proposed framework may be applied to many situations.

8.2   A MODEL FOR THE MARGINAL DISTRIBUTIONS

It is well known that the residuals obtained for a GARCH model are generally non-normal. This observation has led to the introduction of fat-tailed distributions for innovations. Nelson (1991) considers the generalised error distribution, while Bollerslev and Wooldridge (1992) focus on student-t innovations. Engle and Gonzalez-Rivera (1991) model residuals non-parametrically. Even though these contributions recognise the fact that errors have fat tails, they generally do not render higher moments time-varying, i.e. the parameters of the error distribution are assumed to be constant over time.

8.2.1   Hansen's skewed student-t distribution

Hansen (1994) was the first to propose a GARCH model, in which the first four moments are conditional and time-varying. For this purpose, he introduces a generalisation of the student-t distribution that allows the distribution to be asymmetric while maintaining the assumption of a zero mean and unit variance. The conditioning is obtained by expressing parameters as functions of past realisations. Some extensions to this seminal contribution may be found in Theodossiou (1998) and Jondeau and Rockinger (2003a).

Harvey and Siddique (1999) have proposed an alternative specification, based on a non-central student-t distribution. This distribution is designed so that skewness depends on the noncentrality parameter and the degree-of-freedom parameter. However, the difference between the two models is noteworthy. On one hand, Hansen's distribution has a zero mean and unit variance, and the two parameters controlling asymmetry and fat-tailedness are allowed to vary over time. On the other hand, in Harvey and Siddique, innovations are non-standardised, skewness is directly rendered conditional and is therefore time-varying, while kurtosis is not modelled. Note also that the specification of the skewed student-t distribution adopted by Lambert and Laurent (2002) corresponds to the distribution proposed by Hansen, but with a different parametrisation of the asymmetry parameter.

Hansen's skewed student-t distribution is defined by

$$d(z; \eta, \lambda) = \begin{cases} bc \left(1 + \frac{1}{\eta-2} \left(\frac{bz+a}{1-\lambda}\right)^2\right)^{-\frac{\eta+1}{2}} & \text{if } z < -a/b \\ bc \left(1 + \frac{1}{\eta-2} \left(\frac{bz+a}{1+\lambda}\right)^2\right)^{-\frac{\eta+1}{2}} & \text{if } z \geq -a/b \end{cases} \tag{8.1}$$

where

$$a \equiv 4\lambda c \frac{\eta-2}{\eta-1}, \qquad b^2 \equiv 1 + 3\lambda^2 - a^2, \qquad c \equiv \frac{\Gamma\left(\frac{\eta+1}{2}\right)}{\sqrt{\pi(\eta-2)}\Gamma\left(\frac{\eta}{2}\right)}$$

and η and λ denote the degree-of-freedom parameter and the asymmetry parameter respectively. If a random variable Z has the density $d(z; \eta, \lambda)$, we will write $Z \sim ST(z; \eta, \lambda)$.

Inspection of the various formulas reveals that this density is defined for $2 < \eta < \infty$ and $-1 < \lambda < 1$. Furthermore, it encompasses a large set of conventional densities. For instance, if $\lambda = 0$, Hansen's distribution is reduced to the traditional student-t distribution, which is not skewed. If, in addition, $\eta \to \infty$, the student-t distribution reduces to the normal density.

It is well known that a traditional student-t distribution with η degrees of freedom allows for the existence of all moments up to the ηth. Therefore, given the restriction $\eta > 2$, Hansen's skewed student-t distribution is well defined and its second moment exists.

Proposition 1   *If $Z \sim ST(z; \eta, \lambda)$, then Z has zero mean and unit variance.*

Proof   See Hansen (1994).   ■

Proposition 2   *Introduce $m_2 = 1 + 3\lambda^2$, $m_3 = 16c\lambda(1 + \lambda^2)(\eta - 2)^2/[(\eta - 1)(\eta - 3)]$, defined if $\eta > 3$, and $m_4 = 3(\eta - 2)(1 + 10\lambda^2 + 5\lambda^4)/(\eta - 4)$, defined if $\eta > 4$. The higher moments of Z are given by:*

$$E[Z^3] = [m_3 - 3a\,m_2 + 2a^3]/b^3 \tag{8.2}$$

$$E[Z^4] = [m_4 - 4a\,m_3 + 6a^2 m_2 - 3a^4]/b^4 \tag{8.3}$$

Proof   See Jondeau and Rockinger (2003a).   ■

Since Z has zero mean and unit variance, we obtain that skewness (Sk) and kurtosis (Ku) are directly related to the third and fourth moments: $Sk[Z] = E[Z^3]$ and $Ku[Z] = E[Z^4]$.

We emphasise that the density and the various moments do not exist for all parameters. Given the way asymmetry is introduced, we must have $-1 < \lambda < 1$. As already mentioned, the distribution is meaningful only if $\eta > 2$. Furthermore, careful scrutiny of the algebra yielding Equations (8.2) and (8.3) shows that skewness and kurtosis exist if $\eta > 3$ and $\eta > 4$ respectively. The domain over which skewness and kurtosis are well defined is characterised in Jondeau and Rockinger (2003a).[3] The relation between skewness and kurtosis and λ, and η, is a complex one. If one starts with a symmetric distribution, an increase only of λ will yield a skewed and leptokurtic distribution. For a given distribution, if η increases, then both tails of the distribution will increase. Now, if both $|\lambda|$ and η increase simultaneously, the tail on the side with the same sign as λ will unambiguously increase, while the effect on the other tail is ambiguous. In contrast, if $|\lambda|$ decreases while η increases, then the tail on the side with the opposite sign to λ will increase, whereas the impact on the other tail is ambiguous. Given a time series of parameters, a graphical inspection of the densities may yield precious indications as to how the densities evolve.

In the continuous-time finance literature, asset prices are often assumed to follow a Brownian motion combined with jumps. This translates into returns data with occasionally very large realisations. Our model captures such instances since, if η is small, e.g. close to 2, not even skewness exists.

---

[3] In empirical applications, we will only impose that $\eta > 2$ and let the data decide if, for a given time period, a specific moment exists or not.

8.2.2 The cdf of the skewed student-*t* distribution

The copula involves marginal cumulative distributions rather than densities. For this reason, we now derive the cdf of Hansen's skewed student-*t* distribution. To do so, we recall that the conventional student-*t* distribution is defined by

$$t(x; \eta) = \frac{\Gamma\left(\frac{\eta+1}{2}\right)}{\Gamma\left(\frac{\eta}{2}\right)} \frac{1}{\sqrt{\pi\eta}} \left(1 + \frac{x^2}{\eta}\right)^{-\frac{\eta+1}{2}}$$

where η is the degree-of-freedom parameter. Numerical evaluation of the cdf of the conventional student-*t* is well known, and procedures are provided in most software packages. We write the cdf of a student-*t* distribution with η degrees of freedom as

$$A(y; \eta) = \int_{-\infty}^{y} t(x, \eta)\, dx$$

The following proposition presents the cdf of the skewed student-*t* distribution.

Proposition 3 *Let $D(z; \eta, \lambda) = \Pr[Z < z]$, where Z has the skewed student-t distribution given by (8.1). Then $D(z; \eta, \lambda)$ is defined as*

$$D(z; \eta, \lambda) = \begin{cases} (1-\lambda)A\left(\frac{bz+a}{1-\lambda}\sqrt{\frac{\eta}{\eta-2}}; \eta\right) & \text{if } z < -a/b \\ (1+\lambda)A\left(\frac{bz+a}{1+\lambda}\sqrt{\frac{\eta}{\eta-2}}; \eta\right) - \lambda & \text{if } z \geq -a/b \end{cases}$$

Proof Let $w/\sqrt{\eta} = (bz+a)/[(1-\lambda)\sqrt{\eta-2}]$. The result then follows from the change of variable in Equation (8.1) of z into w. ∎

8.2.3 A GARCH model with time-varying skewness and kurtosis

Let $\{r_t\}$, $t = 1, \cdots, T$, be the returns of a given asset. A marginal model with a skewed student-*t* distribution with time-varying volatility, skewness and kurtosis may be defined as

$$r_t = \mu_t + \varepsilon_t \tag{8.4}$$

$$\varepsilon_t = \sigma_t z_t \tag{8.5}$$

$$\sigma_t^2 = a_0 + b_0^+ (\varepsilon_{t-1}^+)^2 + b_0^- (\varepsilon_{t-1}^-)^2 + c_0 \sigma_{t-1}^2 \tag{8.6}$$

$$z_t \sim ST(z_t; \eta_t, \lambda_t) \tag{8.7}$$

Equation (8.4) decomposes the return of time t into a conditional mean, μ_t, and an innovation, ε_t. The conditional mean is captured with ten lags of r_t and day-of-the-week dummies. Equation (8.5) then defines the innovation as the product between conditional volatility, σ_t, and a residual, z_t, with zero mean and unit variance. The next equation, (8.6), determines the dynamics of volatility. Such a specification, which is designed to capture the so-called leverage effect, has been suggested by Glosten, Jagannathan and Runkle (1993). In a similar spirit, one may mention Campbell and Hentschel (1992), Gouriéroux and Monfort (1992), Engle and Ng (1993) and Zakoïan (1994). We use the notation $\varepsilon_t^+ = \max(\varepsilon_t, 0)$ and $\varepsilon_t^- = \max(-\varepsilon_t, 0)$. For positivity and stationarity of the volatility process to be guaranteed, parameters are assumed to satisfy the following constraints: $a_0 > 0$, b_0^+, b_0^-, $c_0 \geq 0$, and $c_0 + \left(b_0^+ + b_0^-\right)/2 < 1$. Equation (8.7) specifies that residuals have a skewed student-t distribution with time-varying parameters η_t and λ_t.

Many specifications could be used for η_t and λ_t. To ensure that η_t and λ_t remain within their authorised range, we consider an unrestricted dynamic where the parameters are denoted by $\tilde{\eta}_t$ and $\tilde{\lambda}_t$ that we constrain via a logistic map, i.e. $\eta_t = g_{]L_\eta, U_\eta[}(\tilde{\eta}_t)$ and $\lambda_t = g_{]L_\lambda, U_\lambda[}(\tilde{\lambda}_t)$.[4] The general unrestricted model that we estimate is given by

$$\tilde{\eta}_t = a_1 + b_1^+ \varepsilon_{t-1}^+ + b_1^- \varepsilon_{t-1}^- + c_1 \tilde{\eta}_{t-1} \tag{8.8}$$

$$\tilde{\lambda}_t = a_2 + b_2^+ \varepsilon_{t-1}^+ + b_2^- \varepsilon_{t-1}^- + c_2 \tilde{\lambda}_{t-1} \tag{8.9}$$

The type of functional specification that should be retained in general is discussed in Jondeau and Rockinger (2003a). In that paper, it is first shown that an autoregressive model expressed as such, i.e. without the logistic map on which one would impose possibly thousands of constraints to guarantee that the parameters are always defined, yields a degenerate solution, i.e. no dynamics are possible: all coefficients of the variables must be zero. Next, that paper presents a procedure on how to avoid identification problems. For instance, if, in the estimation of Equation (8.8), the parameters b_1^+ and b_1^- are found to be statistically insignificant, then the parameter c_1 is not identified. In a numerical estimation, this may yield spuriously a highly significant c_1. Finally, a small simulation experiment in Jondeau and Rockinger (2003a) shows that the model estimates well the true DGP.

The model (8.4)–(8.9) can be estimated easily via the usual maximum-likelihood estimation procedure. To increase the speed of the estimation and enhance the numerical precision, analytical gradients may be implemented. The expression of these gradients is presented in Jondeau and Rockinger (2003a).

8.3   COPULA DISTRIBUTION FUNCTIONS

8.3.1   Generalities

To illustrate the usefulness of copulas, we consider two random variables X_1 and X_2 with continuous marginal cdfs $F_1(x_1) = Pr[X_1 \leq x_1]$ and $F_2(x_2) = Pr[X_2 \leq x_2]$. The random variables may also have a joint distribution function, $H(x_1, x_2) = Pr[X_1 < x_1, X_2 < x_2]$. All the cdfs, $F_i(\cdot)$ and $H(\cdot, \cdot)$ range in the interval $[0, 1]$. In some cases, a multivariate distribution exists, so that the function $H(\cdot, \cdot)$ has an explicit expression. One such case is the multivariate normal distribution. In many cases, however, a description of the margins $F_i(\cdot)$ is relatively easy to obtain, whereas an explicit expression of the joint distribution $H(\cdot, \cdot)$ may be difficult to obtain. In such a context, copulas provide a useful way to link margins into a multivariate distribution function.

We now turn to a more formal definition of copulas. We would like to emphasise from the outset that many results developed in this chapter extend to a higher dimensional framework. Some of the results, however, hold in the bivariate framework only.[5]

---

[4] The logistic map, $g_{]L, U[}(x) = L + (U - L)(1 + e^{-x})^{-1}$ maps $\mathcal{R}$ into the interval $]L, U[$. In practice, we use the bounds $L_\eta = 2.001$, $U_\eta = 30$ for η and $L_\lambda = -0.9998$, $U_\lambda = 0.9998$ for λ.
[5] The following definition and proposition may be found in Nelsen (1999, p. 8).

Definition 1   *A two-dimensional copula is a function $C : [0,1]^2 \rightarrow [0,1]$ with the three following properties:*

1. $C(u_1, u_2)$ *is increasing in u_1 and u_2.*
2. $C(0, u_2) = C(u_1, 0) = 0$, $C(1, u_2) = u_2$, $C(u_1, 1) = u_1$.
3. $\forall u_1, u_1', u_2, u_2'$ *in* $[0,1]$ *such that $u_1 < u_1'$ and $u_2 < u_2'$, we have $C(u_1', u_2') - C(u_1', u_2) - C(u_1, u_2') + C(u_1, u_2) \geq 0$.*

Point 1 states that, when one marginal distribution is constant, the joint probability will increase provided that the other marginal distribution increases. Point 2 states that if one margin has zero probability of occuring then it must be the same for the joint occurrence. Also, if, on the contrary, one margin is certain to occur, then the probability of a joint occurrence is determined by the remaining margin probability. Property 3 indicates that, if u_1 and u_2 both increase, then the joint probability also increases. This property is, therefore, a multivariate extension of the condition that a cdf is increasing.

Furthermore, if we set $u_i = F_i(x_i)$, then $C(F_1(x_1), F_2(x_2))$ yields a description of the joint distribution of X_1 and X_2. Having obtained this intuitive definition, we can now propose the two following properties.

Proposition 4   *If u_1 and u_2 are independent, then $C(u_1, u_2) = u_1 u_2$.*

Proof   The proof of this property follows immediately from the definition of independent random variables.   ∎

Theorem 1   *(Sklar's Theorem for continuous distributions). Let H be a joint distribution function with margins F_1 and F_2. Then, there exists a copula C such that, for all real numbers x_1 and x_2, one has the equality*

$$H(x_1, x_2) = C(F_1(x_1), F_2(x_2)) \tag{8.10}$$

Furthermore, if F_1 and F_2 are continuous, then C is unique. Conversely, if F_1 and F_2 are distributions, then the function H defined by Equation (8.10) is a joint distribution function with margins F_1 and F_2.

Proof   The proof of this theorem first appeared in Sklar (1959). A relatively simple proof may be found in Schweizer and Sklar (1974).   ∎

This theorem highlights the importance of copulas for empirical research. In this work, we use the "conversely" part of the theorem and construct a multivariate density from marginal ones.

8.3.2   Construction of the estimated copula functions

An abundant taxonomy of copula functions has emerged in the literature in order to fit most situations that can be encountered in practice, e.g. Joe (1997). In this chapter we illustrate the usefulness of copulas in the modelling of the dependency structure, using three well-known copula functions – Plackett's, the Gaussian and the student-t copulas, which are characterised by a single dependency parameter. The three copula functions are symmetric. Therefore, when the dependency parameter is assumed to be constant, large joint positive realisations have the same probability of occurrence as large joint negative realisations. In Section 8.4.1, we relax this assumption by allowing the dependency parameter to be conditional on past realisations. Another important issue concerns the dependency of the copula in the tails of the distribution. Since we focus on how the dependency of international markets varies after some joint realisations, we do not want to put particular emphasis on extreme events. Such an issue has been addressed already, using an alternative methodology, by Longin and Solnik (2001). Therefore, we consider copula functions that have different characteristics in terms of tail dependence. The Plackett and Gaussian copulas do not have tail dependence, while the student-t copula has such a tail dependence (see, for instance, Embrechts, Lindskog and McNeil, 2003).

We begin with a brief description of how Plackett's copula is constructed.[6] In Figure 8.1, we assume that we have two random variables X_1 and X_2. Both variables may take two discrete states, say high and low. As indicated in the figure, we associate probabilities a, b, c and d to the various simultaneous realisations. Intuitively, if the probabilities are high along the 45° diagonal, then we would have a positive dependence between the two random variables. Indeed, if one state is high, the other state will be high as well. In contrast, if there are as many observations along the (a, b) diagonal as along the (c, d) diagonal, then the random variables may be considered independent.

These observations suggest defining $\theta = ab/cd$ as a natural measure of dependency. If $\theta = 1$, there will be independence; if $\theta < 1$, dependence will be negative; and if $\theta > 1$,

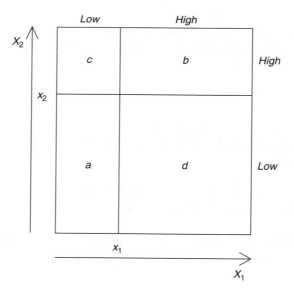

Figure 8.1   A (2,2) contingency table.

[6] We follow the derivation of Nelsen (1999, p. 79–89). See Plackett (1965) for the seminal work.

dependence will be positive. The states labelled 'Low' are associated with the marginal cdfs $F_1(x_1)$ and $F_2(x_2)$ in $[0, 1]$. Assuming that θ does not depend on x_1 and x_2 yields the following expression for the joint cdf of X_1 and X_2

$$C(u_1, u_2; \theta) = \begin{cases} \frac{1+(\theta-1)(u_1+u_2)-\sqrt{[1+(\theta-1)(u_1+u_2)]^2-4u_1u_2\theta(\theta-1)}}{2(\theta-1)} & \text{if } \theta \neq 1 \\ u_1 u_2 & \text{if } \theta = 1 \end{cases}$$

defined for $\theta > 0$. It may be verified that C satisfies the three conditions that define a copula function. As a consequence, the function $C(F_1(x_1), F_2(x_2); \theta)$ is the joint cdf of X_1 and X_2. It is easy to establish the density of Plackett's copula as

$$c(u_1, u_2; \theta) \equiv \frac{\partial^2 C(u_1, u_2; \theta)}{\partial u_1 \partial u_2} = \frac{\theta[1+(u_1-2u_1u_2+u_2)(\theta-1)]}{\left([1+(\theta-1)(u_1+u_2)]^2-4u_1u_2\theta(\theta-1)\right)^{\frac{3}{2}}}$$

It is worth noticing that θ is only defined for positive values. In numerical applications, this restriction is easily implemented by using a logarithmic transform of θ. In this case, independency corresponds to a value of $\ln(\theta) = 0$. When $\ln(\theta)$ is positive (negative), we have positive (negative) dependency.

The Gaussian copula is defined by the cdf

$$C(u_1, u_2; \rho) = \Phi_\rho\left(\Phi^{-1}(u_1), \Phi^{-1}(u_2)\right)$$

and the density

$$c(u_1, u_2; \rho) = \frac{1}{\sqrt{1-\rho^2}} \exp\left(-\frac{1}{2}\psi'\left(\Omega^{-1}-I_2\right)\psi\right)$$

where $\psi = \left(\Phi^{-1}(u_1), \Phi^{-1}(u_2)\right)'$ and Ω is the $(2, 2)$ correlation matrix with ρ as correlation between u_1 and u_2. Φ_ρ is the bivariate standardised Gaussian cdf with correlation ρ, while Φ is the univariate standardised Gaussian cdf.

Similarly, the student-t copula is defined by the cdf

$$C(u_1, u_2; \rho, n) = T_{\rho,n}\left(t_n^{-1}(u_1), t_n^{-1}(u_2)\right)$$

and the density

$$c(u_1, u_2; \rho, n) = \frac{1}{\sqrt{1-\rho^2}} \frac{\Gamma\left(\frac{n+2}{2}\right)\Gamma\left(\frac{n}{2}\right)}{\left(\Gamma\left(\frac{n+1}{2}\right)\right)^2} \frac{\left(1+\frac{1}{n}\psi'\Omega^{-1}\psi\right)^{-\frac{n+2}{2}}}{\prod_{i=1}^2\left(1+\frac{1}{n}\psi_i^2\right)^{-\frac{n+1}{2}}}$$

where $\psi = \left(t_n^{-1}(u_1), t_n^{-1}(u_2)\right)'$. $T_{\rho,n}$ is the bivariate student-t cdf with n degrees of freedom and correlation ρ, while t_n is the univariate student-t cdf with degree-of-freedom parameter n.

In Figure 8.2, we display examples of contour plots associated with the density of the Plackett, Gaussian and student-t copula functions for the case of positive dependency ($\rho = 0.5$). The contour plots of negative dependency are symmetric with respect to the axis $x_1 = 0$ or $x_2 = 0$. The degree-of-freedom parameter n is set equal to 5. This figure clearly illustrates that the student-t copula is able to capture tail dependence, while the Plackett and Gaussian copulas do not provide such a possibility.

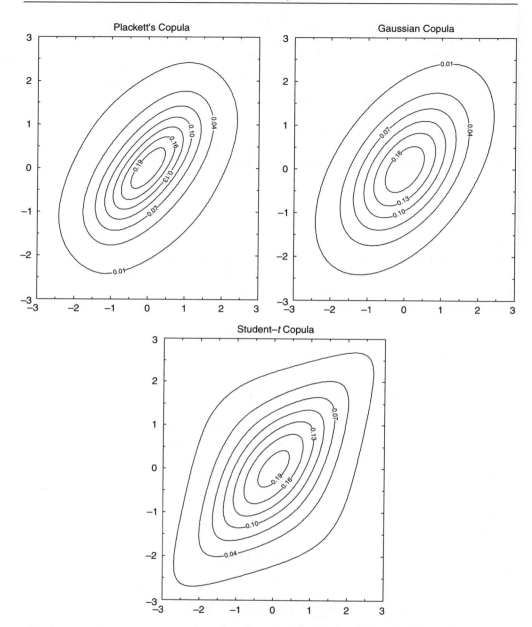

Figure 8.2 Contour plots of Plackett's, Gaussian and student-t copula functions for the case of positive dependency ($\rho = 0.5$). For the student-t copula, the degree-of-freedom parameter n is set equal to 5. The marginal distributions are assumed to be $N(0, 1)$.

8.4 MODELLING DEPENDENCY AND ESTIMATION OF THE MODEL

8.4.1 Conditional dependency

Consider a sample $\{z_{1t}, z_{2t}\}$, $t = 1, \cdots, T$, where z_{it} is assumed to be generated by a skewed student-t distribution with time-varying moments (Equations (8.4)–(8.9)). The cdf and the pdf of residuals z_{it} are thus denoted $F_i(z_{it}; \xi_i) = D(z_{it}; \xi_i)$ and $f_i(z_{it}; \xi_i) = d(z_{it}; \xi_i)$, $i = 1, 2$, respectively, where ξ_i denotes the vector of unknown parameters pertaining to the margin i. We set $u_{it} \equiv F_i(z_{it}; \xi_i)$ for notational convenience. The key observation of this research is that the dependency parameter can be conditioned easily in the case of all the copulas investigated.[7] We define ρ_t as the value taken by the dependency parameter at time t.

Several approaches have been proposed in the literature for modelling the correlation coefficient in a multivariate context. Kroner and Ng (1998), Engle and Sheppard (2001), Engle (2002) and Tse and Tsui (2002) have suggested modelling of covariances or correlations in the context of GARCH models, in which conditional correlation depends on recent cross-products of residuals. We adopt, in the following, a specification close to the dynamic conditional correlation (DCC) model proposed by Engle and Sheppard (2001) and Cappiello, Engle and Sheppard (2003) in their modelling of Pearson's correlation in a GARCH context. In this model, the conditional correlation matrix, denoted $\mathbf{R}_t$, is defined by:

$$\mathbf{R}_t = \mathbf{Q}_t^{*-1} \mathbf{Q}_t \mathbf{Q}_t^{*-1} \tag{8.11}$$

$$\mathbf{Q}_t = (1 - \alpha - \beta) \bar{\mathbf{Q}} + \alpha (z_{t-1} z_{t-1}') + \beta \mathbf{Q}_{t-1}$$

where $\bar{\mathbf{Q}} = E[z_t z_t']$ is the unconditional covariance matrix of residuals $z_t = (z_{1t}, z_{2t})'$ and

$$\mathbf{Q}_t^* = \begin{pmatrix} \sqrt{q_{11t}} & 0 \\ 0 & \sqrt{q_{22t}} \end{pmatrix}$$

is the diagonal matrix composed of the square root of the diagonal elements of $\mathbf{Q}_t$. In the bivariate case, the off-diagonal element of $\mathbf{R}_t$ is simply given by $\rho_t = q_{12t}/\sqrt{q_{11t} q_{22t}}$. The normalisation by $\mathbf{Q}_t^*$ in Equation (8.11) is intended to express the conditional correlation matrix directly from the conditional covariance matrix.[8] Parameters α and β are assumed to satisfy $0 \le \alpha, \beta \le 1$ and $\alpha + \beta \le 1$. Once these restrictions are imposed, the conditional correlation matrix is guaranteed to be positive definite during the optimisation.

Following Cappiello, Engle and Sheppard (2003), we also investigated an asymmetric dynamic conditional correlation (ADCC) model, which can be written as follows

$$\mathbf{R}_t = \mathbf{Q}_t^{*-1} \mathbf{Q}_t \mathbf{Q}_t^{*-1} \tag{8.12}$$

$$\mathbf{Q}_t = [(1 - \alpha - \beta) \bar{\mathbf{Q}} - \alpha^- \bar{\mathbf{Q}}^-] + \alpha (z_{t-1} z_{t-1}') + \alpha^- (z_{t-1}^- z_{t-1}^{-\prime}) + \beta \mathbf{Q}_{t-1}$$

where $\bar{\mathbf{Q}}^- = E[z_t^- z_t^{-\prime}]$ and $z_t^- = (\max(-z_{1t}, 0), \max(-z_{2t}, 0))'$. This model incorporates the stylized fact that large joint negative shocks are more likely to affect subsequent

---

[7] As shown below, the student-t copula is preferred to the Gaussian and Plackett's copulas. Consequently, we will investigate the modelling of the dependency structure for the student-t copula only.

[8] In our context, $\mathbf{Q}_t^*$ is close to unit matrix, since residuals z_t have been preliminarily standardised.

correlation than large joint positive shocks. Consequently, the parameter α^- is expected to be positive.

8.4.2   Estimation in a copula framework

We now briefly describe how the parameter vector of the dependency structure can be estimated. The copula function is assumed to depend on a set of unknown parameters through the function $G\left(z_{1t-1}, z_{2t-1}; \xi_c\right)$. Therefore, $\xi_c = (\rho, \alpha, \beta, n)'$ for the DCC specification, and $\xi_c = (\rho, \alpha, \alpha^-, \beta, n)'$ for the ADCC specification. We set $\xi = (\xi_1', \xi_2', \xi_c')'$. The joint density of an observation (z_{1t}, z_{2t}) is thus

$$l\left(\xi\right) = c\left(F_1\left(z_{1t}; \xi_1\right), F_2\left(z_{2t}; \xi_2\right); G\left(z_{1t-1}, z_{2t-1}; \xi_c\right)\right) \times f_1\left(z_{1t}; \xi_1\right) \times f_2\left(z_{2t}; \xi_2\right)$$

As a consequence, the log-likelihood of a sample becomes

$$L(\xi) = \sum_{t=1}^{T} \ln\left[c\left(F_1\left(z_{1t}; \xi_1\right), F_2\left(z_{2t}; \xi_2\right); G\left(z_{1t-1}, z_{2t-1}; \xi_c\right)\right)\right]$$

$$+ \sum_{t=1}^{T}\sum_{i=1}^{2} \ln f_i\left(z_{it}; \xi_i\right) \tag{8.13}$$

Maximum likelihood involves maximising the log-likelihood function (8.13) simultaneously over all parameters, yielding parameter estimates denoted $\hat{\xi}_{\mathrm{ML}} = \left(\hat{\xi}_1', \hat{\xi}_2', \hat{\xi}_c'\right)'$, such that

$$\hat{\xi}_{\mathrm{ML}} = \arg\max L\left(\xi\right)$$

In some applications, however, this estimation method may be difficult to implement, because of a large number of unknown parameters or of the complexity of the model.[9] In such a case, it may be necessary to adopt a two-step ML procedure, also called inference functions for margins. This approach, which has been introduced by Shih and Louis (1995), Joe and Xu (1996) and Riboulet, Roncalli and Bouyé (2000), can be viewed as the ML estimation of the dependence structure given the estimated margins. Patton (2006) shows that the two-step estimator $\tilde{\xi}_{\mathrm{TS}} = \left(\tilde{\xi}_1', \tilde{\xi}_2', \tilde{\xi}_c'\right)'$ is asymptotically efficient and normal. First, parameters pertaining to the marginal distributions are estimated separately:

$$\tilde{\xi}_i \in \arg\max \sum_{t=1}^{T} \ln f_i\left(z_{it}; \xi_i\right) \qquad i = 1, 2 \tag{8.14}$$

Then, parameters pertaining to the copula function are estimated by solving:

$$\tilde{\xi}_c \in \arg\max \sum_{t=1}^{T} \ln c\left(F_1\left(z_{1t}; \tilde{\xi}_1\right), F_2\left(z_{2t}; \tilde{\xi}_2\right); G\left(z_{1t-1}, z_{2t-1}; \tilde{\xi}_c\right)\right)$$

---

[9] The dependency parameter of the copula function may be a convoluted expression of the parameters. In such a case, an analytical expression of the gradient of the likelihood might not exist. Therefore, only numerical gradients may be computable, implying a dramatic slowing down of the numerical procedure.

8.5   EMPIRICAL RESULTS

8.5.1   The data

We investigate the interactions between five major stock indices. The labels are SP for the S&P 500, NIK for the Nikkei stock index, FTSE for the Financial Times stock index, DAX for the Deutsche Aktien Index and CAC for the French Cotation Automatique Continue index. Our sample covers the period from January 1st, 1980 to December 31st, 1999.

All the data are from Datastream, sampled at a daily frequency. To eliminate spurious correlation generated by holidays, we eliminated from the database those observations when a holiday occurred at least for one country. This reduced the sample from 5479 observations to 4578. Note that such an observation would not affect the dependency between stock markets during extreme events. Yet it would affect the estimation of the return marginal distribution and, subsequently, the estimation of the distribution of the copula. In particular, the estimation of the copula would be distorted to account for the excessive occurrence of zero returns in the distribution. To take into account the fact that international markets have different trading hours, we use once-lagged US returns. This does not affect the correlation with European markets significantly (because trading times are partially overlapping), but increases the correlation between the S&P and the Nikkei from 0.1 to 0.26. Preliminary estimations also revealed that the crash of October 1987 was of such importance that the dynamics of our model would be very much influenced by this event. For the S&P, on that date the index dropped by 22 %. The second largest drop was only 9 %. For this reason, we eliminated the data between October 17th and 24th. This reduces the sample by six observations to a total of 4572 observations.

Table 8.1 provides summary statistics on market-index returns. Returns are defined as $100 \times \ln\left(P_t / P_{t-1}\right)$, where P_t is the value of the index at time t. Therefore, the number of

Table 8.1   Summary statistics on daily stock-market returns. Mean, Std, Sk and XKu denote the mean, the standard deviation, the skewness and the excess kurtosis of returns, respectively. Standard errors are computed using a GMM-based procedure. Wald Stat. is the Wald statistic, which tests the null hypothesis that skewness and excess kurtosis are jointly equal to zero. It is distributed, under the null, as a $\chi^2(2)$. Min and Max represent the minimum and maximum of centred and reduced returns, while $q1$, $q5$, $q95$ and $q99$ represent the 1, 5, 95 and 99 percentiles. The 1 %, 5 %, 95 % and 99 % percentiles for a normal distribution are -2.3263, -1.6449, 1.6449 and 2.3263. The $LM(K)$ statistic for heteroskedasticity is obtained by regressing squared returns on K lags. $QW(K)$ is the Box–Ljung statistic for serial correlation, corrected for heteroskedasticity, computed with K lags. Since international markets have different trading hours, the correlation matrix is computed using once-lagged US returns. Significance is denoted by superscripts at the 1 % ([a]), 5 % ([b]) and 10 % ([c]) levels

	SP	NIK	FTSE	DAX	CAC
Mean	0.049[a]	−0.002	0.044[a]	0.044[b]	0.041[b]
s.e.	(0.014)	(0.018)	(0.014)	(0.018)	(0.019)
Std	0.963[a]	1.244[a]	0.923[a]	1.211[a]	1.190[a]
s.e.	(0.026)	(0.039)	(0.020)	(0.042)	(0.042)
Sk	−0.399[b]	0.167	−0.164	−0.720[b]	−0.683[b]
s.e.	(0.186)	(0.226)	(0.103)	(0.299)	(0.362)

Table 8.1   Continued

	SP	NIK	FTSE	DAX	CAC
XKu	5.147[a]	6.006[a]	2.082[a]	8.604[a]	8.369[b]
s.e.	(1.389)	(1.785)	(0.525)	(3.132)	(3.550)
Wald Stat.	17.454[a]	28.072[a]	15.837[a]	7.581[b]	6.022[b]
p-val.	(0.000)	(0.000)	(0.000)	(0.023)	(0.049)
Min	−8.642	−7.234	−6.389	−13.710	−13.910
$q1$	−2.487	−3.534	−2.341	−3.310	−3.280
$q5$	−1.496	−2.049	−1.438	−1.840	−1.826
$q95$	1.559	1.848	1.417	1.778	1.846
$q99$	2.506	3.427	2.277	2.998	2.870
Max	4.989	12.430	5.440	7.288	8.225
LM(1)	82.745[a]	151.046[a]	103.585[a]	222.750[a]	113.279[a]
p-val.	(0.000)	(0.000)	(0.000)	(0.000)	(0.000)
LM(5)	188.927[a]	351.829[a]	315.646[a]	318.219[a]	345.317[a]
p-val.	(0.000)	(0.000)	(0.000)	(0.000)	(0.000)
QW(5)	13.187[b]	4.901	17.264[a]	10.161[c]	10.404[c]
p-val.	(0.022)	(0.428)	(0.004)	(0.071)	(0.065)
QW(10)	22.526[b]	10.238	25.574[a]	18.515[b]	21.470[b]
p-val.	(0.013)	(0.420)	(0.004)	(0.047)	(0.018)
Correlation matrix					
SP	1	0.258	0.272	0.317	0.269
NIK	0.258	1	0.248	0.276	0.245
FTSE	0.272	0.248	1	0.475	0.524
DAX	0.317	0.276	0.475	1	0.554
CAC	0.269	0.245	0.524	0.554	1

observations is the same for all markets, and the series do not contain days when the market was closed. We begin with the serial dependency of returns. The $LM(K)$ statistic tests whether the squared return is serially correlated up to lag K. This statistic clearly indicates that ARCH effects are likely to be found in all market returns. Also, when considering the Ljung– Box statistic, $QW(K)$, after correction for heteroskedasticity, we obtain that, in most cases, returns are serially correlated. We obtain clear indication of such autocorrelation for the SP, the FTSE and the CAC.

Now we consider the unconditional moments of the various series. All the standard errors have been computed with a GMM-based procedure. We notice that for all series, except the Nikkei, skewness is negative. Moreover, considering excess kurtosis, XKu, we observe a significant positive parameter for all the series. This indicates that all the series display fatter tails than the Gaussian distribution. The Wald statistics of the joint test of significance of skewness and excess kurtosis corroborate this finding.[10]

Finally, Table 8.1 displays the unconditional Pearson correlations. This matrix indicates that rather high dependency is likely to be found between market returns. The correlation is smallest between the Nikkei and the CAC, and largest between the DAX and the CAC.

---

[10] When the 1987 crash is not removed, the SP distribution is characterised by a very strong asymmetry (with a skewness equal to −2.55) and fat tails (with an excess kurtosis as high as 57). Yet, in that case, due to uncertainty around higher-moment point estimates, the Wald test would no longer reject normality.

8.5.2 Estimation of the marginal model

Table 8.2 presents the results of the general model in which volatility, skewness and kurtosis are allowed to vary over time. First, the different magnitude of b_1^+ and b_1^- shows that a negative return has a stronger effect on subsequent volatility than a positive return of the same magnitude. This is the well-known leverage effect, documented by Campbell and Hentschel (1992), Glosten, Jagannathan and Runkle (1993) and Zakoïan (1994). These findings cannot be compared directly with Harvey and Siddique (1999). Their model strongly differs from ours in the choice of error distribution and of model specification. They also use data that differ from ours. In our estimations, the introduction of time-varying skewness does not alter

Table 8.2 Parameter estimates and residual summary statistics for the model with a skewed student-t distribution and time-varying higher moments. Parameters are defined in Equations (8.6), (8.8) and (8.9). The table also shows goodness-of-fit statistics, following Diebold, Gunther and Tay (1998). The first part contains the LM test statistics for the null of no serial correlation of moments of the u_{it}. It is defined as $(T - 20) R^2$, where R^2 is the coefficient of determination of the regression of $(u_{it} - \bar{u}_i)^k$ on 20 own lags, for $k = 1, \ldots, 4$. Under the null, the statistic is distributed as a $\chi^2 (20)$. The table also shows the test statistic, DGT, for the null hypothesis that the cdf of residuals is Uniform(0, 1). Under the null, the statistic is distributed as a $\chi^2 (20)$. Finally, the table presents the log-likelihood (lnL) and the AIC and SIC information criteria. LRT(6) is the LR test statistic for the null hypothesis that skewness and kurtosis are constant over time. Under the null, the statistic is distributed as a $\chi^2 (6)$

	SP	NIK	FTSE	DAX	CAC
Volatility equation					
a_0	0.006^a	0.016^a	0.021^a	0.022^a	0.022^a
	(0.002)	(0.003)	(0.005)	(0.006)	(0.006)
b_0^+	0.043^a	0.044^a	0.045^a	0.081^a	0.067^a
	(0.010)	(0.011)	(0.010)	(0.016)	(0.013)
b_0^-	0.071^a	0.154^a	0.085^a	0.125^a	0.107^a
	(0.012)	(0.020)	(0.012)	(0.018)	(0.014)
c_0	0.941^a	0.897^a	0.910^a	0.887^a	0.900^a
	(0.009)	(0.012)	(0.013)	(0.014)	(0.012)
Degree-of-freedom equation					
a_1	-0.510^a	-0.972^a	0.390	-0.496^b	-0.429
	(0.198)	(0.373)	(0.466)	(0.242)	(0.230)
b_1^+	-0.616^a	-0.181^c	-0.994^a	-0.664^a	-0.436^a
	(0.149)	(0.098)	(0.291)	(0.136)	(0.126)
b_1^-	0.060	0.318	-0.414	0.001	0.326
	(0.174)	(0.282)	(0.358)	(0.098)	(0.369)
c_1	0.628^a	0.496^a	0.049	0.422^a	0.626^a
	(0.130)	(0.167)	(0.453)	(0.154)	(0.142)
Asymmetry parameter equation					
a_2	-0.084^c	-0.228^a	-0.117^a	-0.046	-0.057^c
	(0.049)	(0.083)	(0.033)	(0.051)	(0.034)
b_2^+	0.239^a	0.109^b	0.271^a	-0.033	0.083^c
	(0.071)	(0.050)	(0.056)	(0.091)	(0.047)
b_2^-	-0.088^c	-0.106^c	-0.058	-0.100^b	-0.033
	(0.051)	(0.057)	(0.042)	(0.050)	(0.031)
c_2	0.253	-0.475^c	0.745^a	0.508^c	0.669^a
	(0.178)	(0.254)	(0.075)	(0.304)	(0.159)

Table 8.2 Continued

	SP	NIK	FTSE	DAX	CAC
Summary statistics					
LM test for no serial correlation of ...					
first moments	30.934[c]	26.119	19.201	32.978[b]	24.599
second moments	22.487	16.221	15.327	14.356	19.027
third moments	24.877	26.879	20.815	28.561[c]	17.422
fourth moments	20.840	18.078	10.752	7.188	13.688
DGT(20)	18.886	19.719	24.208	30.004[c]	12.152
p-val.	(0.464)	(0.412)	(0.188)	(0.052)	(0.879)
InL	-5770.644	-6489.164	-5776.923	-6601.303	-6634.668
LRT(6)	39.518	18.813	38.495	21.700	14.539
p-val.	(0.000)	(0.004)	(0.000)	(0.001)	(0.024)
AIC	2.535	2.850	2.538	2.899	2.914
SIC	2.552	2.867	2.555	2.916	2.931

the asymmetry of news on volatility. In Harvey and Siddique (1999), the result depends on the series used.

Second, the impact of large returns (of either sign) on the subsequent distribution is measured via λ_t and η_t. A discussion of the actual impact on skewness and kurtosis of past returns is not straightforward, because the asymmetry parameter, λ_t, and the tail-fatness parameter, η_t, are closely entangled. The unrestricted dynamics of $\tilde{\lambda}_t$ and $\tilde{\eta}_t$ get mapped into λ_t and η_t with the logistic map. For most markets, except the FTSE, we obtain an estimate of the persistence parameter c_1 ranging between 0.4 and 0.65. The negative sign of b_1^+ suggests that, subsequent to large positive realisations, tails thin down. In contrast, we do not obtain significant estimates of b_1^-, although the point estimate is generally positive.

The asymmetric impact of large returns on the distribution is measured by the dynamics of λ_t. We find that, in general, past positive returns enlarge the right tail while past negative returns enlarge the left tail. The effect of positive returns is slightly larger than the effect of negative returns, although not always significantly. Furthermore, for European stock markets, we find persistence in the asymmetry parameter. If we combine the effects of λ_t and η_t in the light of the discussion of Section 8.2, we conclude that past negative shocks tend to increase the left tail, whereas past positive shocks have an ambiguous impact on the right tail.

As a diagnostic check, the table also reports the goodness-of-fit test for the general distribution. We follow Diebold, Gunther and Tay (1998), henceforth denoted DGT, who suggested that, if the marginal distributions are correctly specified, the margins u_{1t} and u_{2t} should be iid Uniform $(0, 1)$. The test is performed in two steps. First, we evaluate whether u_{1t} and u_{2t} are serially correlated. For this purpose, we examine the serial correlations of $(u_{it} - \bar{u}_i)^k$, for $k = 1, \ldots, 4$.[11] We thus regress $(u_{it} - \bar{u}_i)^k$ on 20 lags of the variable. The LM test statistic is defined as $(T - 20) R^2$, where R^2 is the coefficient of determination of the regression and is distributed, under the null, as a $\chi^2 (20)$. We find that the LM tests for serial correlation of margins do not reject the null hypothesis of no serial correlation.

Second, we test the null hypothesis that u_{it} is distributed as a Uniform $(0, 1)$. Hence, we cut the empirical and theoretical distributions into N bins and test whether the two distributions significantly differ on each bin. Table 8.2 reports the DGT test statistic for various

---

[11] Zero correlation is equivalent to independence only under Gaussianity. The correlogram is, therefore, only hinting at possible independence.

distributions with p-values computed with $N - 1$ degrees of freedom.[12] When we consider the case $N = 20$ bins, we do not reject the null hypothesis that the theoretical distribution provides a good fit of the empirical distribution for any return series, at the 5 % level.

Figure 8.3 displays the evolution of the η_t and λ_t parameters for the SP and the CAC, respectively. As far as the asymmetry parameter, λ_t, is concerned, we recall that λ_t is constrained to the range -1 to 1. We observe that the distribution of the SP return is characterised by large movements in asymmetry.

8.5.3 Estimation of the multivariate model

8.5.3.1 The model with constant dependency parameter

For each stock-index pair, we estimate the multivariate model. In Figure 8.4 we present scatterplots of the marginal cumulative distribution functions u_{1t} and u_{2t} for the SP–NIK and for the FTSE–CAC, respectively. We notice that, except for the region where one margin is large and the other small, the unit square is rather uniformly filled with realisations. In both figures, there is a higher concentration in the corners along the diagonal. This clustering corresponds to the observation that correlation is higher in the tails. Certain studies have focused on the strength of correlation in the tails (see Longin and Solnik, 2001; Ang and Chen, 2002). This is, however, not the scope of this research. We will investigate whether, subsequent to some joint realisation, a similar joint realisation can be expected.

It should be emphasised that these scatterplots do not reveal anything about temporal dependency. To establish if a temporal dependency exists, it is necessary to estimate a dynamic model such as (8.11). We now turn to the discussion of the parameter estimates.

In Table 8.3, Panel A, we report several statistics on the estimation of the copula with constant dependency parameter. We report parameter estimates of the copula functions: $\ln(\theta)$ and the associated implied Spearman's rho for Plackett's copula,[13] the dependency parameter ρ for the Gaussian copula and the dependency parameter ρ as well as the degree-of-freedom parameter n for the student-t copula. For all market pairs, the estimate of the dependency parameter is found to be positive and significant. For Plackett's copula, this result is confirmed by the value of the implied Spearman's rho. It can be compared with the empirical value of the correlation between margins reported in the last row of the table. The two estimates are very close to one another, suggesting that the chosen copulas provide a rather good description of the dependency between the markets under study. We also performed a goodness-of-fit test to investigate whether a given copula function is able to fit the dependence structure observed in the data, along the lines of DGT.[14] For all market pairs, we obtain that the student-t copula fits the data very well, since the null hypothesis is never rejected. In contrast, the Gaussian copula is unable to adjust the dependence structure between European markets, while Plackett's copula is unable to fit the dependency structure for any market pair.

---

[12] As shown by Vlaar and Palm (1993), under the null, the correct distribution of the DGT test statistic is bounded between a $\chi^2(N-1)$ and a $\chi^2(N-K-1)$, where K is the number of estimated parameters.

[13] Spearman's rho is defined as Pearson's correlation between margins. It is related to θ through the relation

$$\varrho_S = \frac{\theta+1}{\theta-1} - \frac{2\theta}{(\theta-1)^2 \ln(\theta)}$$

The standard error of the implied ϱ_S is computed with the delta method.

[14] The reported DGT test statistics are computed by splitting the joint distribution as a (5,5) square and by evaluating for each bin whether the empirical and theoretical distributions differ significantly.

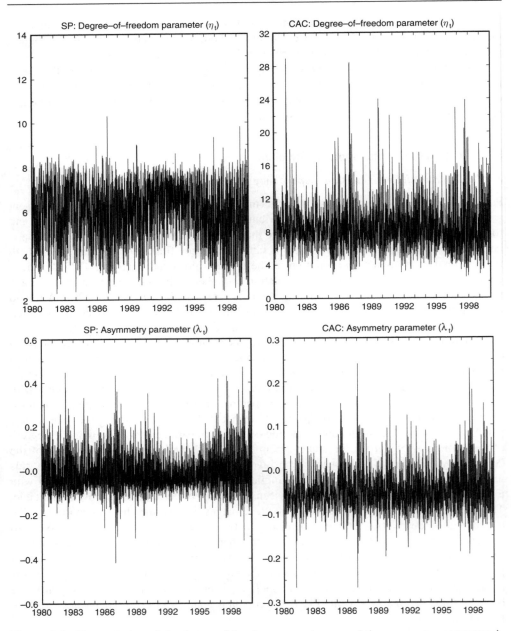

Figure 8.3 The evolution of the degree-of-freedom parameter η_t and the asymmetry parameter λ_t for the SP and the CAC indices.

To provide further insight on the ability of the chosen copulas to fit the data, we report the log-likelihood, the AIC and SIC information criteria. We also present the LRT statistic for the null hypothesis that the degree-of-freedom parameter of the student-t copula is infinite, so that the student-t copula reduces to the Gaussian copula. For all market pairs, we obtain

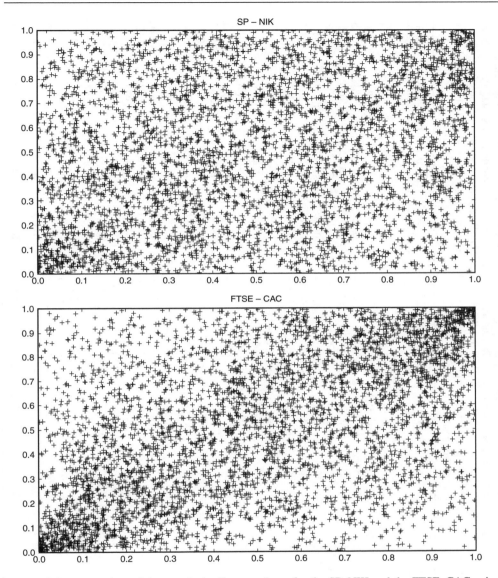

Figure 8.4 Scatterplots of the marginal cdfs u_{1t} and u_{2t}, for the SP–NIK and the FTSE–CAC pairs, respectively.

that the log-likelihood of the Gaussian copula is larger than that of Plackett's copula. Since the two functions have the same number of parameters to be estimated, the Gaussian copula would be selected on the basis of information criteria. As regards the student-t copula, comparison with the Gaussian one can be based both on the information criteria and on the LR test. With both tests, we select the student-t copula. As will be shown later on, this result is consistent with the finding that the dependency is stronger in the tails of the distribution than in the middle of the distribution.

Table 8.3 Parameter estimates for the copula functions when the dependency parameter is assumed to be constant over time. Parameters are θ and the associated Spearman's rho for Plackett's, ρ for the Gaussian and ρ and n for the student-t copula. The table also reports the test statistic for the null hypothesis that the cdf of residuals is Uniform(0, 1). Under the null, the statistic is distributed as a χ^2 (25). We also report the log-likelihood (lnL) as well as the AIC and SIC information criteria. For the student-t copula, LRT is the LR test statistic for the null hypothesis that $1/n = 0$. Finally, the last row presents empirical ρ, that is the Pearson's correlation between residuals

	SP/NIK	SP/FTSE	SP/DAX	SP/CAC	NIK/FTSE	NIK/DAX	NIK/CAC	FTSE/DAX	FTSE/CAC	DAX/CAC
				Panel A: Plackett's copula						
ln(θ)	0.717	0.675	0.875	0.819	0.580	0.749	0.628	1.236	1.560	1.456
s.e.	(0.043)	(0.043)	(0.042)	(0.043)	(0.044)	(0.043)	(0.044)	(0.041)	(0.040)	(0.041)
Spearman's rho	0.235	0.222	0.285	0.267	0.191	0.245	0.207	0.392	0.481	0.454
s.e.	(0.014)	(0.014)	(0.013)	(0.013)	(0.014)	(0.014)	(0.014)	(0.012)	(0.011)	(0.011)
DGT(25)	554.931[a]	561.754[a]	510.231[a]	469.966[a]	668.069[a]	535.778[a]	627.749[a]	503.023[a]	518.067[a]	540.786[a]
lnL	129.45	116.83	197.15	167.41	82.63	139.73	98.17	385.69	612.62	531.66
AIC	−0.056	−0.051	−0.086	−0.073	−0.036	−0.061	−0.043	−0.168	−0.268	−0.232
SIC	−0.055	−0.049	−0.084	−0.071	−0.034	−0.059	−0.041	−0.167	−0.266	−0.231
				Panel B: Gaussian copula						
ρ	0.253	0.240	0.305	0.275	0.199	0.253	0.212	0.406	0.488	0.459
s.e.	(0.014)	(0.014)	(0.013)	(0.013)	(0.014)	(0.014)	(0.014)	(0.012)	(0.010)	(0.011)
DGT(25)	28.770	14.780	23.944	16.069	38.162[b]	32.885	34.239[c]	41.312[b]	42.424[b]	54.217[a]
lnL	148.94	135.13	220.39	178.40	91.82	148.41	104.30	408.67	620.63	536.47
AIC	−0.065	−0.059	−0.096	−0.078	−0.040	−0.064	−0.045	−0.178	−0.271	−0.234
SIC	−0.063	−0.057	−0.095	−0.076	−0.038	−0.063	−0.044	−0.177	−0.270	−0.233
				Panel C: student-t copula						
ρ	0.251	0.239	0.304	0.275	0.197	0.251	0.211	0.406	0.494	0.465
s.e.	(0.014)	(0.014)	(0.014)	(0.014)	(0.015)	(0.014)	(0.015)	(0.013)	(0.012)	(0.012)
n	25.649	23.773	18.425	12.939	12.446	17.895	14.742	9.320	6.975	6.666
s.e.	(10.313)	(9.056)	(5.380)	(2.794)	(2.612)	(5.256)	(3.590)	(1.522)	(0.851)	(0.779)
DGT(25)	25.789	16.985	24.228	12.346	33.496[c]	24.211	33.362[c]	22.513	21.147	27.427
lnL	152.449	139.052	227.500	191.420	105.704	155.314	114.909	433.927	667.453	592.095
LRT	7.027	7.847	14.215	26.035	27.761	13.811	21.221	50.507	93.655	111.256
p-val.	(0.008)	(0.005)	(0.000)	(0.000)	(0.000)	(0.000)	(0.000)	(0.000)	(0.000)	(0.000)
AIC	−0.066	−0.060	−0.099	−0.083	−0.045	−0.067	−0.049	−0.189	−0.291	−0.258
SIC	−0.063	−0.057	−0.096	−0.080	−0.043	−0.064	−0.047	−0.186	−0.288	−0.255
empirical ρ	0.232	0.222	0.285	0.261	0.183	0.239	0.201	0.383	0.470	0.440

Since the student-t copula dominates the Plackett and Gaussian ones, we focus from now on only on the student-t copula. Notice that we performed the same estimations as the ones reported with the other copulas under investigation.

8.5.3.2 *The model with dynamic dependency parameter*

The last issue we address in this chapter is the persistence in the dependency parameter. Thus, we estimate the DCC and ADCC models, given by Equations (8.11) and (8.12) respectively, for the student-t copula. Results are reported in Table 8.4. When considering first the DCC model (Panel A), we notice that the persistence parameter, β, ranges between 0.88 and 0.99. The effect of the past residuals, measured by α, is, in general, significantly positive. Inspection of the persistence measure $(\alpha + \beta)$ suggests that persistence in dependency is high between European stock markets, but also for pairs involving the SP.

Estimates of the asymmetric DCC model (Panel B) reveal the following features. On one hand, for European market pairs or pairs involving the SP, no asymmetry in conditional correlation emerges, with parameters α as well as α^- being insignificantly different from zero. On the other hand, the LR test statistics for the null hypothesis of no asymmetry in conditional correlation is rejected for pairs including the NIK. In this case, only negative shocks have a significant impact on subsequent correlation.

In Figure 8.5, we display the evolution of the parameter ρ_t obtained with the ADCC model, for the SP–NIK, the NIK–DAX, the FTSE–DAX and the FTSE–CAC pairs. For markets involving the SP or NIK, we do not observe a significant trend in dependency. In contrast, the dynamics of dependency between European market pairs has increased dramatically during the period under study. The dependency ρ_t increased from about 0.2 in 1980 to about 0.7 in 2000 for the FTSE–DAX, as well as the FTSE–CAC, pairs. Another interesting result is the asymmetry in the dependency structure found for most market pairs involving the NIK. As the pattern of dependency between the NIK and the DAX clearly indicates, negative shocks are followed by a subsequent increase in the dependency structure.

8.6 FURTHER RESEARCH TOPICS

We have developed in this chapter a framework, based on copula functions, to model dependency between time series, when univariate distributions are complicated and cannot easily be extended to a multivariate setup. We use this methodology to investigate the dependency between daily stock-market returns. We first provide empirical evidence that the distribution of daily returns may be well described by the skewed student-t distribution, with volatility, skewness and kurtosis varying over time. In such a context, modelling several returns simultaneously using the multivariate extension of this distribution would be extremely cumbersome. So, we use copula functions to join these complicated univariate distributions. This approach leads to a multivariate distribution that fits the data quite well, without involving time-consuming estimations. Finally, we describe how the dependency parameter can be rendered conditional and we propose a DCC model to describe the dynamics of the dependency parameter. We obtain evidence that the dependency between large stock markets is time-varying and persistent, in particular between European markets.

Table 8.4 Parameter estimates for the student-t copula when the dynamics of the dependency parameter ρ is given (Panel A) by the DCC model (Equation (8.11)) and (Panel B) by the ADCC model (Equation (8.12)). LRT is the LR test statistic for the null hypothesis that $\alpha^- = 0$. We also report the log-likelihood and the AIC and SIC information criteria

	SP/NIK	SP/FTSE	SP/DAX	SP/CAC	NIK/FTSE	NIK/DAX	NIK/CAC	FTSE/DAX	FTSE/CAC	DAX/CAC
Panel A: Dynamic conditional correlation model										
β	0.969	0.965	0.952	0.972	0.953	0.882	0.910	0.981	0.983	0.962
s.e.	(0.011)	(0.200)	(0.013)	(0.014)	(0.045)	(0.047)	(0.047)	(0.004)	(0.003)	(0.005)
α	0.015	0.001	0.019	0.010	0.008	0.031	0.021	0.016	0.016	0.030
s.e.	(0.004)	(0.005)	(0.005)	(0.004)	(0.005)	(0.010)	(0.008)	(0.003)	(0.003)	(0.004)
n	27.029	24.032	18.711	13.098	12.681	18.154	14.918	11.191	9.911	9.653
s.e.	(11.072)	(9.766)	(5.496)	(2.712)	(2.716)	(5.491)	(3.643)	(2.013)	(1.642)	(1.556)
lnL	170.551	139.219	242.884	197.812	107.148	168.435	121.266	510.535	833.147	734.227
AIC	−0.073	−0.059	−0.104	−0.085	−0.045	−0.072	−0.051	−0.222	−0.363	−0.319
SIC	−0.067	−0.054	−0.099	−0.079	−0.039	−0.066	−0.046	−0.216	−0.357	−0.314
Panel B: asymmetric dynamic conditional correlation model										
β	0.971	0.919	0.954	0.974	0.996	0.924	0.938	0.985	0.982	0.959
s.e.	(0.010)	(0.092)	(0.013)	(0.013)	(0.002)	(0.024)	(0.022)	(0.003)	(0.003)	(0.005)
α	0.011	0.008	0.020	0.011	−0.004	0.003	−0.005	0.007	0.012	0.025
s.e.	(0.005)	(0.008)	(0.007)	(0.005)	(0.002)	(0.008)	(0.006)	(0.003)	(0.004)	(0.005)
α	0.011	−0.019	−0.003	−0.003	0.009	0.047	0.045	0.013	0.008	0.014
s.e.	(0.008)	(0.011)	(0.008)	(0.006)	(0.003)	(0.016)	(0.013)	(0.005)	(0.006)	(0.008)
n	27.928	23.796	18.762	13.074	13.113	19.360	16.412	11.134	9.918	9.544
s.e.	(11.658)	(9.657)	(5.515)	(2.704)	(2.879)	(6.153)	(4.381)	(2.024)	(1.647)	(1.537)
lnL	171.389	141.579	242.920	197.929	112.346	174.669	128.009	513.298	834.061	735.331
LRT	1.677	4.720	0.072	0.234	10.395	12.469	13.485	5.526	1.829	2.208
p-val.	(0.195)	(0.030)	(0.788)	(0.629)	(0.001)	(0.000)	(0.000)	(0.019)	(0.176)	(0.137)
AIC	−0.073	−0.060	−0.105	−0.085	−0.047	−0.075	−0.054	−0.223	−0.363	−0.320
SIC	−0.068	−0.055	−0.099	−0.079	−0.042	−0.069	−0.049	−0.217	−0.357	−0.314

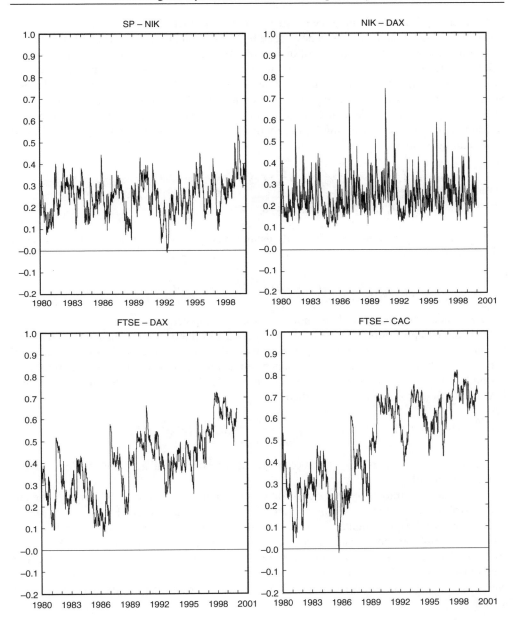

Figure 8.5   The evolution of the parameter ρ_t obtained with the asymmetric DCC model (8.12), for the SP–NIK, the NIK–DAX, the FTSE–DAX and the FTSE–CAC pairs.

Now, let's discuss other fields where our model can be useful. First, this framework may be used to investigate the spillover of large realisations in emerging markets. The volatility spillovers among such markets have been investigated, for instance, in Bekaert and Harvey (1995) and in Rockinger and Urga (2001). The focus on extreme realisations may provide further insights.

Another application of our model is the conditional asset allocation in a non-Gaussian framework. Such a model has been developed by Rubinstein (1973). Kraus and Litzenberger (1976) provide a first empirical test of this model. Barone-Adesi (1985) shows how a model involving higher moments can be obtained with the assumption of a quadratic market model. Ingersoll (1990) treats the topic at textbook level. Harvey and Siddique (2000) provide tests of these models. Further theoretical elements are brought forward by Jurczenko and Maillet (2001 and 2006). To implement asset allocation in a non-Gaussian world, it is necessary to compute expressions involving higher moments. Such expressions will typically involve computations such as

$$
m_{ijt} = \int_{z_{1t} \in \mathcal{R}} \int_{z_{2t} \in \mathcal{R}} z_{1t}^i z_{2t}^j \, c(F_1\,(z_{1t};\,\xi_1)\,,F_2\,(z_{2t};\,\xi_2)\,;\,G\,(z_{1t-1},z_{2t-1};\,\xi_c))
$$
$$
\times f_1\,(z_{1t};\,\xi_1) \times f_2\,(z_{2t};\,\xi_2)\,\mathrm{d}z_{1t}\,\mathrm{d}z_{2t}
$$

Such integrals may be evaluated efficiently using a change in variables $u_{it} = F_i\,(z_{it};\,\xi_i)$. With this change, we get

$$
m_{ijt} = \int_{u_{1t} \in [0,1]} \int_{u_{2t} \in [0,1]} (F_1^{-1}(u_{1t}))^i (F_2^{-1}(u_{2t}))^j \times c(u_{1t}, u_{2t};\, \rho_t)\mathrm{d}u_{1t}\,\mathrm{d}u_{2t}
$$

Once the model is estimated, these moments can be computed.

Still another application may be found in value-at-risk applications. There, it is necessary to compute the probability that a portfolio exceeds a given threshold. Again, once the marginal models are known, the exceedance probability may be computed numerically as a simple integration, using the fact that, if the pair (Z_{1t}, Z_{2t}) has some joint distribution function $C(F_1\,(z_{1t};\,\xi_1)\,,F_2\,(z_{2t};\,\xi_2))$, then

$$
Pr[\delta Z_{1t} + (1-\delta)Z_{2t} > \omega] = \int_{\delta z_{1t} + (1-\delta)z_{2t} > \omega} \mathrm{d}C\,(F_1\,(z_{1t};\,\xi_1)\,,F_2\,(z_{2t};\,\xi_2)\,;\,\rho_t)
$$

Again, this expression is easy to implement numerically. Similarly, one could compute expected shortfall.

Furthermore, a straightforward extension of our framework could yield a model for the joint distribution of returns, volume and duration between transactions. For instance, Marsh and Wagner (2000) investigate the return-volume dependence when extreme events occur. For this purpose, one could use a trivariate copula or proceed in successive steps. First, one could model the dependency between volume and duration using a first copula. Then, in a second step, one could link this copula to the return series through another copula. Hence, our model may be adapted to settings where the data of each margin are not of the same nature.

ACKNOWLEDGEMENTS

Eric Jondeau (formerly at the Banque de France) is from the University of Lausanne and the Swiss:Finance:Institute. Michael Rockinger (a former consultant for the Banque de France) is from the University of Lausanne, the Swiss:Finance:Institute and CEPR. He acknowledges help from the HEC-Paris Foundation, as well as the Swiss National Science Foundation through NCCR (Financial Valuation and Risk Management). We are grateful to Sanvi

Avouyi-Dovi, Giovanni Barone-Adesi, Patrick Gagliardini, Christian Gouriéroux, Bertrand Maillet, Jean-Michel Zakoïan, as well as an anonymous referee for precious comments. The usual disclaimer applies. The Banque de France does not necessarily endorse the views expressed in this chapter.

REFERENCES

Adcock, C. J. (2002) Asset Pricing and Portfolio Selection Based on the Multivariate Skew-Student Distribution, University of Sheffield Working Paper.

Ang, A. and J. Chen (2002) Asymmetric Correlations of Equity Portfolios, *Journal of Financial Economics* **63**(3), 443–494.

Azzalini, A. and A. Capitanio (2003) Distributions Generated by Perturbation of Symmetry with Emphasis on a Multivariate Skew *T* Distribution, *Journal of the Royal Statistical Society: Series B* **65**(2), 367–389.

Barone-Adesi, G. (1985) Arbitrage Equilibrium with Skewed Asset Returns, *Journal of Financial and Quantitative Analysis* **20**(3), 299–313.

Bauwens, L. and S. Laurent (2005) A New Class of Multivariate Skew Densities, with Application to GARCH Model, *Journal of Business and Economic Statistics* **23**(3), 346–354.

Bekaert, G. and C. L. Harvey (1995) Time-Varying World Market Integration, *Journal of Finance* **50**(2), 403–444.

Bera, A. K. and S. Kim (2002) Testing Constancy of Correlation and other Specifications of the BGARCH Model with an Application to International Equity Returns, *Journal of Empirical Finance* **9**(2), 171–195.

Bollerslev, T. (1986) Generalized Autoregressive Conditional Heteroskedasticity, *Journal of Econometrics* **31**(3), 307–327.

Bollerslev, T. and J. M. Wooldridge (1992) Quasi-Maximum Likelihood Estimation and Inference in Dynamic Models with Time-Varying Covariances, *Econometric Reviews* **11**(2), 143–172.

Brooks, C., S. P. Burke and G. Persand (2005) Autoregressive Conditional Kurtosis, *Journal of Financial Econometrics* **3**(3), 399–421.

Campbell, J. Y. and L. Hentschel (1992) No News Is Good News: An Asymmetric Model of Changing Volatility, *Journal of Financial Economics* **31**(3), 281–318.

Cappiello, L., R. F. Engle and K. Sheppard (2003) Asymmetric Dynamics in the Correlations of Global Equity and Bond Returns, ECB Working Paper 204.

Denuit, M. and O. Scaillet (2004) Nonparametric Tests for Positive Quadrant Dependence, *Journal of Financial Econometrics* **2**(3), 422–450.

Diebold, F. X., T. A. Gunther and A. S. Tay (1998) Evaluating Density Forecasts with Applications to Financial Risk Management, *International Economic Review* **39**(4), 863–883.

Embrechts, P., A. J. McNeil and D. Straumann (1999) Correlation and Dependency in Risk Management: Properties and Pitfalls, Working Paper, ETH Zurich.

Embrechts, P., F. Lindskog and A. J. McNeil (2003) Modelling Dependence with Copulas and Applications to Risk Management. In: *Handbook of Heavy Tailed Distributions in Finance*, S. T. Rachev (Ed.), Elsevier/North-Holland, Amsterdam.

Engle, R. F. (1982) Auto-Regressive Conditional Heteroskedasticity with Estimates of the Variance of United Kingdom Inflation, *Econometrica* **50**(4), 987–1007.

Engle, R. F. (2002) Dynamic Conditional Correlation: A Simple Class of Multivariate Generalized Autoregressive Conditional Heteroskedastic Models, *Journal of Business and Economic Statistics* **20**, 339–350.

Engle, R. F. and G. Gonzalez-Rivera (1991) Semi-Parametric ARCH Models, *Journal of Business and Economic Statistics* **9**(4), 345–359.

Engle, R. F. and V. K. Ng (1993) Measuring and Testing the Impact of News on Volatility, *Journal of Finance* **48**(5), 1749–1778.

Engle, R. F. and K. Sheppard (2001) Theoretical and Empirical Properties of Dynamic Conditional Correlation Multivariate GARCH, NBER Working Paper 8554.

Gagliardini, P. and C. Gouriéroux (2002) Duration Time Series Models with Proportional Hazard, CREST Working Paper 2002–21.

Glosten, R. T., R. Jagannathan and D. Runkle (1993) On the Relation between the Expected Value and the Volatility of the Nominal Excess Return on Stocks, *Journal of Finance* **48**(5), 1779–1801.

Gouriéroux, C. and A. Monfort (1992) Qualitative Threshold ARCH Models, *Journal of Econometrics* **52**(1–2), 159–199.

Hamao, Y., R. W. Masulis and V. K. Ng (1990) Correlations in Price Changes and Volatility Across International Stock Markets, *Review of Financial Studies* **3**(2), 281–307.

Hansen, B. E. (1994) Autoregressive Conditional Density Estimation, *International Economic Review* **35**(3), 705–730.

Harvey, C. R. and A. Siddique (1999) Autoregressive Conditional Skewness, *Journal of Financial and Quantitative Analysis* **34**(4), 465–487.

Harvey, C. R. and A. Siddique (2000) Conditional Skewness in Asset Pricing Tests, *Journal of Finance* **55**(3), 1263–1295.

Hwang, S. and M. Salmon (2002) An Analysis of Performance Measures Using Copulae. In: *Performance Measurement in Finance: Firms, Funds, and Managers*, J. K. Knight and S. Satchell (Eds), Butterworth-Heinemann, London.

Ingersoll, J. Jr (1990) *Theory of Financial Decision Making*, Rowman and Littlefield, Totowa, New Jersey.

Joe, H. (1997) *Multivariate Models and Dependence Concepts*, Chapman & Hall, London.

Joe, H. and J. J. Xu (1996) The Estimation Method of Inference Functions for Margins for Multivariate Models, Technical Report 166, Department of Statistics, University of British Columbia.

Jondeau, E. and M. Rockinger (2003a) Conditional Volatility, Skewness, and Kurtosis: Existence, Persistence, and Comovements, *Journal of Economic Dynamics and Control* **27**(10), 1699–1737.

Jondeau, E. and M. Rockinger (2003b) User's Guide, *Journal of Economic Dynamics and Control* **27**(10), 1739–1742.

Jurczenko, E. and B. Maillet (2001) The 3-CAPM: Theoretical Foundations and a Comparison of Asset Pricing Models in a Unified Framework. In: *Developments in Forecast Combination and Portfolio Choice*, C. Dunis, J. Moody and A. Timmermann (Eds.), John Wiley & Sons, Ltd, Chichester pp. 239–273.

Jurczenko, E. and B. Maillet (2006) The 4-Moment CAPM: In between Asset Pricing and Asset Allocation. In: *Multi-moment Assest Allocation and Pricing Models*, E. Jurczenko and B. Maillet (Eds), Wiley, Chapter 6.

Kraus, A. and R. H. Litzenberger (1976) Skewness Preference and the Valuation of Risk Assets, *Journal of Finance* **31**(4), 1085–1100.

Kroner, K. F. and V. K. Ng (1998) Modeling Asymmetric Comovements of Asset Returns, *Review of Financial Studies* **11**(4), 817–844.

Lambert, P. and S. Laurent (2002) Modeling Skewness Dynamics in Series of Financial Data Using Skewed Location-Scale Distributions, Working Paper, Université Catholique de Louvain and Université de Liège.

Li, D. X. (2000) On Default Correlation: A Copula Function Approach, *Journal of Fixed Income* **9**(4), 43–54.

Lindskog, F. (2000) Modelling Dependence with Copulas and Applications to Risk Management, Working Paper, RiskLab, Zürich.

Longin, F. and B. Solnik (1995) Is the Correlation in International Equity Returns Constant: 1960–1990?, *Journal of International Money and Finance* **14**(1), 3–26.

Longin, F. and B. Solnik (2001) Extreme Correlation of International Equity Markets, *Journal of Finance* **56**(2), 649–676.

Malevergne, Y. and D. Sornette (2003) Testing the Gaussian Copula Hypothesis for Financial Assets Dependence, *Quantitative Finance* **3**, 231–250.

Marsh, T. A. and N. Wagner (2000) Return-Volume Dependence and Extremes in International Equity Markets, Working Paper, Haas School of Business.

Nelsen, R. B. (1999) *An Introduction to Copulas*, Springer Verlag, New York.

Nelson, D. B. (1991) Conditional Heteroskedasticity in Asset Returns: A New Approach, *Econometrica* **59**(2), 347–370.

Patton, A. J. (2006) Estimation of Multivariate Models for Time Series of Possibly Different Lengths, *Journal of Applied Econometrics* **21**(2), 147–173.

Plackett, R. L. (1965) A Class of Bivariate Distributions, *Journal of the American Statistical Association* **60**, 516–522.

Premaratne, G. and A. K. Bera (2000) Modeling Asymmetry and Excess Kurtosis in Stock Return Data, Working Paper, University of Illinois.

Riboulet, G., T. Roncalli and E. Bouyé (2000) Copulas for Finance: A Reading Guide and Some Applications, Working Paper, Groupe de Recherche Opérationnelle, Crédit Lyonnais.

Rockinger, M. and E. Jondeau (2002) Entropy Densities with an Application to Autoregressive Conditional Skewness and Kurtosis, *Journal of Econometrics* **106**(1), 119–142.

Rockinger, M. and G. Urga (2001) A Time-Varying Parameter Model to Test for Predictability and Integration in the Stock Markets of Transition Economies, *Journal of Business and Economic Statistics* **19**(1), 73–84.

Rosenberg, J. V. (2003) Nonparametric Pricing of Multivariate Contingent Claims, *Journal of Derivatives* **10**(3), 9–26.

Rubinstein, M. E. (1973) The Fundamental Theorem of Parameter-Preference Security Valuation, *Journal of Financial and Quantitative Analysis* **8**(1), 61–69.

Sahu, S. K., D. K. Dey and M. D. Branco (2003) A New Class of Multivariate Skew Distributions with Applications to Bayesian Regression Models, *Canadian Journal of Statistics* **31**, 129–150.

Schweizer, B. and A. Sklar (1974) Operations on Distribution Functions Not Derivable from Operations on Random Variables, *Studia Mathematica* **52**, 43–52.

Shih, J. H. and T. A. Louis (1995) Inferences on the Association Parameter in Copula Models for Bivariate Survival Data, *Biometrics* **51**, 1384–1399.

Sklar, A. (1959) Fonctions de répartition à *n* dimensions et leurs marges, *Publications de l'Institut Statistique de l'Université de Paris* **8**, 229–231.

Susmel, R. and R. F. Engle (1994) Hourly Volatility Spillovers between International Equity Markets, *Journal of International Money and Finance* **13**(1), 3–25.

Theodossiou, P. (1998) Financial Data and the Skewed Generalized *T* Distribution, *Management Science* **44**(12–1), 1650–1661.

Tibiletti, L. (1995) Beneficial Changes in Random Variables via Copulas: An Application to Insurance, *Geneva Papers on Risk and Insurance Theory* **20**, 191–202.

Tse, Y. K. (2000) A Test for Constant Correlations in a Multivariate GARCH Model, *Journal of Econometrics* **98**(1), 107–127.

Tse, Y. K. and A. K. C. Tsui (2002) A Multivariate Generalized Autoregressive Conditional Heteroskedasticity Model with Time-Varying Correlations, *Journal of Business and Economics Statistics* **20**(3), 351–362.

Vlaar, P. J. G. and F. C. Palm (1993) The Message in Weekly Exchange Rates in the European Monetary System: Mean Reversion, Conditional Heteroskedasticity, and Jumps, *Journal of Business and Economic Statistics* **11**(3), 351–360.

Zakoïan, J. M. (1994) Threshold Heteroskedastic Models, *Journal of Economic Dynamics and Control* **18**(5), 931–955.

9

A Test of the Homogeneity of Asset pricing Models

Giovanni Barone-Adesi, Patrick Gagliardini and Giovanni Urga

ABSTRACT

Tests of multi-moment asset pricing models impose linear constraints in the risk-return space. In this chapter we derive the relevant statistics and test the restriction in a multivariate setting.

9.1 INTRODUCTION

Expected returns on financial assets are usually modelled as linear functions of covariances of returns with some systematic risk factors. Sharpe (1964), Lintner (1965), Black (1972), Merton (1973), Kraus and Litzenberger (1976), Ross (1976), Breeden (1979), Barone-Adesi (1985), Jagannathan and Wang (1996) and Harvey and Siddique (2000) have proposed several formulations of this general paradigm. See Campbell (2000) for a recent survey on the field of asset pricing. Most of the empirical tests to date have produced negative or ambiguous results. These findings have spurred renewed interest in evaluating the statistical properties of methodologies currently available. Among recent studies, Shanken (1992) and Kan and Zhang (1999a, 1999b) highlight relevant sources of ambiguity embodied in these commonly employed methodologies.

It appears that only preliminary knowledge of the return-generating process may lead to the design of reliable tests. Because this condition is never met in practice, researchers are forced to choose between powerful tests that are misleading in the presence of possible model misspecifications or more tolerant tests, such as the ones based on the stochastic discount factor methodology, that have limited power. The first choice may lead not only to the rejection of correct models, but also to the acceptance of irrelevant factors as sources of systematic risk, as noted by Kan and Zhang (1999a, 1999b). On the other hand, the choice of the stochastic discount factor methodology fails to discriminate among competing models and often leads to very large confidence intervals for estimated risk premia (Cochrane, 1996; Kan and Zhang, 1999a, 1999b).

Multi-moment Asset Allocation and Pricing Models   Edited by E. Jurczenko and B. Maillet
© 2006 John Wiley & Sons, Ltd

In addition to these methodological difficulties, a number of anomalous empirical regularities have been detected. Banz (1981) relates expected returns to firm size, Fama and French (1995) link expected returns to the ratio of book-to-market value. Some of these anomalies fade over time, others seem to be more persistent, raising the possibility that they are due to omitted systematic risk factors. These pricing anomalies may be related to the possibility that useless factors appear to be priced. Of course it is also possible that pricing anomalies proxy for omitted factors. While statistical tests do not allow us to choose among these two possible explanations of pricing anomalies, Kan and Zhang (1999a, 1999b) suggest that perhaps large increases in R^2 and persistence of sign and size of coefficients over time are most likely to be associated with truly priced factors.

To investigate the effects of possible misspecifications of the return-generating process on tests of asset pricing models, in this chapter we study the portfolios used by Jagannathan and Wang (1996). One hundred portfolios sorted by beta and size to maximise the spread of observed betas are available. To test for the extent of misspecification of the return-generating process, we nest the usual market model into the extended version used by Barone-Adesi (1985) and Barone-Adesi, Gagliardini and Urga (2004).

The rest of the chapter is organised as follows. In Section 9.2 we recall the framework of the quadratic market model introduced in Barone-Adesi (1985) and Barone-Adesi, Gagliardini and Urga (2004). Section 9.3 reports the empirical results based on the dataset of Jagannathan and Wang (1996). Section 9.4 concludes.

9.2   THE QUADRATIC MARKET MODEL

The evolution of financial asset returns shows significant co-movements. Factor models try to explain these co-movements by a rather small number of underlying variables, called factors, which have a common effect on the return dynamics. The quadratic market model is an extension of the traditional market model, where market returns and the square of the market returns are the two factors. The model specification is:

$$\mathbf{R}_t = \mathbf{a} + \mathbf{B}\,R_{M,t} + \mathbf{\Gamma}R_{M,t}^2 + \varepsilon_t$$
$$E(\varepsilon_t|\underline{R_{M,t}}) = 0 \tag{9.1}$$

where $\mathbf{R}_t$ is an $N \times 1$ vector of asset returns in period t, $R_{M,t}$ is the return of the market in period t, $\mathbf{a}$ is an $N \times 1$ vector of intercepts and $\mathbf{B}$ and $\mathbf{\Gamma}$ are $N \times 1$ vectors of sensitivities.

The motivation for including the square of the market returns is to account for risk originating from coskewness with the market portfolio. Specifically, the traditional market model postulates that asset returns move proportionally to the market. However, in real financial data we observe violations of this simple specification. Indeed, compared to the linear dependence implied by the market model, some classes of assets show a tendency to have higher (lower) returns when the market experiences large absolute returns. Such assets feature positive (negative) coskewness and therefore diminish (increase) the risk of the portfolio with respect to extreme events (see also Kraus and Litzenberger, 1976; Barone-Adesi, 1985; Harvey and Siddique, 2000). The quadratic market model captures possible nonlinearities in the dependence between asset returns and market returns, as well as asymmetries in response to upward and downward market movements.

As we will see in detail in the empirical section, the misspecification arising from neglecting these nonlinearities and asymmetries can produce a significant heterogeneity across portfolios. When the heterogeneity is correlated to variables representing portfolio characteristics such as size, these variables will appear to have explanatory power for the cross-section of expected returns. By taking into account the quadratic term, we are able to control for these heterogeneities. This point also addresses the fact that, if there are similarities in the processes generating the data across and within the portfolio groups, combining the data improves the efficiency of the estimation of the parameters. There exists a huge body of literature in panel data econometrics pointing out the various consequences for inference of neglecting heterogeneity (Robertson and Symons, 1992; Pesaran and Smith, 1995; Baltagi and Griffin, 1997; Hsiao, Pesaran and Tahmiscioglu, 1999; Haque, Pesaran and Sharma, 1999; Pesaran, Shin and Smith, 1999; Baltagi, Griffin and Xiong, 2000 amongst others).

Usual arbitrage pricing considerations (Ross, 1976; Chamberlain and Rothschild, 1983) imply that expected returns of assets following factor model (9.1) approximately satisfy the restriction (Barone-Adesi, 1985):

$$E(\mathbf{R}_t) = \lambda_0 + \mathbf{B}\lambda_1 + \mathbf{\Gamma}\lambda_2 \tag{9.2}$$

where λ_0 is the expected return on a portfolio for which the components β and γ of the vectors $\mathbf{B}$ and $\mathbf{\Gamma}$ are $\beta = \gamma = 0$, while λ_1 and λ_2 are expected excess returns on portfolios perfectly correlated with $R_{M,t}$ and $R_{M,t}^2$. In particular, since the risk-free asset and the first factor, that is the market, satisfy (9.2), it must be that $\lambda_0 = R_F$, the risk-free rate, and $\lambda_1 = E(R_{M,t}) - R_F$. It is important to notice that a similar restriction doesn't hold for the second factor since it is not a traded asset, but it is possible to show (see Barone-Adesi, 1985) that $\lambda_2 < E(R_{M,t}^2)$.

Equation (9.2) implies the restriction

$$\mathbf{a} = \mathbf{S}_N R_F - \mathbf{B} R_F + \mathbf{\Gamma}(\lambda_2 - E(R_{M,t}^2))$$

where $\mathbf{S}_N$ is an $N \times 1$ vector of ones, and imposing it on factor model (9.1) we get

$$\mathbf{R}_t - \mathbf{S}_N R_F = \mathbf{B}(R_{M,t} - R_F) + \mathbf{\Gamma}\left(R_{M,t}^2 + \vartheta_2\right) + \varepsilon_t \tag{9.3}$$

where $\vartheta_2 = \lambda_2 - E(R_{M,t}^2) < 0$. Written for each portfolio separately we have:

$$R_{it} - R_F = \beta_i(R_{M,t} - R_F) + \gamma_i R_{M,t}^2 + \gamma_i \vartheta_2 + \varepsilon_{it} \quad i = 1, \ldots, N$$

which is a nonlinear panel data model.

It is worth noticing that the factors representing time-varying regressors are common to all assets, whereas the equilibrium condition induces a restriction for the cross-section of expected returns through the term $\gamma_i \vartheta_2$. This explains why factor models of this kind are traditionally estimated by combinations of time series and cross-section regressions. Interested readers may refer to Barone-Adesi, Gagliardini and Urga (2004), where estimation and inference methodologies for models (9.1) and (9.3) are presented.

9.3 EMPIRICAL RESULTS

9.3.1 Data description

In this subsection we briefly describe the dataset in Jagannathan and Wang (1996), which we use as a basis for the various empirical exercises concerning the estimation of the quadratic market model.

The dataset consists of percentage monthly returns of 100 portfolios of NYSE and AMEX stocks for the period July 1963–December 1990. The portfolios have been constructed in the following way. For each calendar year, firms are sorted into size deciles based on their market value at the end of June. Firms within each size decile are then sorted into beta deciles, based on a beta estimated using 24 to 60 months of past return data and the CRSP value-weighted index as the market index proxy. For each of these 100 portfolios the return is computed for the following 12 months by equally weighting the returns on stocks in the portfolio.

For our exercise, however, we decided to reaggregate the 100 portfolios in each size decile, in order to obtain ten size-portfolios, ranked in order of increasing size. The basic reason for this is to avoid estimating covariance matrices of large dimension.

Finally, as market return we used the capital-weighted CRSP index over the same period.

9.3.2   Results

In this subsection we report the results of our empirical investigations. Table 9.1 contains the estimated γ_i from the quadratic market model in (9.1) (t-statistics in parentheses: OLS and Newey–West heteroskedasticity and autocorrelation consistent estimator with five lags, respectively). Corresponding adjusted $R^2_{i,Q}$ for each portfolio are reported in Table 9.2 (R^2_i are adjusted R^2 for a regression of portfolio returns on a constant and market returns). In Table 9.3 we report estimates for the coefficients γ_i, ϑ_2, λ_2 for the restricted model in Equation (9.3) (R^2_* denotes the McElroy, 1977 goodness-of-fit measure). Finally, in Table 9.4 we report the estimates of model (9.3) where we introduce an intercept δ in portfolio expected excess returns, which is constant across portfolios.

From the $\widehat{\gamma}_i$ coefficients estimated in the unrestricted model (9.1), the quadratic market model seems to be a valuable extension of the basic market model, since the sensitivities to quadratic market returns appear significantly different from zero. In particular, these sensitivities are negative for small firms and positive for large firms. The findings of a positive dependence of coskewness sensitivities to size in the period 1963–1990 are consistent with the results in Harvey and Siddique (2000). Finally, we notice that the $\widehat{\gamma}_i$ coefficients estimated in the restricted models (Tables 9.3 and 9.4) are similar.

Let us now consider the risk premium for coskewness. The coefficient λ_2 is negative, as expected. In fact, portfolios that tend to have higher positive returns when the market has high absolute returns (positive coskewness) help the investor to reduce the risk for extreme

Table 9.1   Estimated γ_i from the quadratic market model in (9.1)

$\widehat{\gamma}_1 = -0.014$	$\widehat{\gamma}_2 = -0.013$	$\widehat{\gamma}_3 = -0.010$	$\widehat{\gamma}_4 = -0.009$
(-2.12)	(-2.70)	(-2.28)	(-2.44)
(-1.66)	(-1.99)	(-1.90)	(-2.00)
$\widehat{\gamma}_5 = -0.006$	$\widehat{\gamma}_6 = -0.005$	$\widehat{\gamma}_7 = -0.001$	$\widehat{\gamma}_8 = -0.000$
(-1.97)	(-1.65)	(-0.26)	(-0.10)
(-1.33)	(-1.33)	(-0.21)	(-0.08)
$\widehat{\gamma}_9 = 0.000$	$\widehat{\gamma}_{10} = 0.004$		
(0.31)	(3.70)		
(0.30)	(3.38)		

Table 9.2 Adjusted $R_{i,Q}^2$ for each portfolio

$R_{1,Q}^2 = 0.529$ $R_1^2 = 0.524$	$R_{2,Q}^2 = 0.701$ $R_1^2 = 0.695$	$R_{3,Q}^2 = 0.754$ $R_1^2 = 0.750$	$R_{4,Q}^2 = 0.791$ $R_1^2 = 0.787$
$R_{5,Q}^2 = 0.827$ $R_1^2 = 0.826$	$R_{6,Q}^2 = 0.856$ $R_1^2 = 0.855$	$R_{7,Q}^2 = 0.907$ $R_1^2 = 0.907$	$R_{8,Q}^2 = 0.919$ $R_1^2 = 0.920$
$R_{9,Q}^2 = 0.946$ $R_1^2 = 0.946$	$R_{10,Q}^2 = 0.972$ $R_1^2 = 0.971$		

Table 9.3 Estimates for the coefficients γ_i, ϑ_2 and λ_2 for the restricted model in (9.3)

$\widehat{\gamma}_1 = -0.016$ (-2.31)	$\widehat{\gamma}_2 = -0.014$ (-2.81)	$\widehat{\gamma}_3 = -0.010$ (-2.43)	$\widehat{\gamma}_4 = -0.010$ (-2.64)	$\widehat{\gamma}_5 = -0.007$ (-2.15)
$\widehat{\gamma}_6 = -0.005$ (-1.80)	$\widehat{\gamma}_7 = -0.001$ (-0.36)	$\widehat{\gamma}_8 = -0.001$ (-0.40)	$\widehat{\gamma}_9 = 0.000$ (0.26)	$\widehat{\gamma}_{10} = 0.004$ (3.77)
$\widehat{\vartheta}_2 = -25.184$ (-3.16)	$\widehat{\lambda}_2 = -4.560$ (-0.55)	$R_*^2 = 0.8824$		

Table 9.4 Estimates of model (9.3) with an intercept δ in portfolio expected excess returns

$\widehat{\gamma}_1 = -0.016$ (-2.51)	$\widehat{\gamma}_2 = -0.012$ (-2.72)	$\widehat{\gamma}_3 = -0.010$ (-2.43)	$\widehat{\gamma}_4 = -0.010$ (-2.69)	$\widehat{\gamma}_5 = -0.007$ (-2.21)
$\widehat{\gamma}_6 = -0.005$ (-1.82)	$\widehat{\gamma}_7 = -0.001$ (-0.37)	$\widehat{\gamma}_8 = -0.001$ (-0.68)	$\widehat{\gamma}_9 = 0.001$ (0.42)	$\widehat{\gamma}_{10} = 0.004$ (3.95)
$\widehat{\vartheta}_2 = -38.927$ (-3.51)	$\widehat{\lambda}_2 = -18.302$ (-1.62)	$\widehat{\delta} = 0.046$ (1.18)	$R_*^2 = 0.8824$	

events, and therefore command lower expected returns. Since the coefficients $\widehat{\gamma}_i$ are of order 10^{-2}–10^{-3}, the part of expected excess returns due to coskewness is of the order 0.1–1%.

From Table 9.4, the estimated constant δ is not significant statistically. However, its order of magnitude is the same as that of the risk premium for coskewness. Therefore, it doesn't seem appropriate, from an economic point of view, to omit it. Moreover, its omission can cause biases in the estimates of the other parameters. Finally, we remark that the McElroy (1977) R_*^2 is practically identical in the two restricted models.

In order to assess the economic relevance of the quadratic term, we investigate its improvement over the traditional market model, which is characterised by the factor model (9.1) with $\Gamma = 0$. The Capital Asset Pricing Model (CAPM) (Sharpe, 1964 and Lintner, 1965) corresponds to the restrictions

$$\Gamma = 0, \mathbf{a} - (\mathbf{S}_N - \mathbf{B})R_F = 0$$

As noted above, the estimated coefficients $\boldsymbol{\Gamma}$ reported in Table 9.1 are different from zero for some portfolios, rejecting the market model. Moreover, at an explorative level, it is instructive to analyse the vector $\widehat{\mathbf{a}} - (\mathbf{S}_N - \widehat{\mathbf{B}})R_F$, where $\widehat{\mathbf{a}}$ and $\widehat{\mathbf{B}}$ are estimates obtained under model (9.1). The components of this vector, corresponding to the ten portfolios, are reported in annualised percentage in Table 9.5. This estimated vector is considerably different from zero, pointing again to a failure of the CAPM to capture all relevant factors.

We note that the components of vector $\widehat{\mathbf{a}} - (\mathbf{S}_N - \widehat{\mathbf{B}})R_F$ corresponding to small size portfolios are considerably larger than those of big portfolios. The missing factors appear, therefore, in the form of a heterogeneity across portfolios, which is negatively correlated to size. We formally test for this heterogeneity by computing the asymptotic least-squares statistic ξ_T^M for the hypothesis:

$$\exists\, \delta \in \mathbb{R} : \mathbf{a} - (\mathbf{S}_N - \mathbf{B})R_F = \delta \mathbf{S}_N$$

The result is:

$$\xi_T^M = 21.53$$

which is larger than the critical value at 0.05, $\chi^2_{0.95}(9) = 16.90$, rejecting the homogeneity of the unexplained component. The estimates $\widehat{a}_i - (1 - \widehat{B}_i)R_F - \widehat{\delta}$ for each portfolio are reported in Table 9.5 and feature a considerable heterogeneity across portfolios, consistent with the result of the test.

Let us now consider the same homogeneity tests within the quadratic market model. A formal test for the homogeneity of the unexplained expected returns across portfolios gives

$$\xi_T^M = 11.42$$

Table 9.5 The components of the vector corresponding to the ten portfolios in annualised percentages

	Portfolio 1	Portfolio 2	Portfolio 3	Portfolio 4	Portfolio 5
$\widehat{a}_i - (1 - \widehat{B}_i)R_F$	9.62	6.31	5.32	5.70	4.14
$\widehat{a}_i - (1 - \widehat{B}_i)R_F - \widehat{\delta}$	10.01	6.70	5.71	6.09	4.53
$\widehat{a}_i - (1 - \widehat{B}_i)R_F - \widehat{\vartheta}_2\widehat{\Gamma}_i - \widehat{\delta}$	5.07	2.13	2.20	2.70	2.02
$\widehat{a}_i - (1 - \widehat{B}_i)R_F - \widehat{\vartheta}_2\widehat{\Gamma}_i$	5.73	2.76	2.71	3.20	2.43

	Portfolio 6	Portfolio 7	Portfolio 8	Portfolio 9	Portfolio 10	χ^2
$\widehat{a}_i - (1 - \widehat{B}_i)R_F$	2.99	1.10	2.03	0.24	-1.32	
$\widehat{a}_i - (1 - \widehat{B}_i)R_F - \widehat{\delta}$	3.38	1.49	2.42	0.63	-0.93	21.53
$\widehat{a}_i - (1 - \widehat{B}_i)R_F - \widehat{\vartheta}_2\widehat{\Gamma}_i - \widehat{\delta}$	1.39	0.71	1.76	0.17	-0.39	11.42
$\widehat{a}_i - (1 - \widehat{B}_i)R_F - \widehat{\vartheta}_2\widehat{\Gamma}_i$	1.75	0.94	1.98	0.36	-0.30	14.59

whereas the test for no unexplained expected returns gives

$$\xi_T^M = 14.59$$

both smaller than the critical values $\chi_{0.95}^2(8) = 15.51$, and $\chi_{0.95}^2(9) = 16.90$ respectively. The estimates $\widehat{a}_i - (1 - \widehat{B}_i)R_F - \widehat{\vartheta}_2\widehat{\Gamma}_i - \widehat{\delta}$ and $\widehat{a}_i - (1 - \widehat{B}_i)R_F - \widehat{\vartheta}_2\widehat{\Gamma}_i$ are also reported in Table 9.5. The components of these vectors are considerably smaller and more homogeneous than those found within the market model. We conclude, therefore, that once the quadratic term is taken into account, the evidence for unexplained components in expected returns is considerably smaller.

From a methodological point of view, the use of the asymptotic least squares test statistics appears to be a better way than R^2 to compare the quadratic market model with the market model or the CAPM. Indeed, the model that better fits the data is not necessarily the correct model. On the contrary, financial theories are expressed in the form of statistical hypotheses, which can be tested by asymptotic least squares.

9.4 CONCLUSION

In this chapter we consider a two-factor model to study the presence of significant co-movements in the dynamics of asset returns. In addition to the traditional market returns term, the model includes the square of the market returns to account for risk originating from coskewness with the market portfolio, as recent literature (see, for instance, Harvey and Siddique, 2000) also stresses. Using the dataset in Jagannathan and Wang (1996) we show that the quadratic term is able to account for heterogeneities across portfolios otherwise improperly controlled via a simple constant. Moreover, we show that the quadratic term is significant and that the homogeneity hypothesis is accepted only in the presence of this term. These results are consistent with, and reinforce, the empirical findings in Barone-Adesi, Gagliardini and Urga (2004), obtained using a different dataset.

Although there is evidence that the quadratic market model is not a complete description of asset returns, acceptance of homogeneity is supportive of the significance of its contribution.

ACKNOWLEDGEMENTS

Earlier versions of this chapter were presented at the 9th Conference on Panel Data (Geneva, 22–23 June, 2000) and at the Conference on *Multi-moment Capital Asset Pricing Models and Related Topics* (Paris, April 29, 2002). We thank the participants for helpful discussions. M. Rockinger, C. Zhang, R. Morck and an anonymous referee provided us with very useful comments that helped to improve the chapter. Special thanks to the editors, E. Jurczenko and B. Maillet, for their encouragement in preparing this chapter. The usual disclaimer applies. We wish to thank R. Jagannathan and R. Kan for providing us with their dataset. Financial support by the National Centre of Competence in Research "Financial Valuation and Risk Management" (NCCRFINRISK) is gratefully acknowledged.

REFERENCES

Baltagi, B. H. and J. M. Griffin (1997) Pooled Estimators versus their Heterogenous Counterparts in the Context of Dynamic Demand for Gasoline, *Journal of Econometrics* **77**, 303–327.

Baltagi, B. H., J. M. Griffin and W. Xiong (2000) To Pool or not to Pool: Homogenous versus Heterogenous Estimators Applied to Cigarette Demand, *Review of Economics and Statistics* **82**, 117–126.

Banz, R. W. (1981) The Relationship Between Return and Market Value of Common Stocks, *Journal of Financial Economics* **9**, 3–18.

Barone-Adesi, G. (1985) Arbitrage Equilibrium with Skewed Asset Returns, *Journal of Financial and Quantitative Analysis* **20**, 299–313.

Barone-Adesi, G., Gagliardini, P. and G. Urga (2004) Testing Asset Pricing Models with Coskewness, *Journal of Business and Economic Statistics* **22**, 474–485.

Black, F. (1972) Capital Market Equilibrium with Restricted Borrowing, *Journal of Business* **45**, 444–455.

Breeden, D. T. (1979) An Intertemporal Asset Pricing Model with Stochastic Consumption and Investment Opportunities, *Journal of Financial Economics* **7**, 265–296.

Campbell, J. Y. (2000) Asset Pricing at the Millenium, *Journal of Finance* **4**, 1515–1567.

Chamberlain, G. and M. Rothschild (1983) Arbitrage, Factor Structure and Mean Variance Analysis in Large Asset Markets, *Econometrica* **51**, 1281–1301.

Cochrane, J. H. (1996) A Cross-sectional Test of an Investment-based Asset Pricing Model, *Journal of Political Economy* **104**, 572–621.

Fama, E. and K. R. French (1995) Size and Book-to-Market Factors in Earnings and Returns, *Journal of Finance* **50**, 131–155.

Haque, N. U., Pesaran, M. H. and S. Sharma (1999) Neglected Heterogeneity and Dynamics in Cross-Country Saving Regressions. In: *Panel Data Econometrics: Future Directions. Papers in Honour of Prof. Balestra*, J. Krisnakumar and E. Ronchetti (Eds), Elsevier Science.

Harvey, C. R. and A. Siddique (2000) Conditional Skewness in Asset Pricing Tests, *Journal of Finance* **55**, 1263–1295.

Hsiao, C., Pesaran, M. H. and A. K. Tahmiscioglu (1999) Bayes Estimation of Short-Run Coefficients in Dynamic Panel Data Models. In: *Analysis of Panels and Limited Dependent Variable Models: A Volume in Honour of G. S. Maddala*, C. Hsiao, K. Lahiri, L-F. Lee and M.H. Pesaran (Eds), Cambridge University Press, Cambridge.

Jagannathan, R. and Z. Wang (1996) The Conditional CAPM and the Cross-Section of Expected Returns, *Journal of Finance* **51**, 3–53.

Kan, R. and C. Zhang (1999a) GMM Test of Stochastic Discount Factor Models with Useless Factors, *Journal of Financial Economics* **54**, 103–127.

Kan, R. and C. Zhang (1999b) Two-Pass Tests of Asset Pricing Models with Useless Factors, *Journal of Finance* **54**, 203–235.

Kraus, A. and R. Litzenberger (1976) Skewness Preferences and the Valuation of Risk Assets, *Journal of Finance* **31**, 1085–1100.

Lintner, J. (1965) The Valuation of Risk Assets and the Selection of Risky Investments in Stock Portfolios and Capital Budgets, *Review of Economics and Statistics* **47**, 13–37.

McElroy, M. (1977) Goodness of Fit for Seemingly Unrelated Regressions: Glahn's $R^2_{y,x}$ and Hooper's $\bar{r}^2$, *Journal of Econometrics* **6**, 381–387.

Merton, R. C. (1973) An Intertemporal Capital Asset Pricing Model, *Econometrica* **41**, 867–887.

Pesaran, M. H. and R. P. Smith (1995) Estimating Long-Run Relationships from Dynamic Heterogenous Panels, *Journal of Econometrics* **68**, 79–113.

Pesaran, M. H., Shin, Y. and R. P. Smith (1999) Bounds Testing Approaches to the Analysis of Long-Run Relationships, DAE Working Paper 9907, University of Cambridge.

Robertson, D. and J. Symons (1992) Some Strange Properties of Panel Data Estimators, *Journal of Applied Econometrics* **7**, 175–189.

Ross, S. A. (1976) Arbitrage Theory of Capital Asset Pricing, *Journal of Economic Theory* **13**, 341–360.

Shanken, J. (1992) On the Estimation of Beta Pricing Models, *Review of Financial Studies* **5**, 1–33.

Sharpe, W. F. (1964) Capital Asset Prices: A Theory of Market Equilibrium Under Conditions of Risk, *Journal of Finance* **40**, 1189–1196.

Index